D1265540

WINTERS ★ COHEN ★ IRIZARRI ★ POPOV

AMERICATOWN ™

Published by
ARCHAIA ™

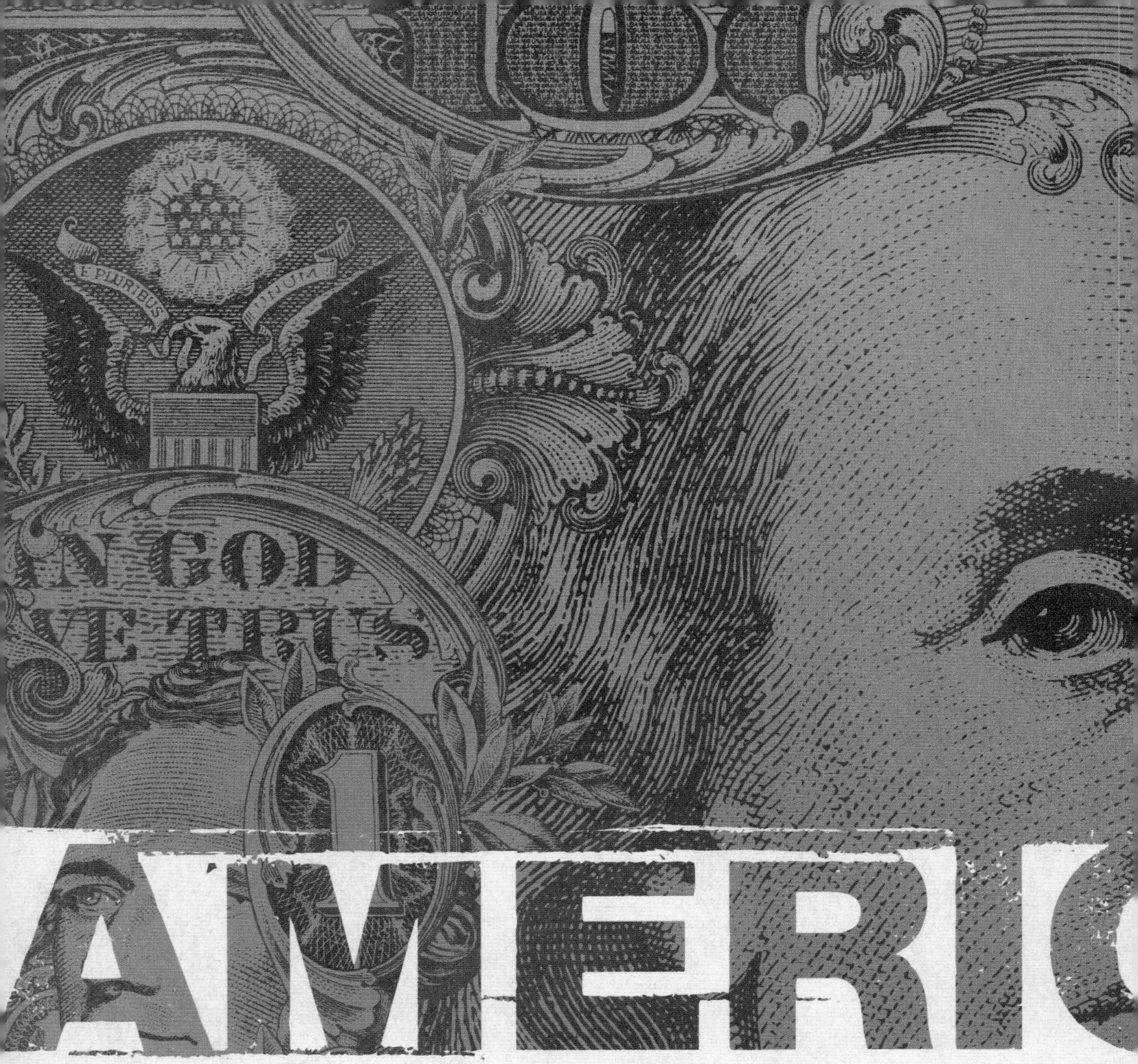
AMERIC

CREATED AND WRITTEN BY

BRADFORD WINTERS

LARRY COHEN

ILLUSTRATED BY

DANIEL IRIZARRI

A TOWN ™

COLORED BY
VLADIMIR POPOV
MATT BATTAGLIA
(ISSUE ONE)

LETTERED BY
SHAWN ALDRIDGE

COVER BY
SCOTT NEWMAN

DESIGNER
JILLIAN CRAB

ASSOCIATE EDITOR
CHRIS ROSA

EDITORS
SIERRA HAHN
IAN BRILL

Ross Richie...CEO & Founder
Matt Gagnon..Editor-In-Chief
Filip Sablik ....President of Publishing & Marketing
Stephen Christy......................President of Development
Lance Kreiter ....VP of Licensing & Merchandising
Phil Barbaro ....VP of Finance
Bryce Carlson .... Managing Editor
Mel Caylo .... Marketing Manager
Scott Newman ....Production Design Manager
Irene Bradish.................................... Operations Manager
Christine Dinh .... Brand Communications Manager
Sierra Hahn ....Senior Editor
Dafna Pleban .... Editor
Shannon Watters .... Editor
Eric Harburn.. Editor
Whitney Leopard ....Associate Editor
Jasmine Amiri ....Associate Editor
Chris Rosa ....Associate Editor
Alex Galer... Assistant Editor
Cameron Chittock ....Assistant Editor
Mary Gumport......................................Assistant Editor
Matthew Levine ....Assistant Editor
Kelsey Dieterich................................ Production Designer
Jillian Crab .... Production Designer
Michelle Ankley................... Production Design Assistant
Grace Park....................... Production Design Assistant
Aaron Ferrara............................... Operations Coordinator
Elizabeth Loughridge ....Accounting Coordinator
José Meza...Sales Assistant
James Arriola....................................... Mailroom Assistant
Holly Aitchison....................................Operations Assistant
Stephanie Hocutt................... Marketing Assistant
Sam Kusek...........................Direct Market Representative

AMERICATOWN, August 2016. Published by Archaia,
a division of Boom Entertainment, Inc. Americatown is
™ & © 2016 Bradford Winters & Larry Cohen. Originally
published in single magazine form as AMERICATOWN
No. 1-8. ™ & © 2015, 2016 Bradford Winters & Larry
Cohen. All rights reserved. Archaia™ and the Archaia
logo are trademarks of Boom Entertainment, Inc.,
registered in various countries and categories. All
characters, events, and institutions depicted herein
are fictional. Any similarity between any of the names,
characters, persons, events, and/or institutions in this
publication to actual names, characters, and persons,
whether living or dead, events, and/or institutions is
unintended and purely coincidental.

BOOM! Studios, 5670 Wilshire Boulevard, Suite 450, Los
Angeles, CA 90036-5679. Printed in China. First Printing.

ISBN: 978-1-60886-873-5, eISBN: 978-1-61398-544-1

BOLIVIA
Santa Cruz de la Sierra
Vallegrande
danez
rija
Tartagal

PARAGUAY
Corumba
Campo Grande
Gral. Eugebui A. Garay
Antonio Joao
Ponta Pora
Concepcion
Asuncion
Formosa
Pilar
Resistencia
Corrientes
Las Garzas
Vera
Ceres
Morteros
ARGENTINA
Santa Fe
Rio Cuarto
Rosario
URUGUAY
Buenos Aires
Las Flores
Olavarria
Puan
la Iris
Pigue
Juarez
Tandil
Zarate
Florida
Negro
Mar del Plata
Necochea
Punta Alta
Pedro Luro
gina
Viedma
he
Rawson
loro Rivadavia

Rondonopolis
Mineiros
Anapolis
Goiania
Luziania
Itumbiara
Cassilandia
Pirapora
Uberlandia
Belo Horizonte
Solviria
Ribeirao Preto
Franca
Sao Carlos
Piracicaba
Maringa
Londrina
Perola
Ponta Grossa
Clevelandia
Sao Paulo
Curitiba
Chapeco
Itajai
Lages
Florianopolis
Criciuma
Novo Hamburgo
Tramandai
Artigas
Rivera
Porto Alegre
Bage
Pelotas
Melo
Rio Grande
Santa Vitoria Do Palmar
Montevideo

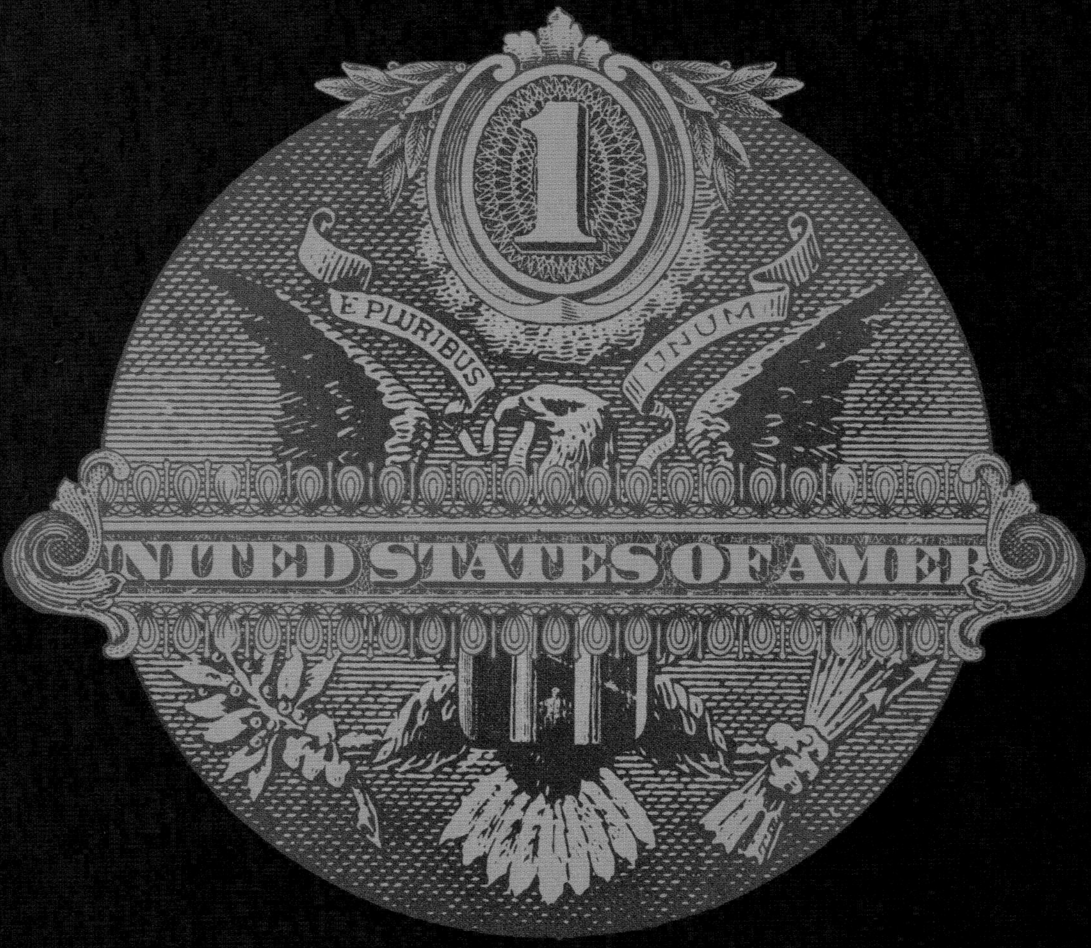
1
E PLURIBUS
UNUM
NITED STATES OF AMER

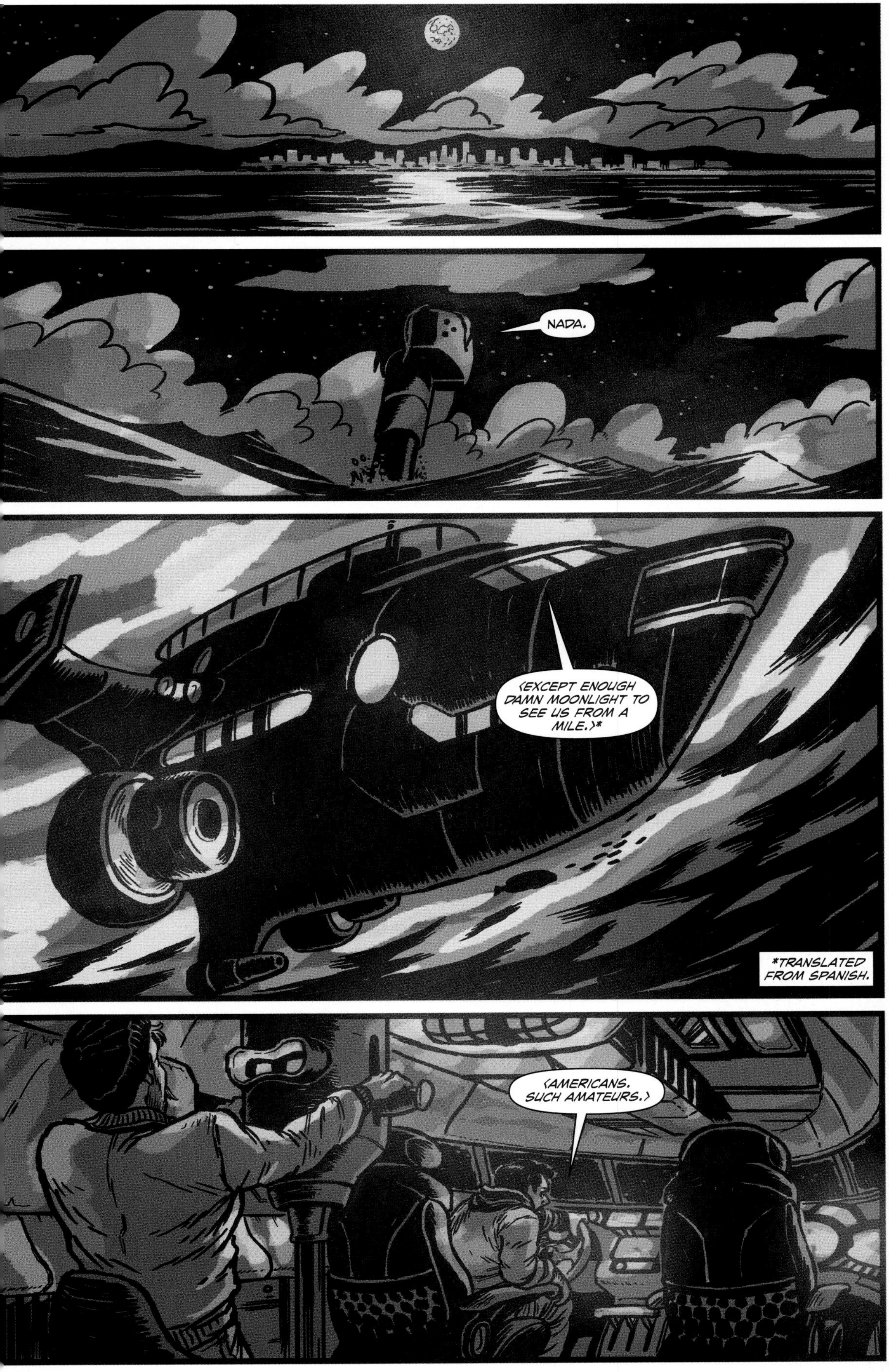
NADA.
‹EXCEPT ENOUGH DAMN MOONLIGHT TO SEE US FROM A MILE.›*
*TRANSLATED FROM SPANISH.
‹AMERICANS. SUCH AMATEURS.›

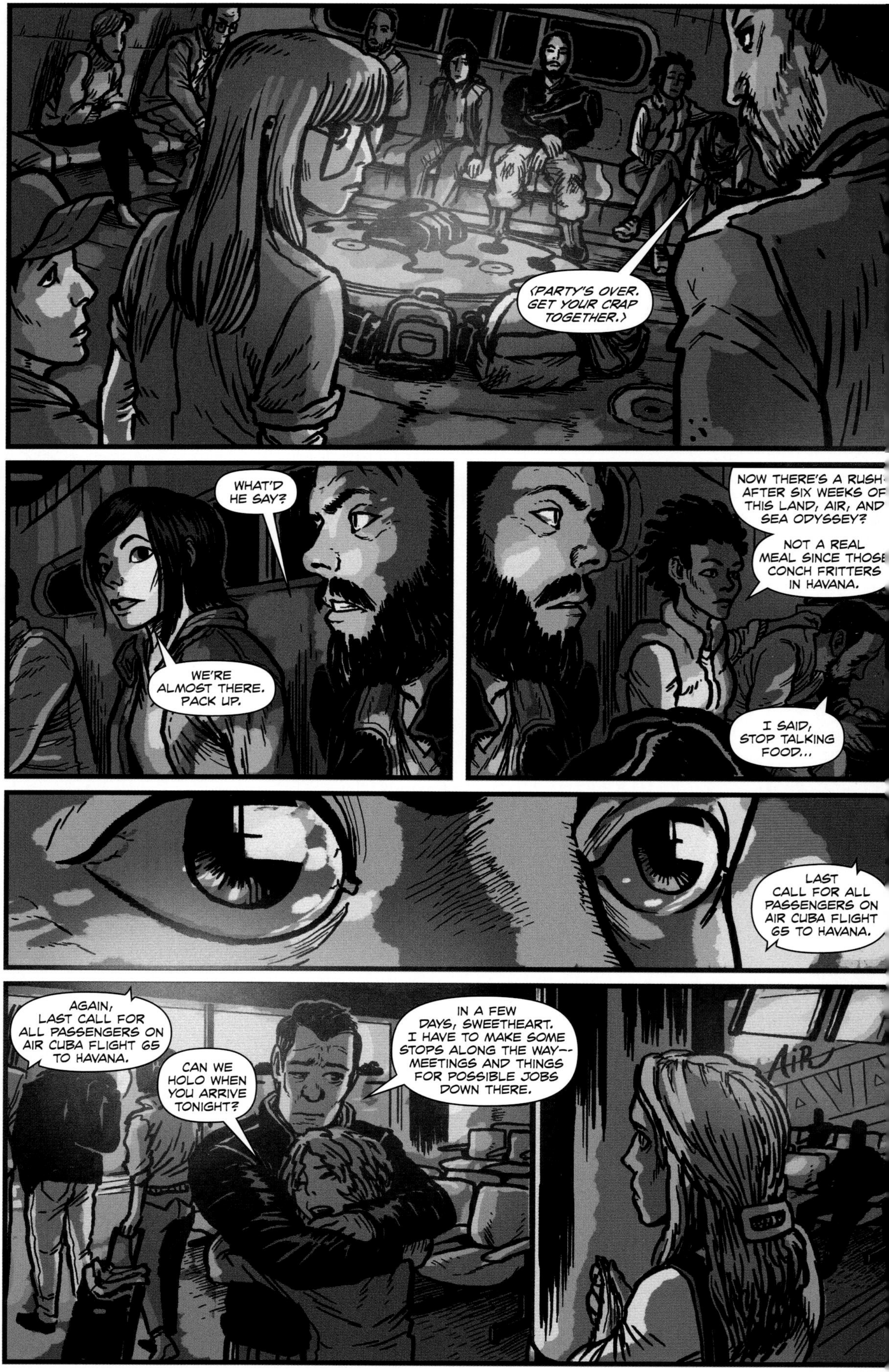

‹PARTY'S OVER. GET YOUR CRAP TOGETHER.›
WHAT'D HE SAY?
WE'RE ALMOST THERE. PACK UP.
NOW THERE'S A RUSH AFTER SIX WEEKS OF THIS LAND, AIR, AND SEA ODYSSEY?
NOT A REAL MEAL SINCE THOSE CONCH FRITTERS IN HAVANA.
I SAID, STOP TALKING FOOD...
LAST CALL FOR ALL PASSENGERS ON AIR CUBA FLIGHT 65 TO HAVANA.
AGAIN, LAST CALL FOR ALL PASSENGERS ON AIR CUBA FLIGHT 65 TO HAVANA.
CAN WE HOLO WHEN YOU ARRIVE TONIGHT?
IN A FEW DAYS, SWEETHEART. I HAVE TO MAKE SOME STOPS ALONG THE WAY-- MEETINGS AND THINGS FOR POSSIBLE JOBS DOWN THERE.

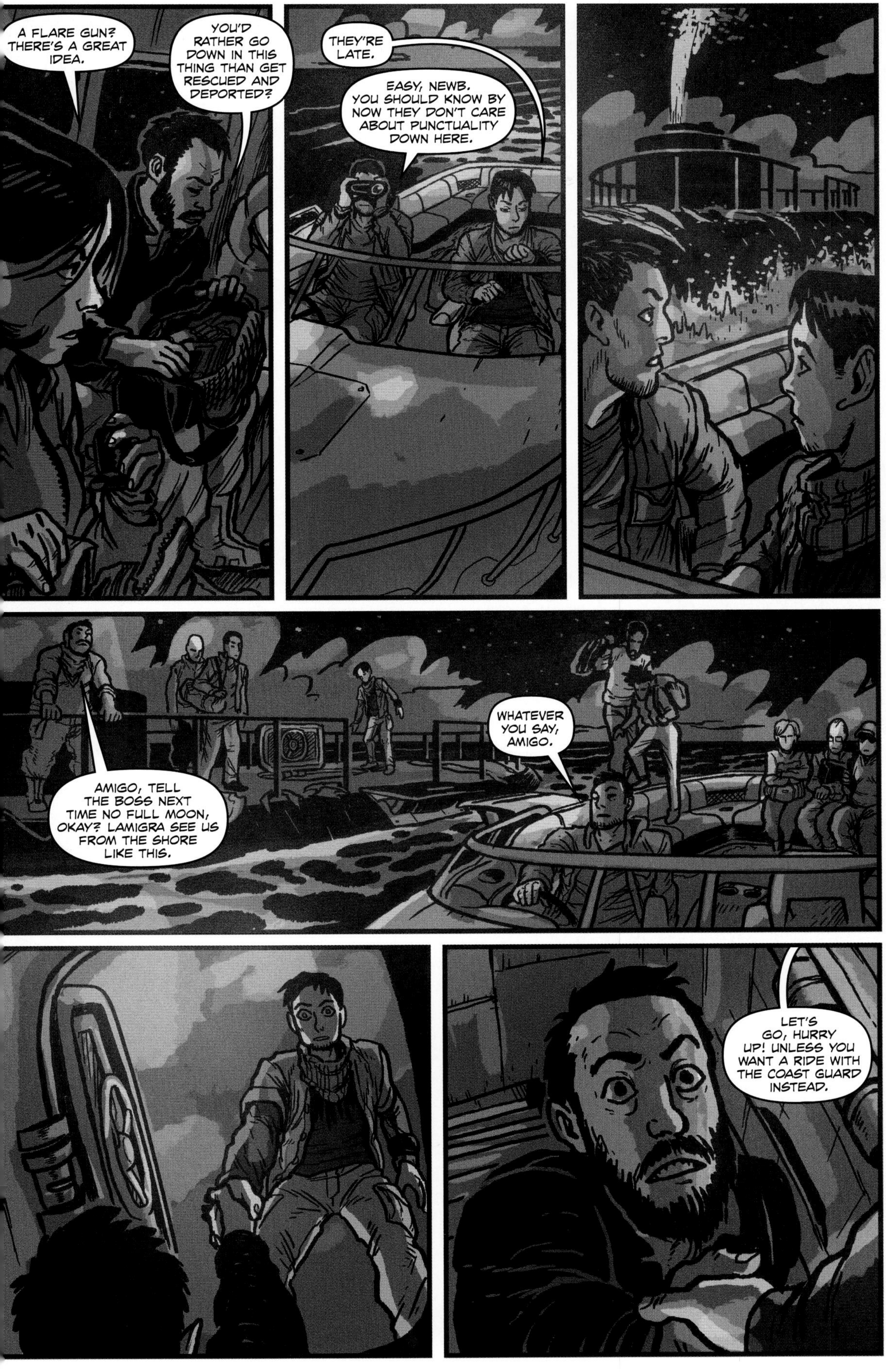
A FLARE GUN? THERE'S A GREAT IDEA.
YOU'D RATHER GO DOWN IN THIS THING THAN GET RESCUED AND DEPORTED?
THEY'RE LATE.
EASY, NEWB. YOU SHOULD KNOW BY NOW THEY DON'T CARE ABOUT PUNCTUALITY DOWN HERE.
AMIGO, TELL THE BOSS NEXT TIME NO FULL MOON, OKAY? LAMIGRA SEE US FROM THE SHORE LIKE THIS.
WHATEVER YOU SAY, AMIGO.
LET'S GO, HURRY UP! UNLESS YOU WANT A RIDE WITH THE COAST GUARD INSTEAD.

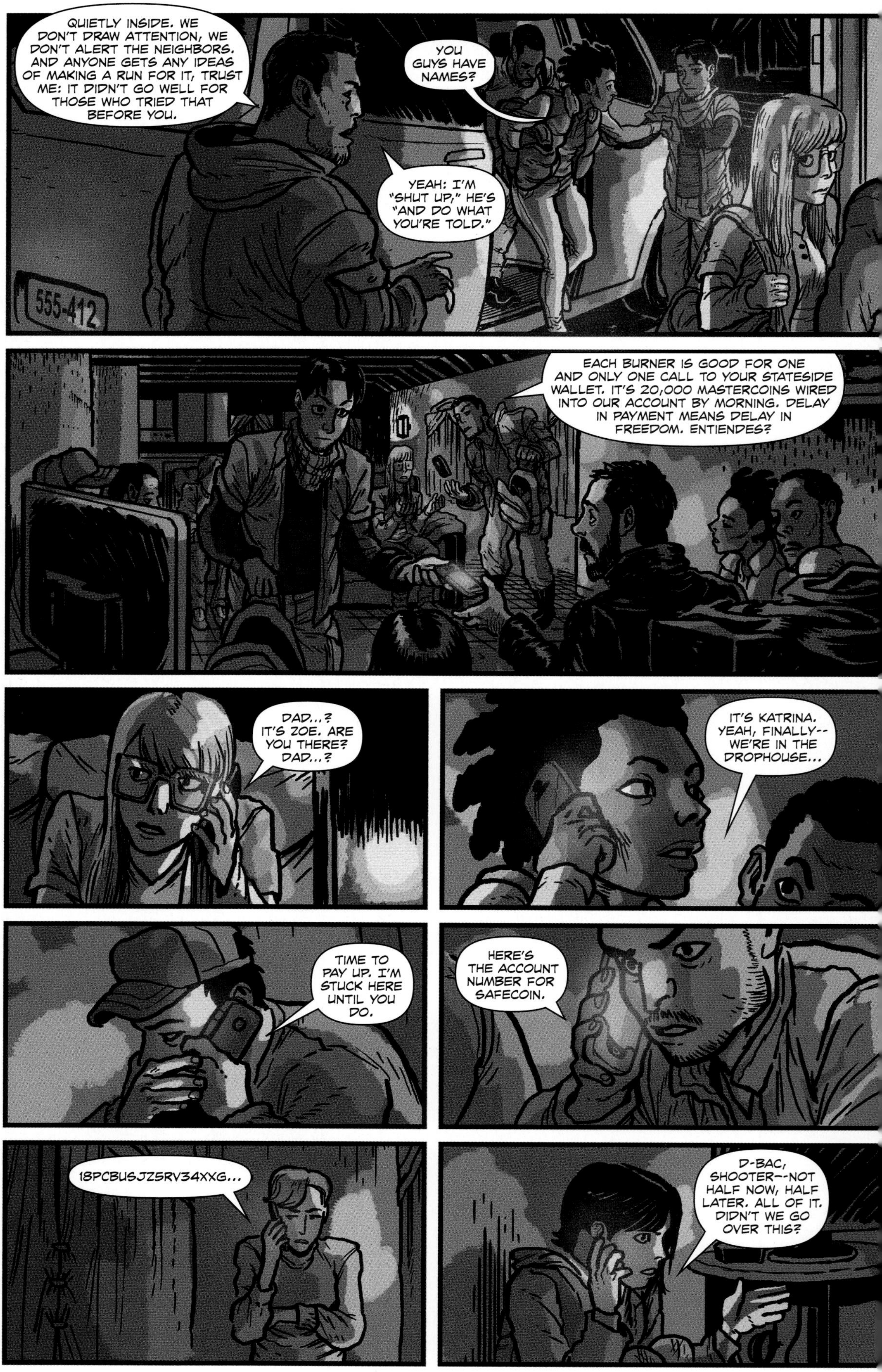
QUIETLY INSIDE. WE DON'T DRAW ATTENTION, WE DON'T ALERT THE NEIGHBORS. AND ANYONE GETS ANY IDEAS OF MAKING A RUN FOR IT, TRUST ME: IT DIDN'T GO WELL FOR THOSE WHO TRIED THAT BEFORE YOU.
YOU GUYS HAVE NAMES?
YEAH: I'M "SHUT UP," HE'S "AND DO WHAT YOU'RE TOLD."
555-412
EACH BURNER IS GOOD FOR ONE AND ONLY ONE CALL TO YOUR STATESIDE WALLET. IT'S 20,000 MASTERCOINS WIRED INTO OUR ACCOUNT BY MORNING. DELAY IN PAYMENT MEANS DELAY IN FREEDOM. ENTIENDES?
DAD...? IT'S ZOE. ARE YOU THERE? DAD...?
IT'S KATRINA. YEAH, FINALLY--WE'RE IN THE DROPHOUSE...
TIME TO PAY UP. I'M STUCK HERE UNTIL YOU DO.
HERE'S THE ACCOUNT NUMBER FOR SAFECOIN.
18PCBUSJZ5RV34XXG...
D-BAC, SHOOTER--NOT HALF NOW, HALF LATER. ALL OF IT. DIDN'T WE GO OVER THIS?

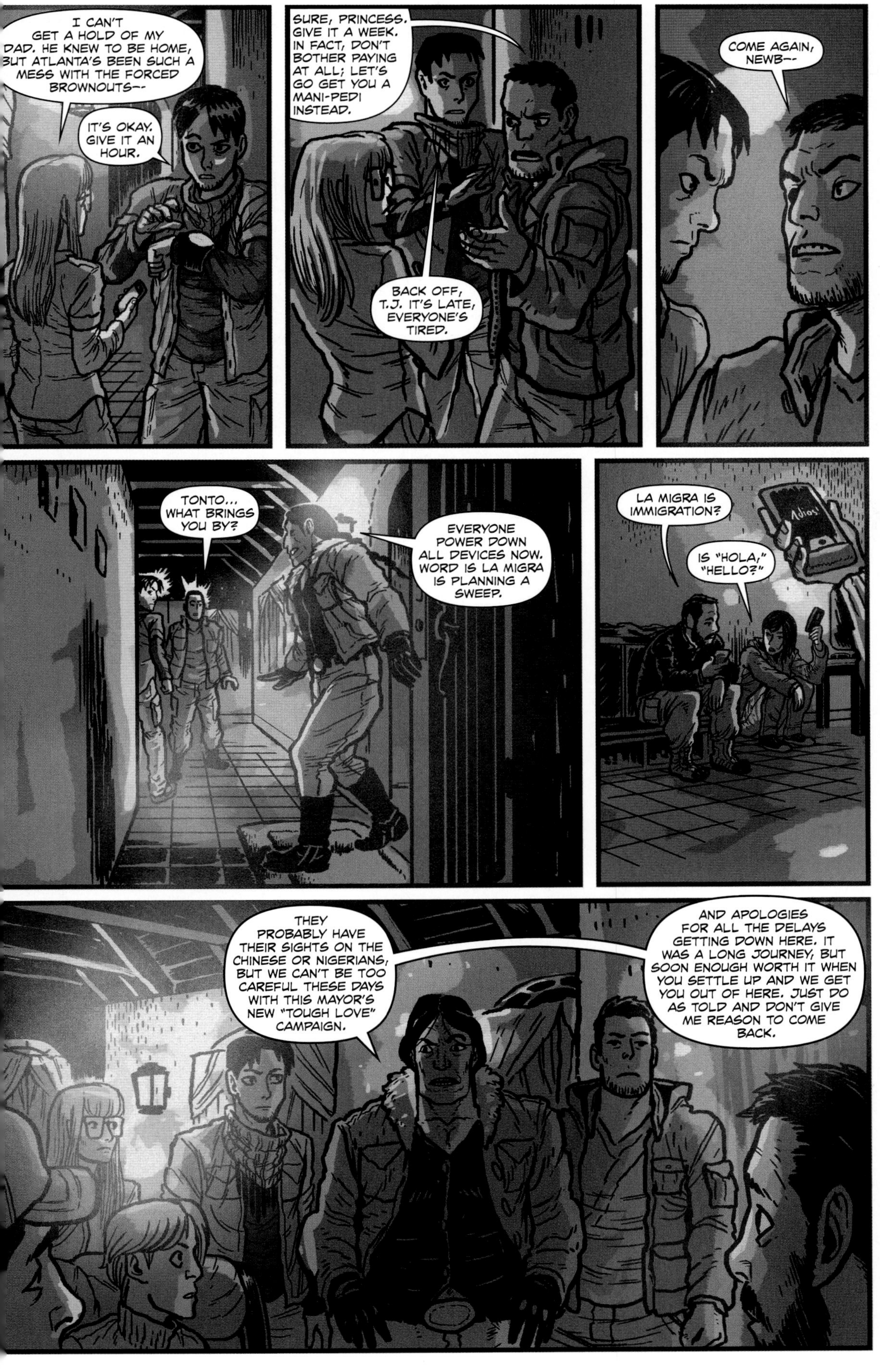
I CAN'T GET A HOLD OF MY DAD. HE KNEW TO BE HOME, BUT ATLANTA'S BEEN SUCH A MESS WITH THE FORCED BROWNOUTS--
IT'S OKAY. GIVE IT AN HOUR.
SURE, PRINCESS. GIVE IT A WEEK. IN FACT, DON'T BOTHER PAYING AT ALL; LET'S GO GET YOU A MANI-PEDI INSTEAD.
BACK OFF, T.J. IT'S LATE, EVERYONE'S TIRED.
COME AGAIN, NEWB--
TONTO... WHAT BRINGS YOU BY?
EVERYONE POWER DOWN ALL DEVICES NOW. WORD IS LA MIGRA IS PLANNING A SWEEP.
LA MIGRA IS IMMIGRATION?
IS "HOLA," "HELLO?"
Adios!
THEY PROBABLY HAVE THEIR SIGHTS ON THE CHINESE OR NIGERIANS, BUT WE CAN'T BE TOO CAREFUL THESE DAYS WITH THIS MAYOR'S NEW "TOUGH LOVE" CAMPAIGN.
AND APOLOGIES FOR ALL THE DELAYS GETTING DOWN HERE. IT WAS A LONG JOURNEY, BUT SOON ENOUGH WORTH IT WHEN YOU SETTLE UP AND WE GET YOU OUT OF HERE. JUST DO AS TOLD AND DON'T GIVE ME REASON TO COME BACK.

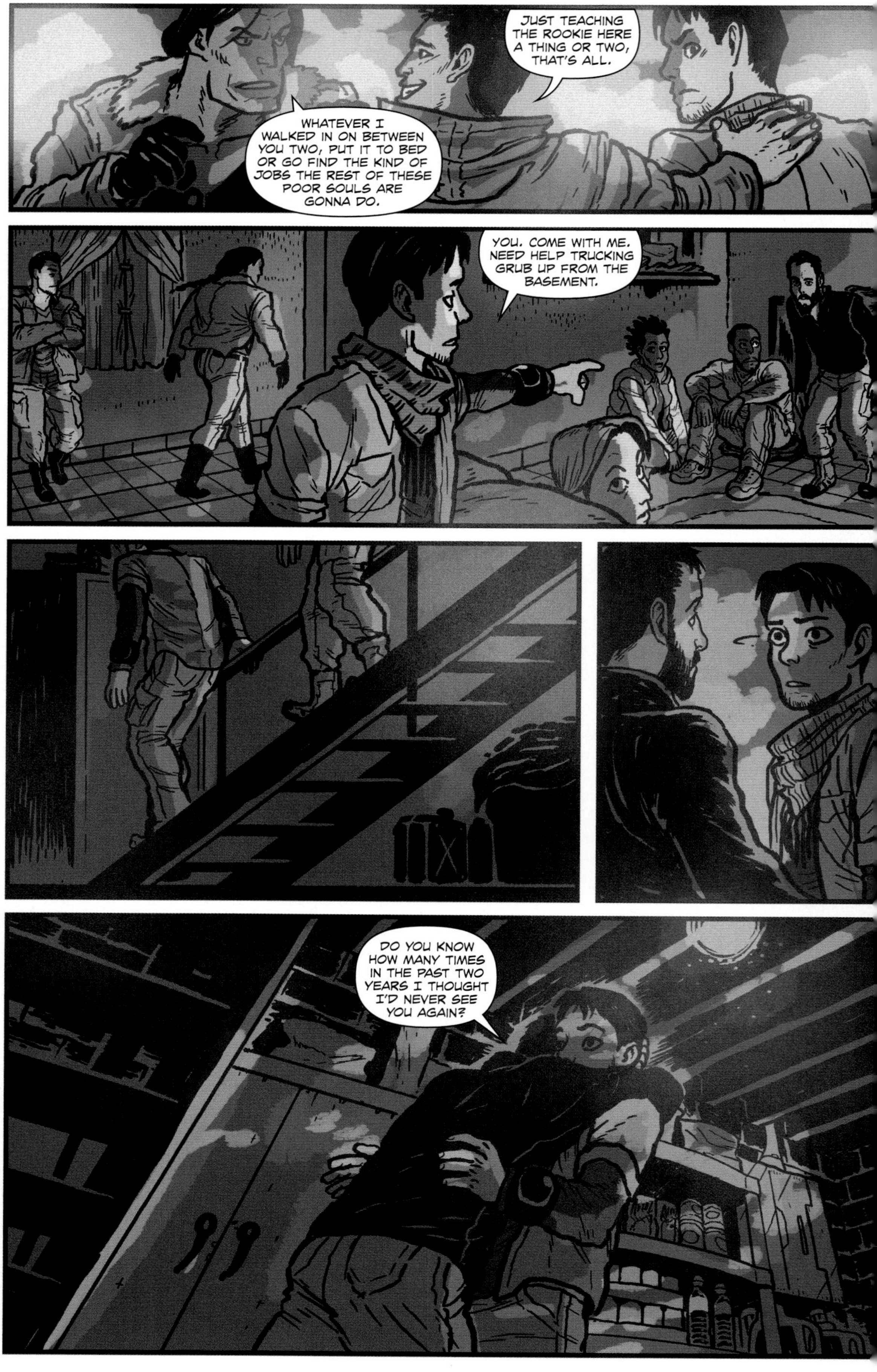
JUST TEACHING THE ROOKIE HERE A THING OR TWO, THAT'S ALL.
WHATEVER I WALKED IN ON BETWEEN YOU TWO, PUT IT TO BED OR GO FIND THE KIND OF JOBS THE REST OF THESE POOR SOULS ARE GONNA DO.
YOU. COME WITH ME. NEED HELP TRUCKING GRUB UP FROM THE BASEMENT.
DO YOU KNOW HOW MANY TIMES IN THE PAST TWO YEARS I THOUGHT I'D NEVER SEE YOU AGAIN?

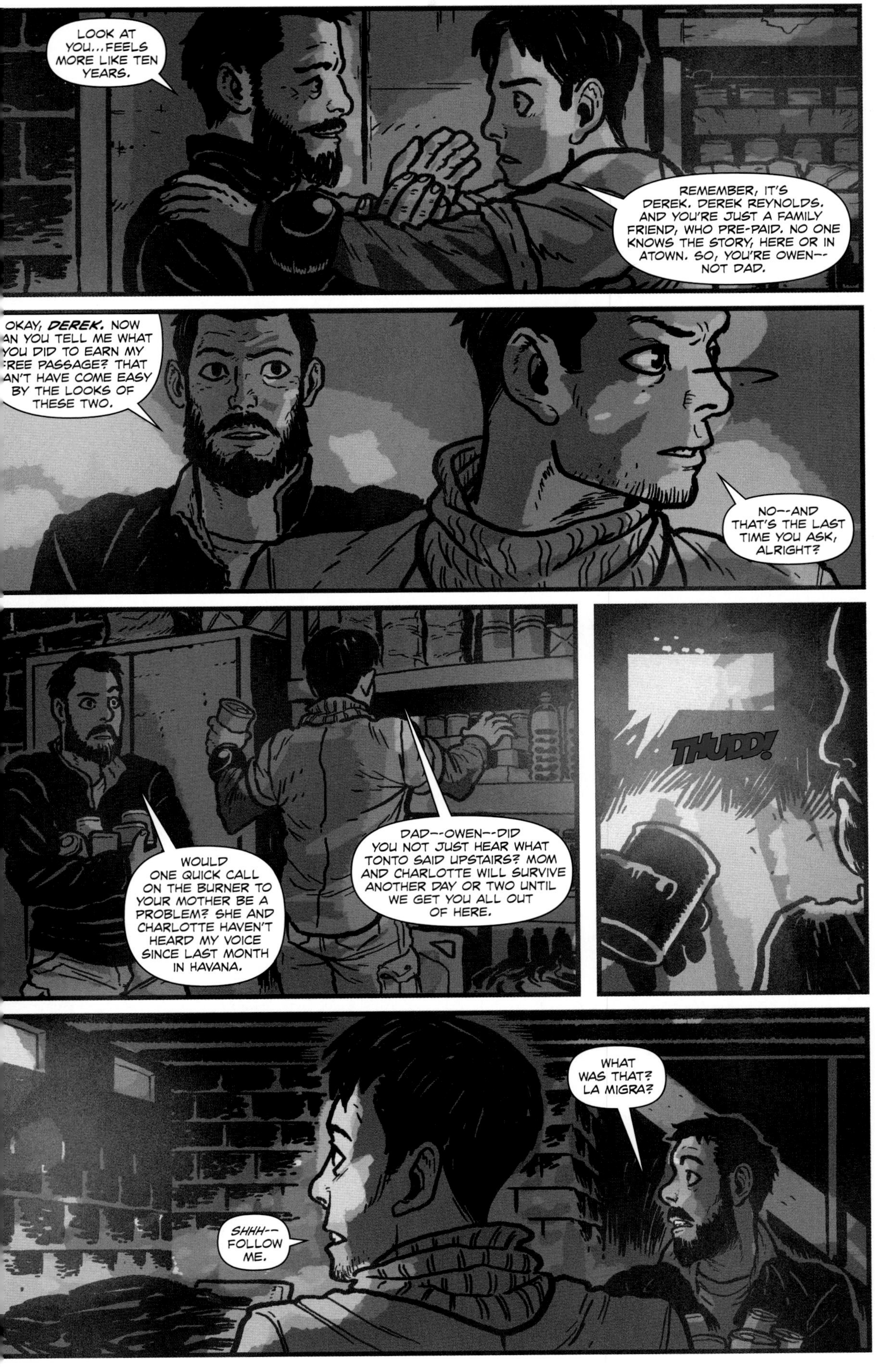
LOOK AT YOU...FEELS MORE LIKE TEN YEARS.
REMEMBER, IT'S DEREK. DEREK REYNOLDS. AND YOU'RE JUST A FAMILY FRIEND, WHO PRE-PAID. NO ONE KNOWS THE STORY, HERE OR IN ATOWN. SO, YOU'RE OWEN-- NOT DAD.
OKAY, DEREK. NOW AN YOU TELL ME WHAT YOU DID TO EARN MY FREE PASSAGE? THAT AN'T HAVE COME EASY BY THE LOOKS OF THESE TWO.
NO--AND THAT'S THE LAST TIME YOU ASK, ALRIGHT?
WOULD ONE QUICK CALL ON THE BURNER TO YOUR MOTHER BE A PROBLEM? SHE AND CHARLOTTE HAVEN'T HEARD MY VOICE SINCE LAST MONTH IN HAVANA.
DAD--OWEN--DID YOU NOT JUST HEAR WHAT TONTO SAID UPSTAIRS? MOM AND CHARLOTTE WILL SURVIVE ANOTHER DAY OR TWO UNTIL WE GET YOU ALL OUT OF HERE.
THUDD!
WHAT WAS THAT? LA MIGRA?
SHHH-- FOLLOW ME.

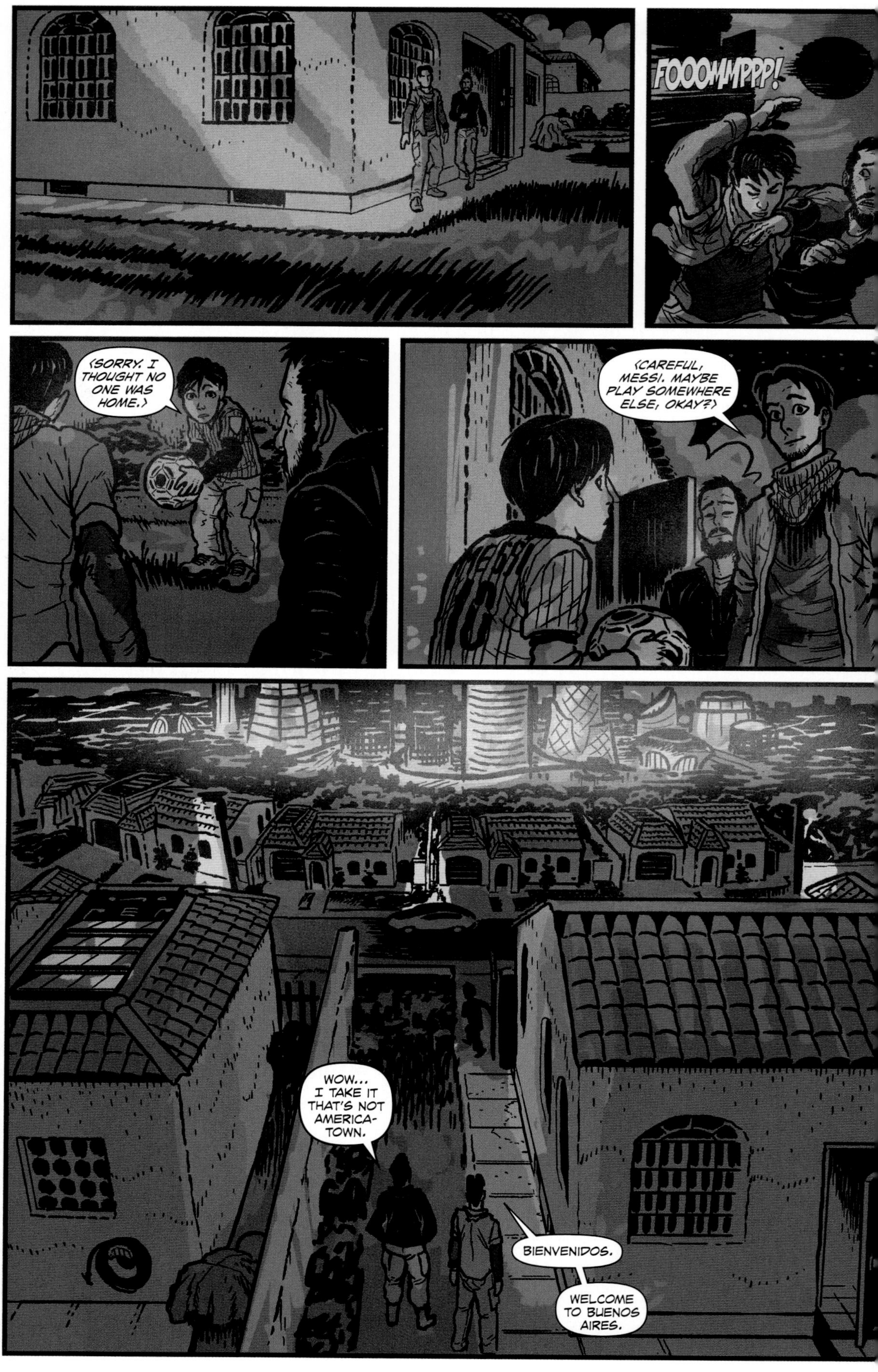
FOOOMMPPP!
‹SORRY. I THOUGHT NO ONE WAS HOME.›
‹CAREFUL, MESSI. MAYBE PLAY SOMEWHERE ELSE, OKAY?›
WOW... I TAKE IT THAT'S NOT AMERICA-TOWN.
BIENVENIDOS.
WELCOME TO BUENOS AIRES.

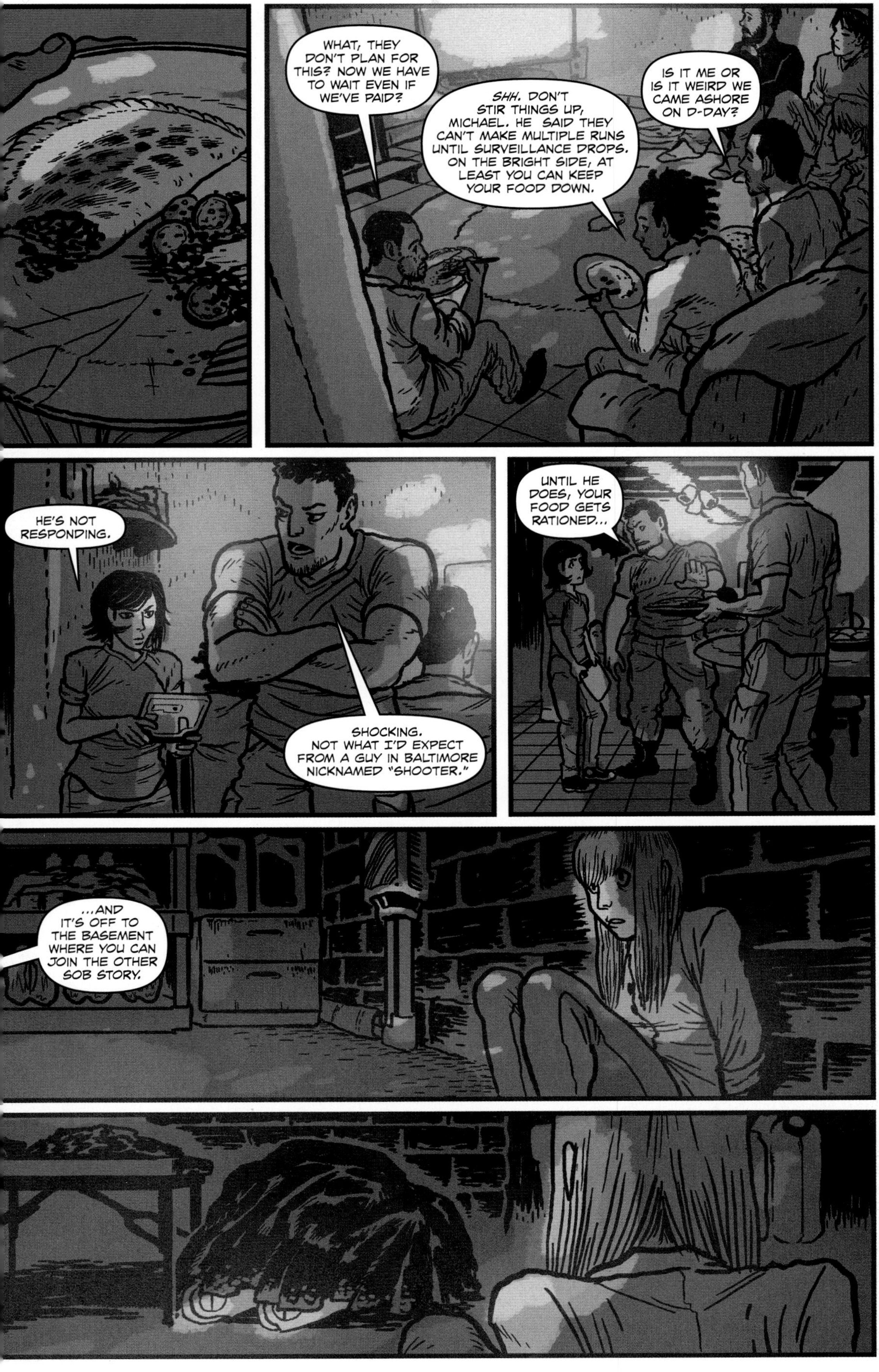
WHAT, THEY DON'T PLAN FOR THIS? NOW WE HAVE TO WAIT EVEN IF WE'VE PAID?
SHH. DON'T STIR THINGS UP, MICHAEL. HE SAID THEY CAN'T MAKE MULTIPLE RUNS UNTIL SURVEILLANCE DROPS. ON THE BRIGHT SIDE, AT LEAST YOU CAN KEEP YOUR FOOD DOWN.
IS IT ME OR IS IT WEIRD WE CAME ASHORE ON D-DAY?
HE'S NOT RESPONDING.
SHOCKING. NOT WHAT I'D EXPECT FROM A GUY IN BALTIMORE NICKNAMED "SHOOTER."
UNTIL HE DOES, YOUR FOOD GETS RATIONED...
...AND IT'S OFF TO THE BASEMENT WHERE YOU CAN JOIN THE OTHER SOB STORY.

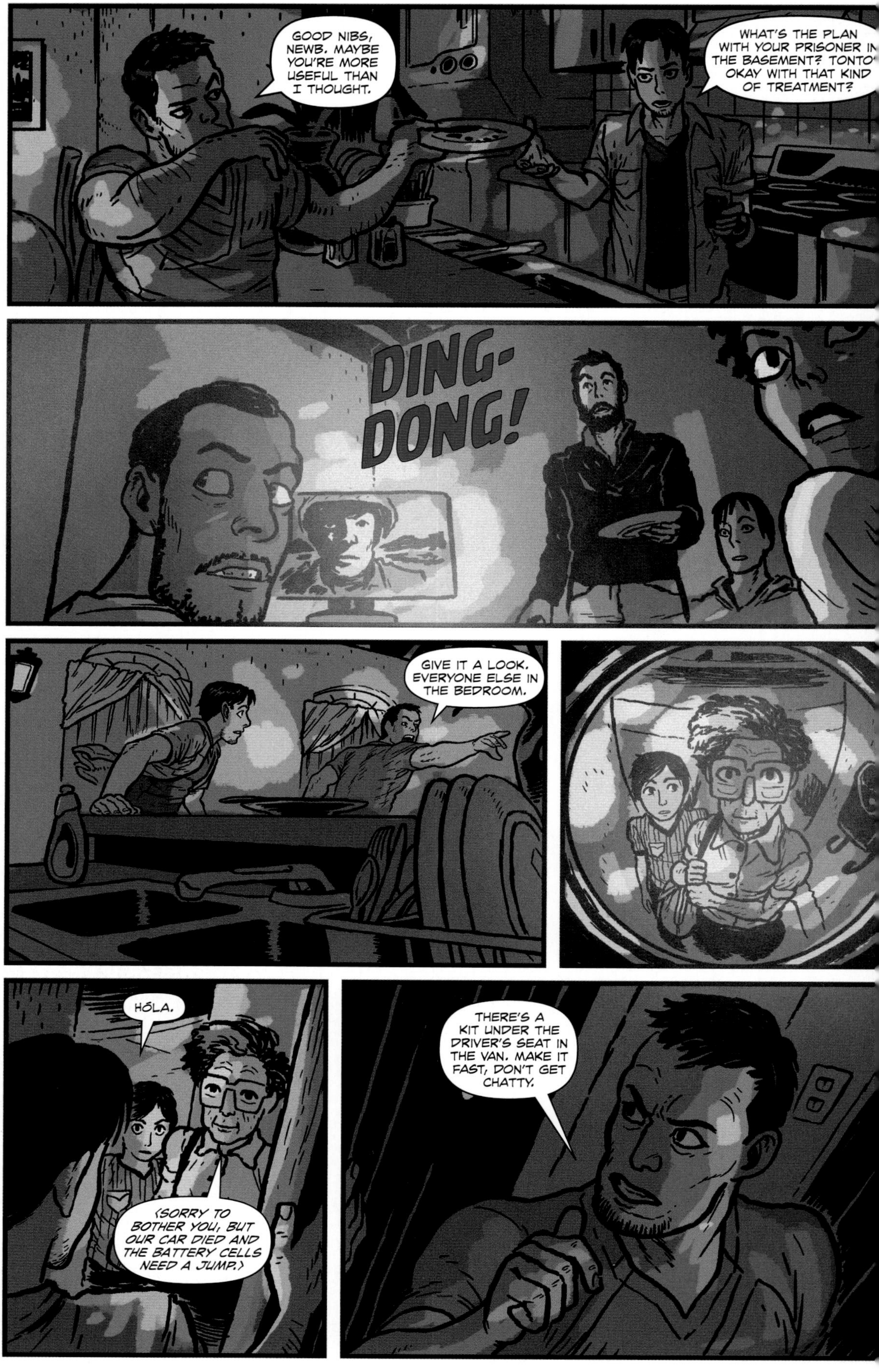
GOOD NIBS, NEWB. MAYBE YOU'RE MORE USEFUL THAN I THOUGHT.
WHAT'S THE PLAN WITH YOUR PRISONER IN THE BASEMENT? TONTO'S OKAY WITH THAT KIND OF TREATMENT?
DING-DONG!
GIVE IT A LOOK. EVERYONE ELSE IN THE BEDROOM.
HÓLA.
‹SORRY TO BOTHER YOU, BUT OUR CAR DIED AND THE BATTERY CELLS NEED A JUMP.›
THERE'S A KIT UNDER THE DRIVER'S SEAT IN THE VAN. MAKE IT FAST, DON'T GET CHATTY.

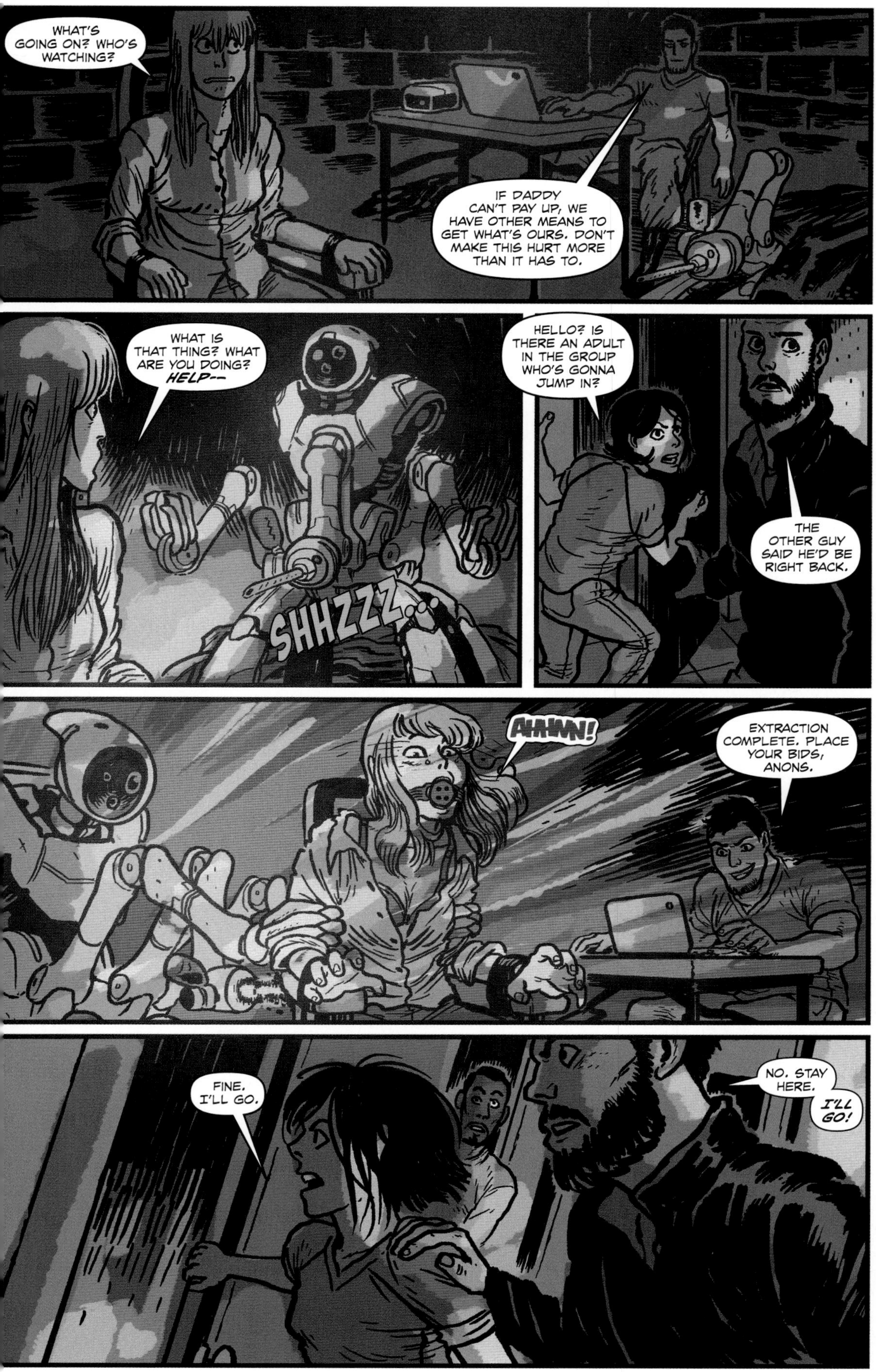
WHAT'S GOING ON? WHO'S WATCHING?
IF DADDY CAN'T PAY UP, WE HAVE OTHER MEANS TO GET WHAT'S OURS. DON'T MAKE THIS HURT MORE THAN IT HAS TO.
WHAT IS THAT THING? WHAT ARE YOU DOING? HELP--
SHHZZZ...
HELLO? IS THERE AN ADULT IN THE GROUP WHO'S GONNA JUMP IN?
THE OTHER GUY SAID HE'D BE RIGHT BACK.
AHHMN!
EXTRACTION COMPLETE. PLACE YOUR BIDS, ANONS.
FINE. I'LL GO.
NO. STAY HERE. I'LL GO!

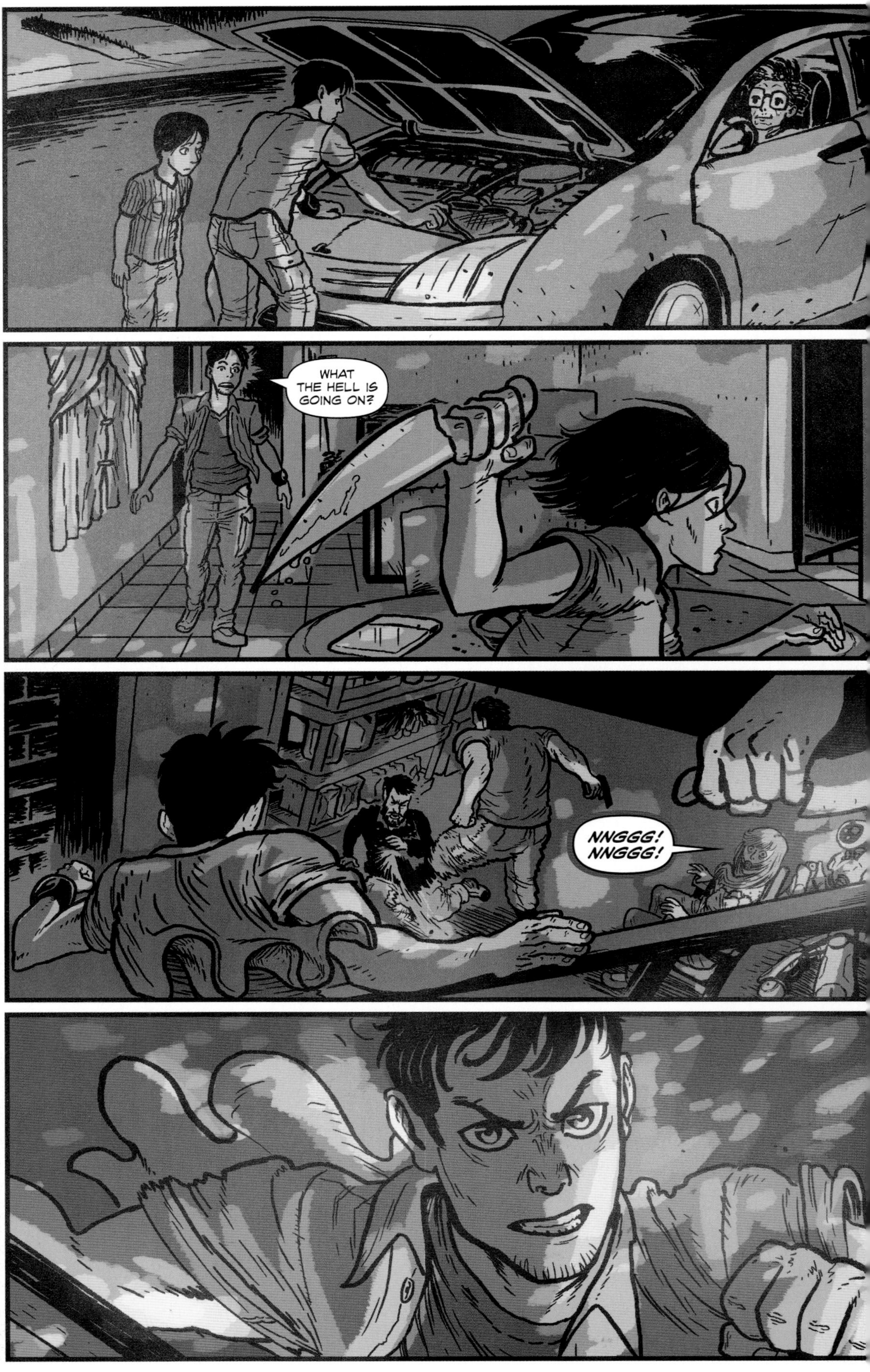
WHAT THE HELL IS GOING ON?
NNGGG! NNGGG!

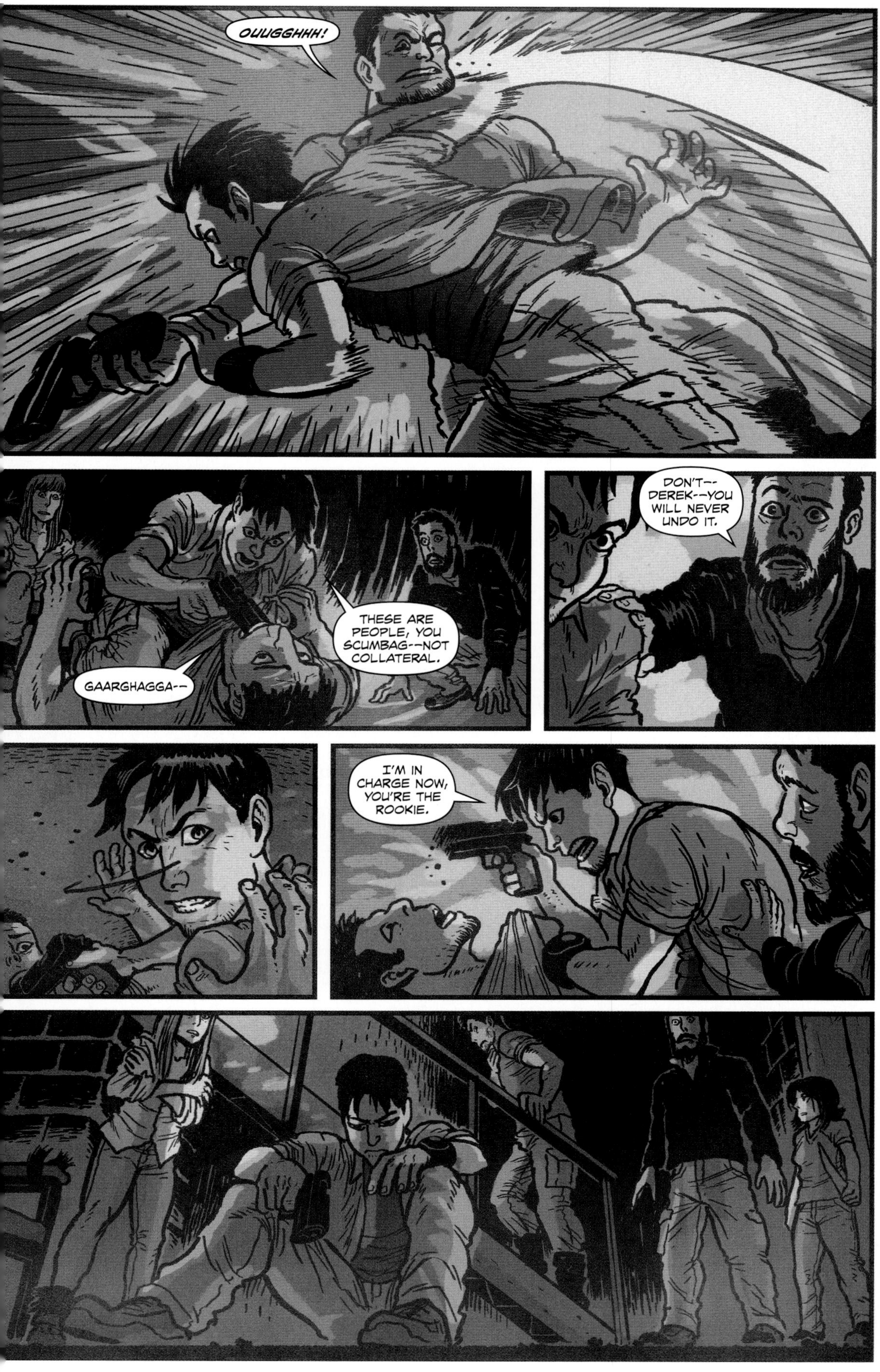
OUUGGHHH!
THESE ARE PEOPLE, YOU SCUMBAG--NOT COLLATERAL.
GAARGHAGGA--
DON'T--DEREK--YOU WILL NEVER UNDO IT.
I'M IN CHARGE NOW, YOU'RE THE ROOKIE.

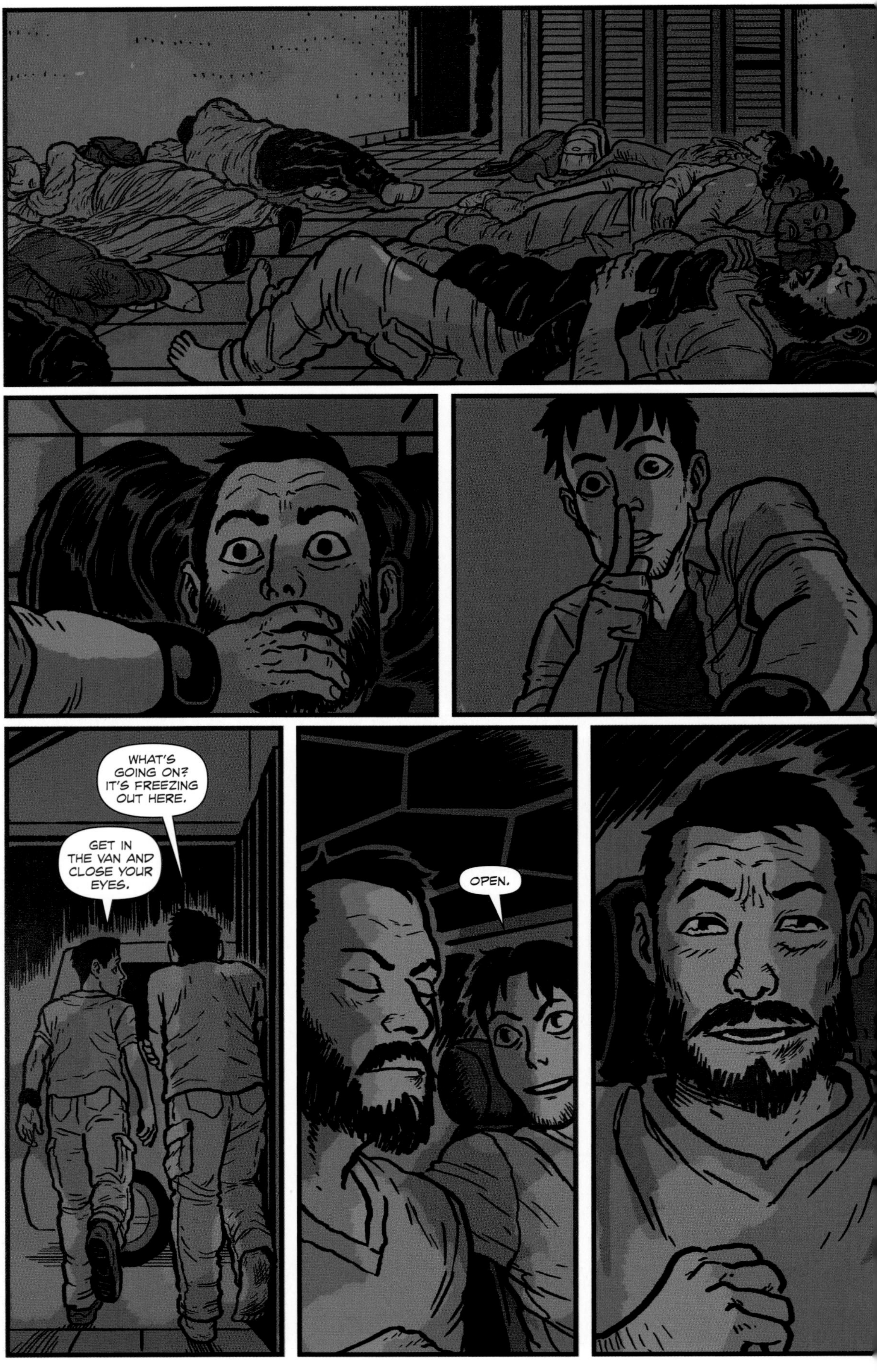
WHAT'S GOING ON? IT'S FREEZING OUT HERE.
GET IN THE VAN AND CLOSE YOUR EYES.
OPEN.

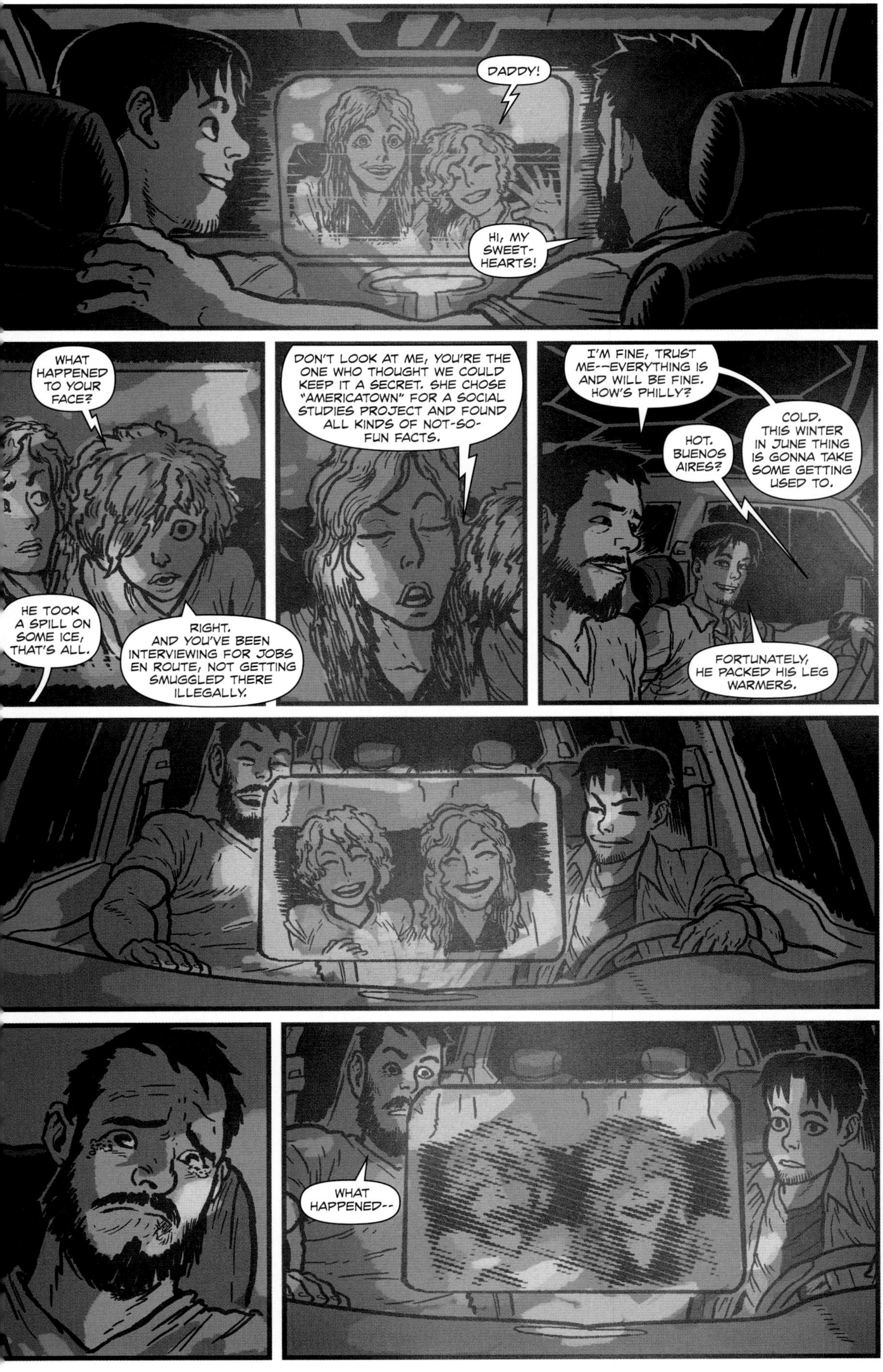
DADDY!
HI, MY SWEET-HEARTS!
WHAT HAPPENED TO YOUR FACE?
HE TOOK A SPILL ON SOME ICE, THAT'S ALL.
RIGHT. AND YOU'VE BEEN INTERVIEWING FOR JOBS EN ROUTE, NOT GETTING SMUGGLED THERE ILLEGALLY.
DON'T LOOK AT ME, YOU'RE THE ONE WHO THOUGHT WE COULD KEEP IT A SECRET. SHE CHOSE "AMERICATOWN" FOR A SOCIAL STUDIES PROJECT AND FOUND ALL KINDS OF NOT-SO-FUN FACTS.
I'M FINE, TRUST ME--EVERYTHING IS AND WILL BE FINE. HOW'S PHILLY?
COLD. THIS WINTER IN JUNE THING IS GONNA TAKE SOME GETTING USED TO.
HOT. BUENOS AIRES?
FORTUNATELY, HE PACKED HIS LEG WARMERS.
WHAT HAPPENED--

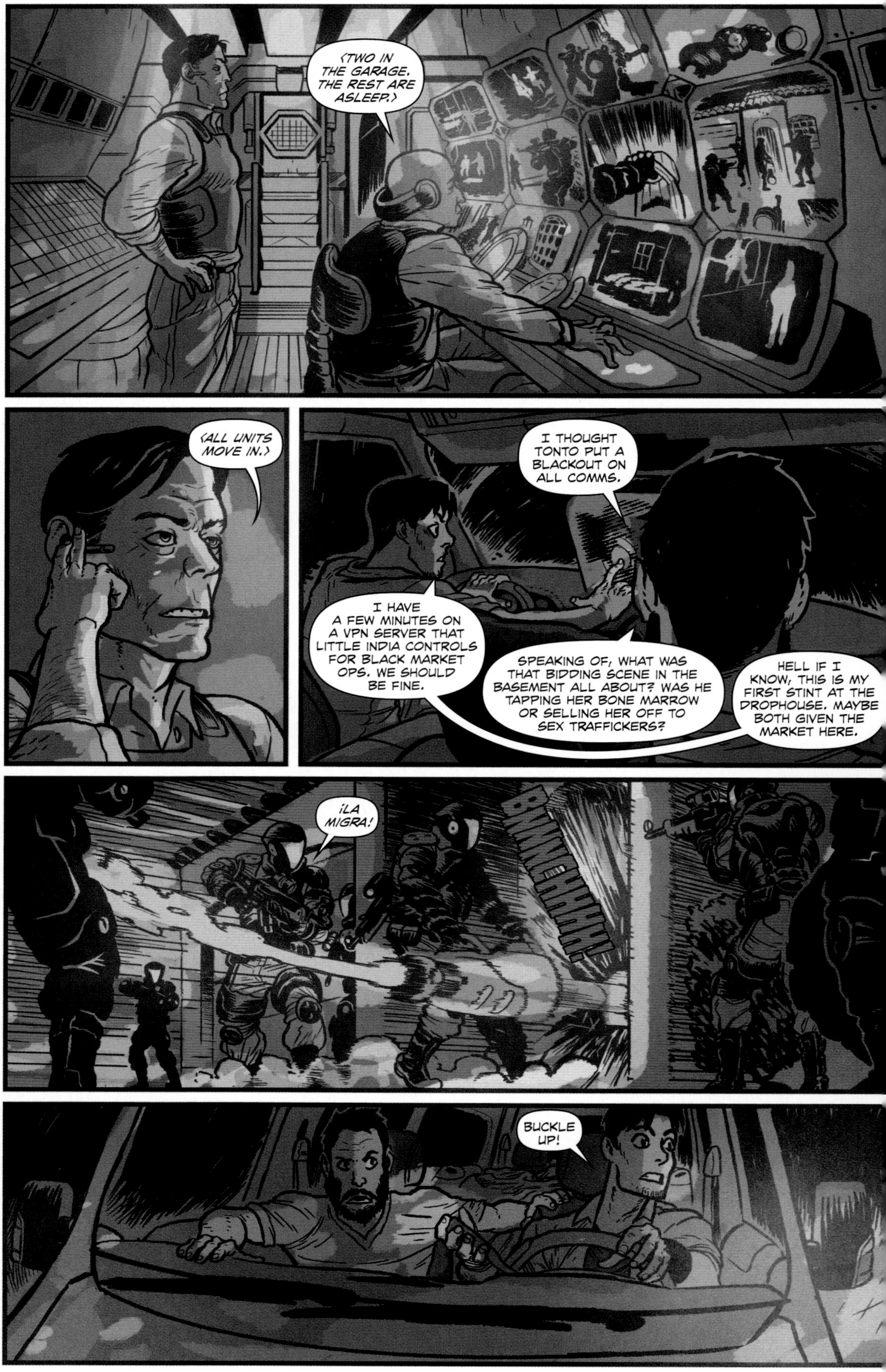

‹TWO IN THE GARAGE. THE REST ARE ASLEEP.›
‹ALL UNITS MOVE IN.›
I THOUGHT TONTO PUT A BLACKOUT ON ALL COMMS.
I HAVE A FEW MINUTES ON A VPN SERVER THAT LITTLE INDIA CONTROLS FOR BLACK MARKET OPS. WE SHOULD BE FINE.
SPEAKING OF, WHAT WAS THAT BIDDING SCENE IN THE BASEMENT ALL ABOUT? WAS HE TAPPING HER BONE MARROW OR SELLING HER OFF TO SEX TRAFFICKERS?
HELL IF I KNOW, THIS IS MY FIRST STINT AT THE DROPHOUSE. MAYBE BOTH GIVEN THE MARKET HERE.
¡LA MIGRA!
BUCKLE UP!

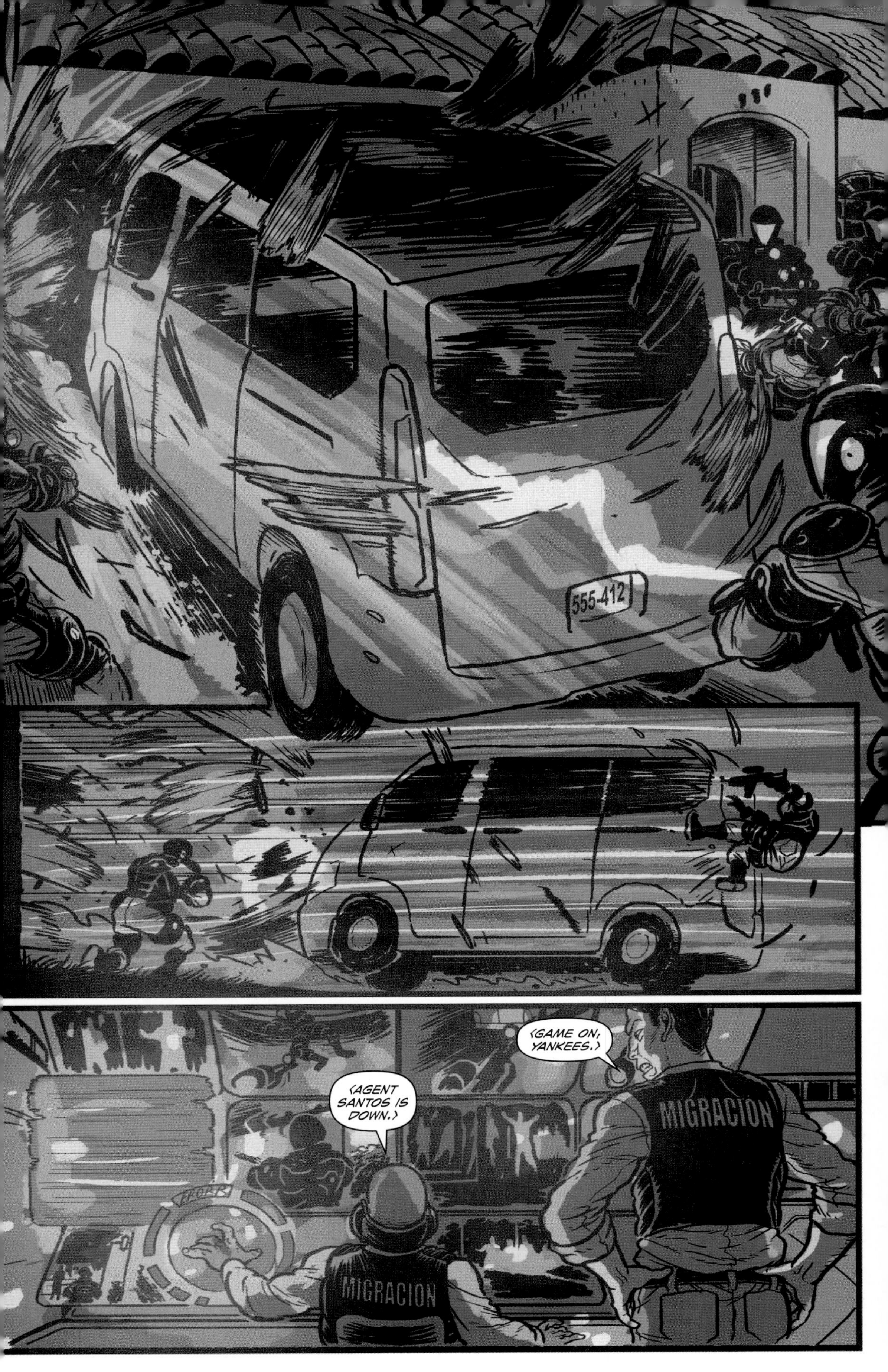
555-412
‹GAME ON, YANKEES.›
‹AGENT SANTOS IS DOWN.›
MIGRACION
MIGRACION

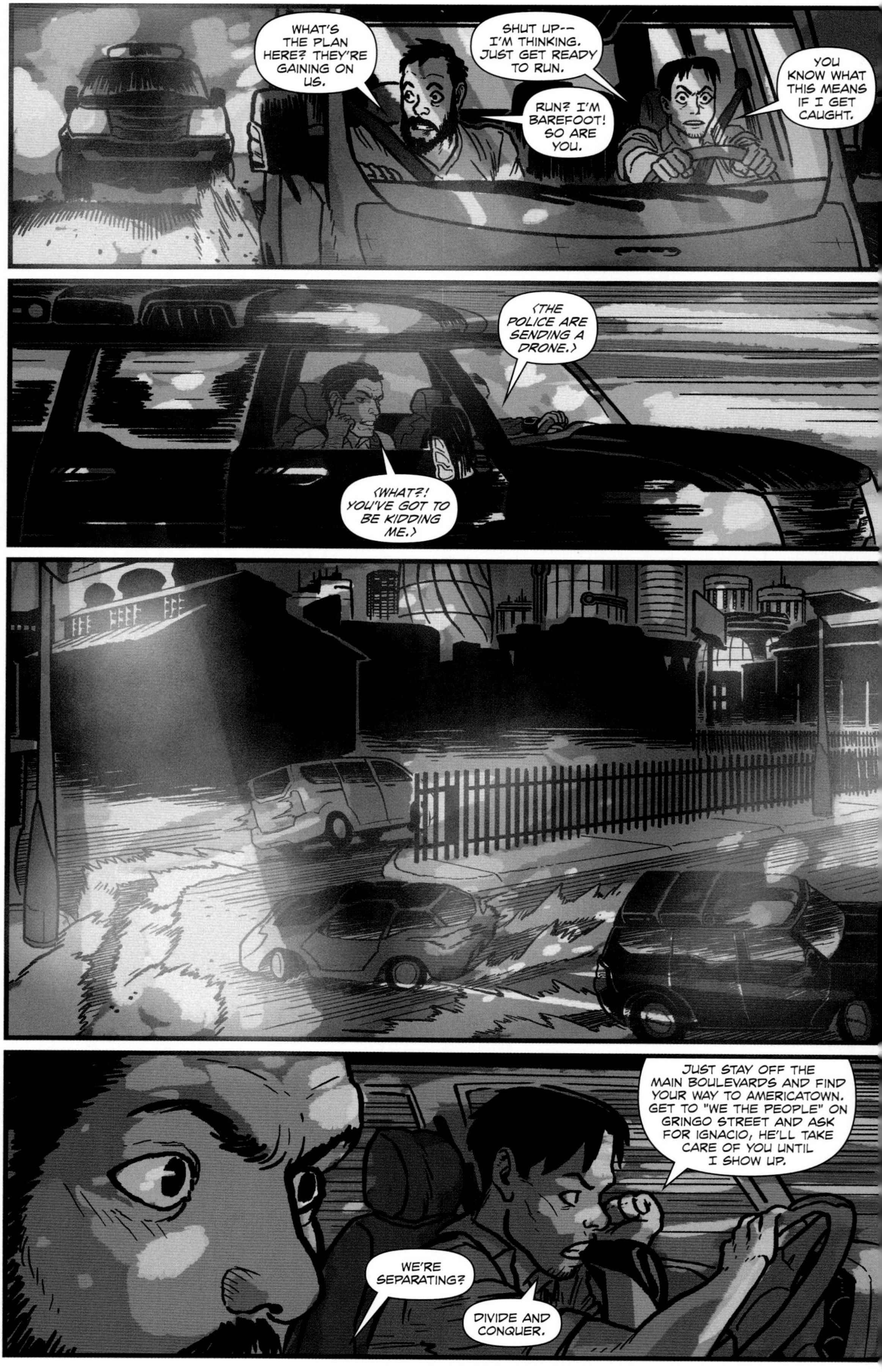
WHAT'S THE PLAN HERE? THEY'RE GAINING ON US.
SHUT UP-- I'M THINKING. JUST GET READY TO RUN.
RUN? I'M BAREFOOT! SO ARE YOU.
YOU KNOW WHAT THIS MEANS IF I GET CAUGHT.
<THE POLICE ARE SENDING A DRONE.>
<WHAT?! YOU'VE GOT TO BE KIDDING ME.>
JUST STAY OFF THE MAIN BOULEVARDS AND FIND YOUR WAY TO AMERICATOWN. GET TO "WE THE PEOPLE" ON GRINGO STREET AND ASK FOR IGNACIO, HE'LL TAKE CARE OF YOU UNTIL I SHOW UP.
WE'RE SEPARATING?
DIVIDE AND CONQUER.

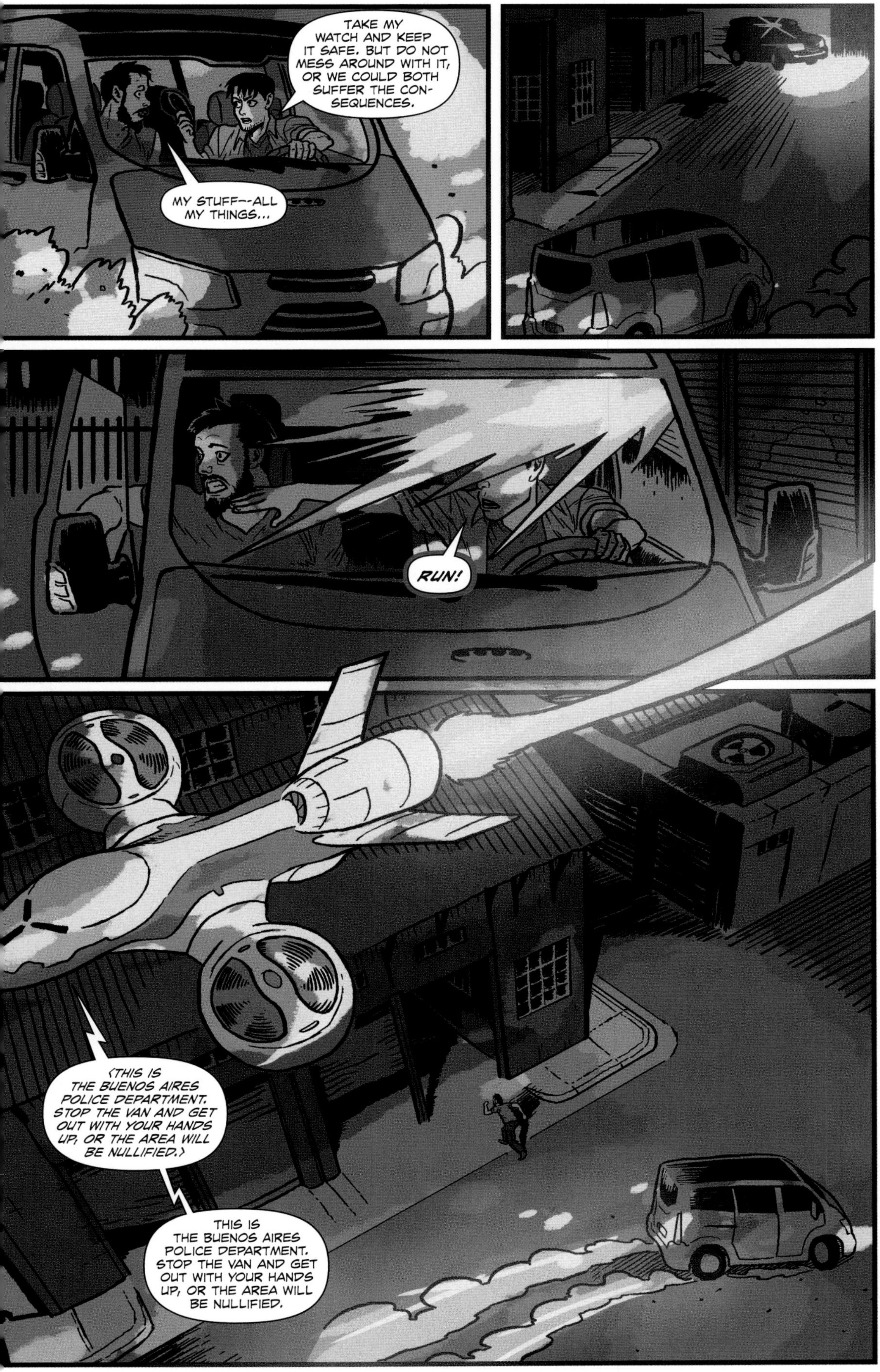
TAKE MY WATCH AND KEEP IT SAFE. BUT DO NOT MESS AROUND WITH IT, OR WE COULD BOTH SUFFER THE CON-SEQUENCES.
MY STUFF--ALL MY THINGS...
RUN!
<THIS IS THE BUENOS AIRES POLICE DEPARTMENT. STOP THE VAN AND GET OUT WITH YOUR HANDS UP, OR THE AREA WILL BE NULLIFIED.>
THIS IS THE BUENOS AIRES POLICE DEPARTMENT. STOP THE VAN AND GET OUT WITH YOUR HANDS UP, OR THE AREA WILL BE NULLIFIED.

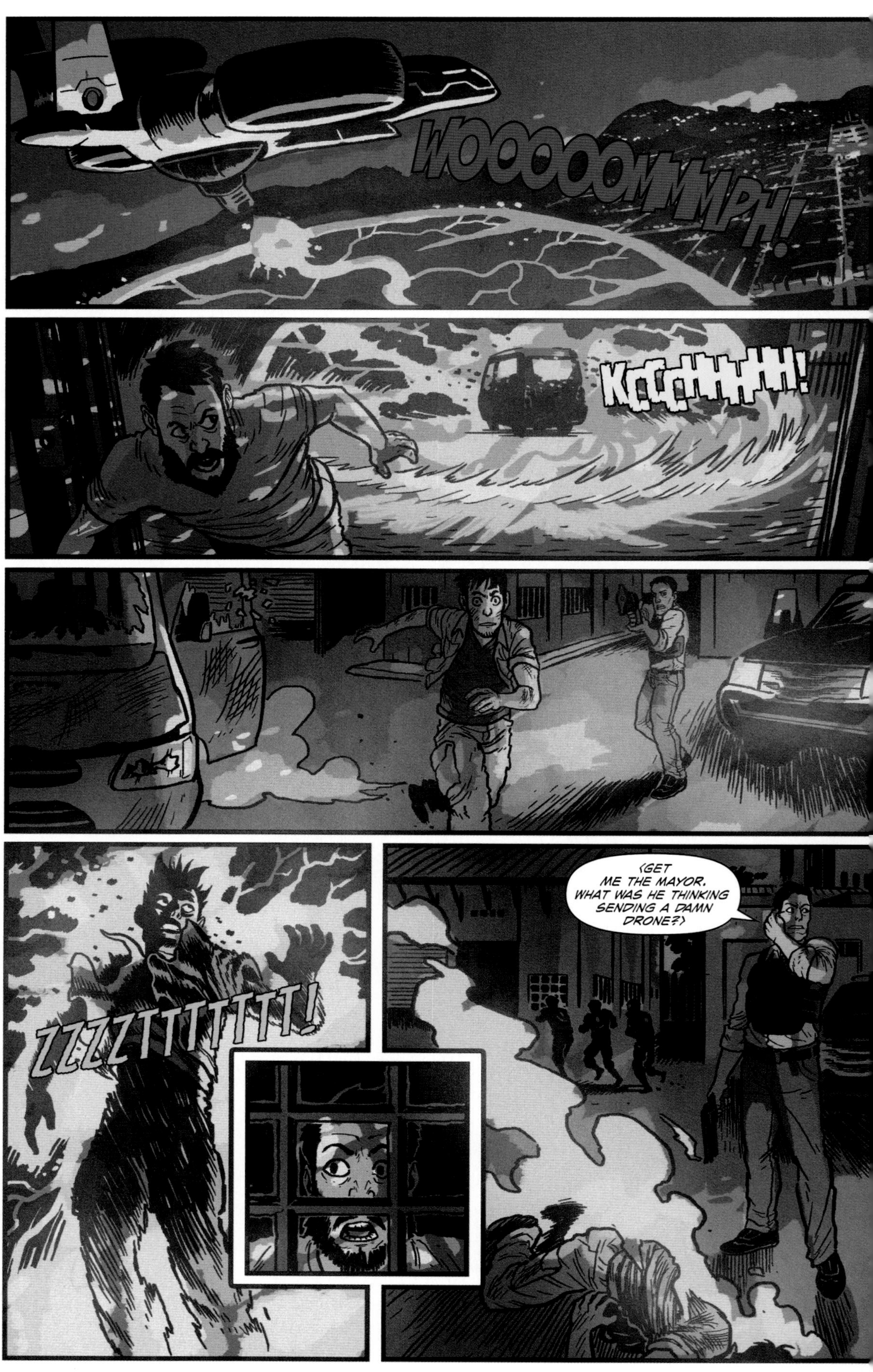
WOOOOOMMMPH!
KCCCHHHHHH!
ZZZZTTTTTTTT!
<GET ME THE MAYOR. WHAT WAS HE THINKING SENDING A DAMN DRONE?>

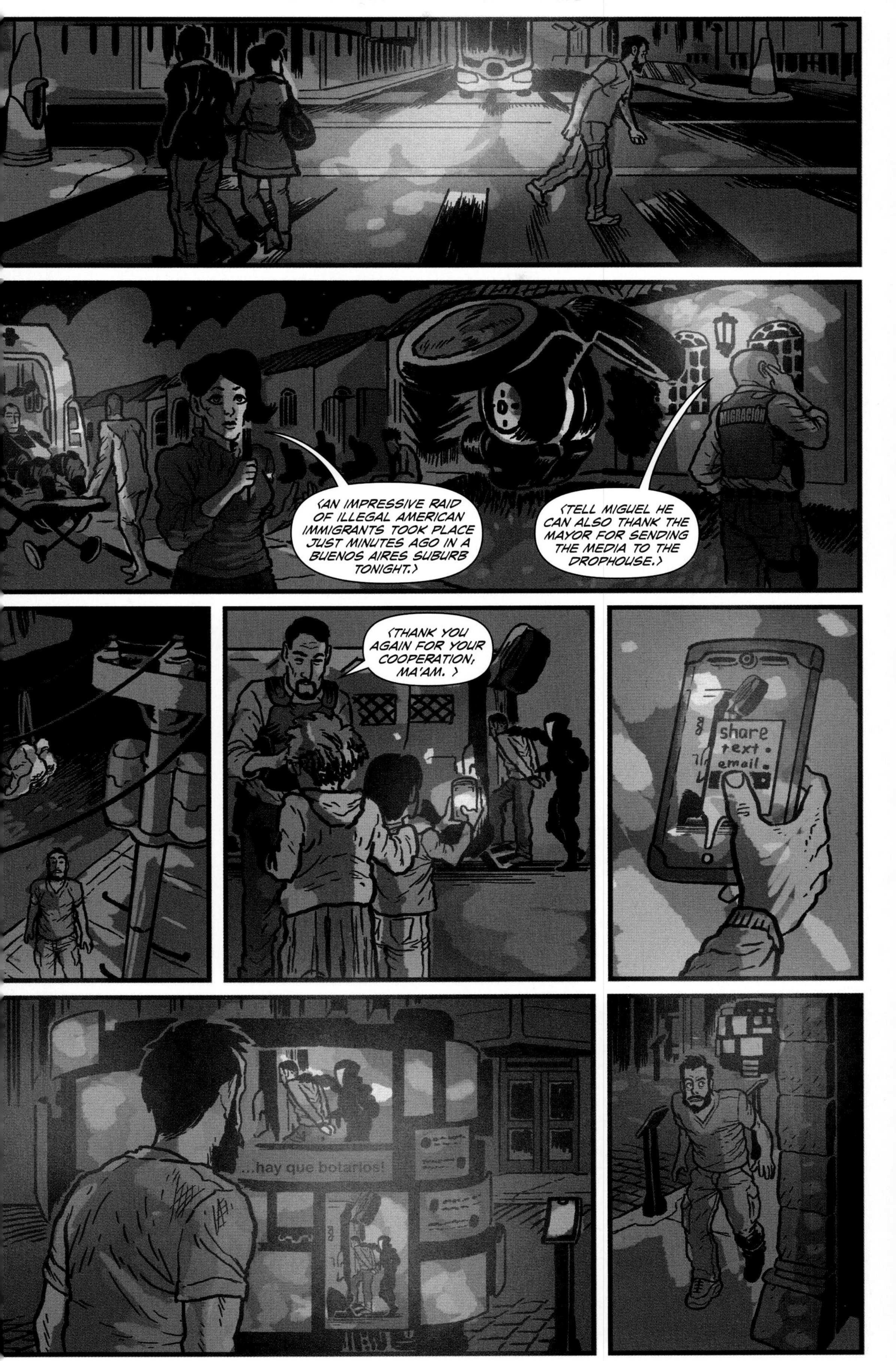

‹AN IMPRESSIVE RAID OF ILLEGAL AMERICAN IMMIGRANTS TOOK PLACE JUST MINUTES AGO IN A BUENOS AIRES SUBURB TONIGHT.›
‹TELL MIGUEL HE CAN ALSO THANK THE MAYOR FOR SENDING THE MEDIA TO THE DROPHOUSE.›
MIGRACIÓN
‹THANK YOU AGAIN FOR YOUR COOPERATION, MA'AM. ›
share
text
email
...hay que botarlos!

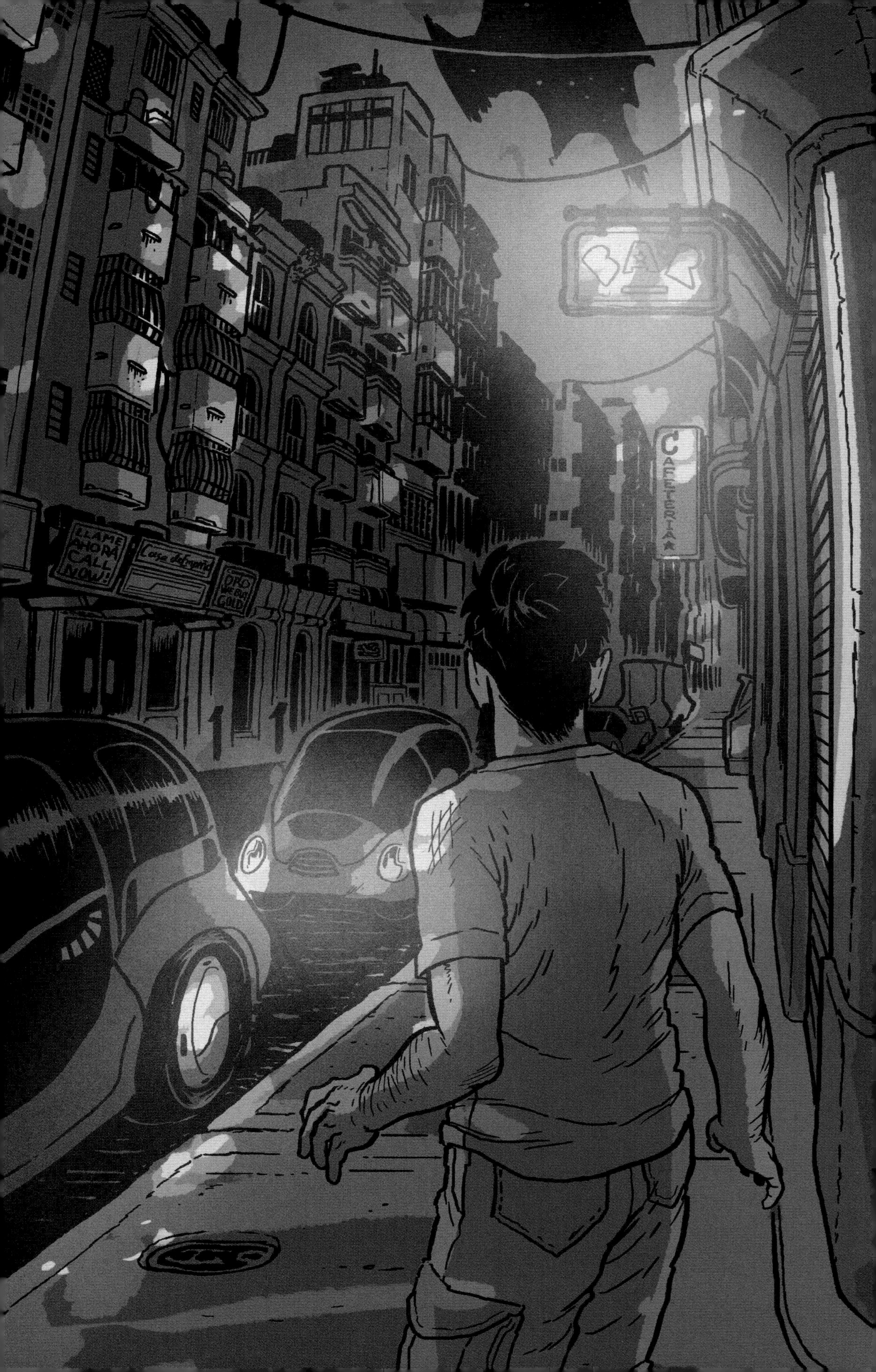
BAR
CAFETERIA
LLAME AHORA CALL NOW!
ORO WE BUY GOLD

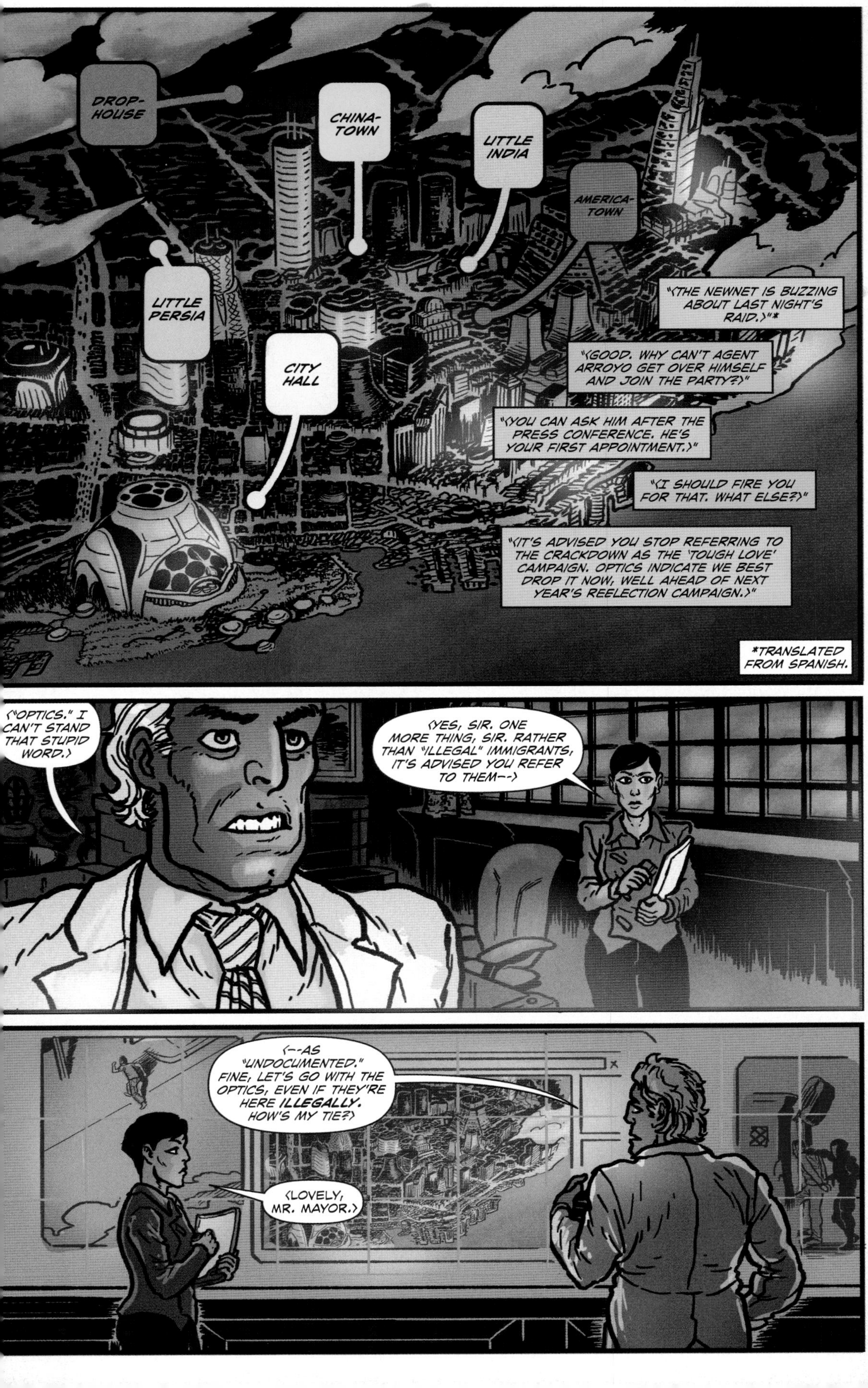

DROP-HOUSE
CHINA-TOWN
LITTLE INDIA
AMERICA-TOWN
LITTLE PERSIA
CITY HALL
"‹THE NEWNET IS BUZZING ABOUT LAST NIGHT'S RAID.›"*
"‹GOOD. WHY CAN'T AGENT ARROYO GET OVER HIMSELF AND JOIN THE PARTY?›"
"‹YOU CAN ASK HIM AFTER THE PRESS CONFERENCE. HE'S YOUR FIRST APPOINTMENT.›"
"‹I SHOULD FIRE YOU FOR THAT. WHAT ELSE?›"
"‹IT'S ADVISED YOU STOP REFERRING TO THE CRACKDOWN AS THE 'TOUGH LOVE' CAMPAIGN. OPTICS INDICATE WE BEST DROP IT NOW, WELL AHEAD OF NEXT YEAR'S REELECTION CAMPAIGN.›"
*TRANSLATED FROM SPANISH.
‹"OPTICS." I CAN'T STAND THAT STUPID WORD.›
‹YES, SIR. ONE MORE THING, SIR. RATHER THAN "ILLEGAL" IMMIGRANTS, IT'S ADVISED YOU REFER TO THEM--›
‹--AS "UNDOCUMENTED." FINE, LET'S GO WITH THE OPTICS, EVEN IF THEY'RE HERE ILLEGALLY. HOW'S MY TIE?›
‹LOVELY, MR. MAYOR.›

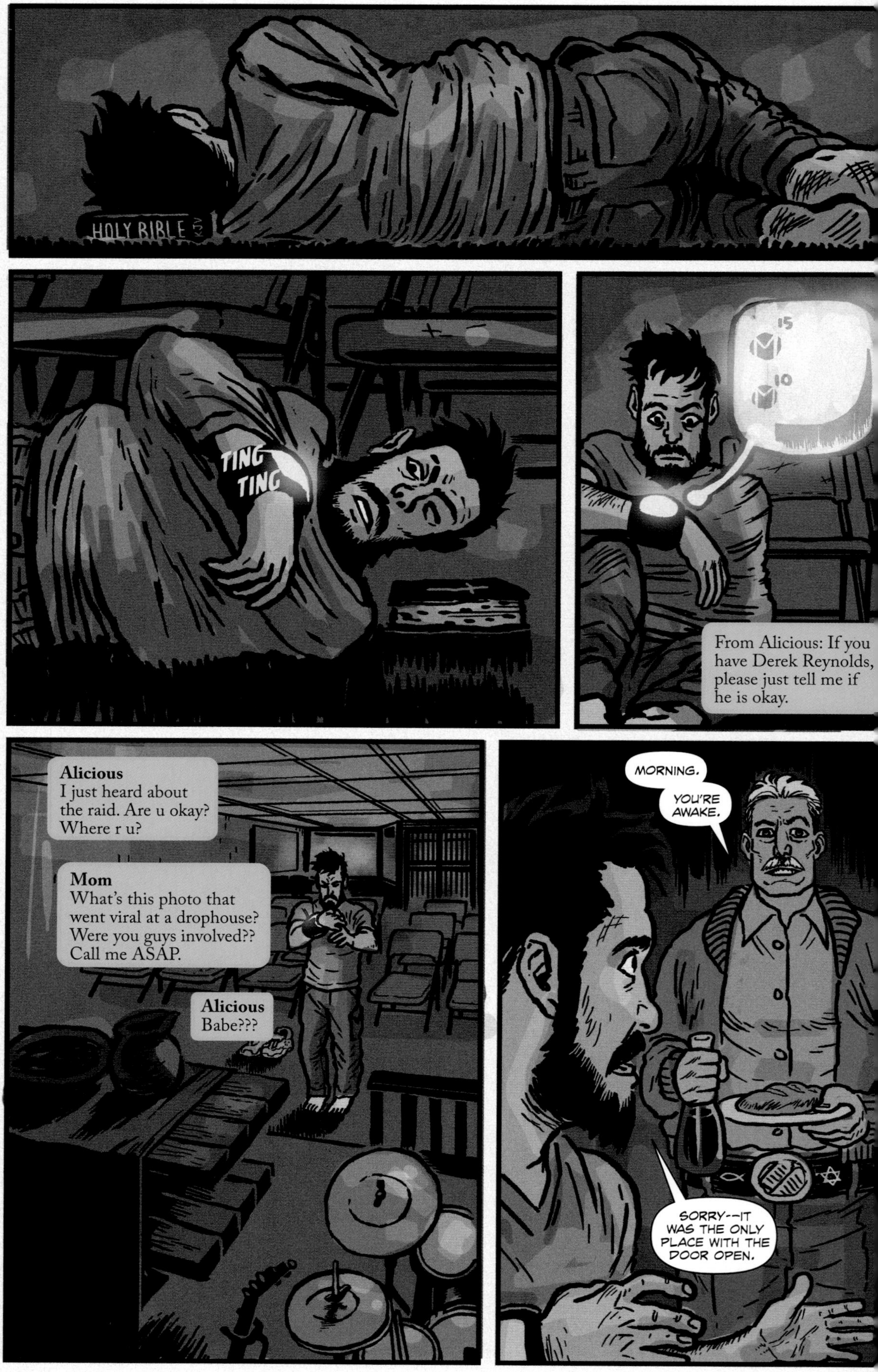
HOLY BIBLE KJV
TING
TING
15
10
From Alicious: If you have Derek Reynolds, please just tell me if he is okay.
Alicious
I just heard about the raid. Are u okay? Where r u?
Mom
What's this photo that went viral at a drophouse? Were you guys involved?? Call me ASAP.
Alicious
Babe???
MORNING.
YOU'RE AWAKE.
SORRY--IT WAS THE ONLY PLACE WITH THE DOOR OPEN.

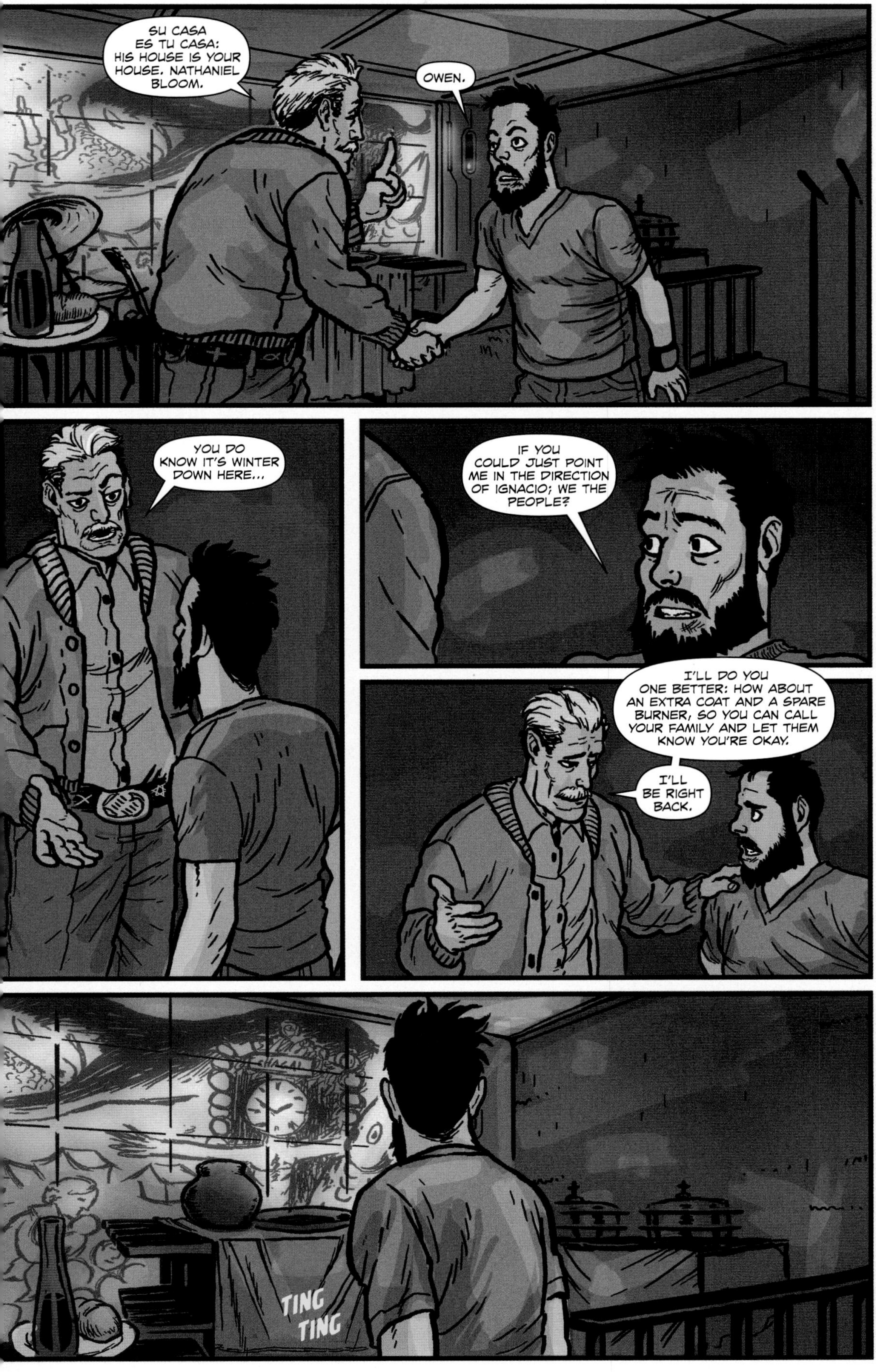
SU CASA ES TU CASA: HIS HOUSE IS YOUR HOUSE. NATHANIEL BLOOM.
OWEN.
YOU DO KNOW IT'S WINTER DOWN HERE...
IF YOU COULD JUST POINT ME IN THE DIRECTION OF IGNACIO; WE THE PEOPLE?
I'LL DO YOU ONE BETTER: HOW ABOUT AN EXTRA COAT AND A SPARE BURNER, SO YOU CAN CALL YOUR FAMILY AND LET THEM KNOW YOU'RE OKAY.
I'LL BE RIGHT BACK.
TING
TING

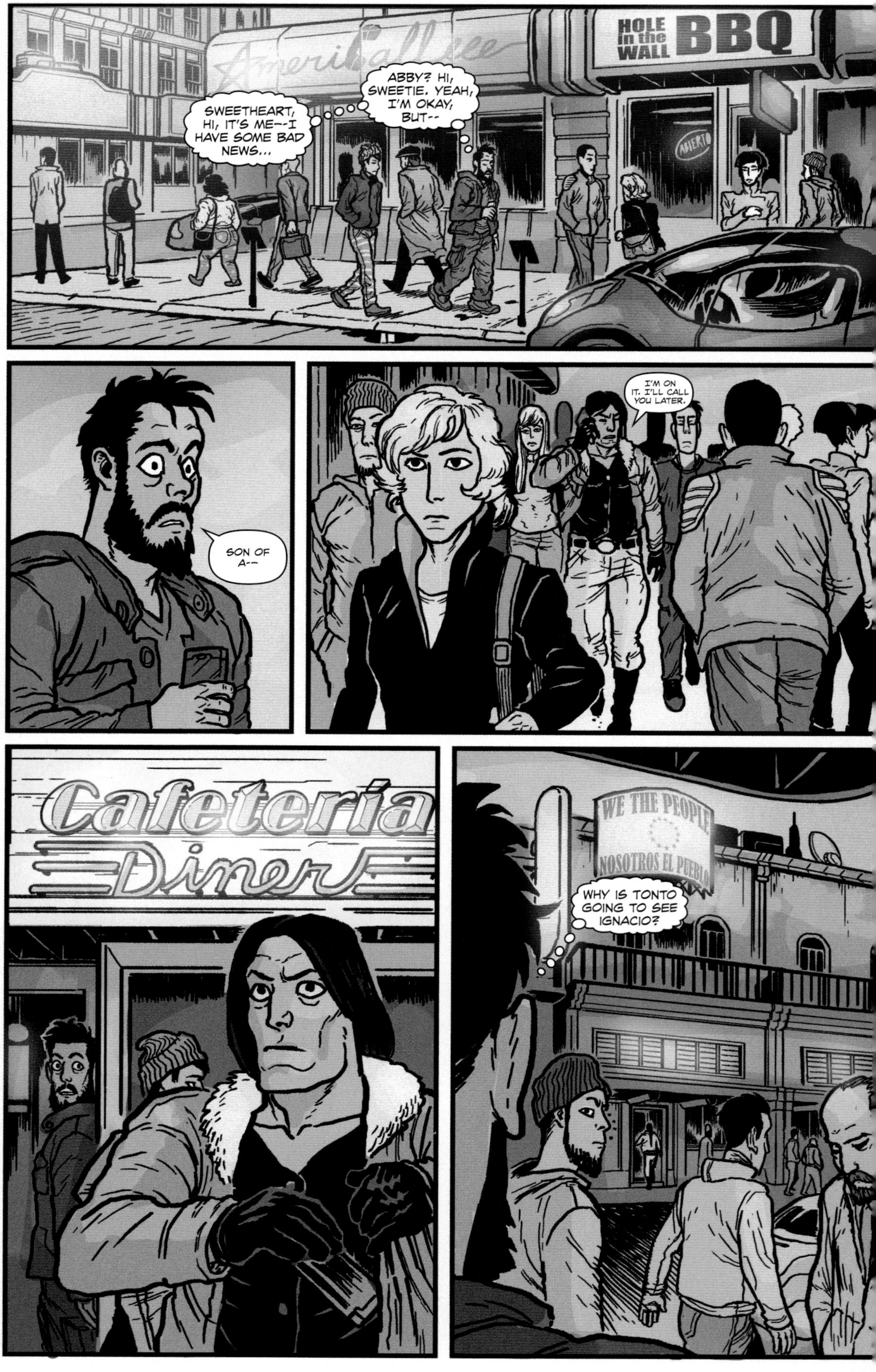
HOLE in the WALL BBQ
ABIERTO
SWEETHEART, HI, IT'S ME--I HAVE SOME BAD NEWS...
ABBY? HI, SWEETIE. YEAH, I'M OKAY, BUT--
SON OF A--
I'M ON IT. I'LL CALL YOU LATER.
Cafeteria
Diner
WE THE PEOPLE
NOSOTROS EL PUEBLO
WHY IS TONTO GOING TO SEE IGNACIO?

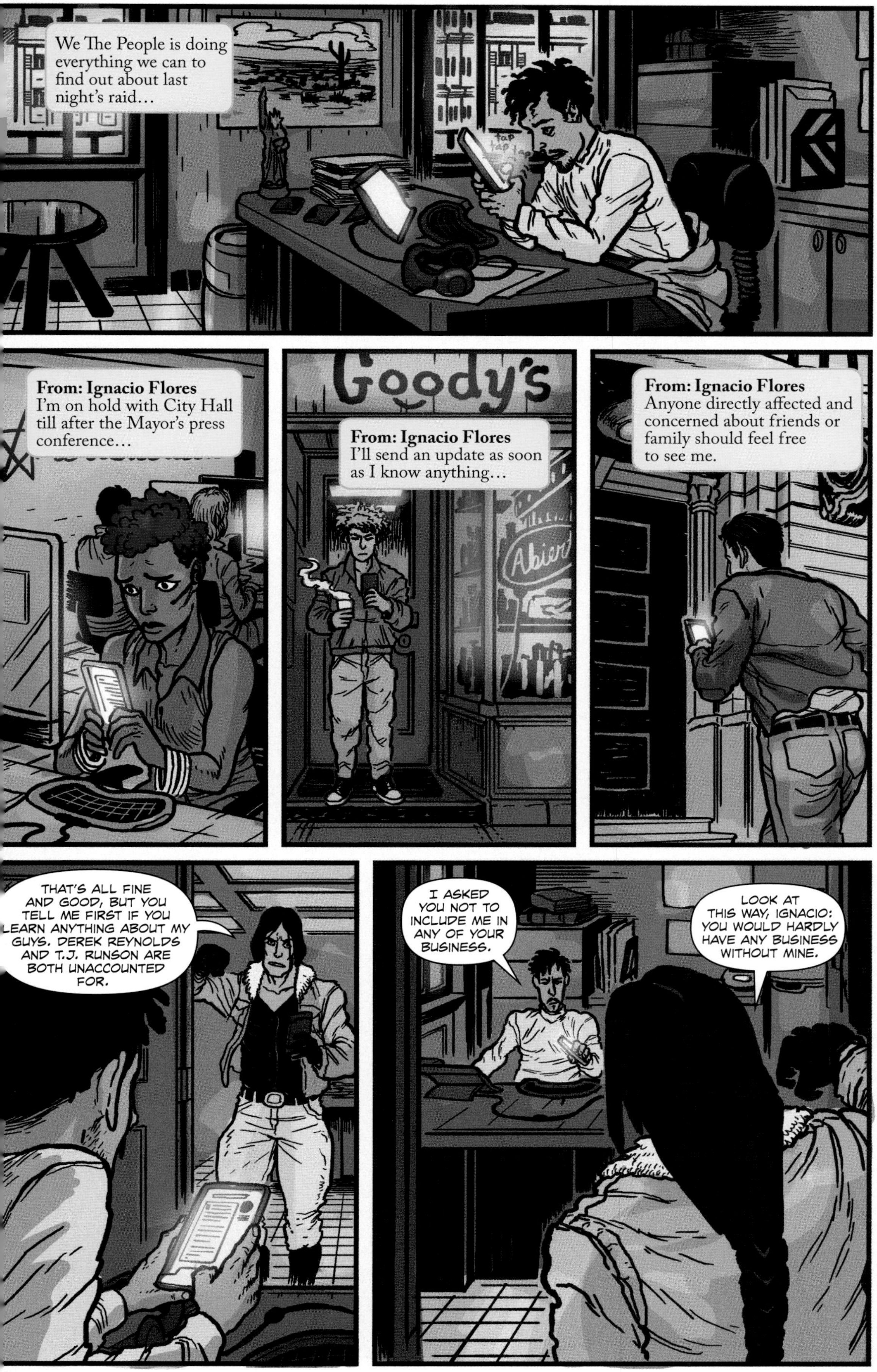
We The People is doing everything we can to find out about last night's raid…
tap tap tap
From: Ignacio Flores
I'm on hold with City Hall till after the Mayor's press conference…
Goody's
From: Ignacio Flores
I'll send an update as soon as I know anything…
From: Ignacio Flores
Anyone directly affected and concerned about friends or family should feel free to see me.
THAT'S ALL FINE AND GOOD, BUT YOU TELL ME FIRST IF YOU LEARN ANYTHING ABOUT MY GUYS. DEREK REYNOLDS AND T.J. RUNSON ARE BOTH UNACCOUNTED FOR.
I ASKED YOU NOT TO INCLUDE ME IN ANY OF YOUR BUSINESS.
LOOK AT THIS WAY, IGNACIO: YOU WOULD HARDLY HAVE ANY BUSINESS WITHOUT MINE.

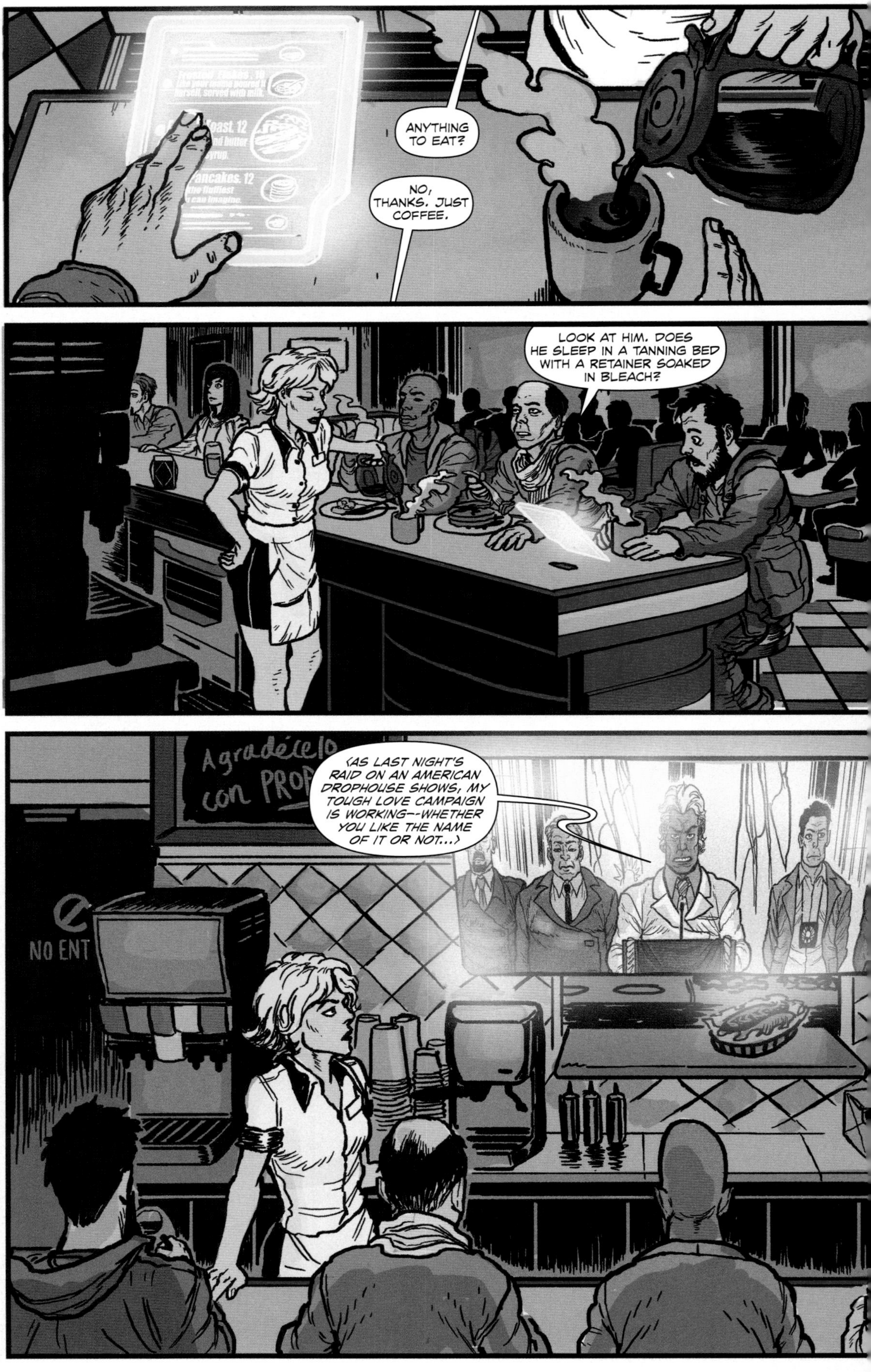
ANYTHING TO EAT?
NO, THANKS. JUST COFFEE.
LOOK AT HIM. DOES HE SLEEP IN A TANNING BED WITH A RETAINER SOAKED IN BLEACH?
Agradécelo con PROP
<AS LAST NIGHT'S RAID ON AN AMERICAN DROPHOUSE SHOWS, MY TOUGH LOVE CAMPAIGN IS WORKING--WHETHER YOU LIKE THE NAME OF IT OR NOT...>
NO ENT

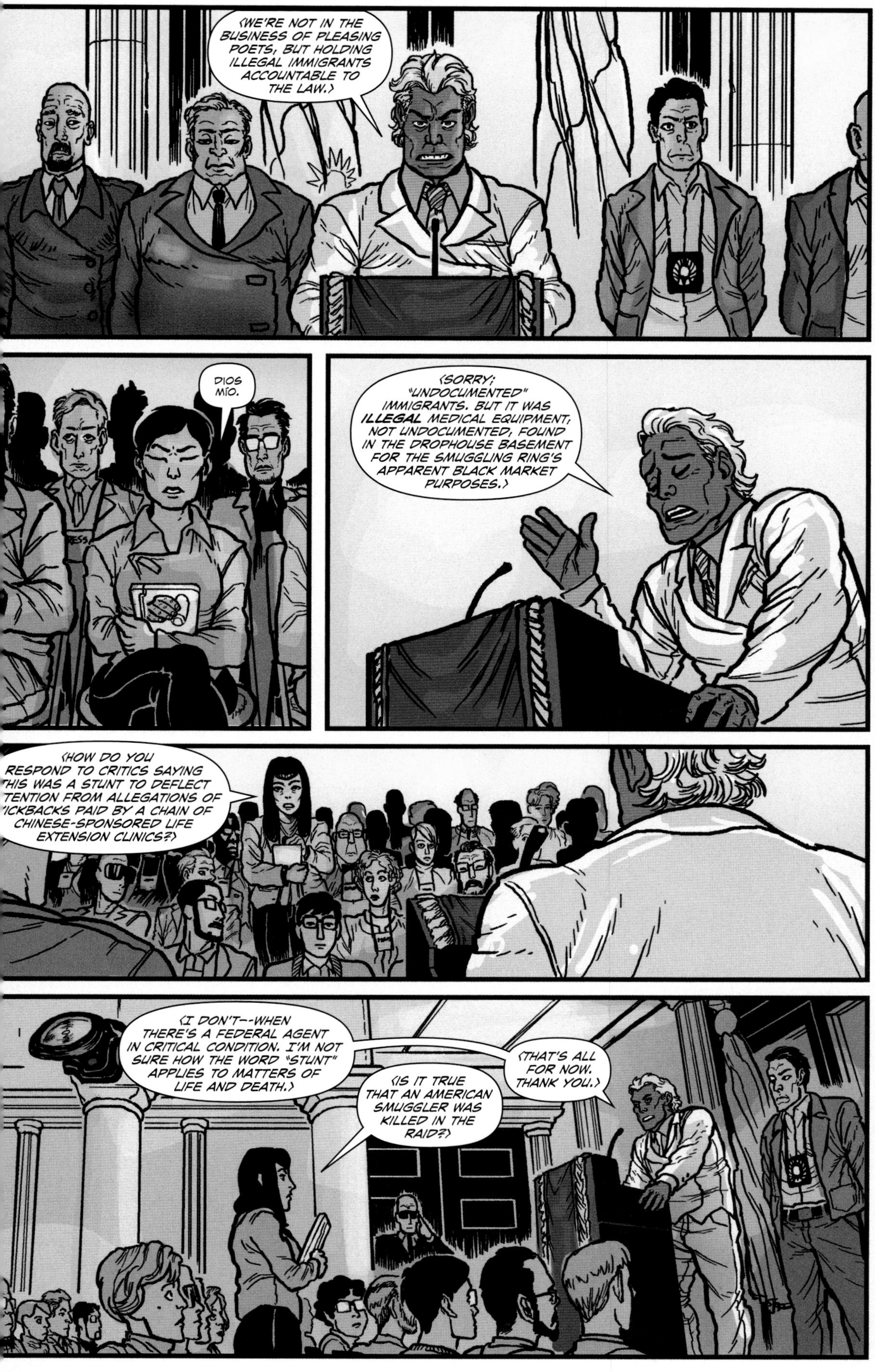
‹WE'RE NOT IN THE BUSINESS OF PLEASING POETS, BUT HOLDING ILLEGAL IMMIGRANTS ACCOUNTABLE TO THE LAW.›
DIOS MÍO.
‹SORRY; "UNDOCUMENTED" IMMIGRANTS. BUT IT WAS ILLEGAL MEDICAL EQUIPMENT, NOT UNDOCUMENTED, FOUND IN THE DROPHOUSE BASEMENT FOR THE SMUGGLING RING'S APPARENT BLACK MARKET PURPOSES.›
‹HOW DO YOU RESPOND TO CRITICS SAYING THIS WAS A STUNT TO DEFLECT TENTION FROM ALLEGATIONS OF ICKBACKS PAID BY A CHAIN OF CHINESE-SPONSORED LIFE EXTENSION CLINICS?›
‹I DON'T--WHEN THERE'S A FEDERAL AGENT IN CRITICAL CONDITION. I'M NOT SURE HOW THE WORD "STUNT" APPLIES TO MATTERS OF LIFE AND DEATH.›
‹IS IT TRUE THAT AN AMERICAN SMUGGLER WAS KILLED IN THE RAID?›
‹THAT'S ALL FOR NOW. THANK YOU.›

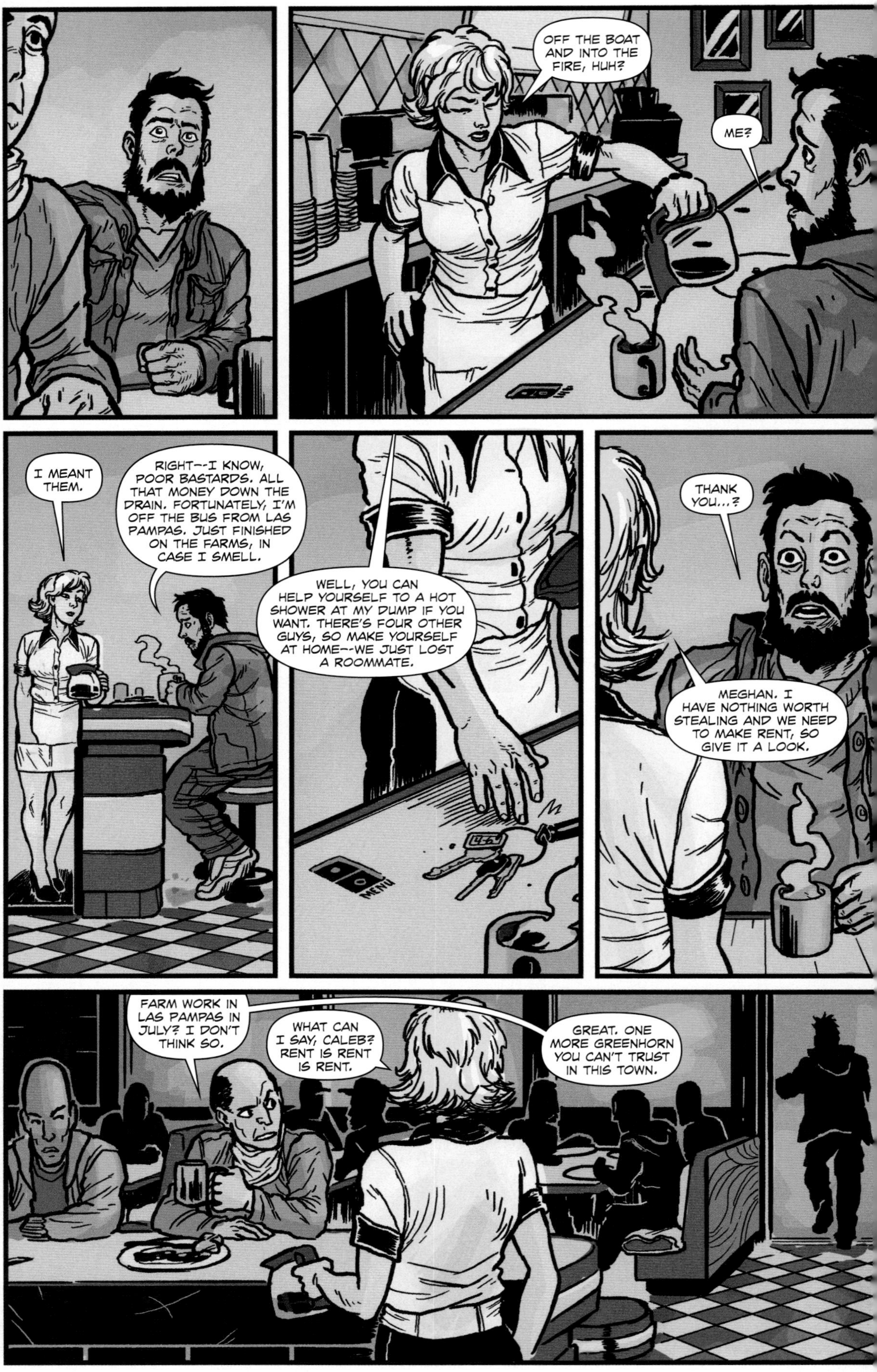
OFF THE BOAT AND INTO THE FIRE, HUH?
ME?
I MEANT THEM.
RIGHT--I KNOW, POOR BASTARDS. ALL THAT MONEY DOWN THE DRAIN. FORTUNATELY, I'M OFF THE BUS FROM LAS PAMPAS. JUST FINISHED ON THE FARMS, IN CASE I SMELL.
WELL, YOU CAN HELP YOURSELF TO A HOT SHOWER AT MY DUMP IF YOU WANT. THERE'S FOUR OTHER GUYS, SO MAKE YOURSELF AT HOME--WE JUST LOST A ROOMMATE.
MENU
THANK YOU...?
MEGHAN. I HAVE NOTHING WORTH STEALING AND WE NEED TO MAKE RENT, SO GIVE IT A LOOK.
FARM WORK IN LAS PAMPAS IN JULY? I DON'T THINK SO.
WHAT CAN I SAY, CALEB? RENT IS RENT IS RENT.
GREAT. ONE MORE GREENHORN YOU CAN'T TRUST IN THIS TOWN.

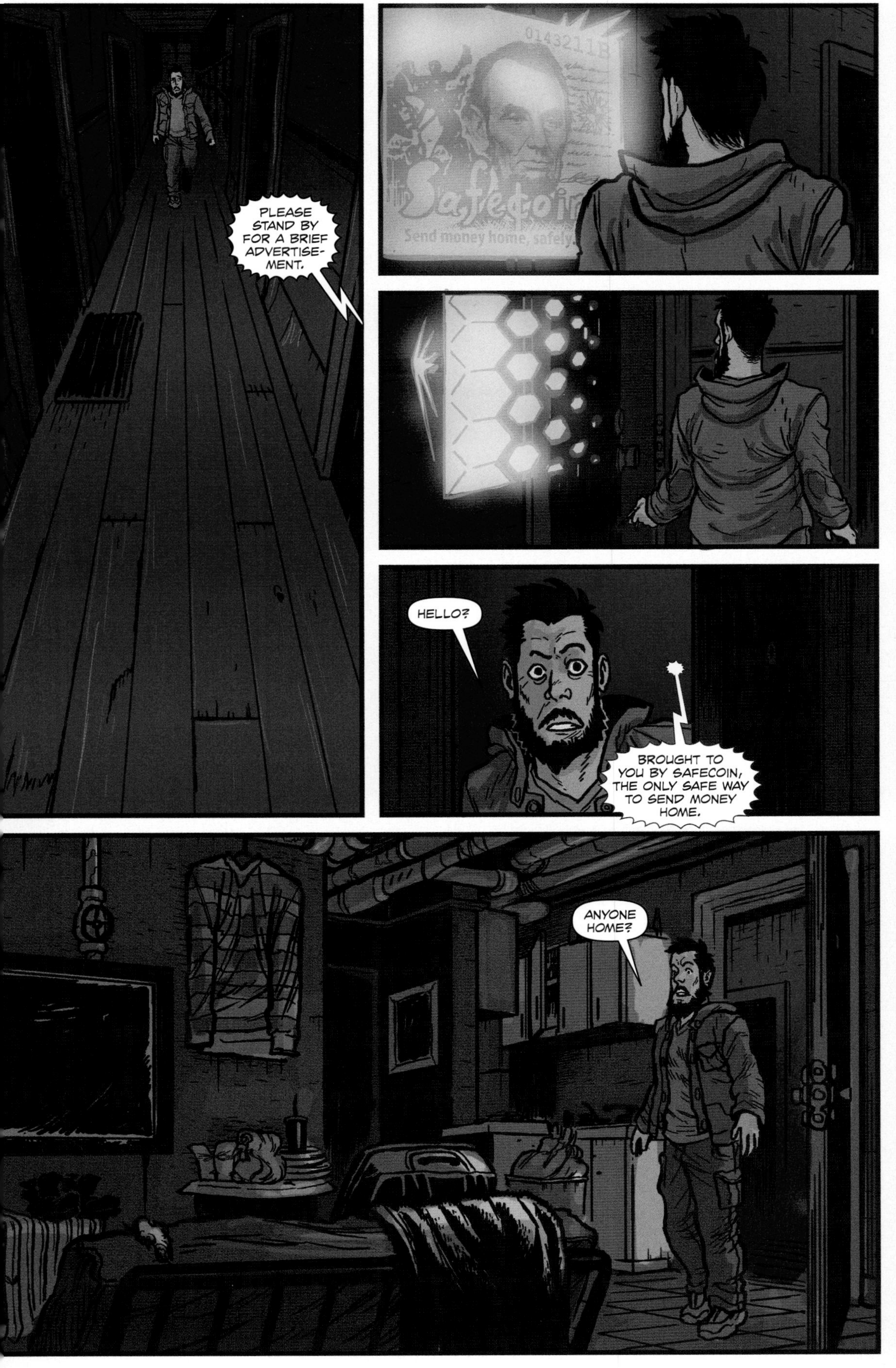
PLEASE STAND BY FOR A BRIEF ADVERTISE-MENT.
01432111B
Safecoin
Send money home, safely.
HELLO?
BROUGHT TO YOU BY SAFECOIN, THE ONLY SAFE WAY TO SEND MONEY HOME.
ANYONE HOME?

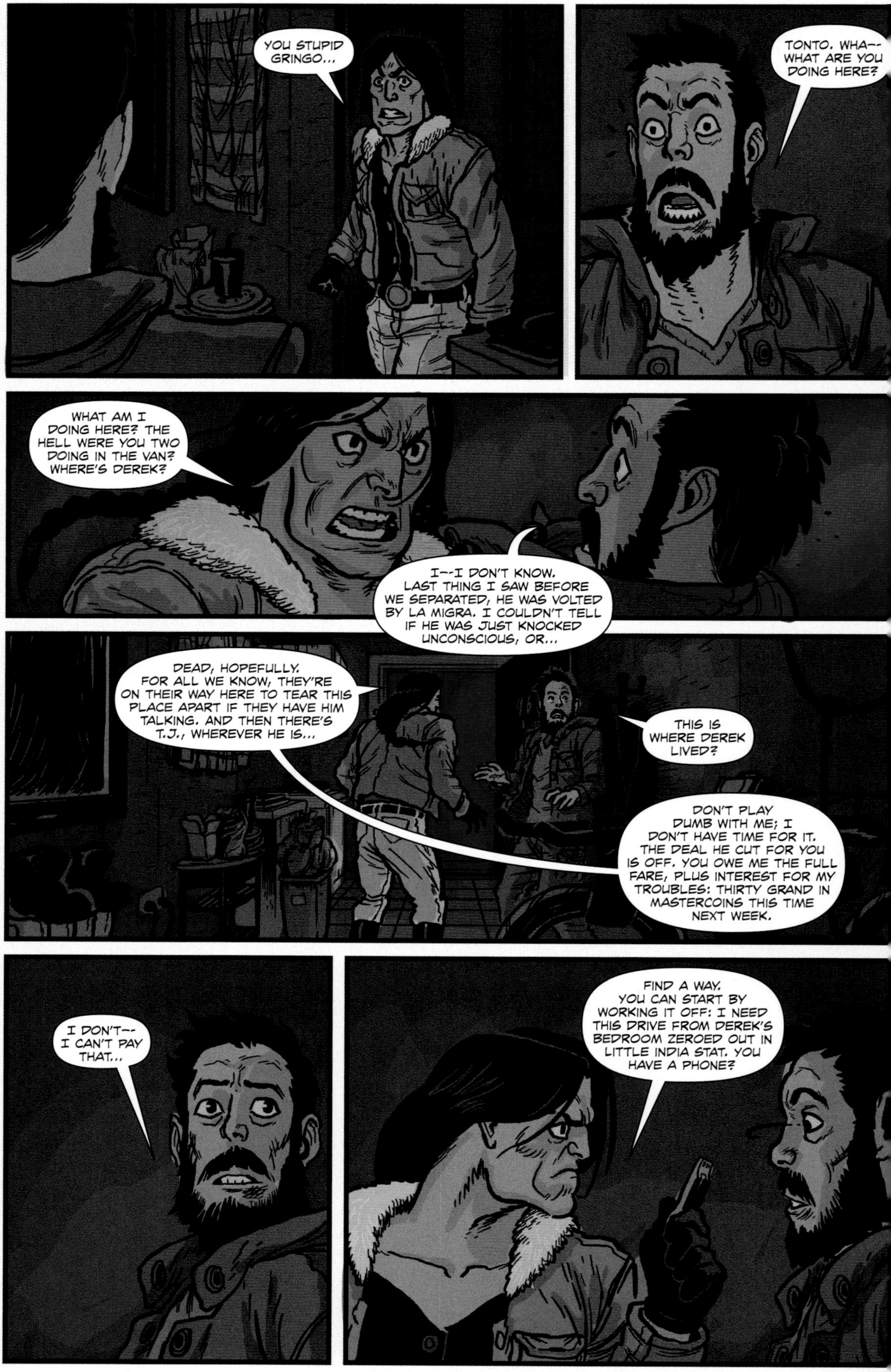
YOU STUPID GRINGO...
TONTO. WHA-- WHAT ARE YOU DOING HERE?
WHAT AM I DOING HERE? THE HELL WERE YOU TWO DOING IN THE VAN? WHERE'S DEREK?
I--I DON'T KNOW. LAST THING I SAW BEFORE WE SEPARATED, HE WAS VOLTED BY LA MIGRA. I COULDN'T TELL IF HE WAS JUST KNOCKED UNCONSCIOUS, OR...
DEAD, HOPEFULLY. FOR ALL WE KNOW, THEY'RE ON THEIR WAY HERE TO TEAR THIS PLACE APART IF THEY HAVE HIM TALKING. AND THEN THERE'S T.J., WHEREVER HE IS...
THIS IS WHERE DEREK LIVED?
DON'T PLAY DUMB WITH ME; I DON'T HAVE TIME FOR IT. THE DEAL HE CUT FOR YOU IS OFF. YOU OWE ME THE FULL FARE, PLUS INTEREST FOR MY TROUBLES: THIRTY GRAND IN MASTERCOINS THIS TIME NEXT WEEK.
I DON'T-- I CAN'T PAY THAT...
FIND A WAY. YOU CAN START BY WORKING IT OFF: I NEED THIS DRIVE FROM DEREK'S BEDROOM ZEROED OUT IN LITTLE INDIA STAT. YOU HAVE A PHONE?

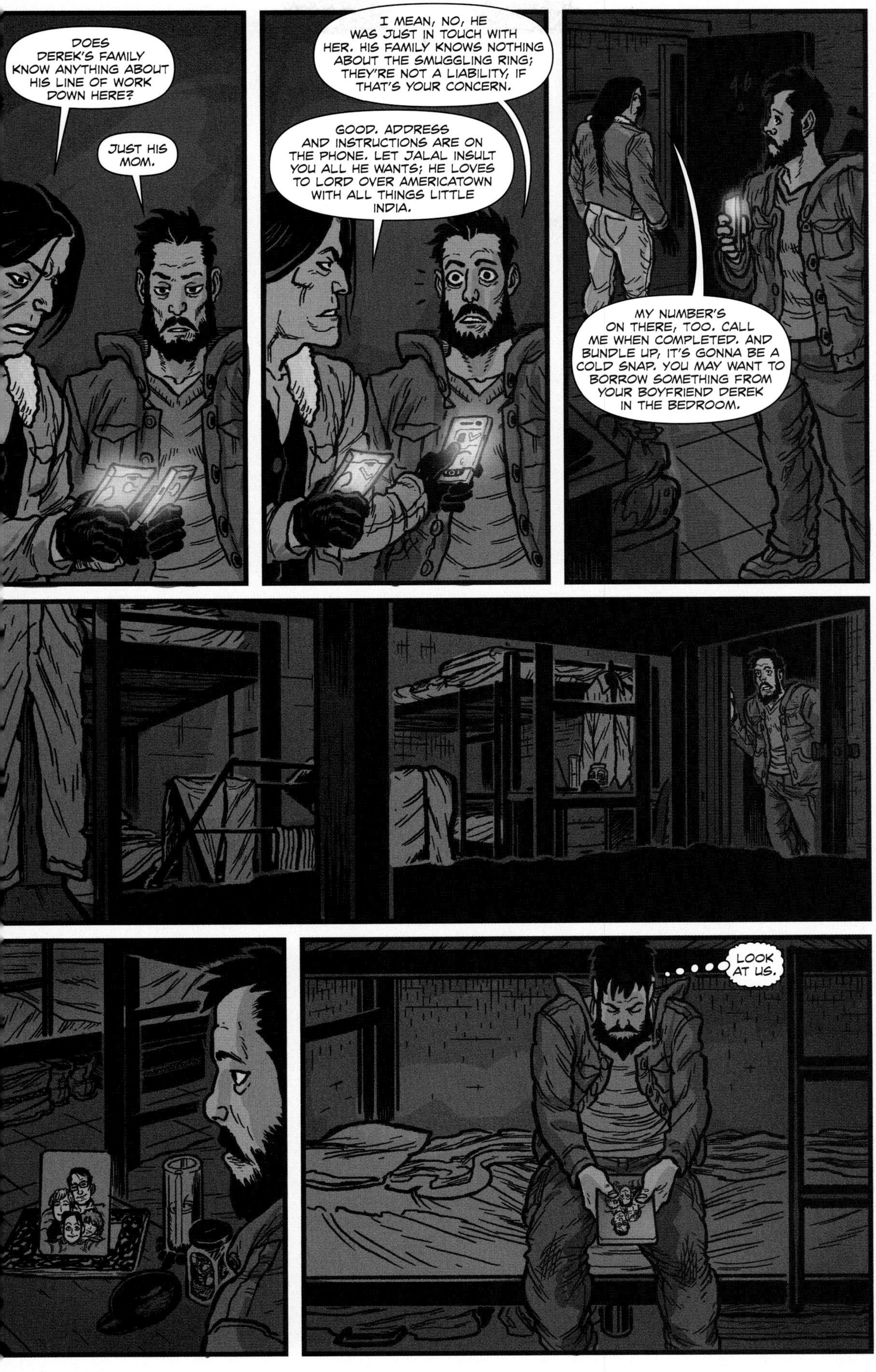
DOES DEREK'S FAMILY KNOW ANYTHING ABOUT HIS LINE OF WORK DOWN HERE?
JUST HIS MOM.
I MEAN, NO, HE WAS JUST IN TOUCH WITH HER. HIS FAMILY KNOWS NOTHING ABOUT THE SMUGGLING RING; THEY'RE NOT A LIABILITY, IF THAT'S YOUR CONCERN.
GOOD. ADDRESS AND INSTRUCTIONS ARE ON THE PHONE. LET JALAL INSULT YOU ALL HE WANTS; HE LOVES TO LORD OVER AMERICATOWN WITH ALL THINGS LITTLE INDIA.
MY NUMBER'S ON THERE, TOO. CALL ME WHEN COMPLETED. AND BUNDLE UP, IT'S GONNA BE A COLD SNAP. YOU MAY WANT TO BORROW SOMETHING FROM YOUR BOYFRIEND DEREK IN THE BEDROOM.
LOOK AT US.

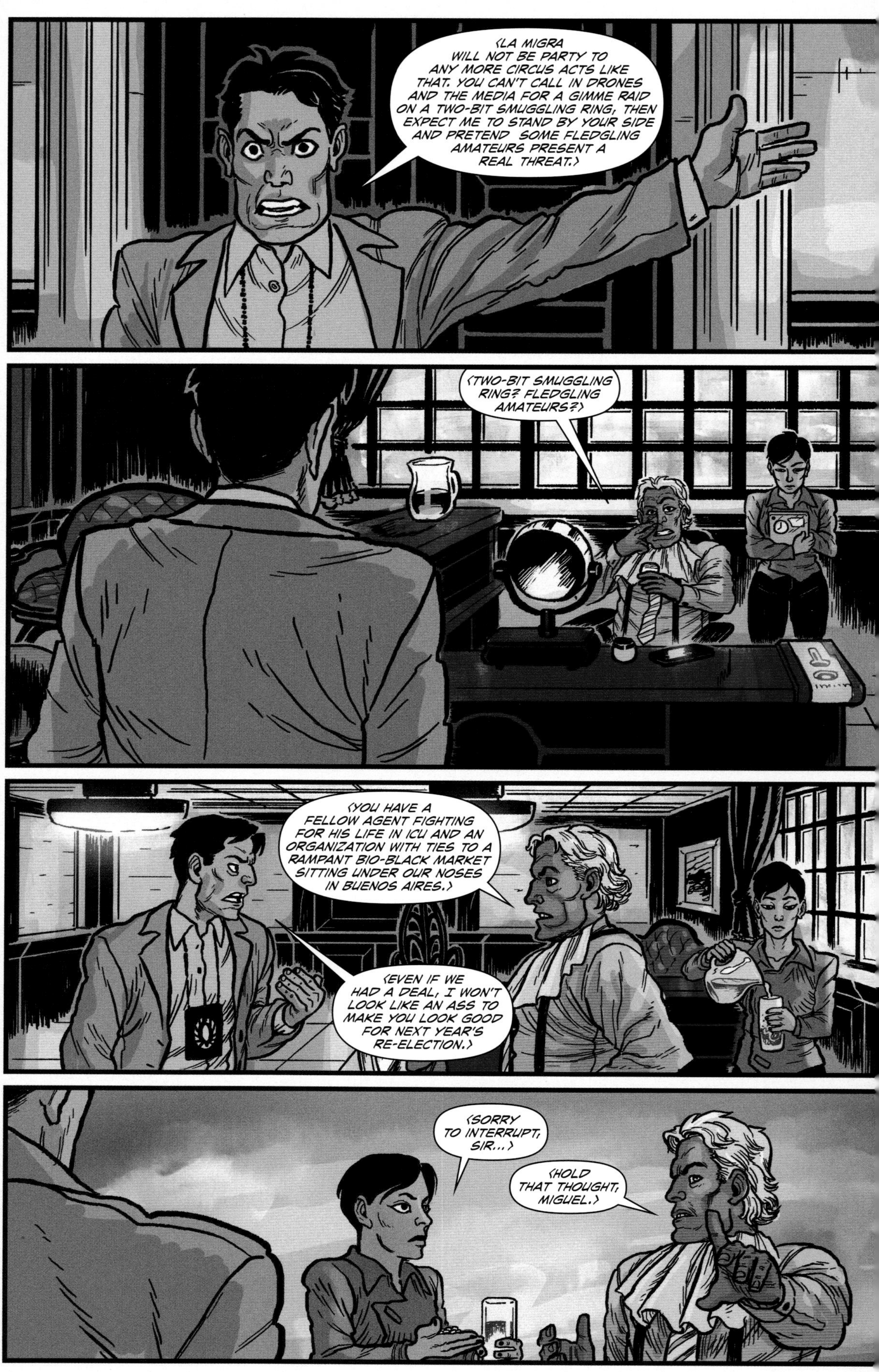
<LA MIGRA WILL NOT BE PARTY TO ANY MORE CIRCUS ACTS LIKE THAT. YOU CAN'T CALL IN DRONES AND THE MEDIA FOR A GIMME RAID ON A TWO-BIT SMUGGLING RING, THEN EXPECT ME TO STAND BY YOUR SIDE AND PRETEND SOME FLEDGLING AMATEURS PRESENT A REAL THREAT.>
<TWO-BIT SMUGGLING RING? FLEDGLING AMATEURS?>
<YOU HAVE A FELLOW AGENT FIGHTING FOR HIS LIFE IN ICU AND AN ORGANIZATION WITH TIES TO A RAMPANT BIO-BLACK MARKET SITTING UNDER OUR NOSES IN BUENOS AIRES.>
<EVEN IF WE HAD A DEAL, I WON'T LOOK LIKE AN ASS TO MAKE YOU LOOK GOOD FOR NEXT YEAR'S RE-ELECTION.>
<SORRY TO INTERRUPT, SIR...>
<HOLD THAT THOUGHT, MIGUEL.>

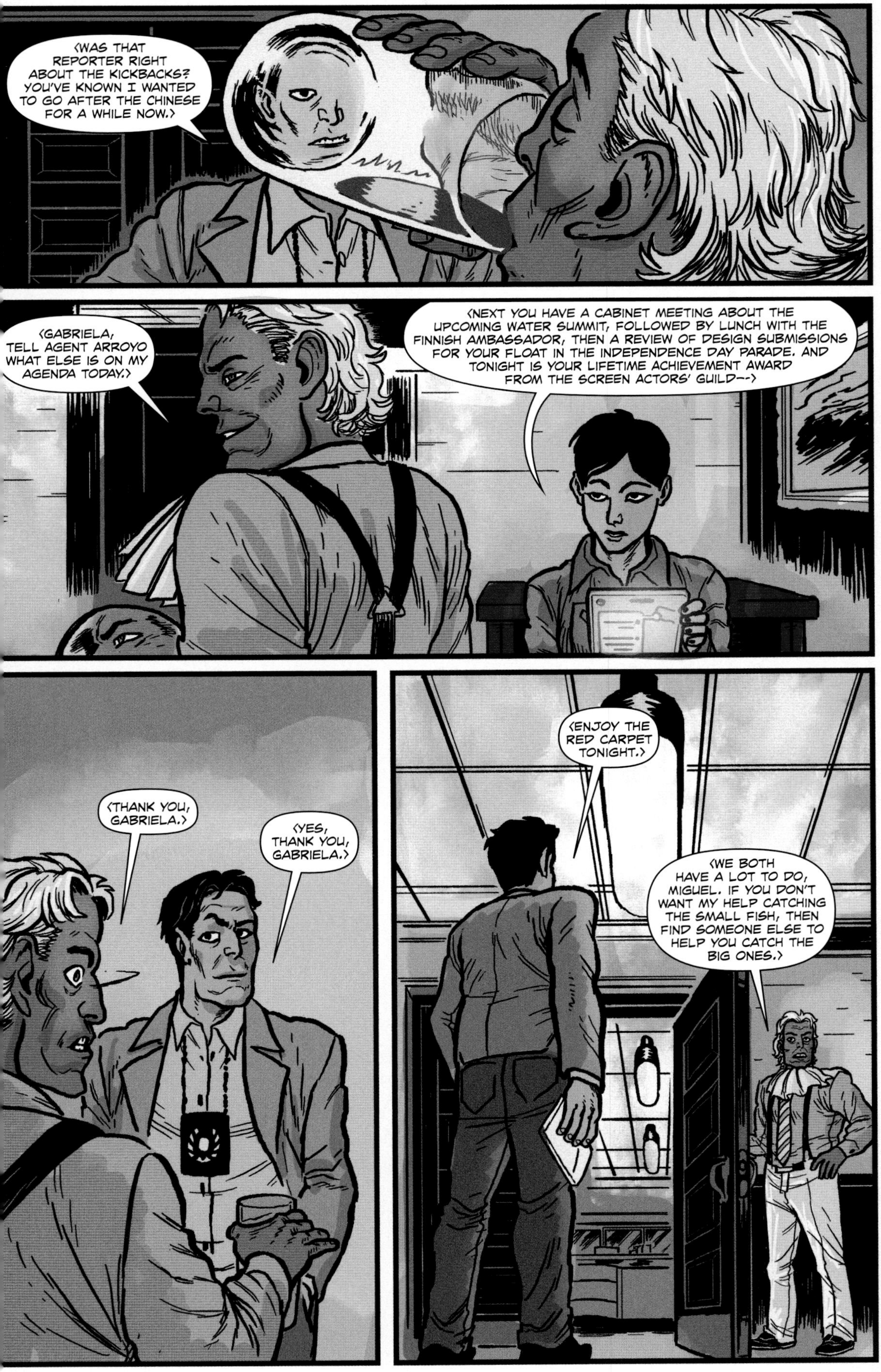
‹WAS THAT REPORTER RIGHT ABOUT THE KICKBACKS? YOU'VE KNOWN I WANTED TO GO AFTER THE CHINESE FOR A WHILE NOW.›
‹GABRIELA, TELL AGENT ARROYO WHAT ELSE IS ON MY AGENDA TODAY.›
‹NEXT YOU HAVE A CABINET MEETING ABOUT THE UPCOMING WATER SUMMIT, FOLLOWED BY LUNCH WITH THE FINNISH AMBASSADOR, THEN A REVIEW OF DESIGN SUBMISSIONS FOR YOUR FLOAT IN THE INDEPENDENCE DAY PARADE. AND TONIGHT IS YOUR LIFETIME ACHIEVEMENT AWARD FROM THE SCREEN ACTORS' GUILD--›
‹THANK YOU, GABRIELA.›
‹YES, THANK YOU, GABRIELA.›
‹ENJOY THE RED CARPET TONIGHT.›
‹WE BOTH HAVE A LOT TO DO, MIGUEL. IF YOU DON'T WANT MY HELP CATCHING THE SMALL FISH, THEN FIND SOMEONE ELSE TO HELP YOU CATCH THE BIG ONES.›

LITTLE INDIA.

EXCUSE ME...

I HAVE A PACKAGE FOR... JALAL?

WHEN IS THAT INDIAN TONTO GOING TO COME HERE HIMSELF?

YOU THINK SELF-HATING JEWS ARE BAD, MOTI?

omfirman Americano muert

en redada de la ma ugada

"ya basta de estos gringos "Que se

WHAT DID THE NEWS JUST SAY?

SOUNDS LIKE AN AMERICAN DIED IN LAST NIGHT'S RAID.

SOMEONE PASS ME A TISSUE.

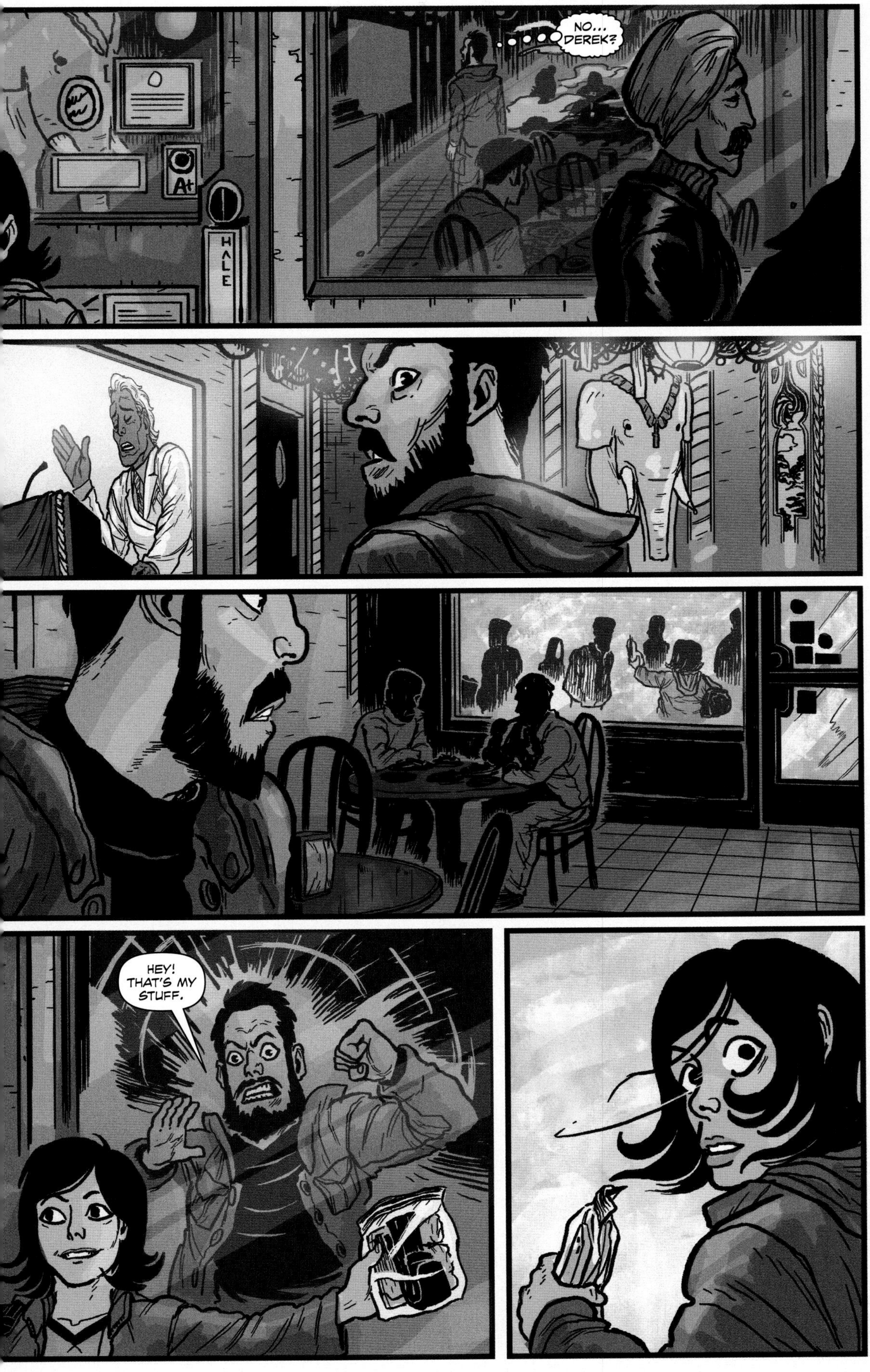
NO... DEREK?
HALE
At
HEY! THAT'S MY STUFF.

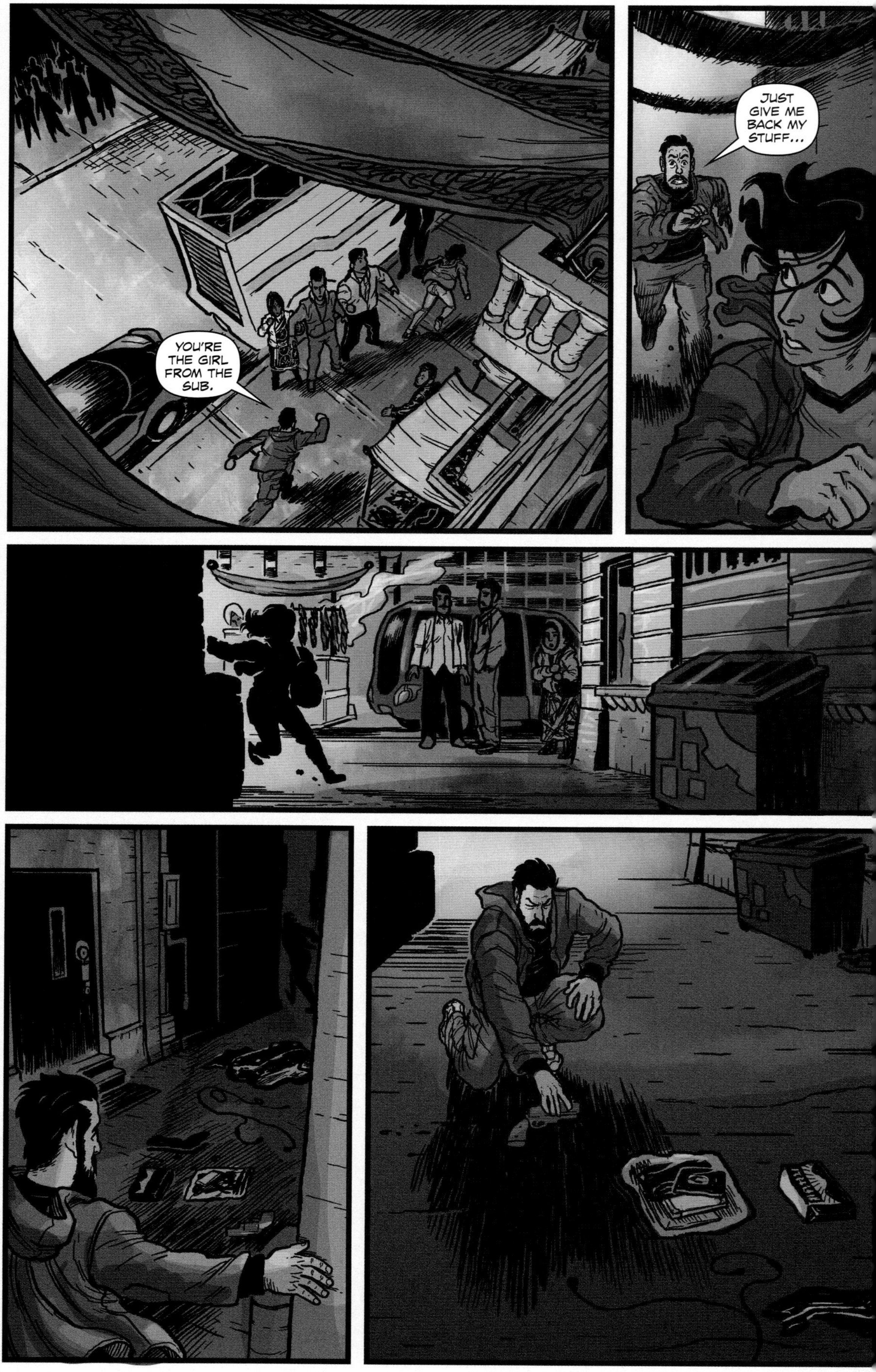
YOU'RE THE GIRL FROM THE SUB.
JUST GIVE ME BACK MY STUFF...

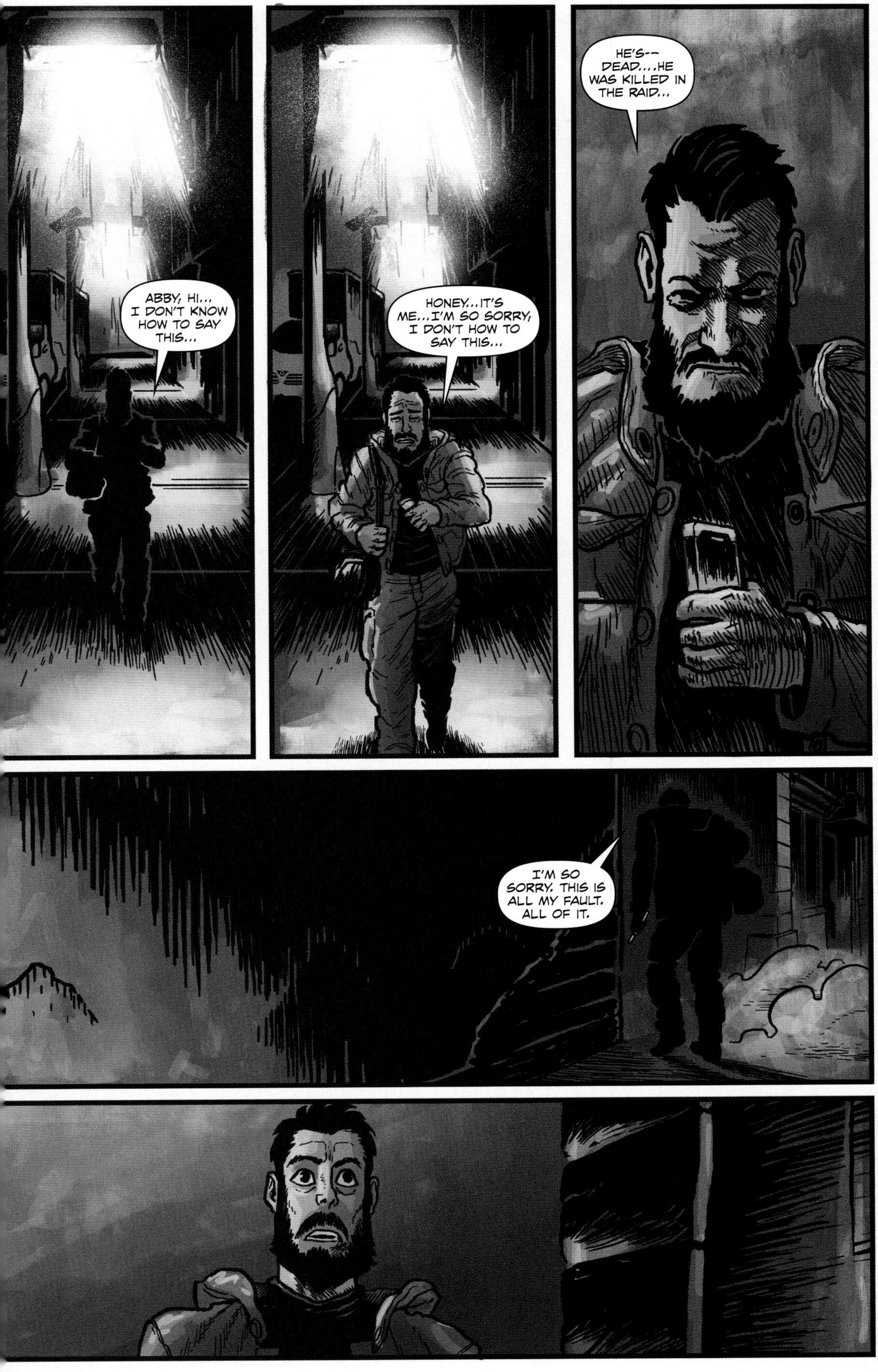
ABBY, HI... I DON'T KNOW HOW TO SAY THIS...
HONEY...IT'S ME...I'M SO SORRY, I DON'T HOW TO SAY THIS...
HE'S-- DEAD....HE WAS KILLED IN THE RAID...
I'M SO SORRY. THIS IS ALL MY FAULT. ALL OF IT.

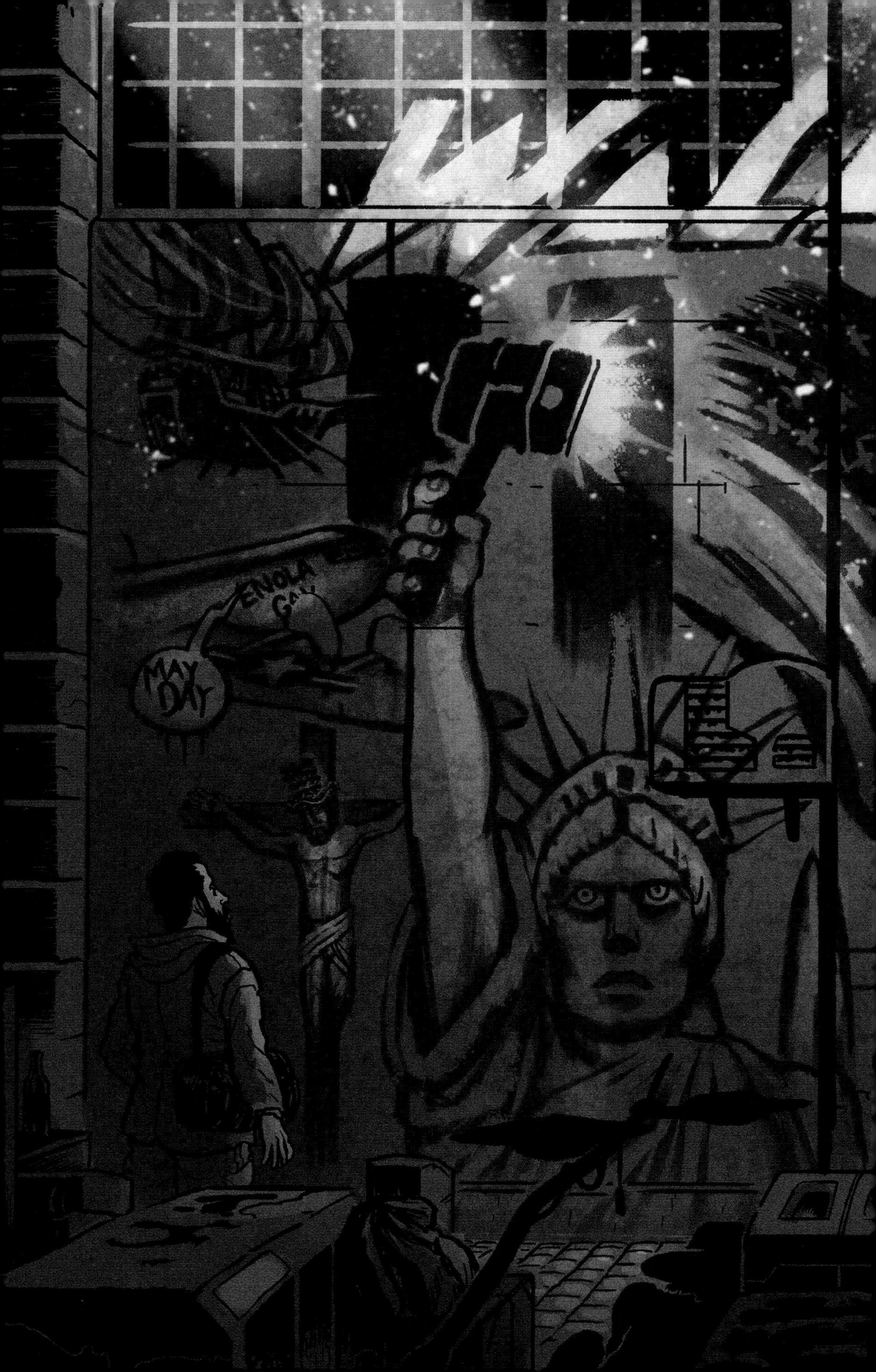
ENOLA GAY
MAY DAY

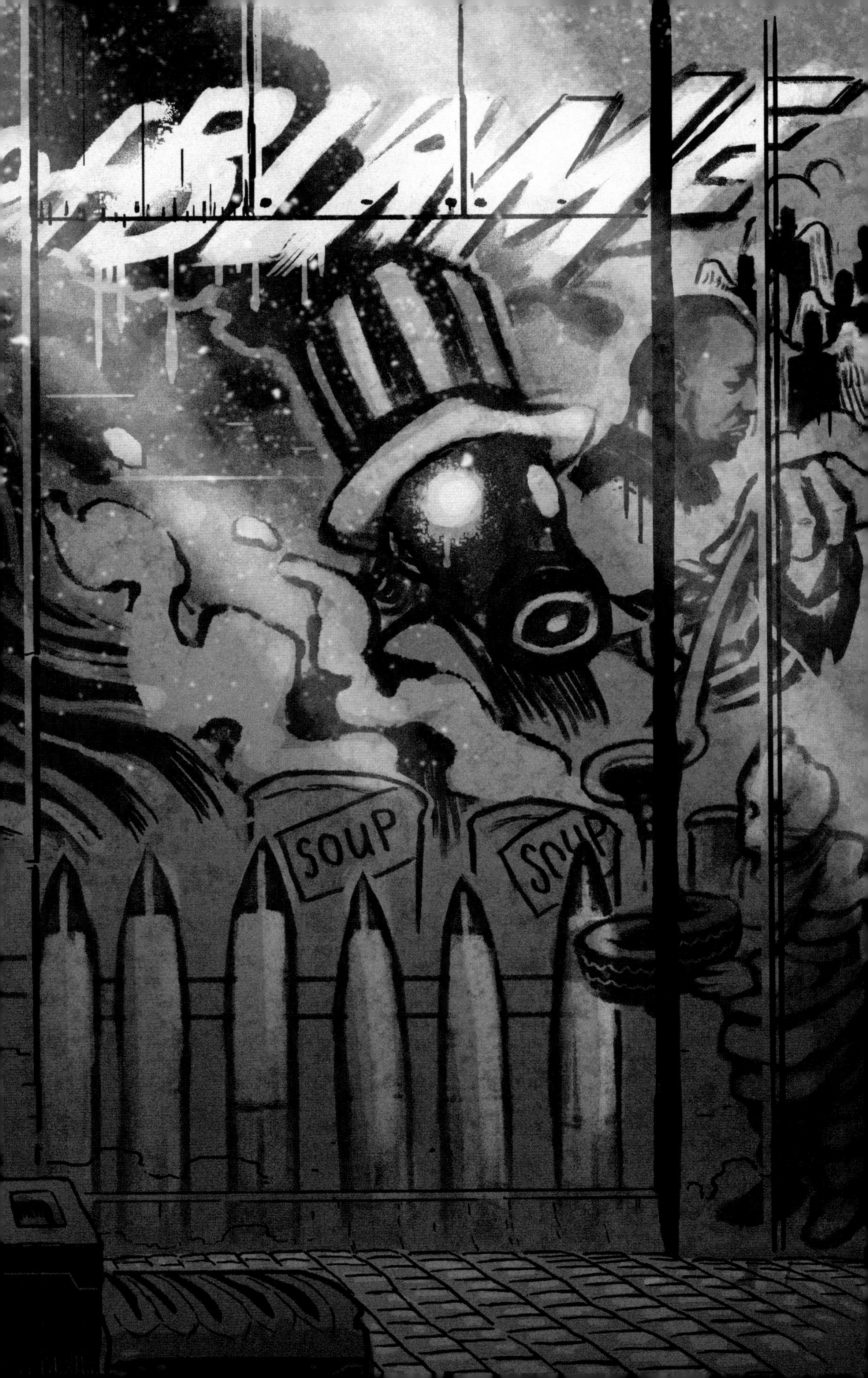
SOUP
SOUP

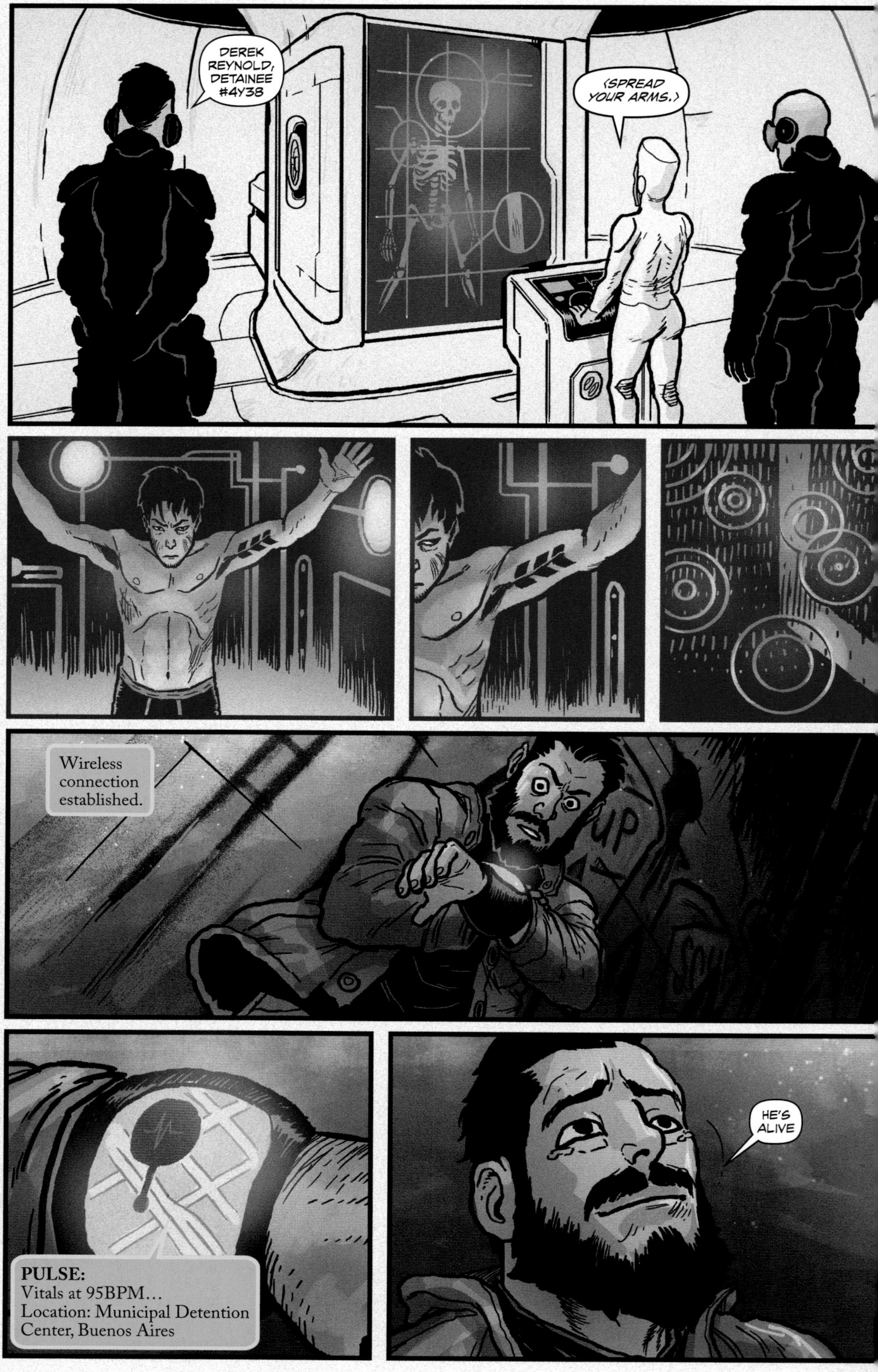
DEREK REYNOLD, DETAINEE #4Y38
⟨SPREAD YOUR ARMS.⟩
Wireless connection established.
UP
PULSE:
Vitals at 95BPM…
Location: Municipal Detention Center, Buenos Aires
HE'S ALIVE

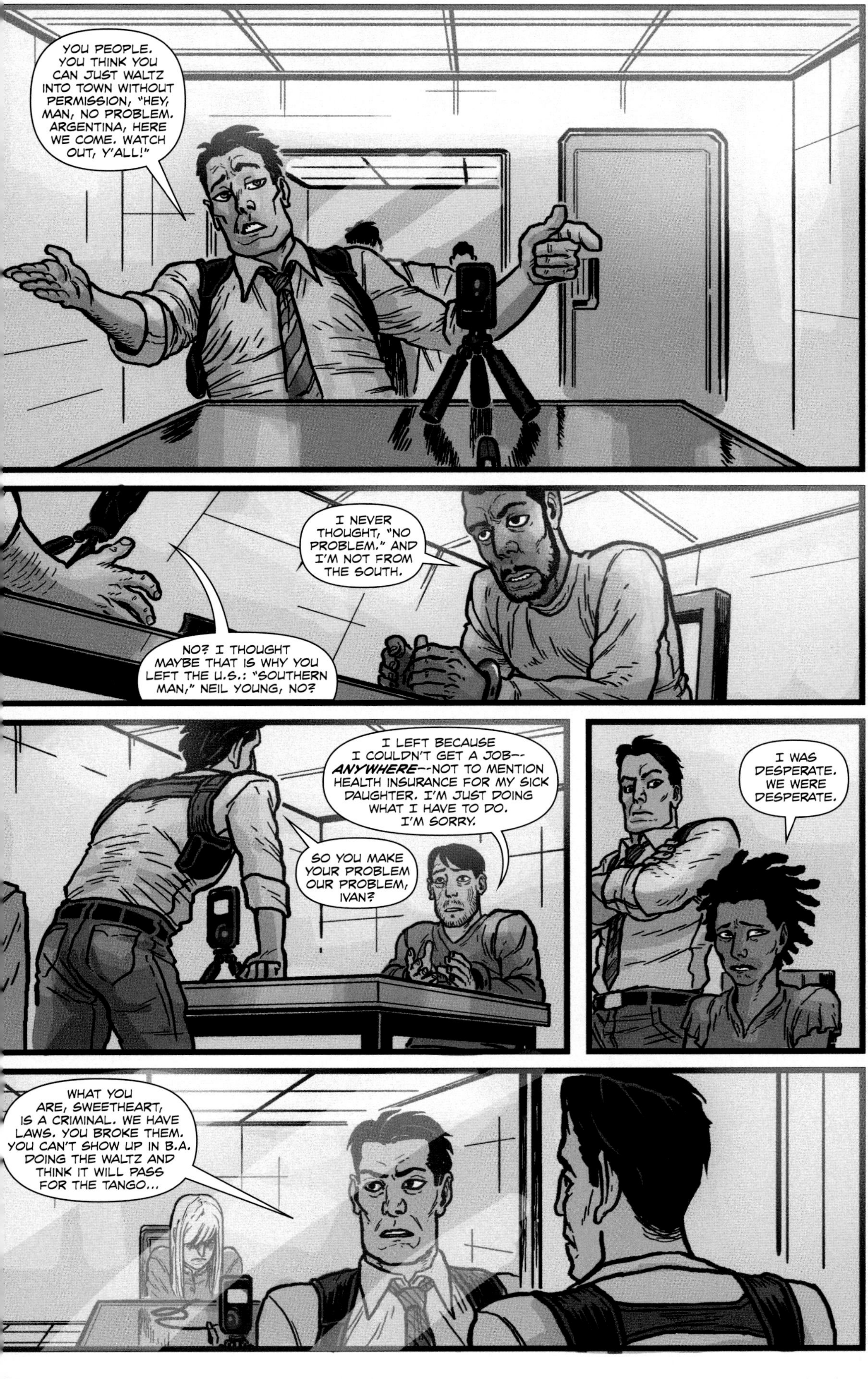
YOU PEOPLE. YOU THINK YOU CAN JUST WALTZ INTO TOWN WITHOUT PERMISSION, "HEY, MAN, NO PROBLEM. ARGENTINA, HERE WE COME. WATCH OUT, Y'ALL!"
I NEVER THOUGHT, "NO PROBLEM." AND I'M NOT FROM THE SOUTH.
NO? I THOUGHT MAYBE THAT IS WHY YOU LEFT THE U.S.: "SOUTHERN MAN," NEIL YOUNG, NO?
I LEFT BECAUSE I COULDN'T GET A JOB-- ANYWHERE--NOT TO MENTION HEALTH INSURANCE FOR MY SICK DAUGHTER. I'M JUST DOING WHAT I HAVE TO DO. I'M SORRY.
SO YOU MAKE YOUR PROBLEM OUR PROBLEM, IVAN?
I WAS DESPERATE. WE WERE DESPERATE.
WHAT YOU ARE, SWEETHEART, IS A CRIMINAL. WE HAVE LAWS. YOU BROKE THEM. YOU CAN'T SHOW UP IN B.A. DOING THE WALTZ AND THINK IT WILL PASS FOR THE TANGO...

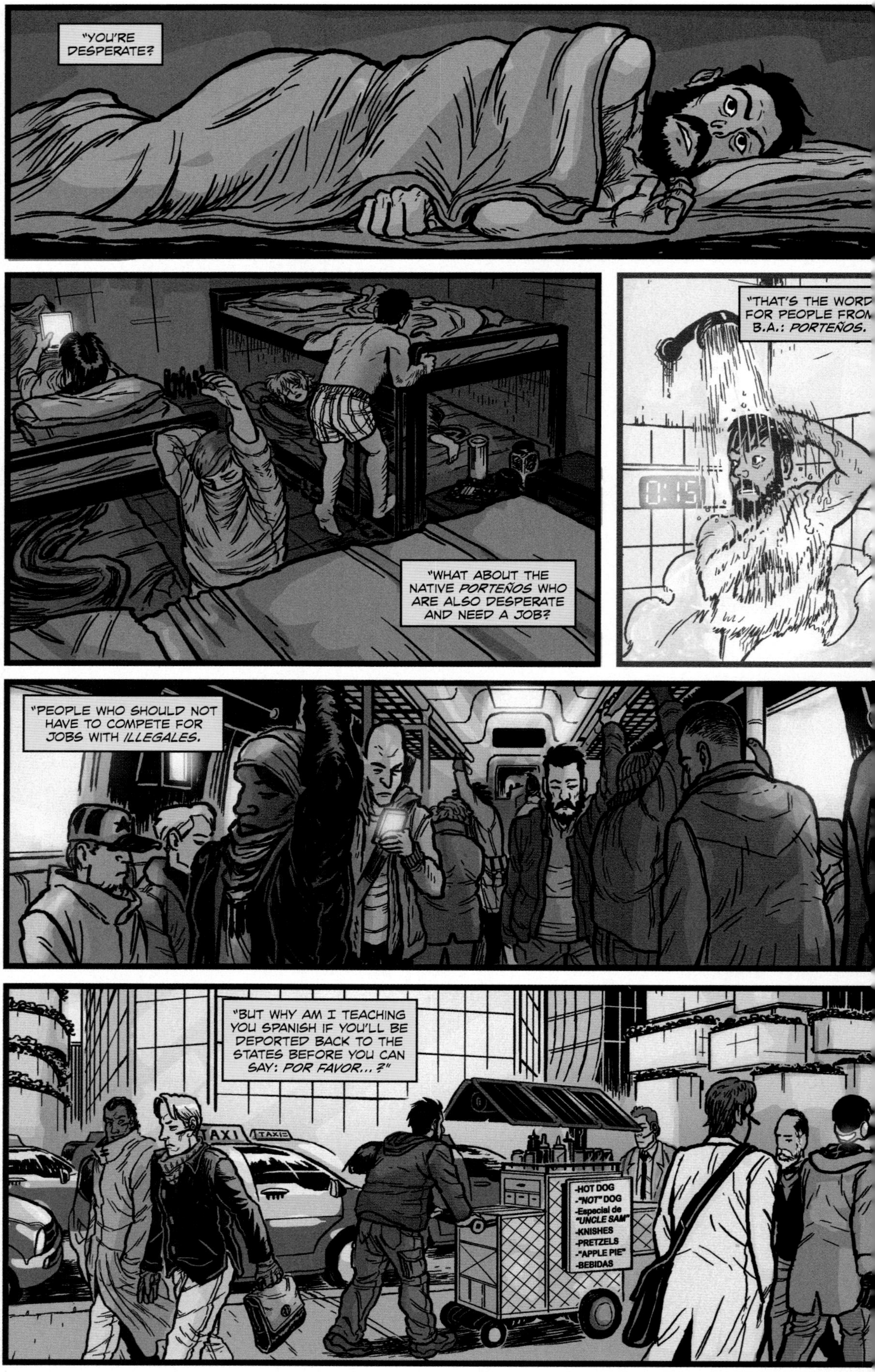
"YOU'RE DESPERATE?
"WHAT ABOUT THE NATIVE *PORTEÑOS* WHO ARE ALSO DESPERATE AND NEED A JOB?
"THAT'S THE WORD FOR PEOPLE FROM B.A.: *PORTEÑOS*.
0:15
"PEOPLE WHO SHOULD NOT HAVE TO COMPETE FOR JOBS WITH *ILLEGALES*.
"BUT WHY AM I TEACHING YOU SPANISH IF YOU'LL BE DEPORTED BACK TO THE STATES BEFORE YOU CAN SAY: *POR FAVOR...?*"
TAXI
TAXI
-HOT DOG
-"NOT" DOG
-Especial de "UNCLE SAM"
-KNISHES
-PRETZELS
-"APPLE PIE"
-BEBIDAS

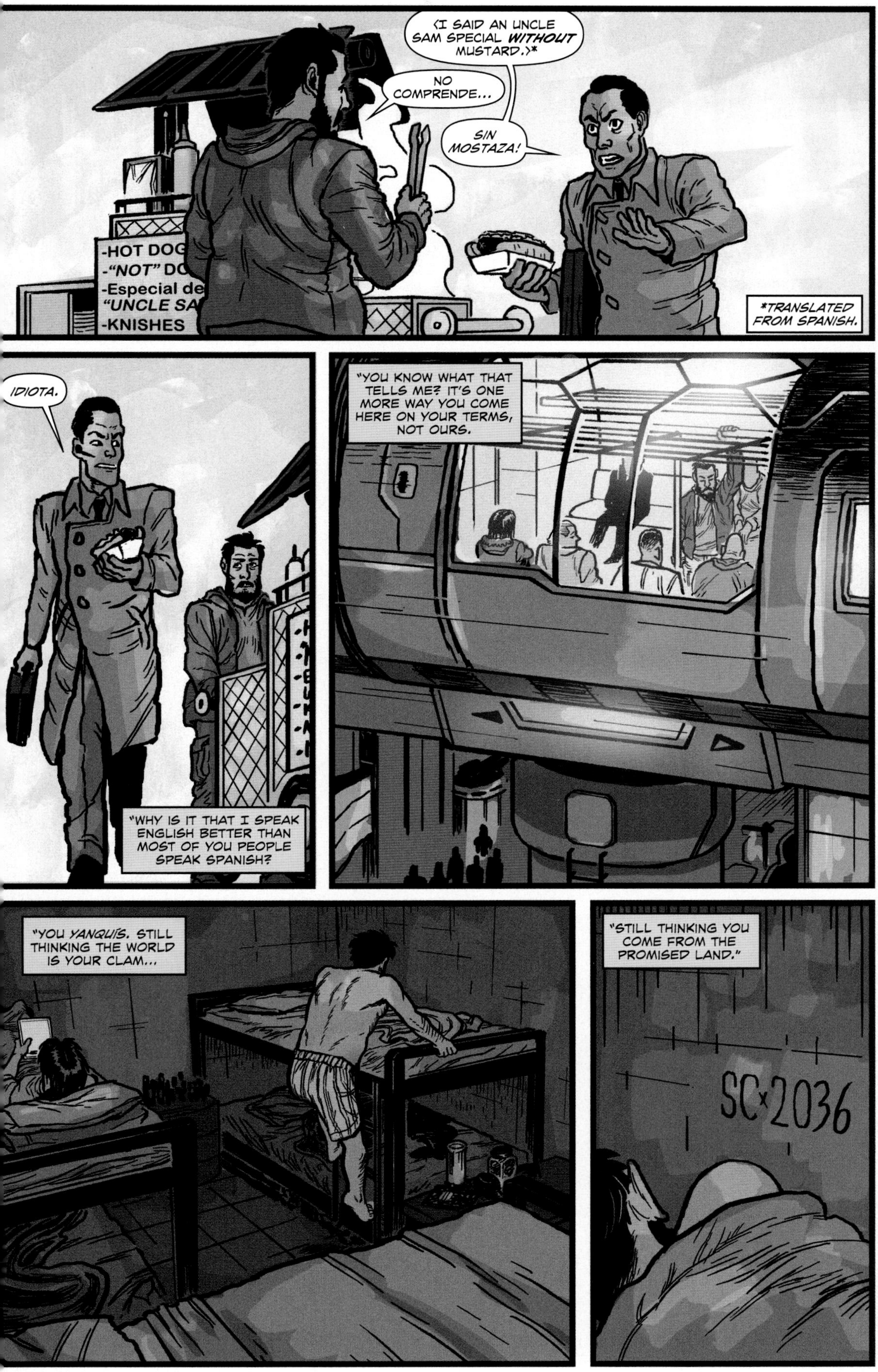

‹I SAID AN UNCLE SAM SPECIAL *WITHOUT* MUSTARD.›*
NO COMPRENDE...
SIN MOSTAZA!
-HOT DOG
-"NOT" DO
-Especial de
"UNCLE SA
-KNISHES
*TRANSLATED FROM SPANISH.
IDIOTA.
"WHY IS IT THAT I SPEAK ENGLISH BETTER THAN MOST OF YOU PEOPLE SPEAK SPANISH?
"YOU KNOW WHAT THAT TELLS ME? IT'S ONE MORE WAY YOU COME HERE ON YOUR TERMS, NOT OURS.
"YOU *YANQUIS*. STILL THINKING THE WORLD IS YOUR CLAM...
"STILL THINKING YOU COME FROM THE PROMISED LAND."
SC×2036

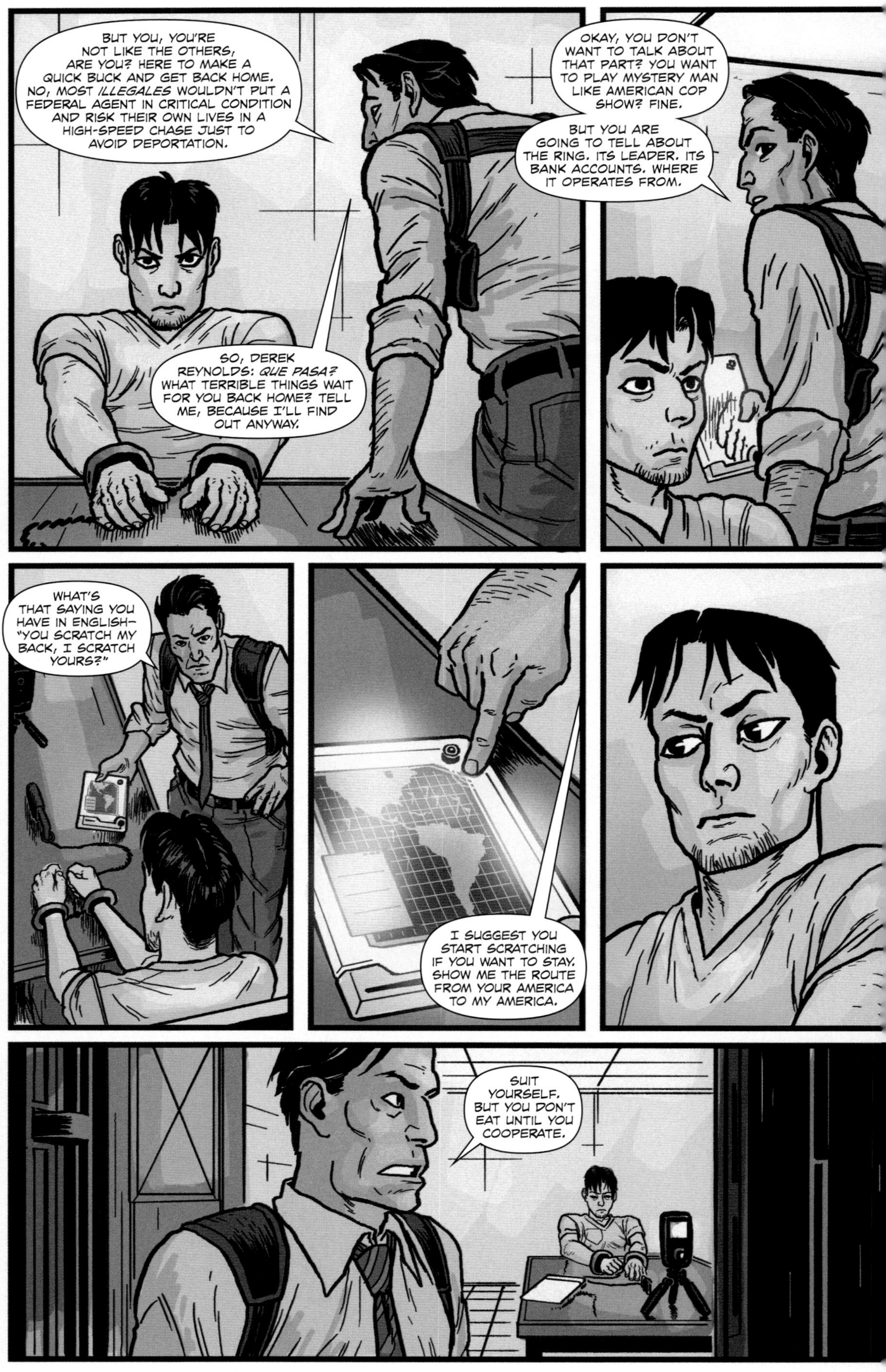
BUT YOU, YOU'RE NOT LIKE THE OTHERS, ARE YOU? HERE TO MAKE A QUICK BUCK AND GET BACK HOME. NO, MOST *ILLEGALES* WOULDN'T PUT A FEDERAL AGENT IN CRITICAL CONDITION AND RISK THEIR OWN LIVES IN A HIGH-SPEED CHASE JUST TO AVOID DEPORTATION.
SO, DEREK REYNOLDS: *QUE PASA?* WHAT TERRIBLE THINGS WAIT FOR YOU BACK HOME? TELL ME, BECAUSE I'LL FIND OUT ANYWAY.
OKAY, YOU DON'T WANT TO TALK ABOUT THAT PART? YOU WANT TO PLAY MYSTERY MAN LIKE AMERICAN COP SHOW? FINE.
BUT YOU ARE GOING TO TELL ABOUT THE RING. ITS LEADER. ITS BANK ACCOUNTS. WHERE IT OPERATES FROM.
WHAT'S THAT SAYING YOU HAVE IN ENGLISH– "YOU SCRATCH MY BACK, I SCRATCH YOURS?"
I SUGGEST YOU START SCRATCHING IF YOU WANT TO STAY. SHOW ME THE ROUTE FROM YOUR AMERICA TO MY AMERICA.
SUIT YOURSELF. BUT YOU DON'T EAT UNTIL YOU COOPERATE.

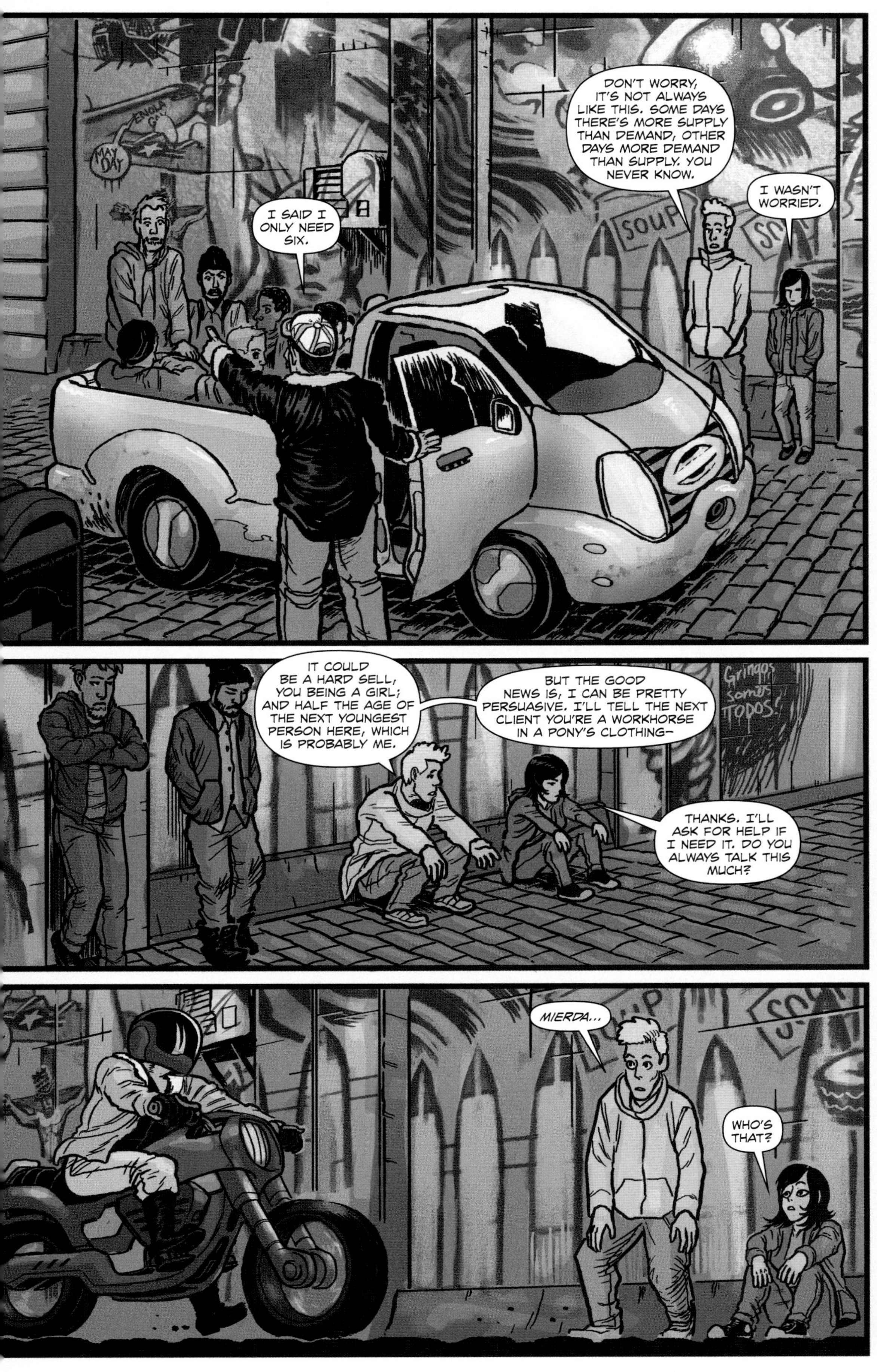
I SAID I ONLY NEED SIX.
DON'T WORRY, IT'S NOT ALWAYS LIKE THIS. SOME DAYS THERE'S MORE SUPPLY THAN DEMAND, OTHER DAYS MORE DEMAND THAN SUPPLY. YOU NEVER KNOW.
I WASN'T WORRIED.
IT COULD BE A HARD SELL, YOU BEING A GIRL; AND HALF THE AGE OF THE NEXT YOUNGEST PERSON HERE, WHICH IS PROBABLY ME.
BUT THE GOOD NEWS IS, I CAN BE PRETTY PERSUASIVE. I'LL TELL THE NEXT CLIENT YOU'RE A WORKHORSE IN A PONY'S CLOTHING–
THANKS. I'LL ASK FOR HELP IF I NEED IT. DO YOU ALWAYS TALK THIS MUCH?
MIERDA...
WHO'S THAT?

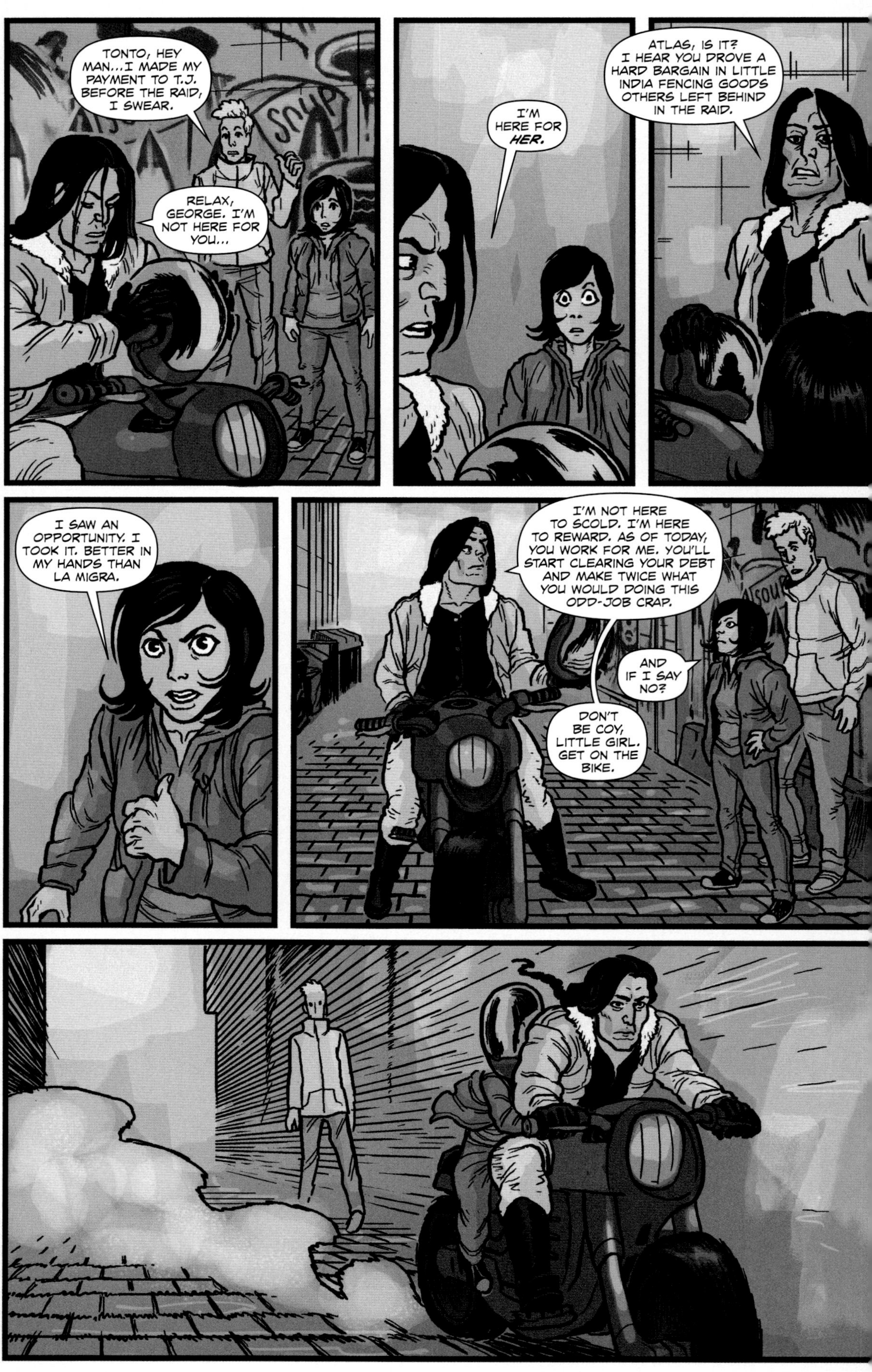
TONTO, HEY MAN...I MADE MY PAYMENT TO T.J. BEFORE THE RAID, I SWEAR.
RELAX, GEORGE. I'M NOT HERE FOR YOU...
I'M HERE FOR HER.
ATLAS, IS IT? I HEAR YOU DROVE A HARD BARGAIN IN LITTLE INDIA FENCING GOODS OTHERS LEFT BEHIND IN THE RAID.
I SAW AN OPPORTUNITY. I TOOK IT. BETTER IN MY HANDS THAN LA MIGRA.
I'M NOT HERE TO SCOLD. I'M HERE TO REWARD. AS OF TODAY, YOU WORK FOR ME. YOU'LL START CLEARING YOUR DEBT AND MAKE TWICE WHAT YOU WOULD DOING THIS ODD-JOB CRAP.
AND IF I SAY NO?
DON'T BE COY, LITTLE GIRL. GET ON THE BIKE.

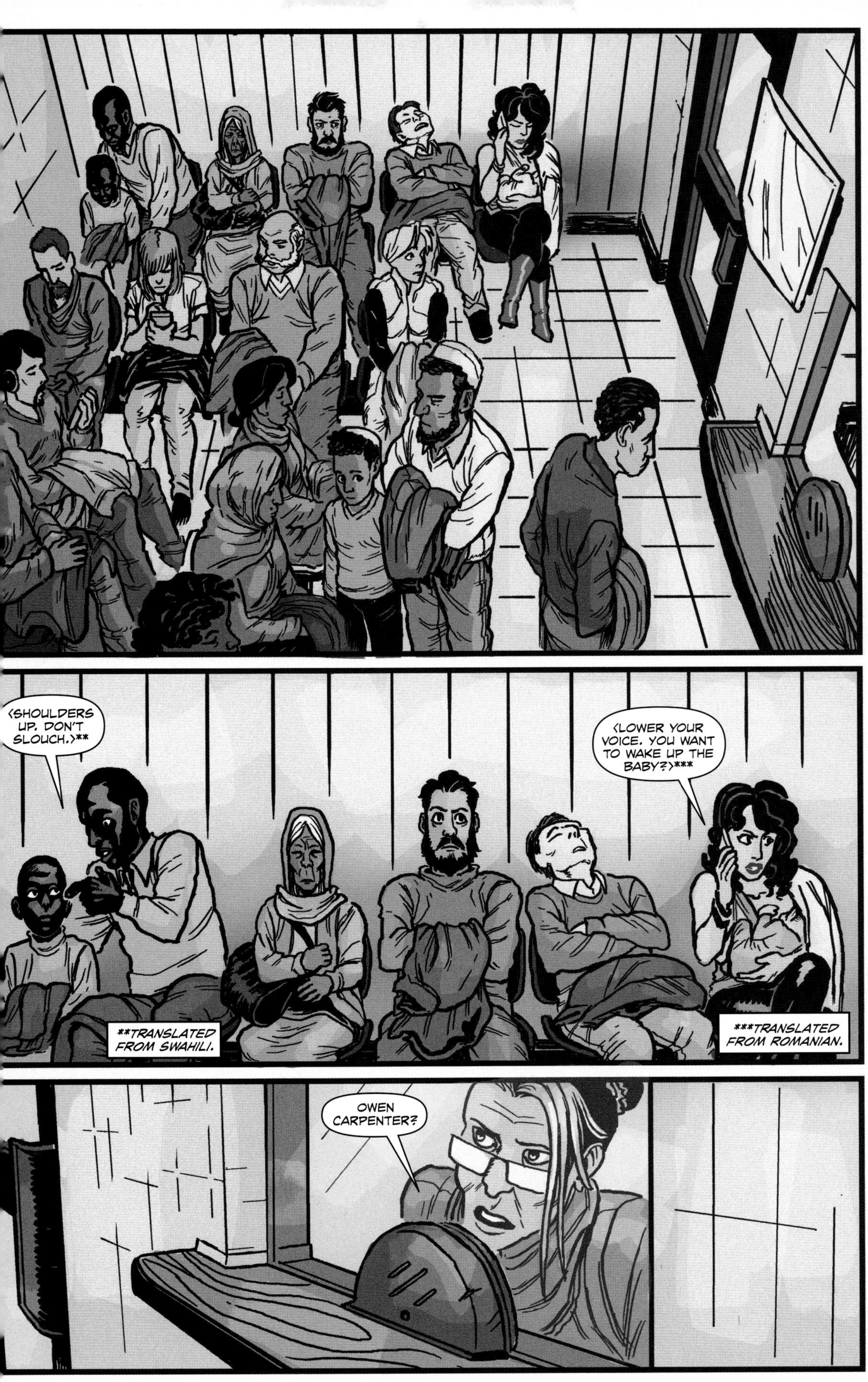
<SHOULDERS UP. DON'T SLOUCH.>**
<LOWER YOUR VOICE. YOU WANT TO WAKE UP THE BABY?>***
**TRANSLATED FROM SWAHILI.
***TRANSLATED FROM ROMANIAN.
OWEN CARPENTER?

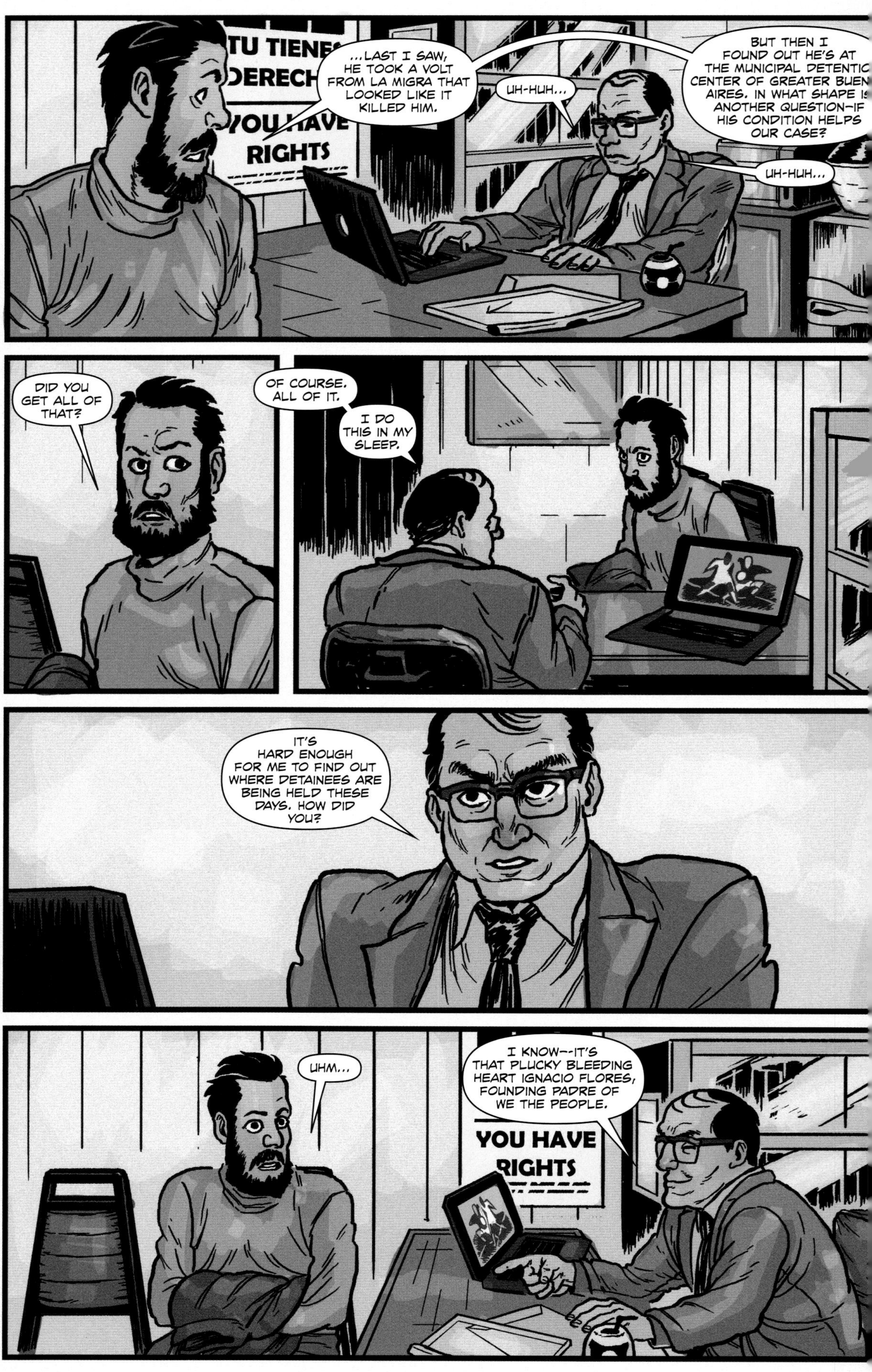
TU TIENES DERECH
YOU HAVE RIGHTS
...LAST I SAW, HE TOOK A VOLT FROM LA MIGRA THAT LOOKED LIKE IT KILLED HIM.
UH-HUH...
BUT THEN I FOUND OUT HE'S AT THE MUNICIPAL DETENTIC CENTER OF GREATER BUEN AIRES. IN WHAT SHAPE IS ANOTHER QUESTION—IF HIS CONDITION HELPS OUR CASE?
UH-HUH...
DID YOU GET ALL OF THAT?
OF COURSE. ALL OF IT.
I DO THIS IN MY SLEEP.
IT'S HARD ENOUGH FOR ME TO FIND OUT WHERE DETAINEES ARE BEING HELD THESE DAYS. HOW DID YOU?
UHM...
I KNOW--IT'S THAT PLUCKY BLEEDING HEART IGNACIO FLORES, FOUNDING PADRE OF WE THE PEOPLE.
YOU HAVE RIGHTS

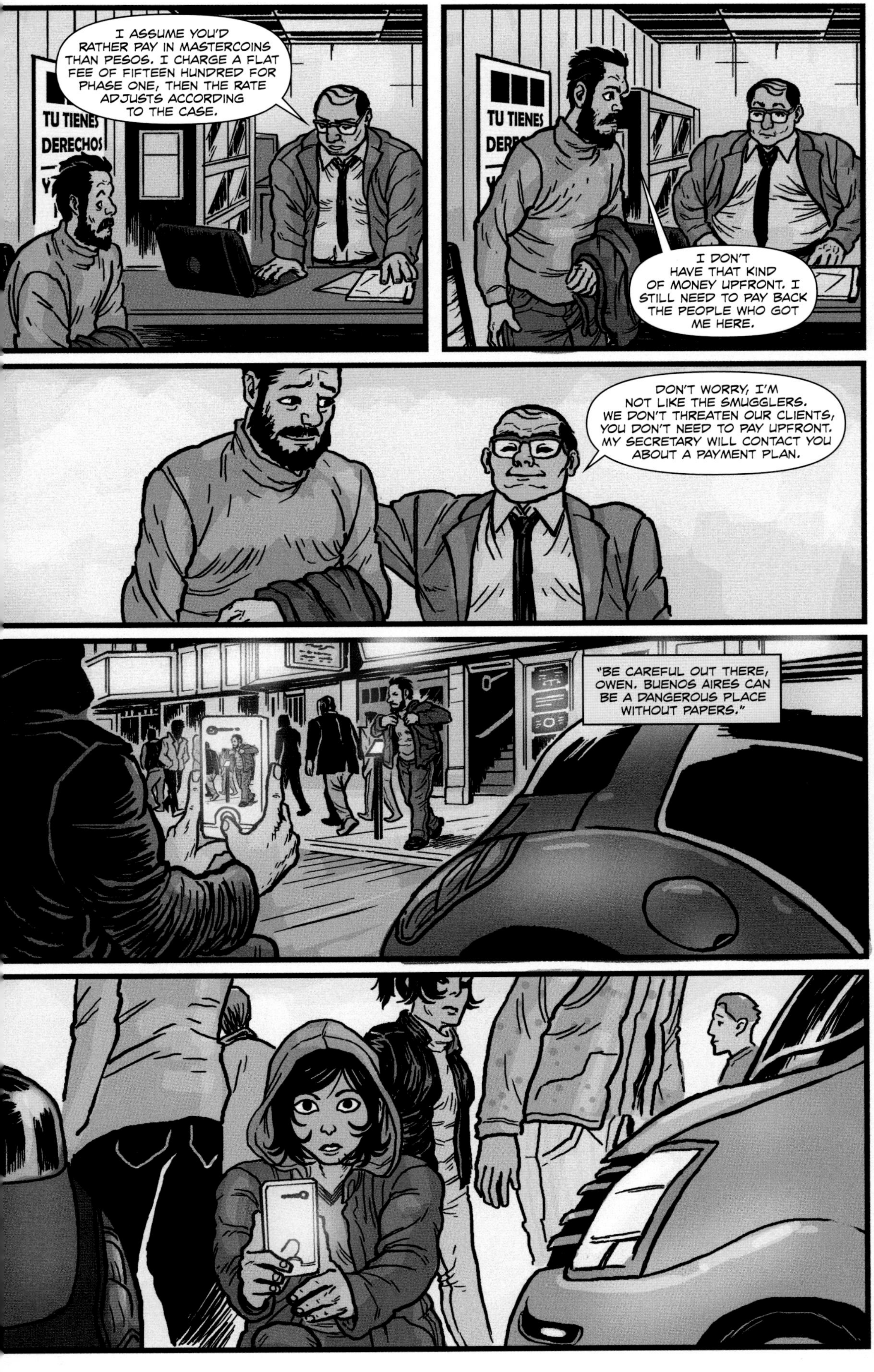
I ASSUME YOU'D RATHER PAY IN MASTERCOINS THAN PESOS. I CHARGE A FLAT FEE OF FIFTEEN HUNDRED FOR PHASE ONE, THEN THE RATE ADJUSTS ACCORDING TO THE CASE.
TU TIENES DERECHOS
I DON'T HAVE THAT KIND OF MONEY UPFRONT. I STILL NEED TO PAY BACK THE PEOPLE WHO GOT ME HERE.
DON'T WORRY, I'M NOT LIKE THE SMUGGLERS. WE DON'T THREATEN OUR CLIENTS, YOU DON'T NEED TO PAY UPFRONT. MY SECRETARY WILL CONTACT YOU ABOUT A PAYMENT PLAN.
"BE CAREFUL OUT THERE, OWEN. BUENOS AIRES CAN BE A DANGEROUS PLACE WITHOUT PAPERS."

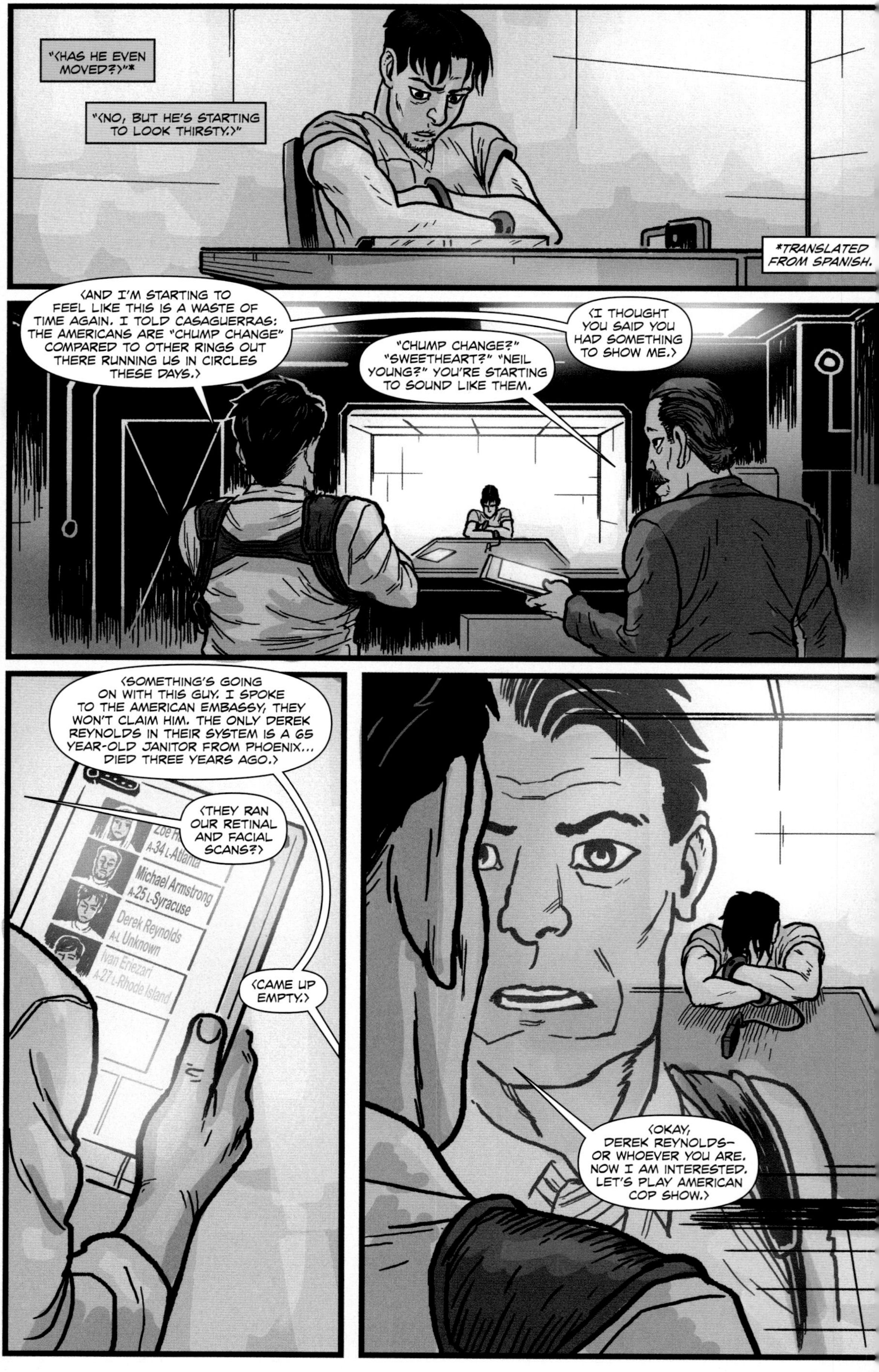
"<HAS HE EVEN MOVED?>"*
"<NO, BUT HE'S STARTING TO LOOK THIRSTY.>"
*TRANSLATED FROM SPANISH.
<AND I'M STARTING TO FEEL LIKE THIS IS A WASTE OF TIME AGAIN. I TOLD CASAGUERRAS: THE AMERICANS ARE "CHUMP CHANGE" COMPARED TO OTHER RINGS OUT THERE RUNNING US IN CIRCLES THESE DAYS.>
<I THOUGHT YOU SAID YOU HAD SOMETHING TO SHOW ME.>
"CHUMP CHANGE?" "SWEETHEART?" "NEIL YOUNG?" YOU'RE STARTING TO SOUND LIKE THEM.
<SOMETHING'S GOING ON WITH THIS GUY. I SPOKE TO THE AMERICAN EMBASSY, THEY WON'T CLAIM HIM. THE ONLY DEREK REYNOLDS IN THEIR SYSTEM IS A 65 YEAR-OLD JANITOR FROM PHOENIX... DIED THREE YEARS AGO.>
<THEY RAN OUR RETINAL AND FACIAL SCANS?>
A-34 L-Atlanta
Michael Armstrong
A-25 L-Syracuse
Derek Reynolds
A-L Unknown
Ivan Eriezari
A-27 L-Rhode Island
<CAME UP EMPTY.>
<OKAY, DEREK REYNOLDS– OR WHOEVER YOU ARE. NOW I AM INTERESTED. LET'S PLAY AMERICAN COP SHOW.>

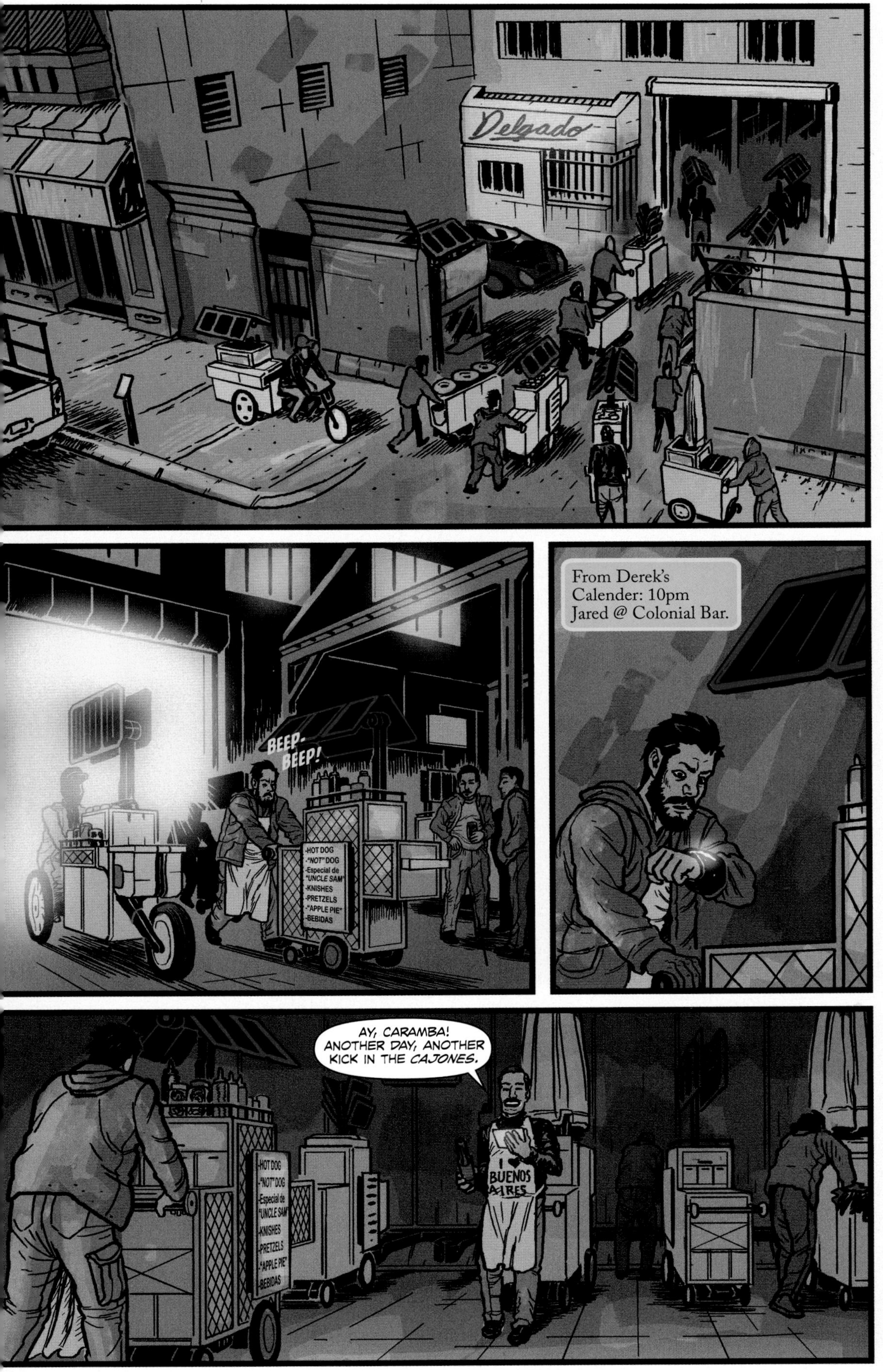
Delgado
BEEP-
BEEP!
-HOT DOG
-"NOT" DOG
-Especial de
"UNCLE SAM"
-KNISHES
-PRETZELS
-"APPLE PIE"
-BEBIDAS
From Derek's Calender: 10pm Jared @ Colonial Bar.
AY, CARAMBA! ANOTHER DAY, ANOTHER KICK IN THE CAJONES.
I ♥ BUENOS AIRES

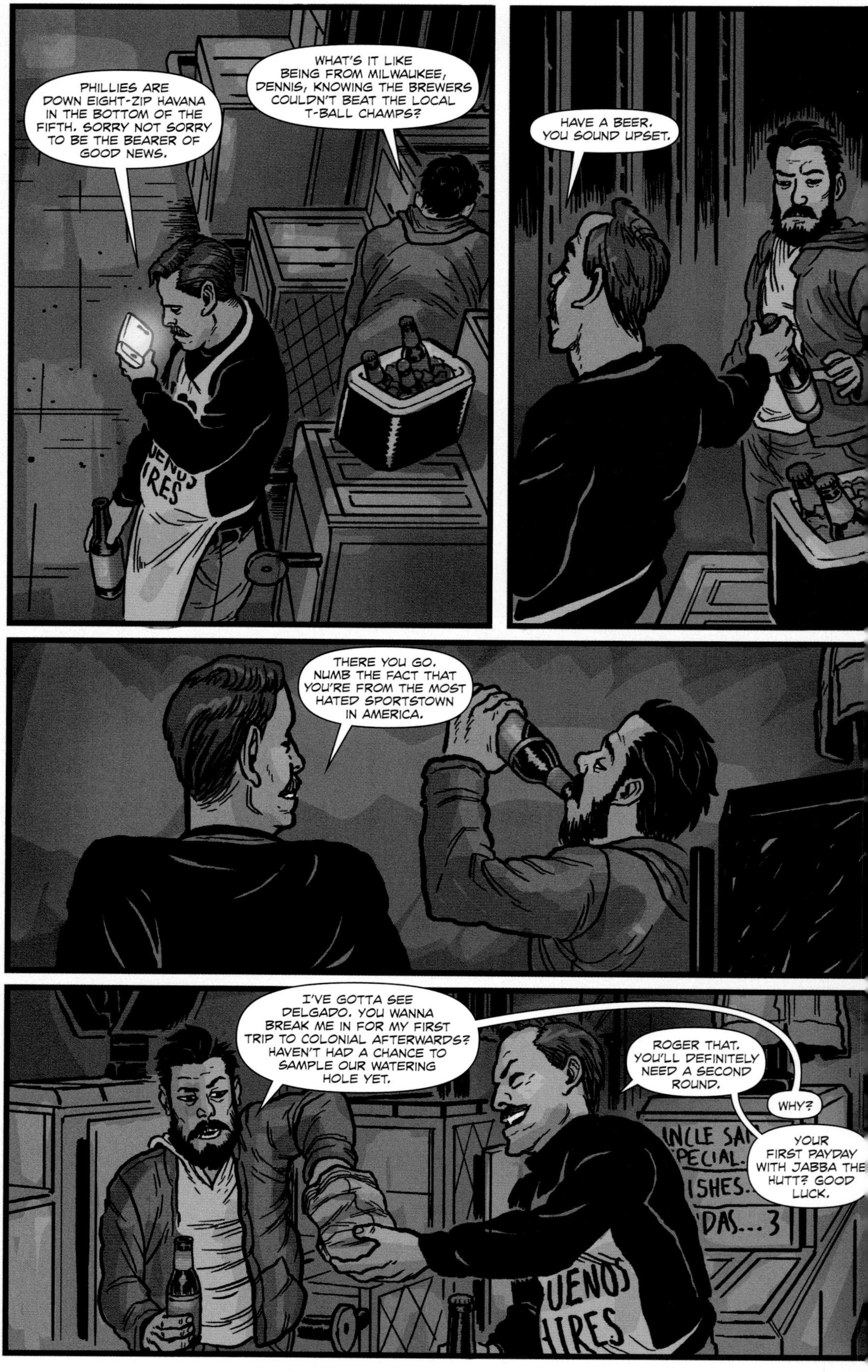
PHILLIES ARE DOWN EIGHT-ZIP HAVANA IN THE BOTTOM OF THE FIFTH. SORRY NOT SORRY TO BE THE BEARER OF GOOD NEWS.
WHAT'S IT LIKE BEING FROM MILWAUKEE, DENNIS, KNOWING THE BREWERS COULDN'T BEAT THE LOCAL T-BALL CHAMPS?
UENOS IRES
HAVE A BEER. YOU SOUND UPSET.
THERE YOU GO. NUMB THE FACT THAT YOU'RE FROM THE MOST HATED SPORTSTOWN IN AMERICA.
I'VE GOTTA SEE DELGADO. YOU WANNA BREAK ME IN FOR MY FIRST TRIP TO COLONIAL AFTERWARDS? HAVEN'T HAD A CHANCE TO SAMPLE OUR WATERING HOLE YET.
ROGER THAT. YOU'LL DEFINITELY NEED A SECOND ROUND.
WHY?
YOUR FIRST PAYDAY WITH JABBA THE HUTT? GOOD LUCK.
UENOS IRES

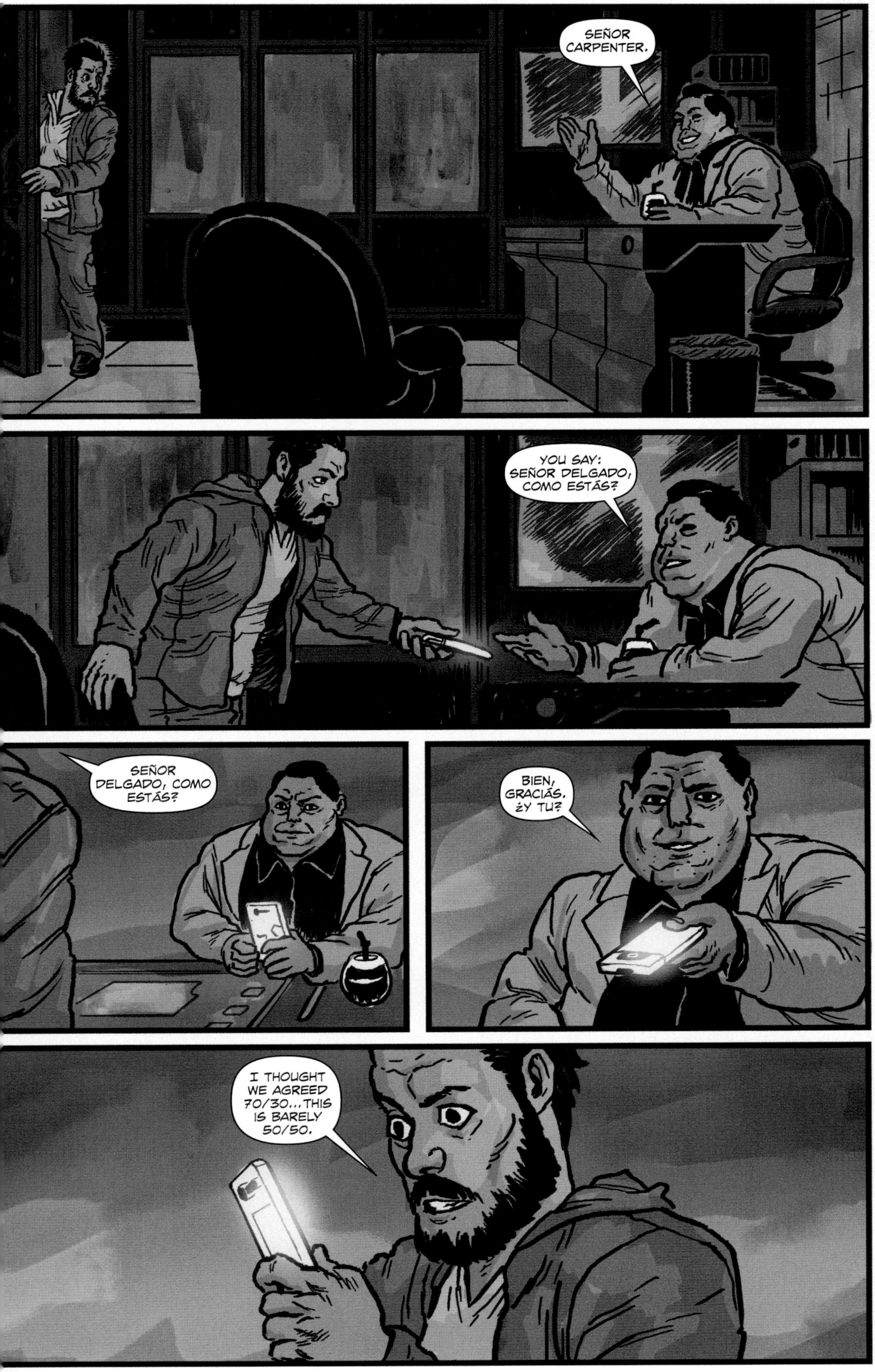
SEÑOR CARPENTER.
YOU SAY: SEÑOR DELGADO, COMO ESTÁS?
SEÑOR DELGADO, COMO ESTÁS?
BIEN, GRACIÁS. ¿Y TU?
I THOUGHT WE AGREED 70/30...THIS IS BARELY 50/50.

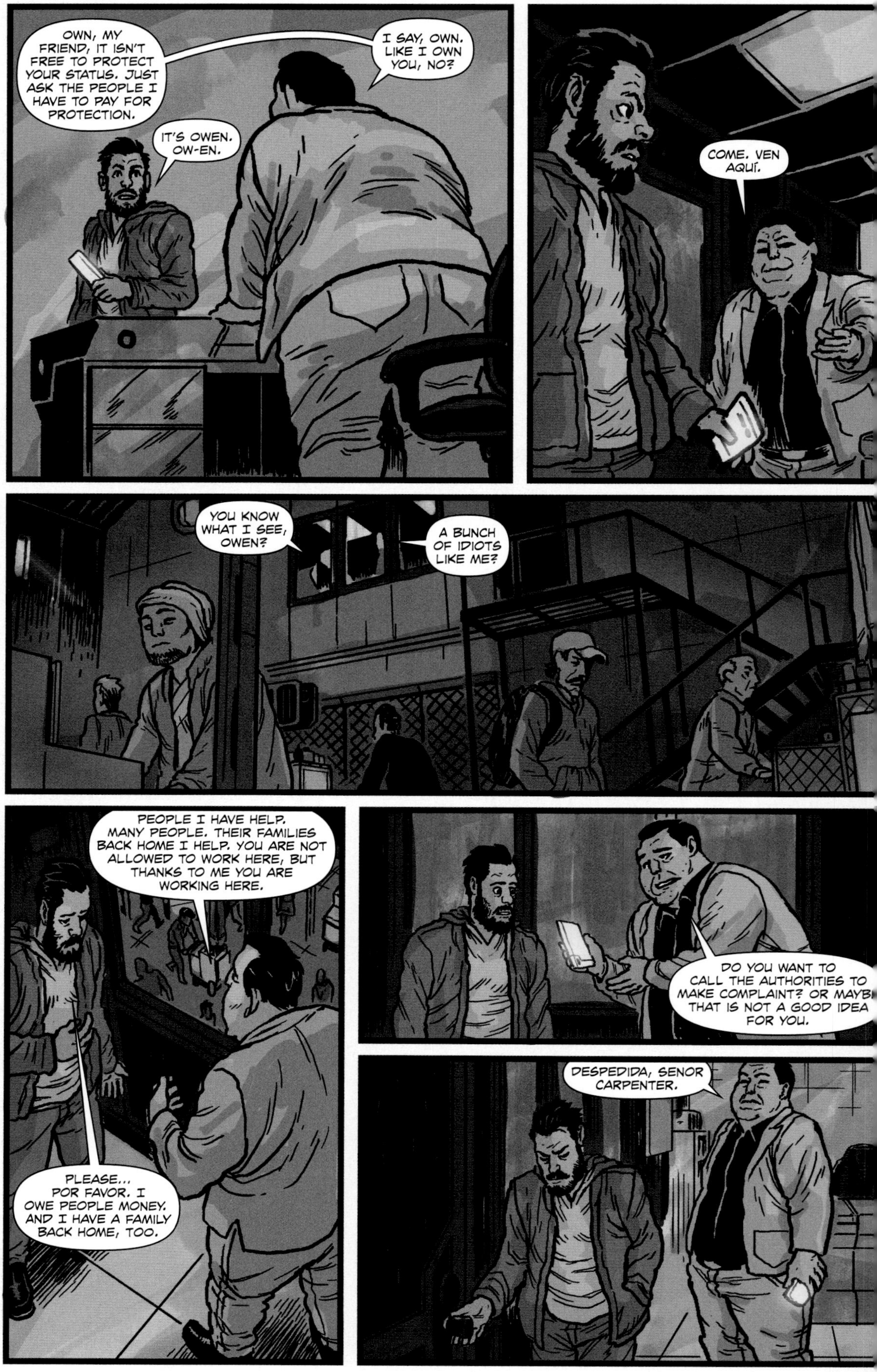
I SAY, OWN. LIKE I OWN YOU, NO?
OWN, MY FRIEND, IT ISN'T FREE TO PROTECT YOUR STATUS. JUST ASK THE PEOPLE I HAVE TO PAY FOR PROTECTION.
IT'S OWEN. OW-EN.
COME. VEN AQUÍ.
YOU KNOW WHAT I SEE, OWEN?
A BUNCH OF IDIOTS LIKE ME?
PEOPLE I HAVE HELP. MANY PEOPLE. THEIR FAMILIES BACK HOME I HELP. YOU ARE NOT ALLOWED TO WORK HERE, BUT THANKS TO ME YOU ARE WORKING HERE.
PLEASE... POR FAVOR. I OWE PEOPLE MONEY. AND I HAVE A FAMILY BACK HOME, TOO.
DO YOU WANT TO CALL THE AUTHORITIES TO MAKE COMPLAINT? OR MAYB THAT IS NOT A GOOD IDEA FOR YOU.
DESPEDIDA, SENOR CARPENTER.

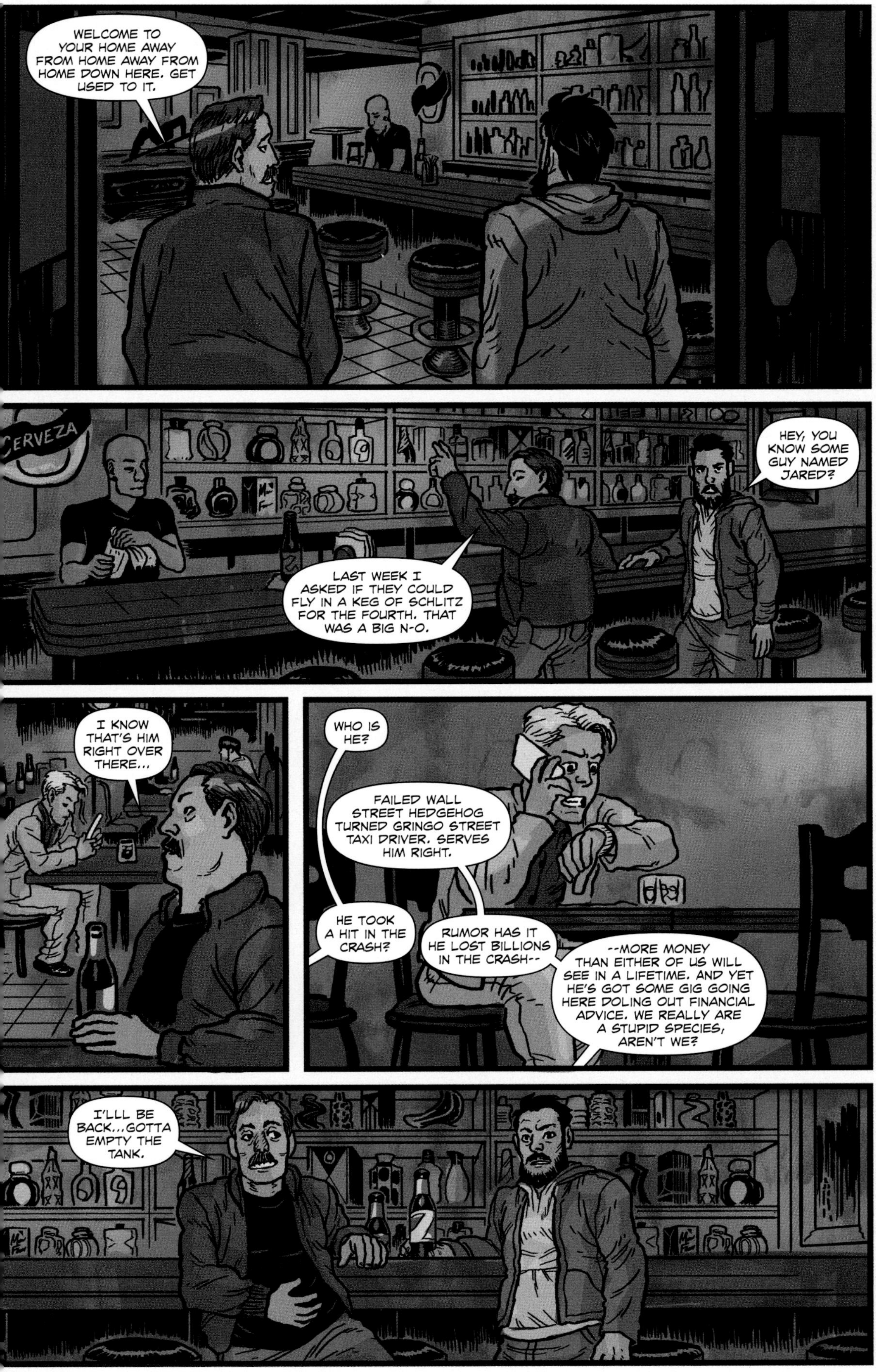
WELCOME TO YOUR HOME AWAY FROM HOME AWAY FROM HOME DOWN HERE. GET USED TO IT.
CERVEZA
HEY, YOU KNOW SOME GUY NAMED JARED?
LAST WEEK I ASKED IF THEY COULD FLY IN A KEG OF SCHLITZ FOR THE FOURTH. THAT WAS A BIG N-O.
I KNOW THAT'S HIM RIGHT OVER THERE...
WHO IS HE?
FAILED WALL STREET HEDGEHOG TURNED GRINGO STREET TAXI DRIVER. SERVES HIM RIGHT.
HE TOOK A HIT IN THE CRASH?
RUMOR HAS IT HE LOST BILLIONS IN THE CRASH--
--MORE MONEY THAN EITHER OF US WILL SEE IN A LIFETIME. AND YET HE'S GOT SOME GIG GOING HERE DOLING OUT FINANCIAL ADVICE. WE REALLY ARE A STUPID SPECIES, AREN'T WE?
I'LLL BE BACK...GOTTA EMPTY THE TANK.

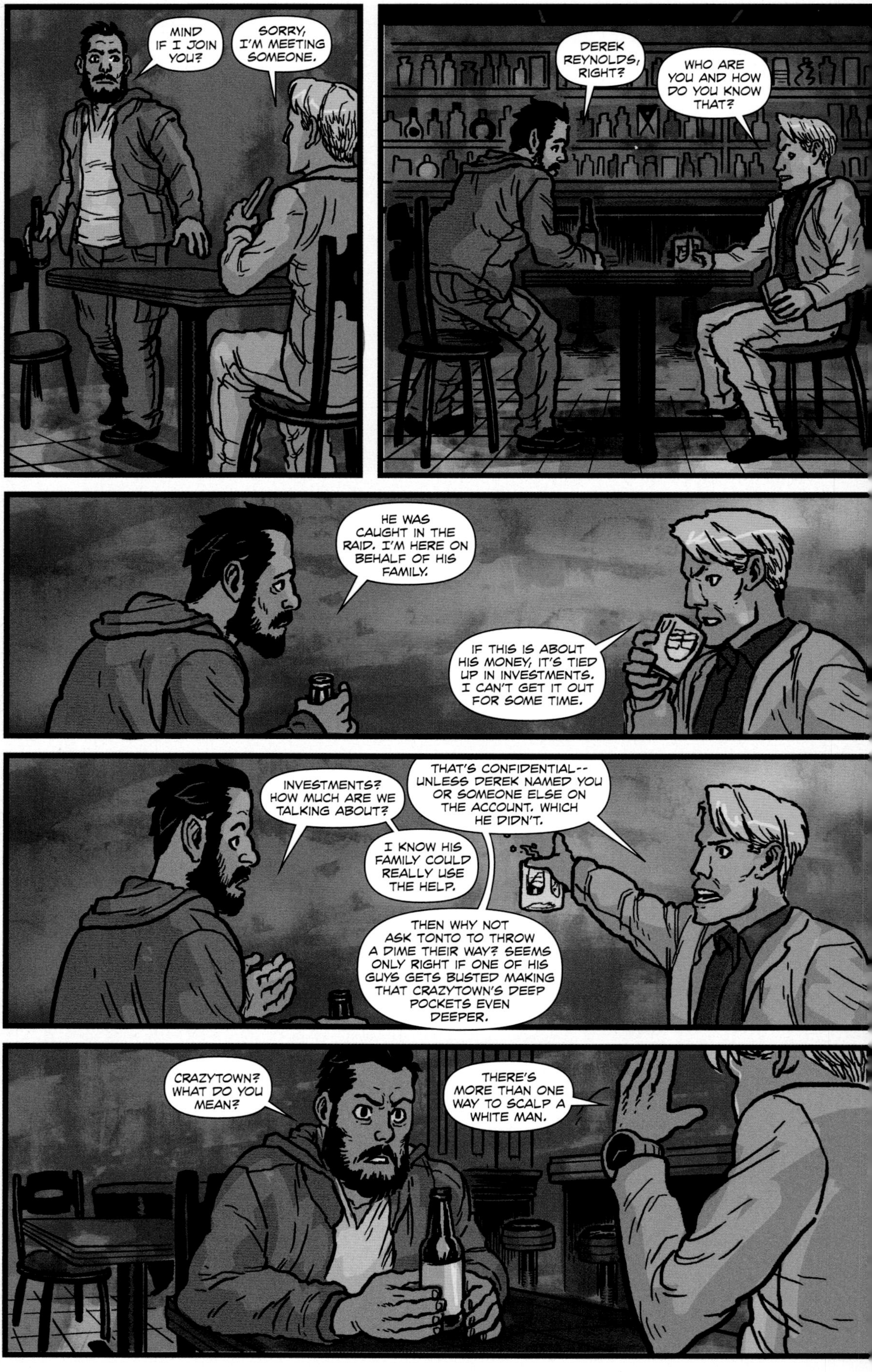
MIND IF I JOIN YOU?
SORRY, I'M MEETING SOMEONE.
DEREK REYNOLDS, RIGHT?
WHO ARE YOU AND HOW DO YOU KNOW THAT?
HE WAS CAUGHT IN THE RAID. I'M HERE ON BEHALF OF HIS FAMILY.
IF THIS IS ABOUT HIS MONEY, IT'S TIED UP IN INVESTMENTS. I CAN'T GET IT OUT FOR SOME TIME.
INVESTMENTS? HOW MUCH ARE WE TALKING ABOUT?
I KNOW HIS FAMILY COULD REALLY USE THE HELP.
THAT'S CONFIDENTIAL--UNLESS DEREK NAMED YOU OR SOMEONE ELSE ON THE ACCOUNT. WHICH HE DIDN'T.
THEN WHY NOT ASK TONTO TO THROW A DIME THEIR WAY? SEEMS ONLY RIGHT IF ONE OF HIS GUYS GETS BUSTED MAKING THAT CRAZYTOWN'S DEEP POCKETS EVEN DEEPER.
CRAZYTOWN? WHAT DO YOU MEAN?
THERE'S MORE THAN ONE WAY TO SCALP A WHITE MAN.

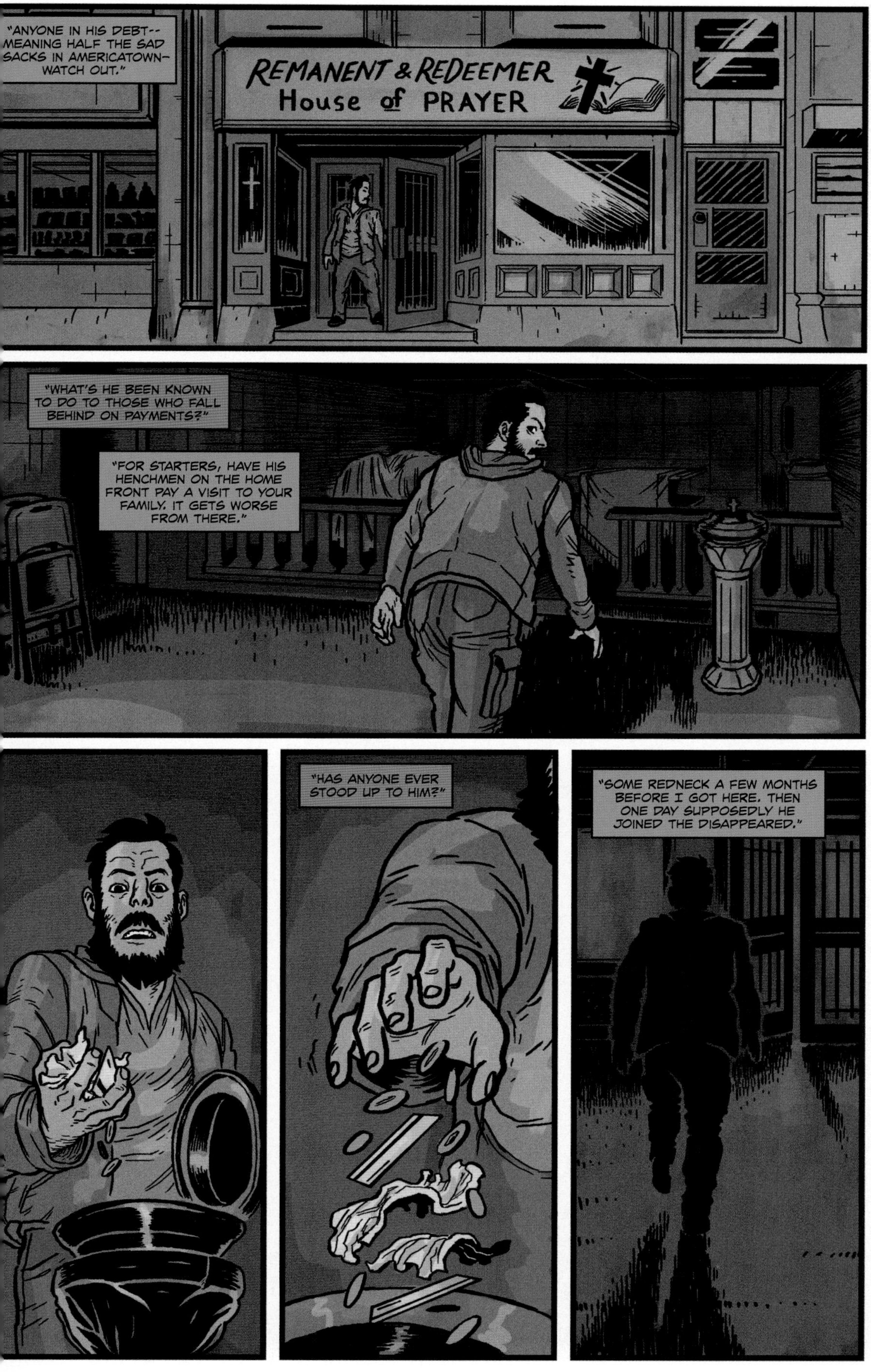
"ANYONE IN HIS DEBT--
MEANING HALF THE SAD
SACKS IN AMERICATOWN-
WATCH OUT."
REMANENT & REDEEMER
House of PRAYER
"WHAT'S HE BEEN KNOWN
TO DO TO THOSE WHO FALL
BEHIND ON PAYMENTS?"
"FOR STARTERS, HAVE HIS
HENCHMEN ON THE HOME
FRONT PAY A VISIT TO YOUR
FAMILY. IT GETS WORSE
FROM THERE."
"HAS ANYONE EVER
STOOD UP TO HIM?"
"SOME REDNECK A FEW MONTHS
BEFORE I GOT HERE. THEN
ONE DAY SUPPOSEDLY HE
JOINED THE DISAPPEARED."

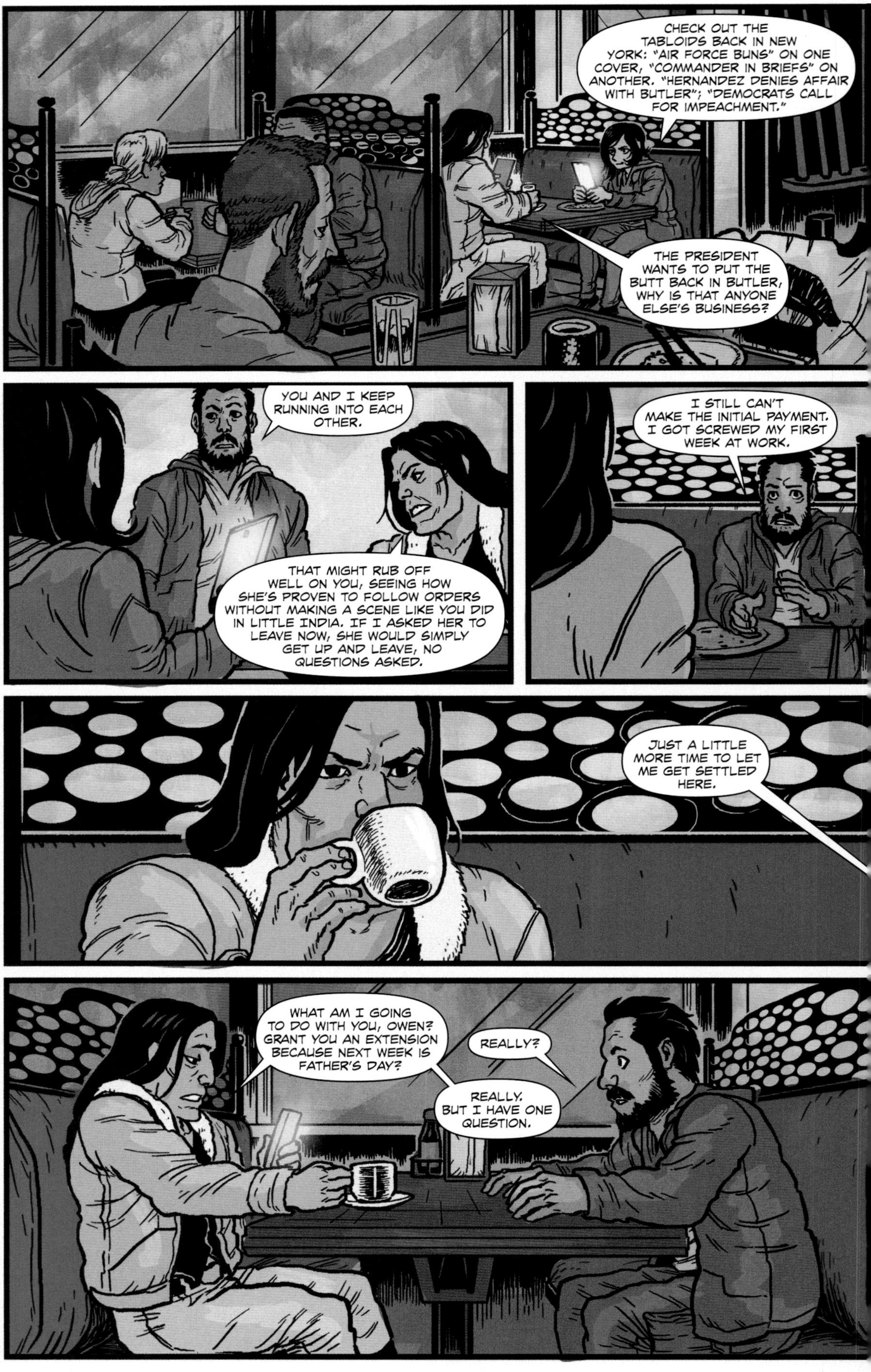
CHECK OUT THE TABLOIDS BACK IN NEW YORK: "AIR FORCE BUNS" ON ONE COVER, "COMMANDER IN BRIEFS" ON ANOTHER. "HERNANDEZ DENIES AFFAIR WITH BUTLER"; "DEMOCRATS CALL FOR IMPEACHMENT."
THE PRESIDENT WANTS TO PUT THE BUTT BACK IN BUTLER, WHY IS THAT ANYONE ELSE'S BUSINESS?
YOU AND I KEEP RUNNING INTO EACH OTHER.
THAT MIGHT RUB OFF WELL ON YOU, SEEING HOW SHE'S PROVEN TO FOLLOW ORDERS WITHOUT MAKING A SCENE LIKE YOU DID IN LITTLE INDIA. IF I ASKED HER TO LEAVE NOW, SHE WOULD SIMPLY GET UP AND LEAVE, NO QUESTIONS ASKED.
I STILL CAN'T MAKE THE INITIAL PAYMENT. I GOT SCREWED MY FIRST WEEK AT WORK.
JUST A LITTLE MORE TIME TO LET ME GET SETTLED HERE.
WHAT AM I GOING TO DO WITH YOU, OWEN? GRANT YOU AN EXTENSION BECAUSE NEXT WEEK IS FATHER'S DAY?
REALLY?
REALLY. BUT I HAVE ONE QUESTION.

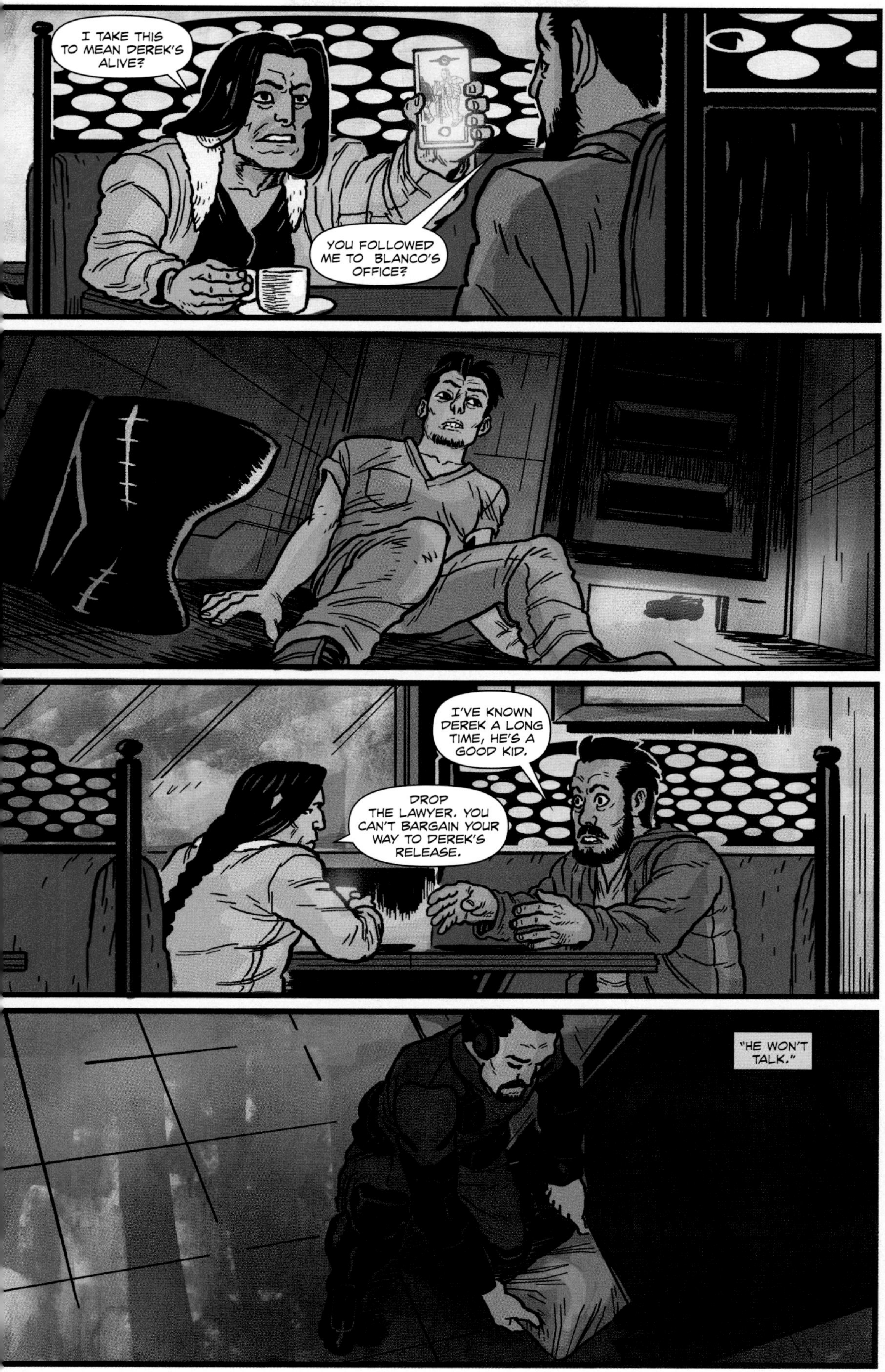
I TAKE THIS TO MEAN DEREK'S ALIVE?
YOU FOLLOWED ME TO BLANCO'S OFFICE?
I'VE KNOWN DEREK A LONG TIME, HE'S A GOOD KID.
DROP THE LAWYER. YOU CAN'T BARGAIN YOUR WAY TO DEREK'S RELEASE.
"HE WON'T TALK."

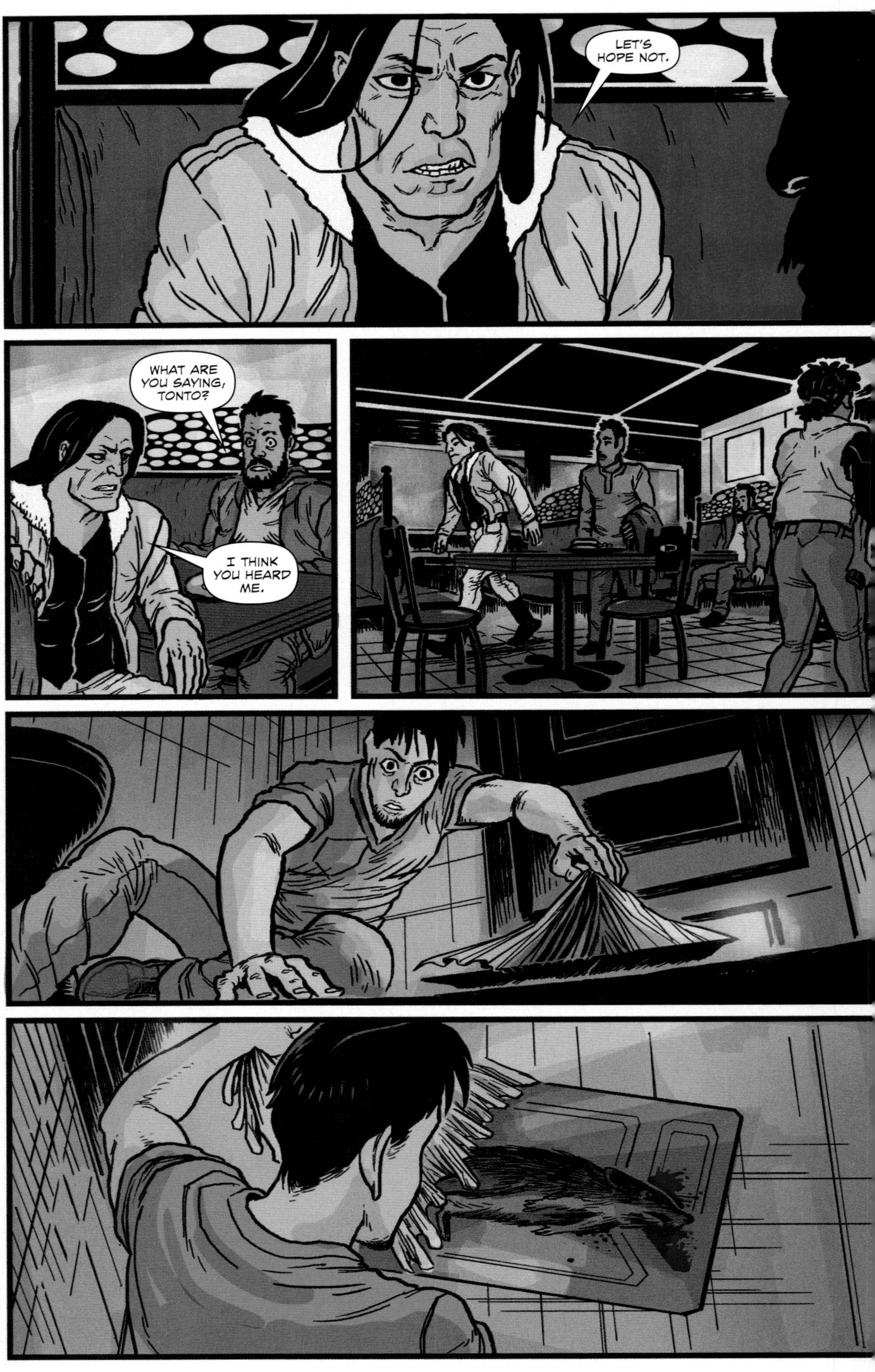
LET'S HOPE NOT.
WHAT ARE YOU SAYING, TONTO?
I THINK YOU HEARD ME.

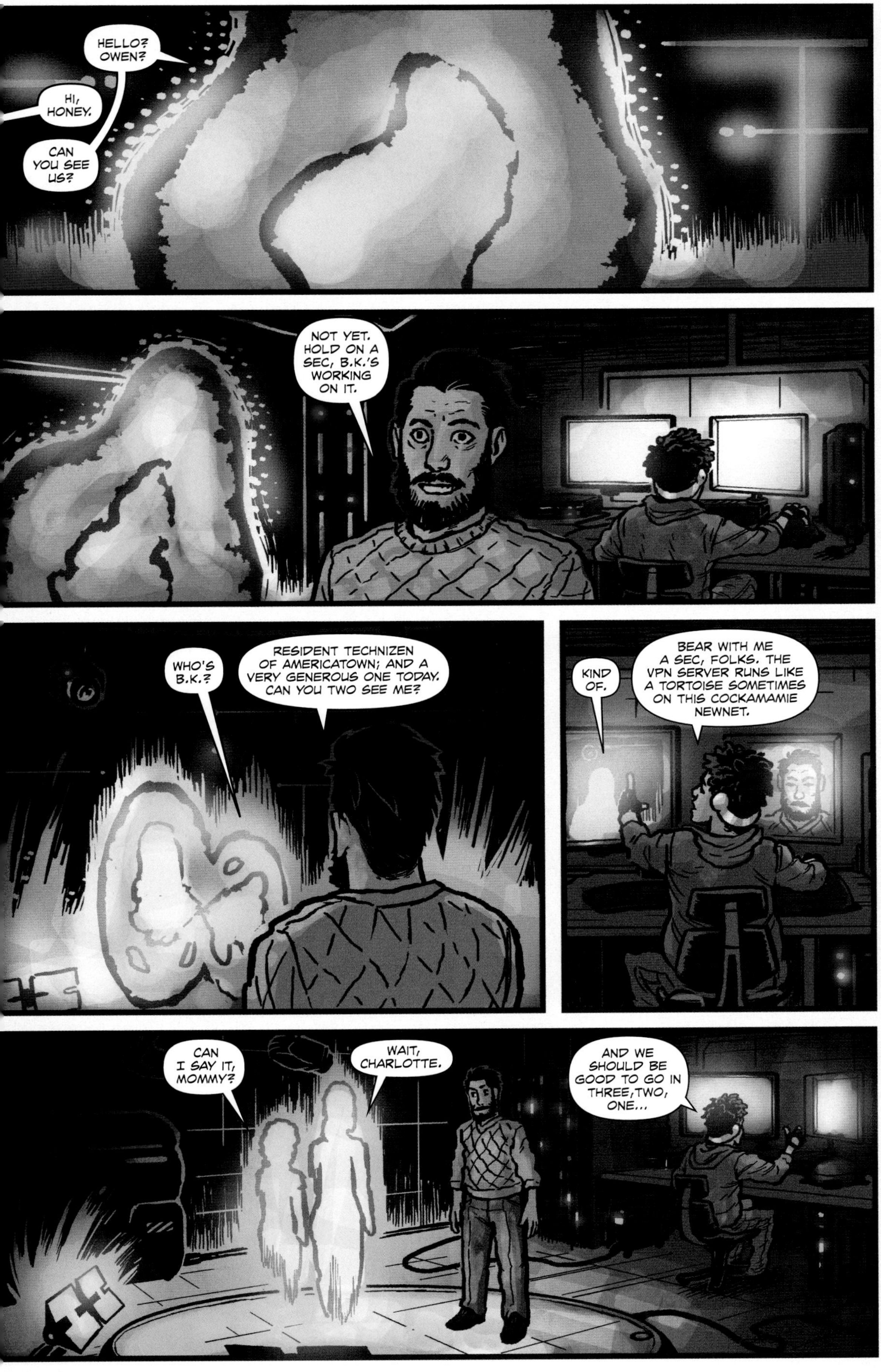
HELLO? OWEN?
HI, HONEY.
CAN YOU SEE US?
NOT YET. HOLD ON A SEC, B.K.'S WORKING ON IT.
WHO'S B.K.?
RESIDENT TECHNIZEN OF AMERICATOWN; AND A VERY GENEROUS ONE TODAY. CAN YOU TWO SEE ME?
KIND OF.
BEAR WITH ME A SEC, FOLKS. THE VPN SERVER RUNS LIKE A TORTOISE SOMETIMES ON THIS COCKAMAMIE NEWNET.
CAN I SAY IT, MOMMY?
WAIT, CHARLOTTE.
AND WE SHOULD BE GOOD TO GO IN THREE, TWO, ONE...

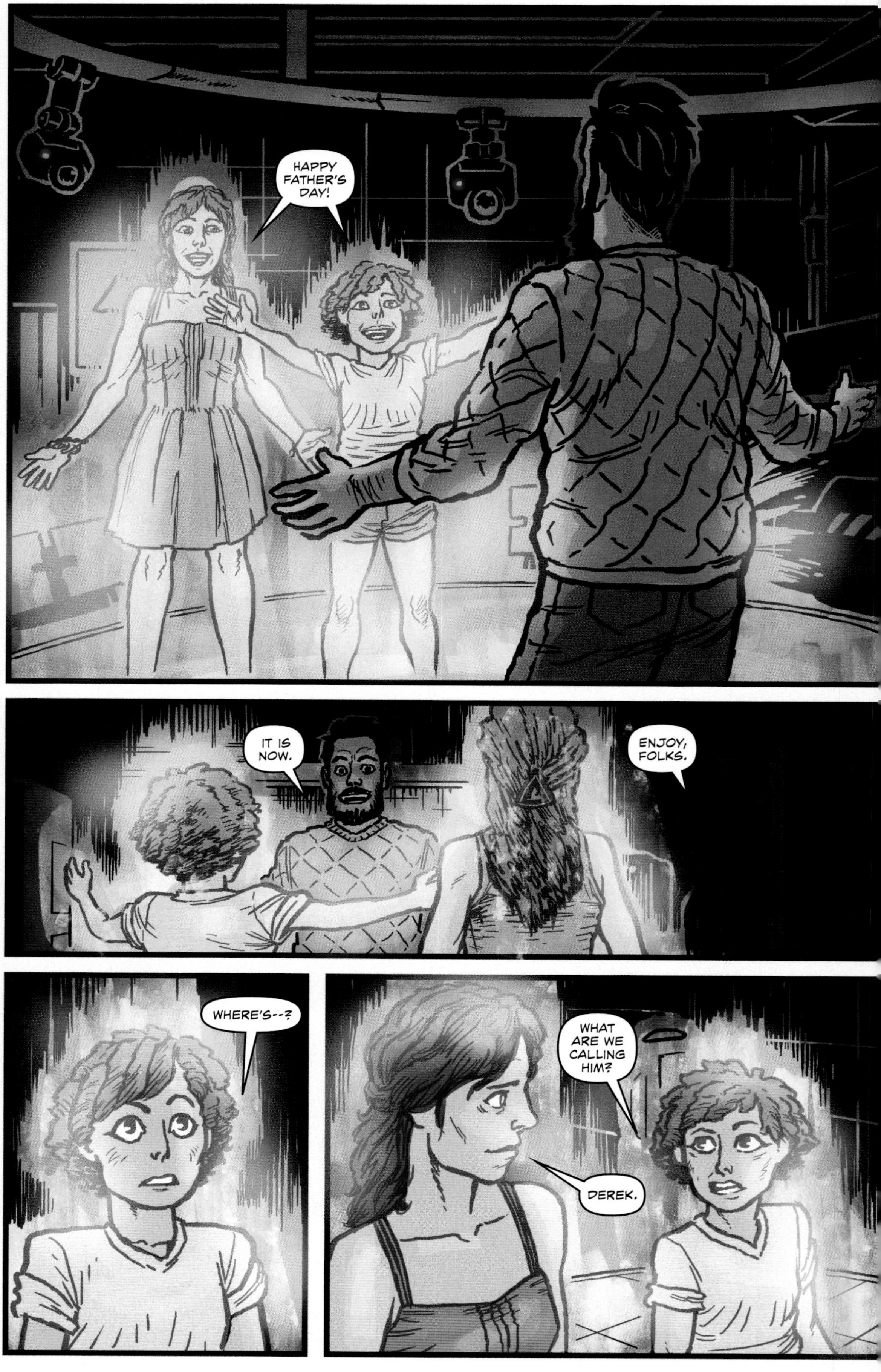
HAPPY FATHER'S DAY!
IT IS NOW.
ENJOY, FOLKS.
WHERE'S--?
WHAT ARE WE CALLING HIM?
DEREK.

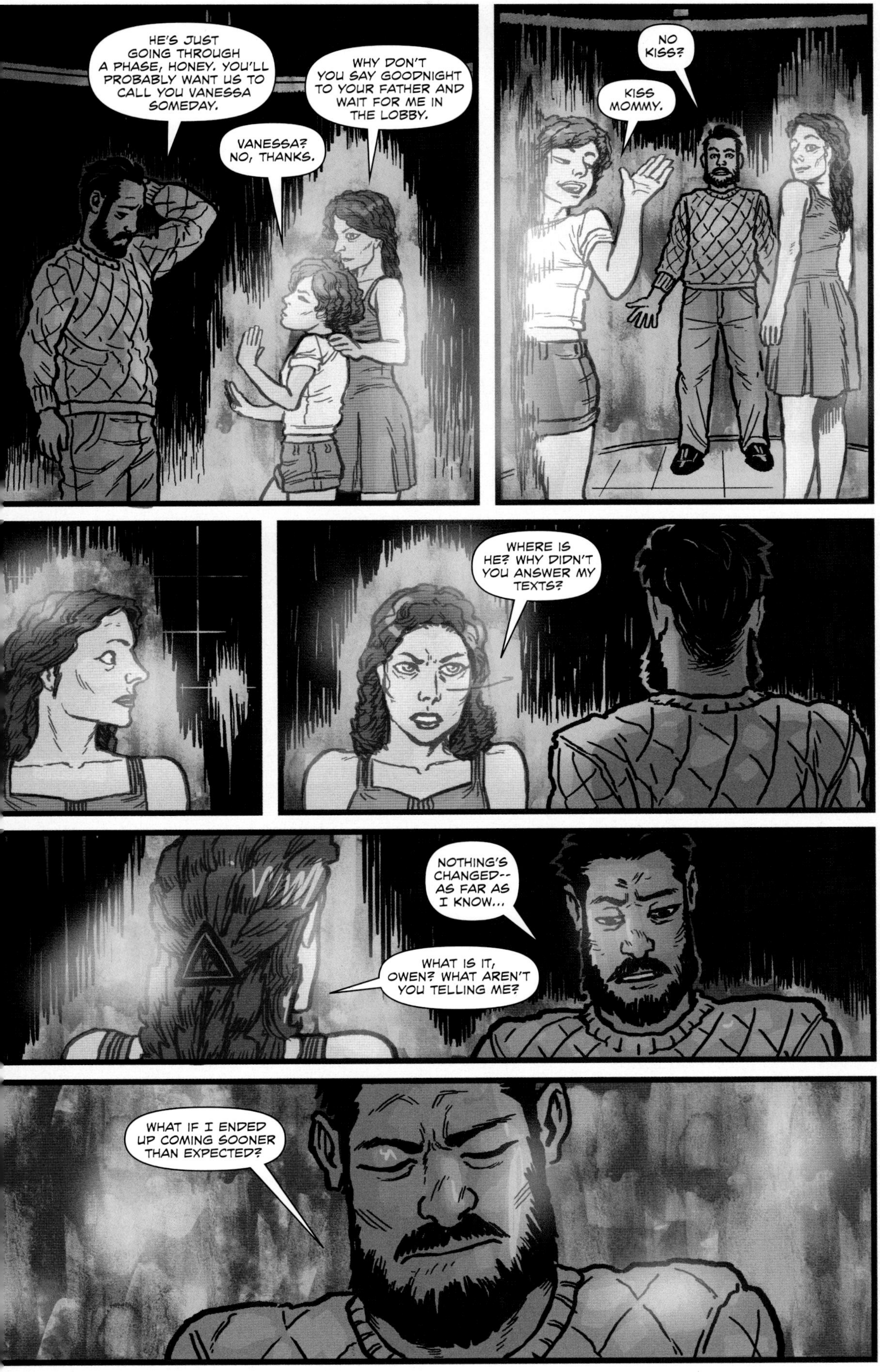
HE'S JUST GOING THROUGH A PHASE, HONEY. YOU'LL PROBABLY WANT US TO CALL YOU VANESSA SOMEDAY.
VANESSA? NO, THANKS.
WHY DON'T YOU SAY GOODNIGHT TO YOUR FATHER AND WAIT FOR ME IN THE LOBBY.
NO KISS?
KISS MOMMY.
WHERE IS HE? WHY DIDN'T YOU ANSWER MY TEXTS?
NOTHING'S CHANGED-- AS FAR AS I KNOW...
WHAT IS IT, OWEN? WHAT AREN'T YOU TELLING ME?
WHAT IF I ENDED UP COMING SOONER THAN EXPECTED?

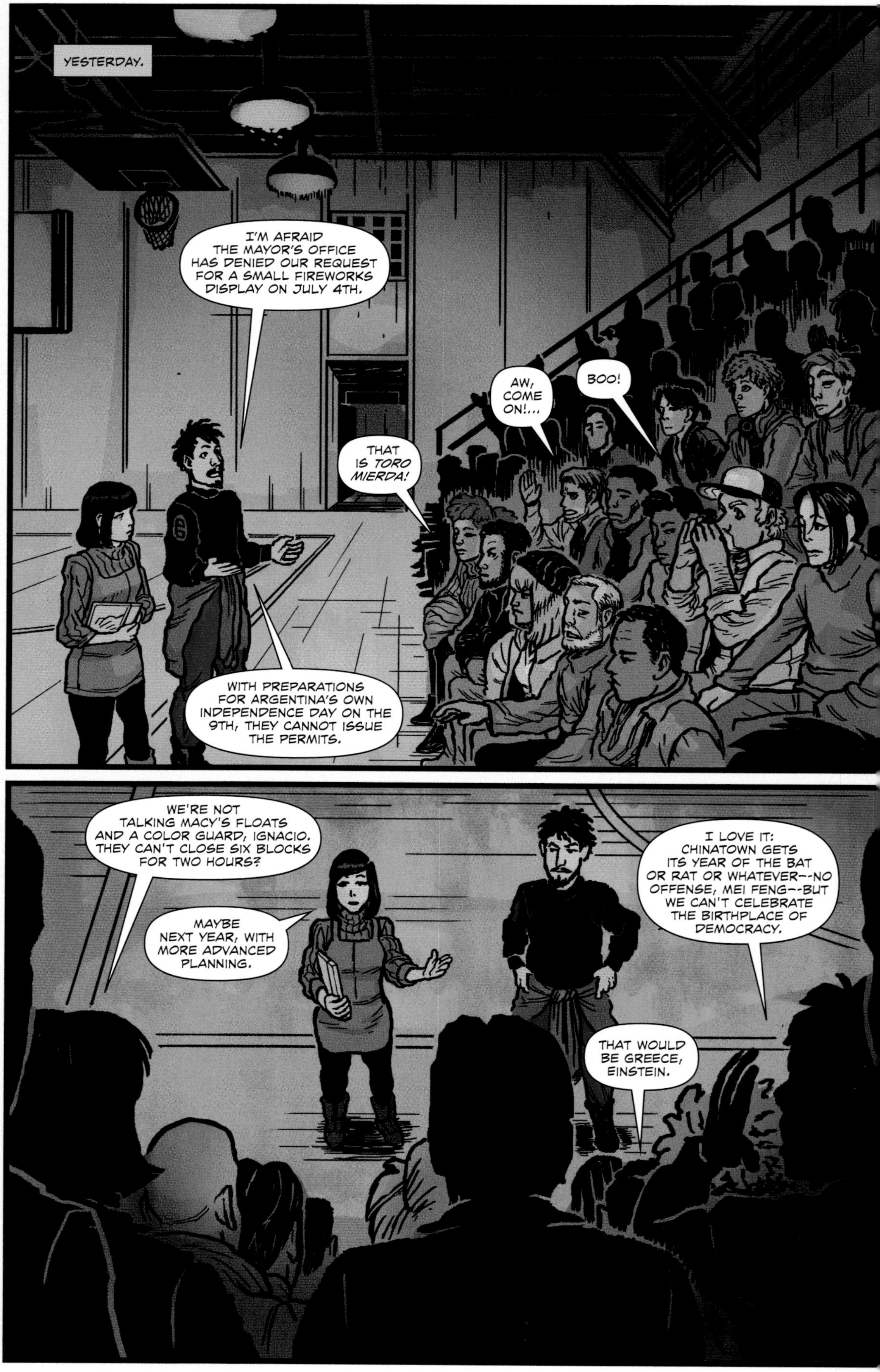
YESTERDAY.
I'M AFRAID THE MAYOR'S OFFICE HAS DENIED OUR REQUEST FOR A SMALL FIREWORKS DISPLAY ON JULY 4TH.
AW, COME ON!...
BOO!
THAT IS *TORO MIERDA!*
WITH PREPARATIONS FOR ARGENTINA'S OWN INDEPENDENCE DAY ON THE 9TH, THEY CANNOT ISSUE THE PERMITS.
WE'RE NOT TALKING MACY'S FLOATS AND A COLOR GUARD, IGNACIO. THEY CAN'T CLOSE SIX BLOCKS FOR TWO HOURS?
MAYBE NEXT YEAR, WITH MORE ADVANCED PLANNING.
I LOVE IT: CHINATOWN GETS ITS YEAR OF THE BAT OR RAT OR WHATEVER--NO OFFENSE, MEI FENG--BUT WE CAN'T CELEBRATE THE BIRTHPLACE OF DEMOCRACY.
THAT WOULD BE GREECE, EINSTEIN.

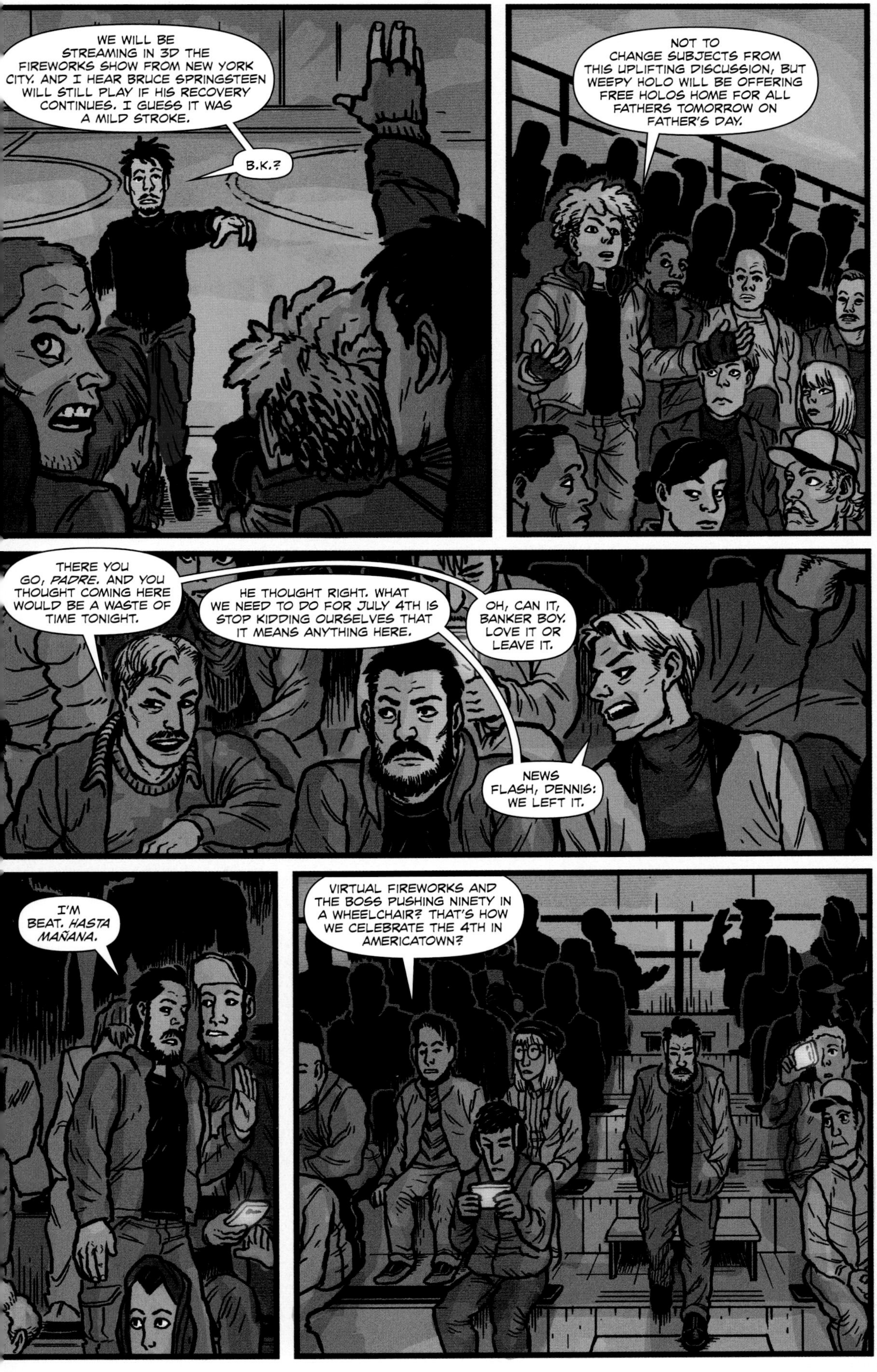
WE WILL BE STREAMING IN 3D THE FIREWORKS SHOW FROM NEW YORK CITY. AND I HEAR BRUCE SPRINGSTEEN WILL STILL PLAY IF HIS RECOVERY CONTINUES. I GUESS IT WAS A MILD STROKE.
B.K.?
NOT TO CHANGE SUBJECTS FROM THIS UPLIFTING DISCUSSION, BUT WEEPY HOLO WILL BE OFFERING FREE HOLOS HOME FOR ALL FATHERS TOMORROW ON FATHER'S DAY.
THERE YOU GO, *PADRE*. AND YOU THOUGHT COMING HERE WOULD BE A WASTE OF TIME TONIGHT.
HE THOUGHT RIGHT. WHAT WE NEED TO DO FOR JULY 4TH IS STOP KIDDING OURSELVES THAT IT MEANS ANYTHING HERE.
OH, CAN IT, BANKER BOY. LOVE IT OR LEAVE IT.
NEWS FLASH, DENNIS: WE LEFT IT.
I'M BEAT. *HASTA MAÑANA.*
VIRTUAL FIREWORKS AND THE BOSS PUSHING NINETY IN A WHEELCHAIR? THAT'S HOW WE CELEBRATE THE 4TH IN AMERICATOWN?

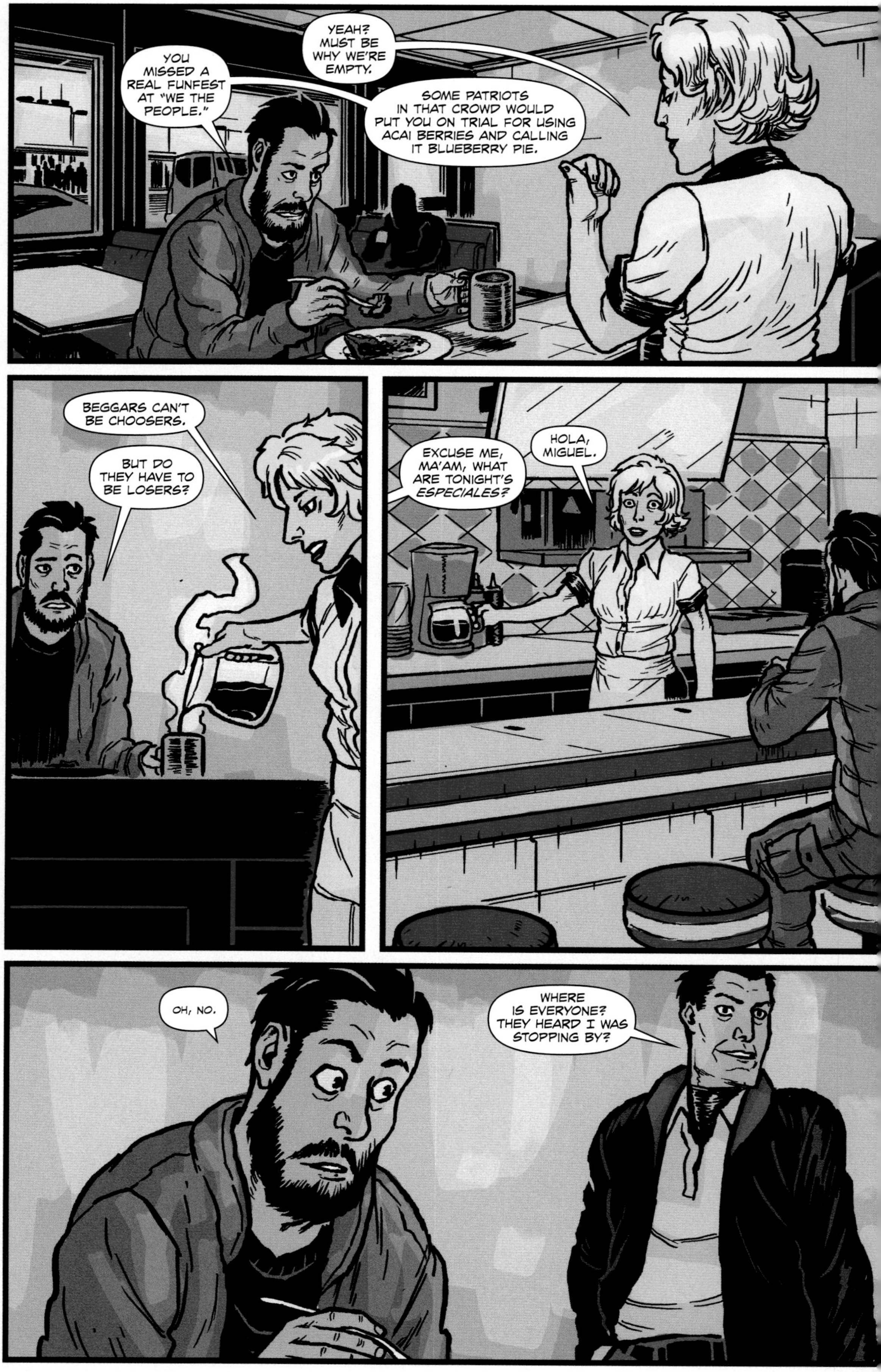
YOU MISSED A REAL FUNFEST AT "WE THE PEOPLE."
YEAH? MUST BE WHY WE'RE EMPTY.
SOME PATRIOTS IN THAT CROWD WOULD PUT YOU ON TRIAL FOR USING ACAI BERRIES AND CALLING IT BLUEBERRY PIE.
BEGGARS CAN'T BE CHOOSERS.
BUT DO THEY HAVE TO BE LOSERS?
EXCUSE ME, MA'AM, WHAT ARE TONIGHT'S *ESPECIALES?*
HOLA, MIGUEL.
OH, NO.
WHERE IS EVERYONE? THEY HEARD I WAS STOPPING BY?

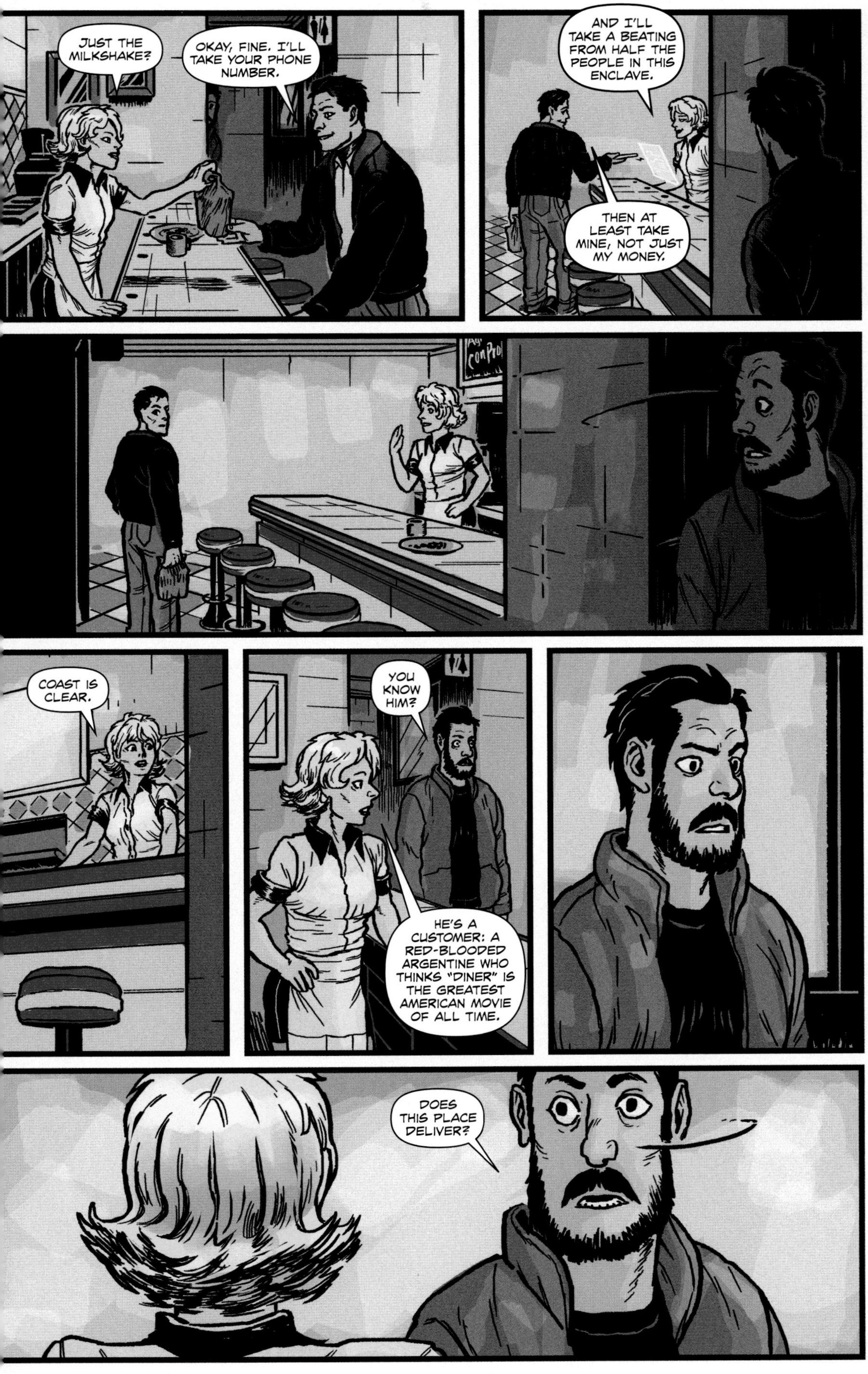
JUST THE MILKSHAKE?
OKAY, FINE. I'LL TAKE YOUR PHONE NUMBER.
AND I'LL TAKE A BEATING FROM HALF THE PEOPLE IN THIS ENCLAVE.
THEN AT LEAST TAKE MINE, NOT JUST MY MONEY.
COAST IS CLEAR.
YOU KNOW HIM?
HE'S A CUSTOMER: A RED-BLOODED ARGENTINE WHO THINKS "DINER" IS THE GREATEST AMERICAN MOVIE OF ALL TIME.
DOES THIS PLACE DELIVER?

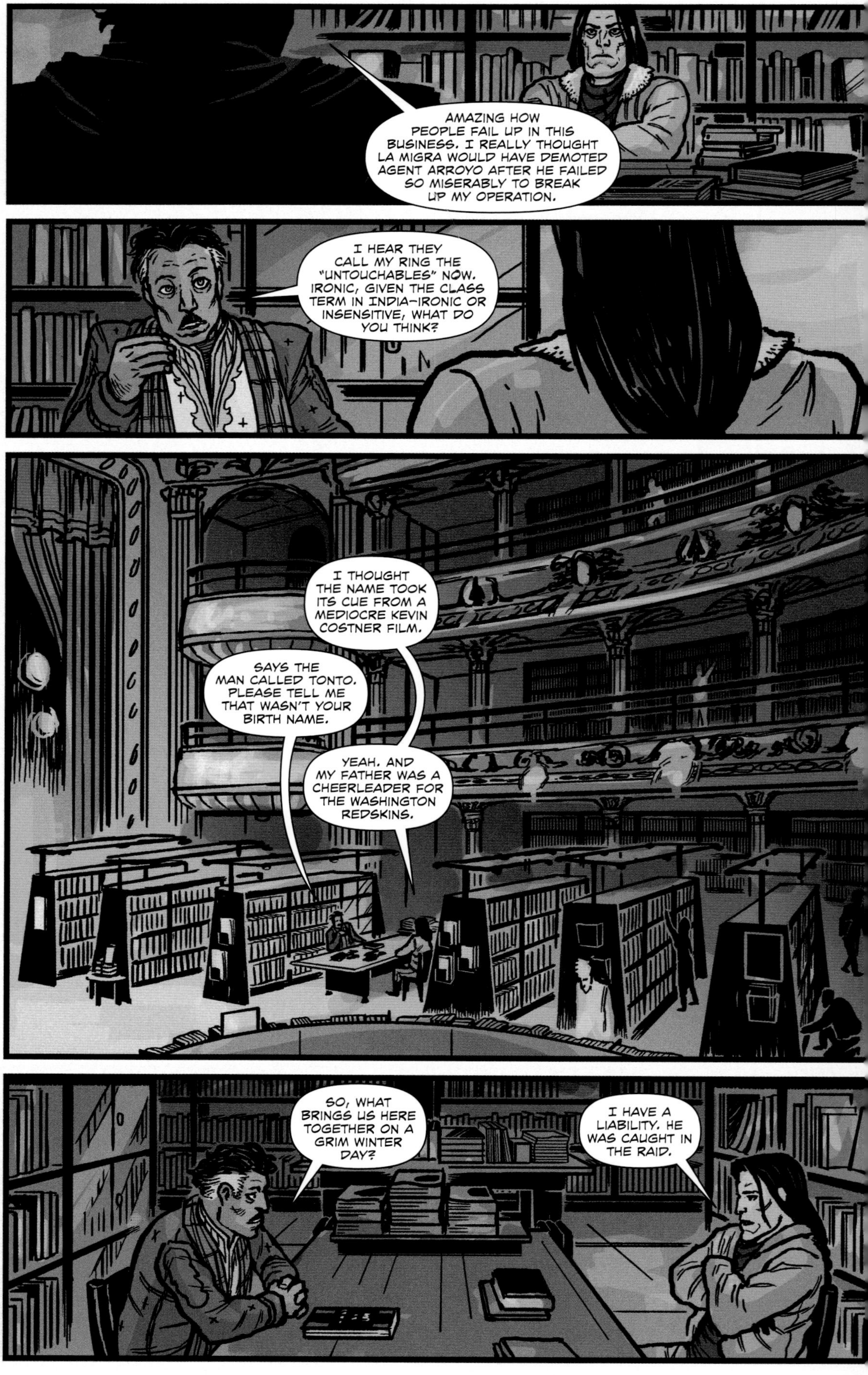
AMAZING HOW PEOPLE FAIL UP IN THIS BUSINESS. I REALLY THOUGHT LA MIGRA WOULD HAVE DEMOTED AGENT ARROYO AFTER HE FAILED SO MISERABLY TO BREAK UP MY OPERATION.
I HEAR THEY CALL MY RING THE "UNTOUCHABLES" NOW. IRONIC, GIVEN THE CLASS TERM IN INDIA–IRONIC OR INSENSITIVE, WHAT DO YOU THINK?
I THOUGHT THE NAME TOOK ITS CUE FROM A MEDIOCRE KEVIN COSTNER FILM.
SAYS THE MAN CALLED TONTO. PLEASE TELL ME THAT WASN'T YOUR BIRTH NAME.
YEAH. AND MY FATHER WAS A CHEERLEADER FOR THE WASHINGTON REDSKINS.
SO, WHAT BRINGS US HERE TOGETHER ON A GRIM WINTER DAY?
I HAVE A LIABILITY. HE WAS CAUGHT IN THE RAID.

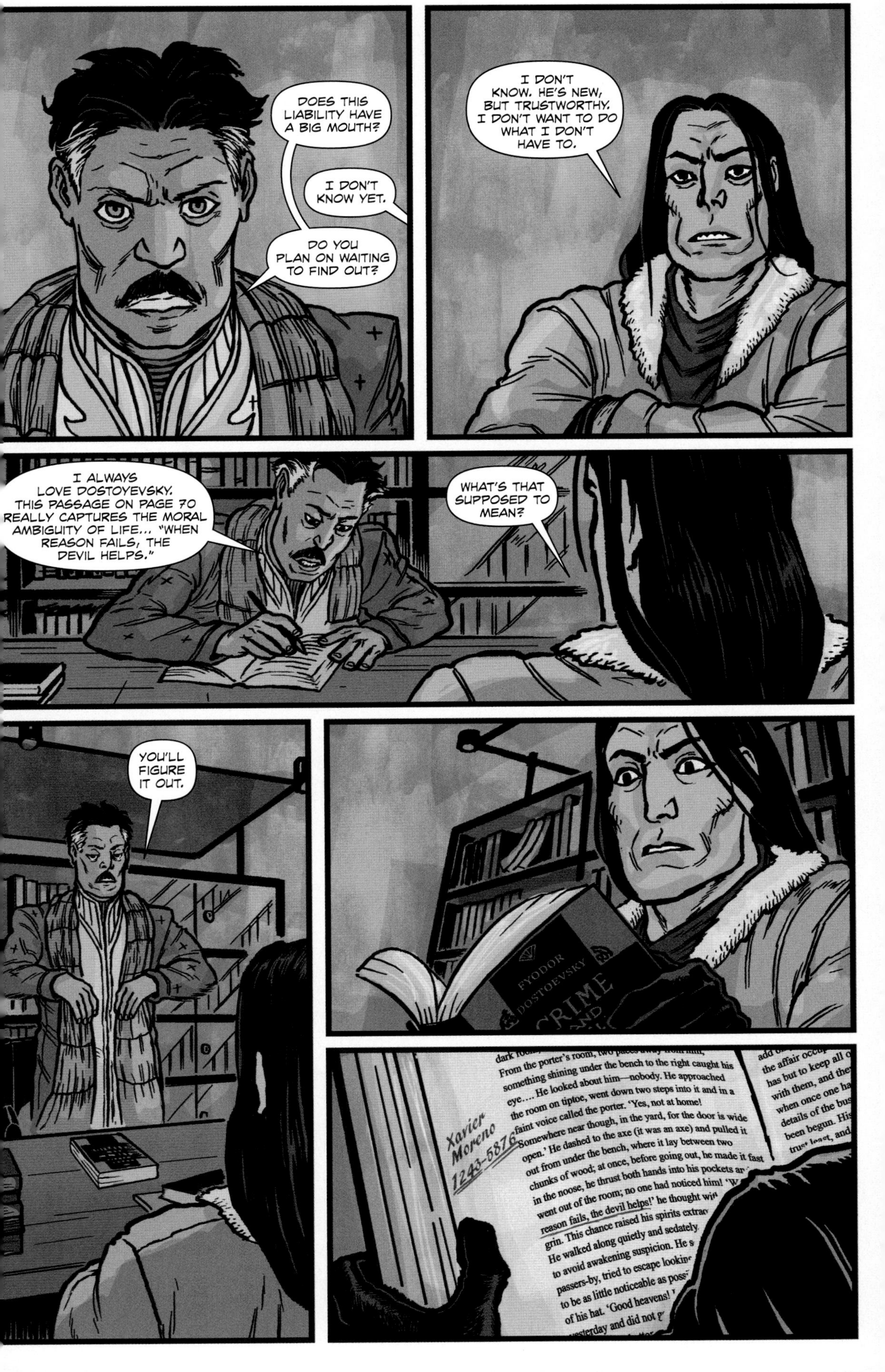

DOES THIS LIABILITY HAVE A BIG MOUTH?
I DON'T KNOW YET.
DO YOU PLAN ON WAITING TO FIND OUT?
I DON'T KNOW. HE'S NEW, BUT TRUSTWORTHY. I DON'T WANT TO DO WHAT I DON'T HAVE TO.
I ALWAYS LOVE DOSTOYEVSKY. THIS PASSAGE ON PAGE 70 REALLY CAPTURES THE MORAL AMBIGUITY OF LIFE... "WHEN REASON FAILS, THE DEVIL HELPS."
WHAT'S THAT SUPPOSED TO MEAN?
YOU'LL FIGURE IT OUT.
FYODOR DOSTOEVSKY
CRIME
From the porter's room, two paces away from him,
something shining under the bench to the right caught his
eye.... He looked about him—nobody. He approached
the room on tiptoe, went down two steps into it and in a
faint voice called the porter. 'Yes, not at home!
Somewhere near though, in the yard, for the door is wide
open.' He dashed to the axe (it was an axe) and pulled it
out from under the bench, where it lay between two
chunks of wood; at once, before going out, he made it fast
in the noose, he thrust both hands into his pockets an
went out of the room; no one had noticed him! 'W
reason fails, the devil helps!' he thought wit
grin. This chance raised his spirits extrao
He walked along quietly and sedately.
He walked along quietly and sedately. He s
to avoid awakening suspicion. He s
passers-by, tried to escape lookin
to be as little noticeable as possi
of his hat. 'Good heavens!
yesterday and did not g
the affair occu
has but to keep all o
with them, and the
when once one ha
details of the bus
been begun. His
trust least, and
Xavier Moreno
1243-5876

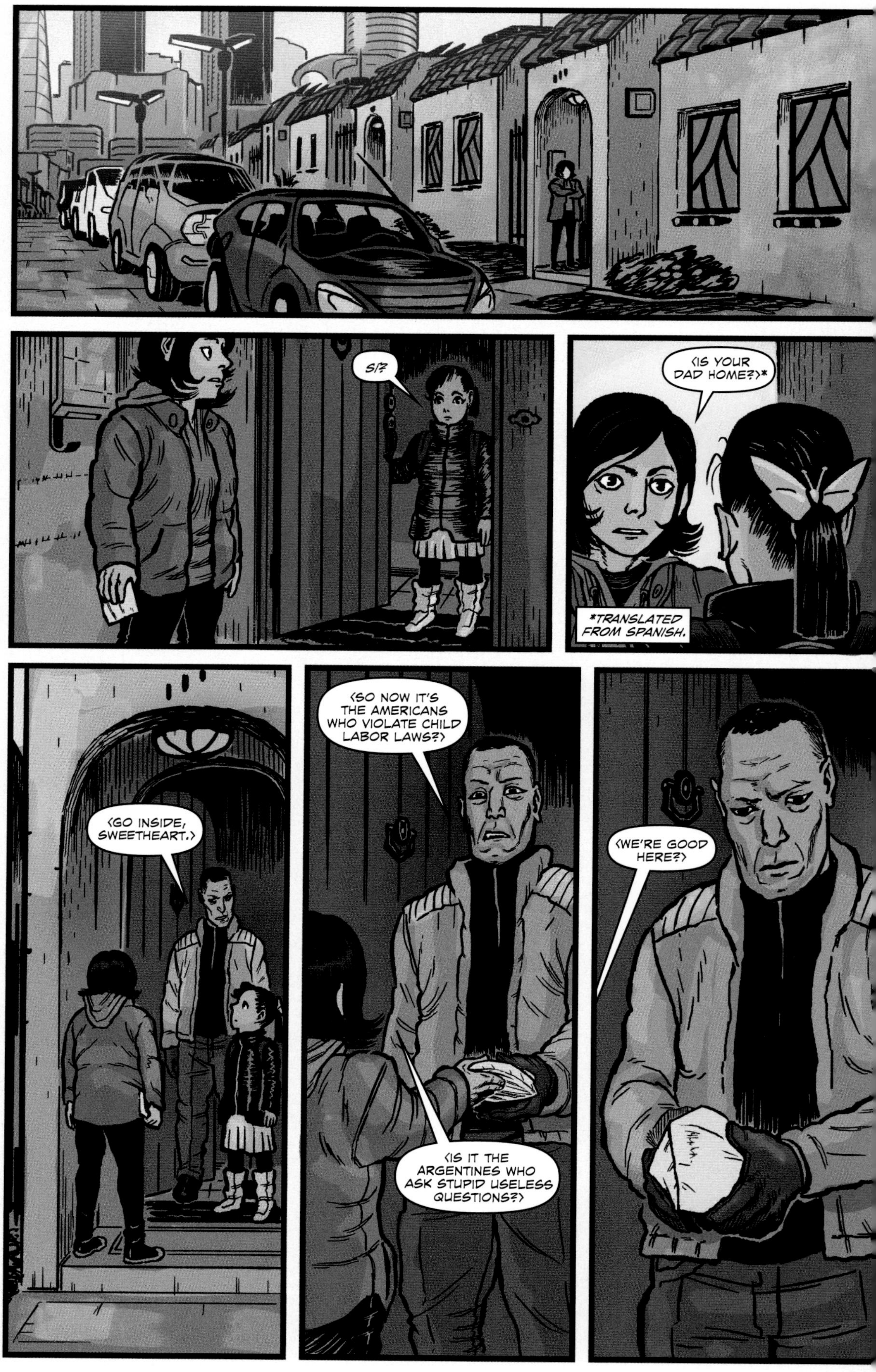
SÍ?
⟨IS YOUR DAD HOME?⟩*
*TRANSLATED FROM SPANISH.
⟨GO INSIDE, SWEETHEART.⟩
⟨SO NOW IT'S THE AMERICANS WHO VIOLATE CHILD LABOR LAWS?⟩
⟨IS IT THE ARGENTINES WHO ASK STUPID USELESS QUESTIONS?⟩
⟨WE'RE GOOD HERE?⟩

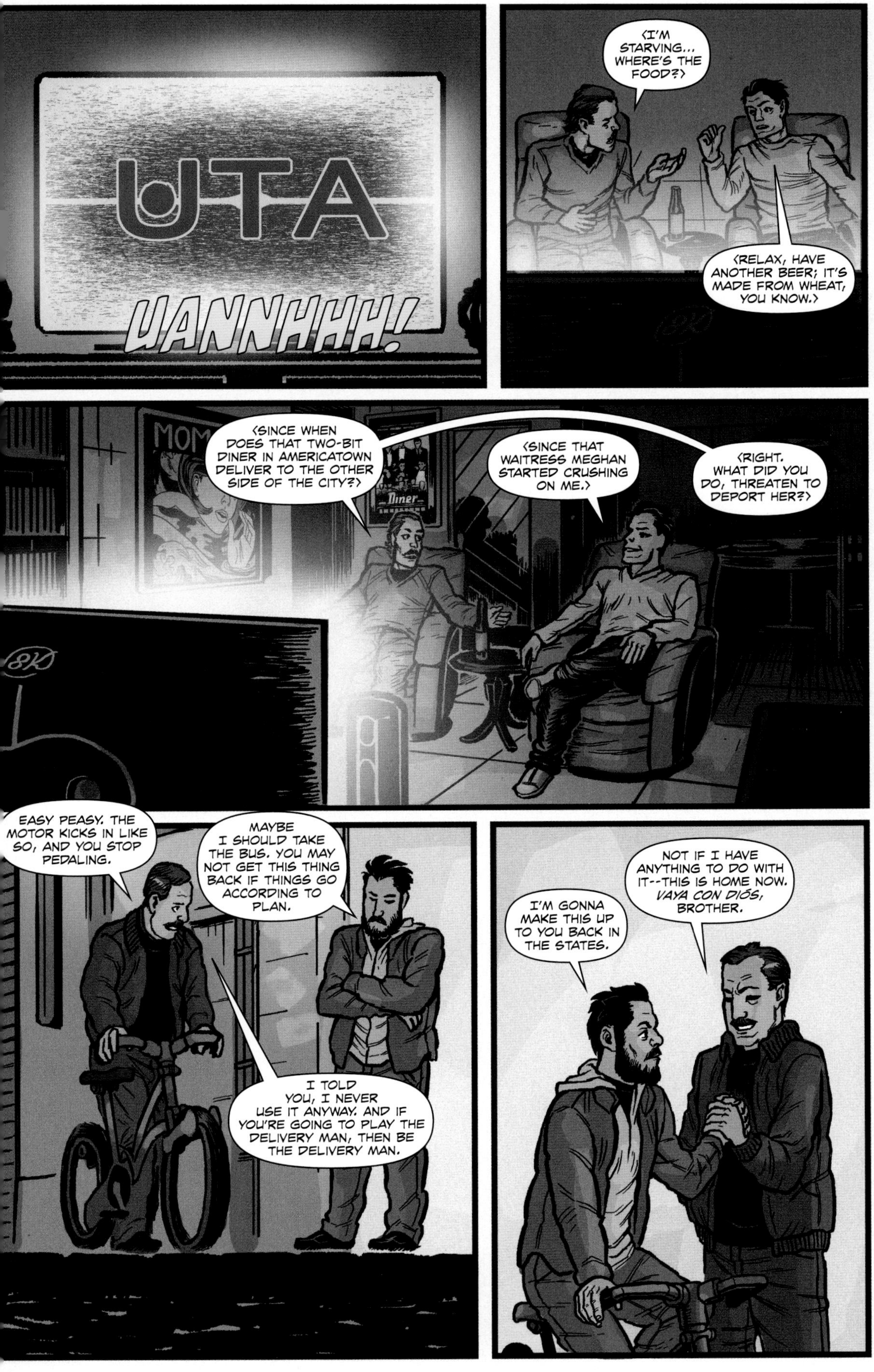
UTA
UANNHHH!
<I'M STARVING... WHERE'S THE FOOD?>
<RELAX, HAVE ANOTHER BEER; IT'S MADE FROM WHEAT, YOU KNOW.>
MOM
Diner
<SINCE WHEN DOES THAT TWO-BIT DINER IN AMERICATOWN DELIVER TO THE OTHER SIDE OF THE CITY?>
<SINCE THAT WAITRESS MEGHAN STARTED CRUSHING ON ME.>
<RIGHT. WHAT DID YOU DO, THREATEN TO DEPORT HER?>
EASY PEASY. THE MOTOR KICKS IN LIKE SO, AND YOU STOP PEDALING.
MAYBE I SHOULD TAKE THE BUS. YOU MAY NOT GET THIS THING BACK IF THINGS GO ACCORDING TO PLAN.
I TOLD YOU, I NEVER USE IT ANYWAY. AND IF YOU'RE GOING TO PLAY THE DELIVERY MAN, THEN BE THE DELIVERY MAN.
I'M GONNA MAKE THIS UP TO YOU BACK IN THE STATES.
NOT IF I HAVE ANYTHING TO DO WITH IT--THIS IS HOME NOW. *VAYA CON DIÓS*, BROTHER.

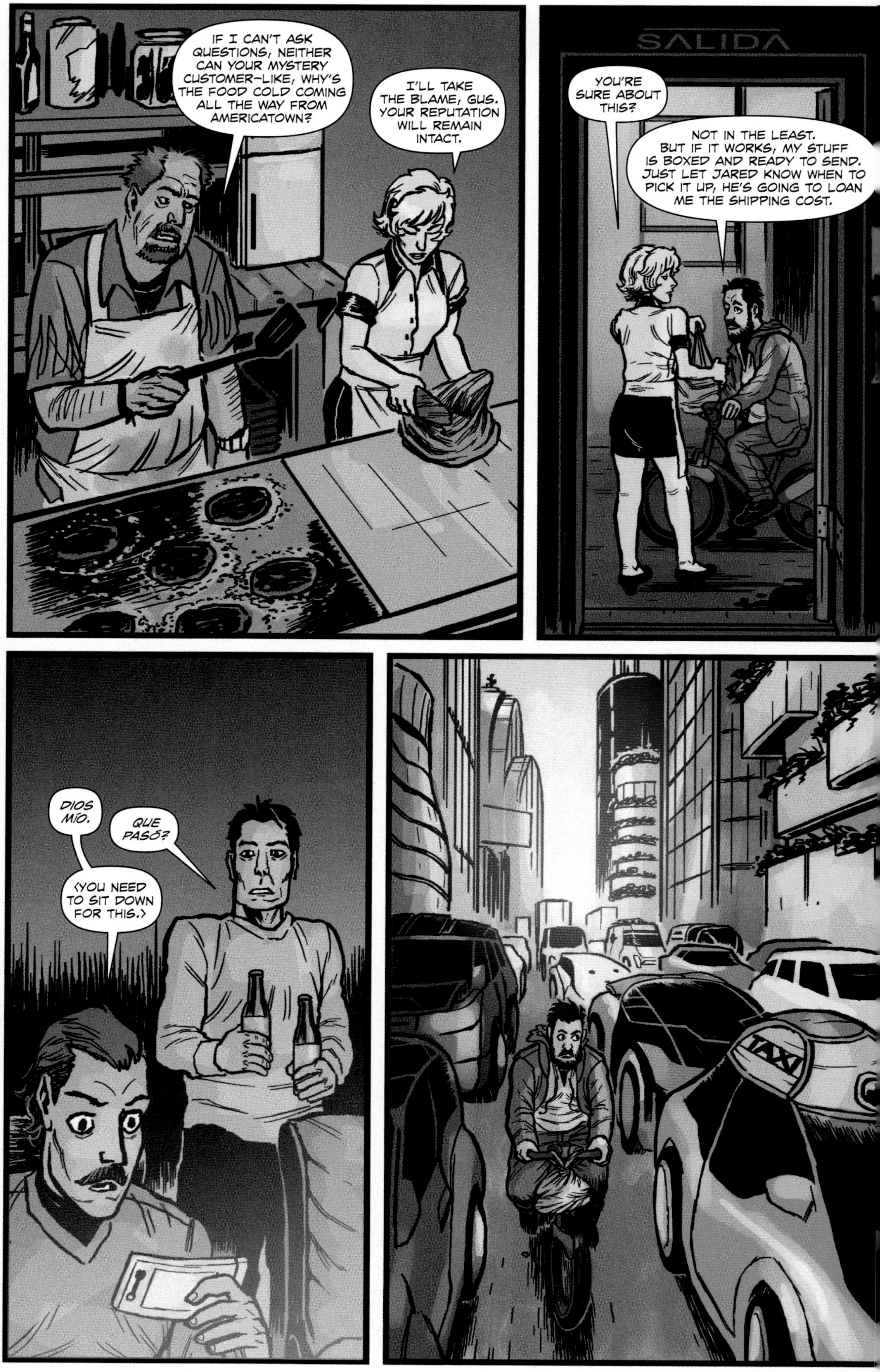
IF I CAN'T ASK QUESTIONS, NEITHER CAN YOUR MYSTERY CUSTOMER—LIKE, WHY'S THE FOOD COLD COMING ALL THE WAY FROM AMERICATOWN?
I'LL TAKE THE BLAME, GUS. YOUR REPUTATION WILL REMAIN INTACT.
SALIDA
YOU'RE SURE ABOUT THIS?
NOT IN THE LEAST. BUT IF IT WORKS, MY STUFF IS BOXED AND READY TO SEND. JUST LET JARED KNOW WHEN TO PICK IT UP, HE'S GOING TO LOAN ME THE SHIPPING COST.
DIOS MÍO.
QUE PASÓ?
‹YOU NEED TO SIT DOWN FOR THIS.›
TAXI

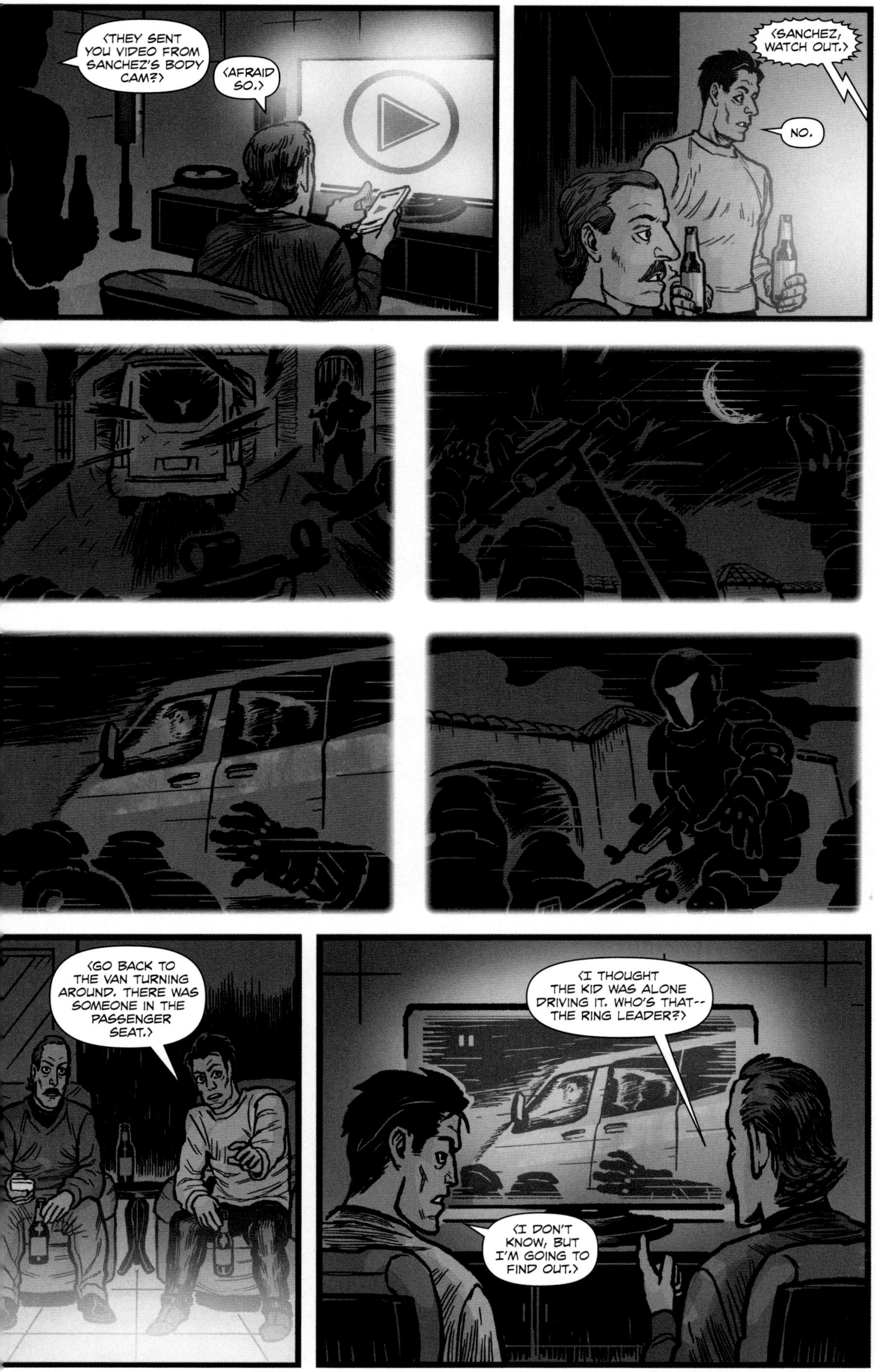
‹THEY SENT YOU VIDEO FROM SANCHEZ'S BODY CAM?›
‹AFRAID SO.›
‹SANCHEZ, WATCH OUT.›
NO.
‹GO BACK TO THE VAN TURNING AROUND. THERE WAS SOMEONE IN THE PASSENGER SEAT.›
‹I THOUGHT THE KID WAS ALONE DRIVING IT. WHO'S THAT-- THE RING LEADER?›
‹I DON'T KNOW, BUT I'M GOING TO FIND OUT.›

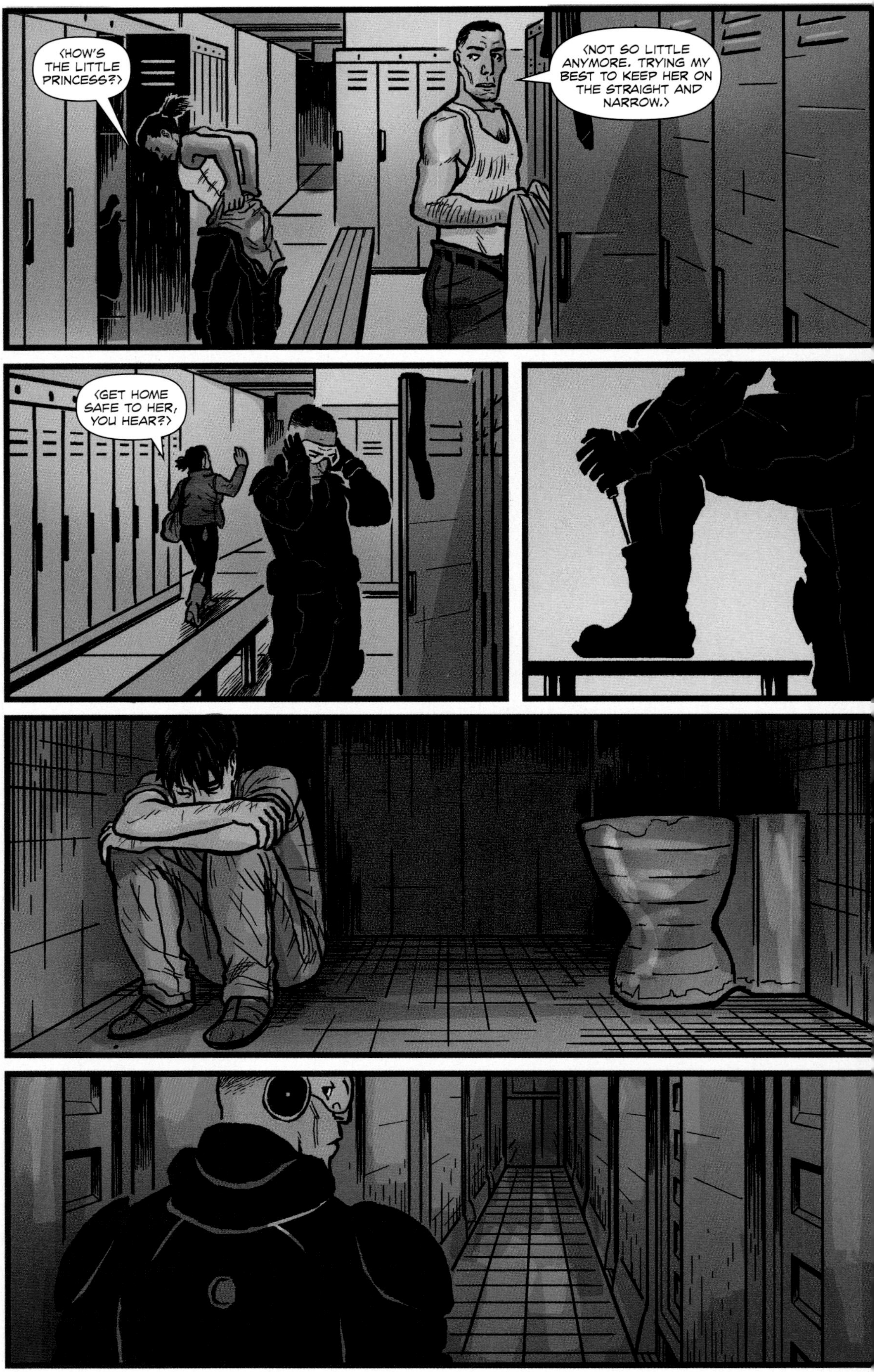
‹HOW'S THE LITTLE PRINCESS?›
‹NOT SO LITTLE ANYMORE. TRYING MY BEST TO KEEP HER ON THE STRAIGHT AND NARROW.›
‹GET HOME SAFE TO HER, YOU HEAR?›

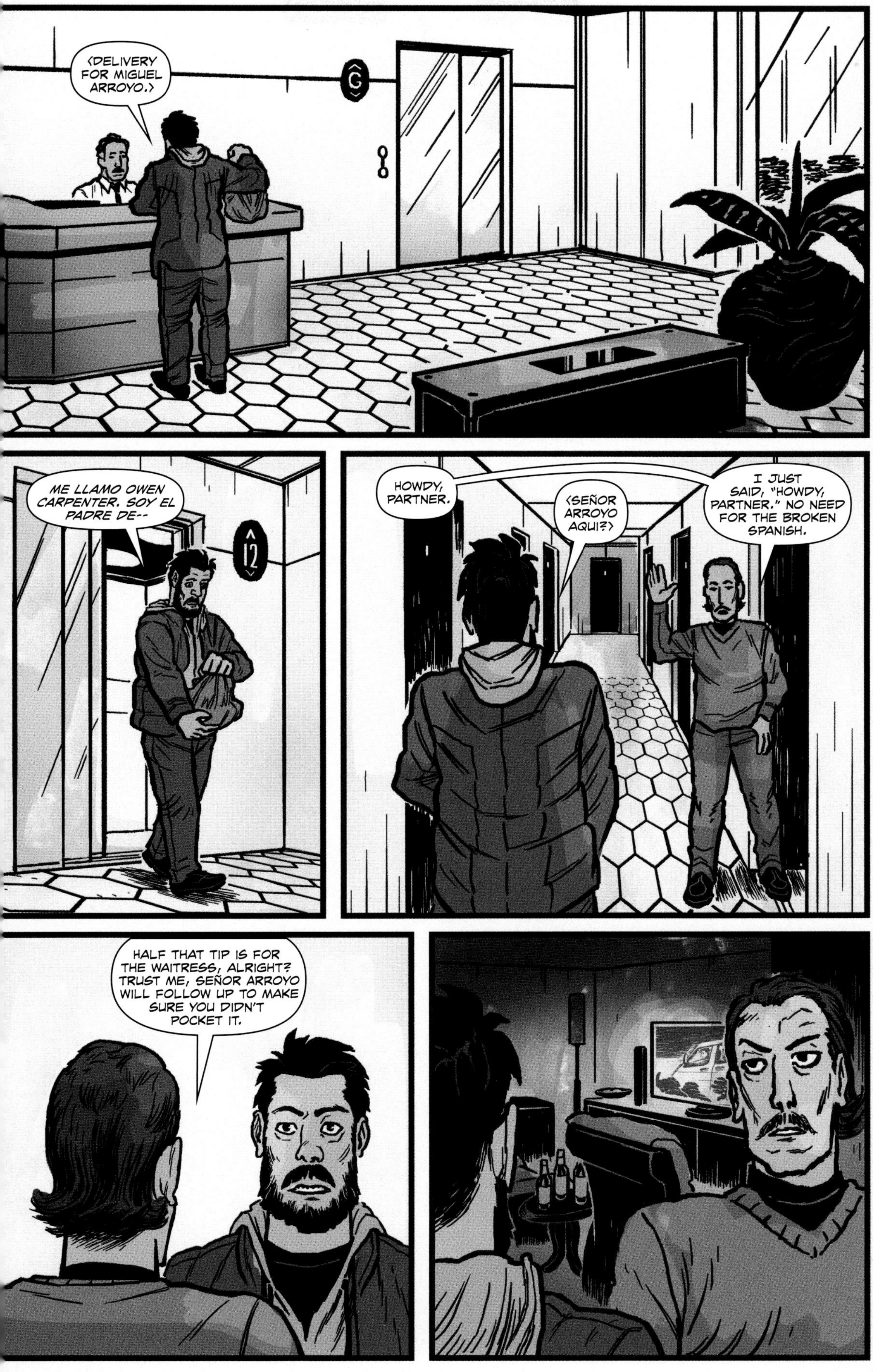
<DELIVERY FOR MIGUEL ARROYO.>
ME LLAMO OWEN CARPENTER. SOY EL PADRE DE--
HOWDY, PARTNER.
<SEÑOR ARROYO AQUI?>
I JUST SAID, "HOWDY, PARTNER." NO NEED FOR THE BROKEN SPANISH.
HALF THAT TIP IS FOR THE WAITRESS, ALRIGHT? TRUST ME, SEÑOR ARROYO WILL FOLLOW UP TO MAKE SURE YOU DIDN'T POCKET IT.

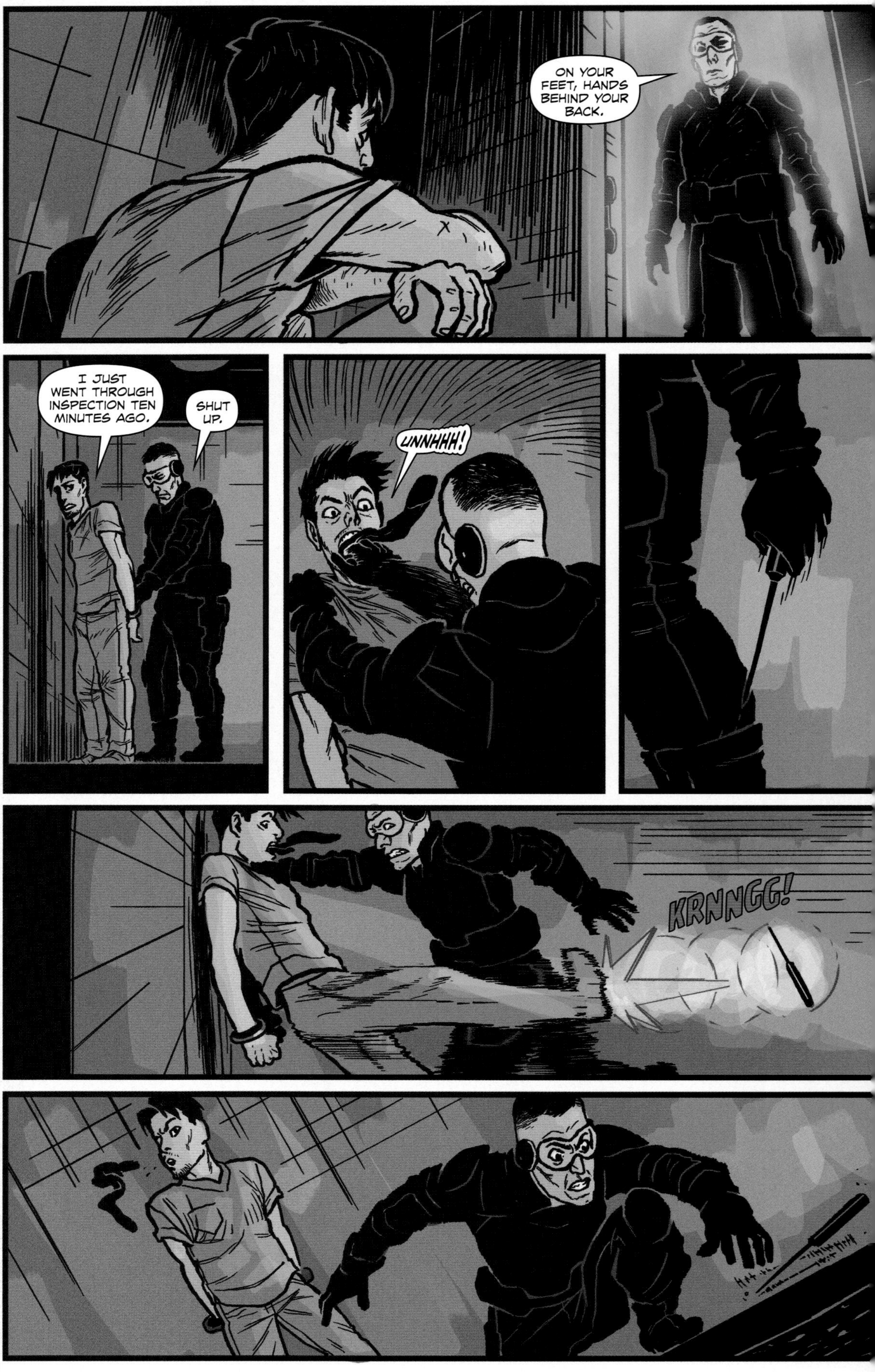
ON YOUR FEET, HANDS BEHIND YOUR BACK.
I JUST WENT THROUGH INSPECTION TEN MINUTES AGO.
SHUT UP.
UNNHHH!
KRNNGG!

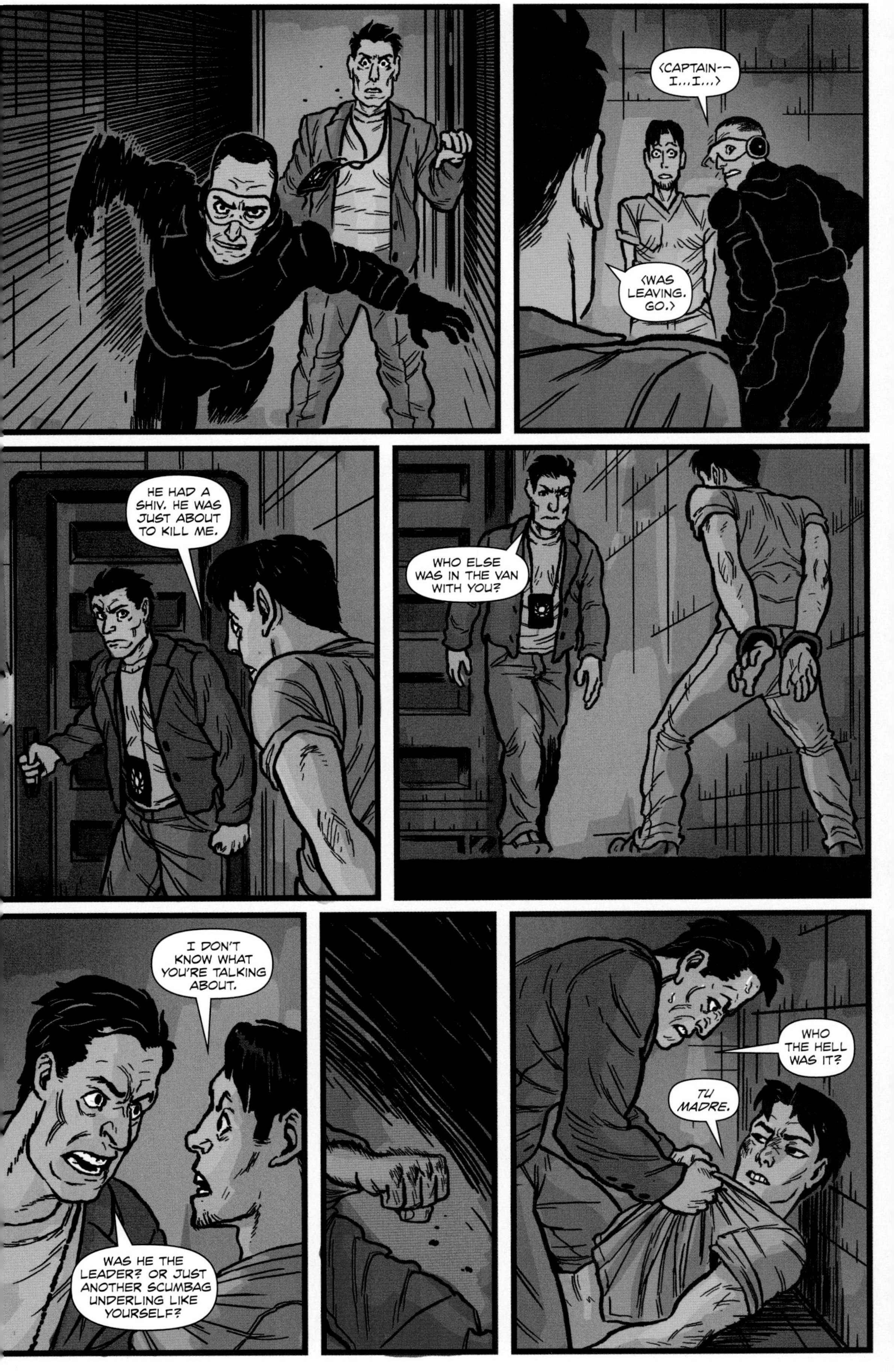
<CAPTAIN-- I...I...>
<WAS LEAVING. GO.>
HE HAD A SHIV. HE WAS JUST ABOUT TO KILL ME.
WHO ELSE WAS IN THE VAN WITH YOU?
I DON'T KNOW WHAT YOU'RE TALKING ABOUT.
WAS HE THE LEADER? OR JUST ANOTHER SCUMBAG UNDERLING LIKE YOURSELF?
WHO THE HELL WAS IT?
TU MADRE.

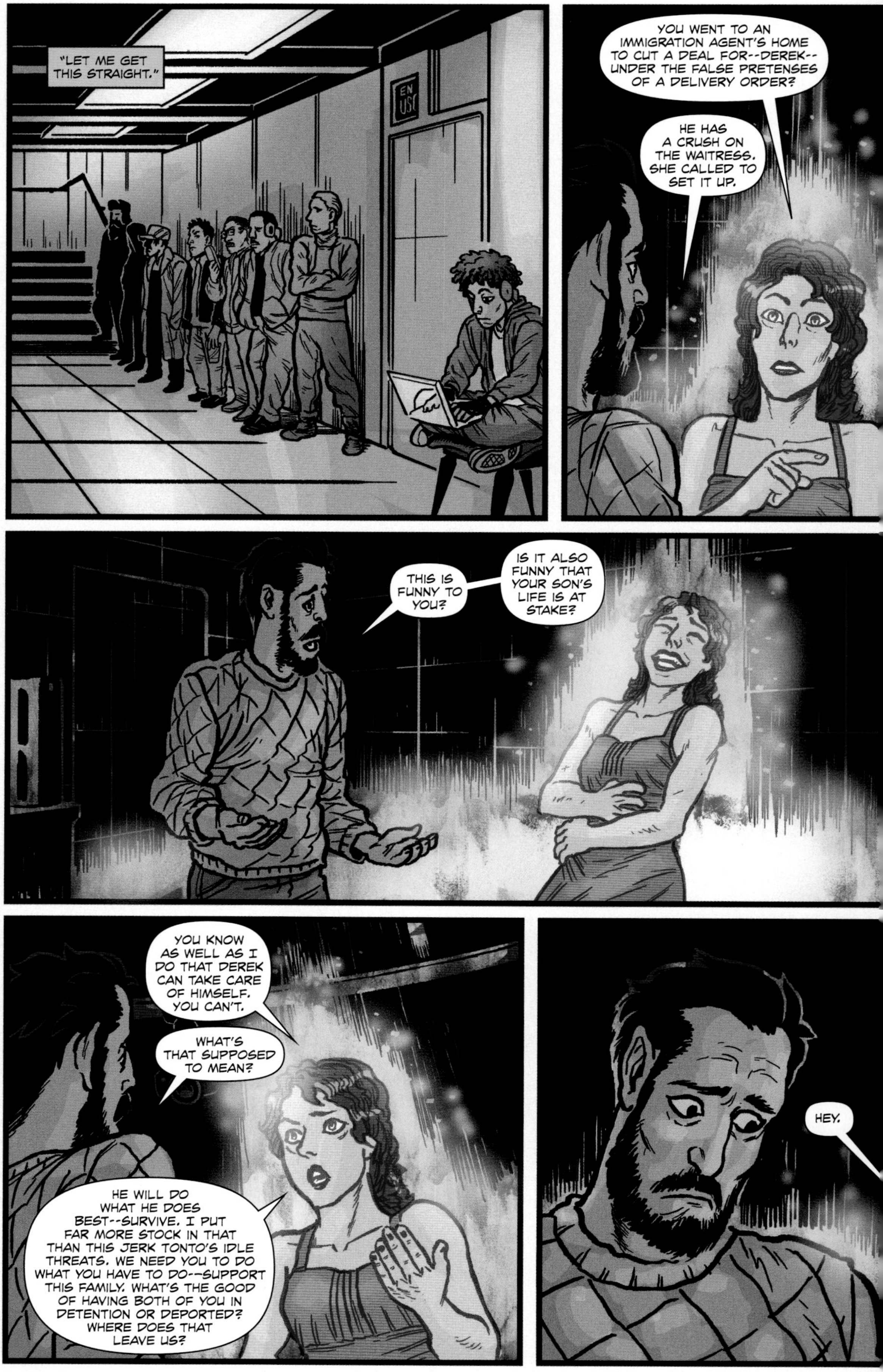
"LET ME GET THIS STRAIGHT."
EN USC
YOU WENT TO AN IMMIGRATION AGENT'S HOME TO CUT A DEAL FOR--DEREK--UNDER THE FALSE PRETENSES OF A DELIVERY ORDER?
HE HAS A CRUSH ON THE WAITRESS. SHE CALLED TO SET IT UP.
THIS IS FUNNY TO YOU?
IS IT ALSO FUNNY THAT YOUR SON'S LIFE IS AT STAKE?
YOU KNOW AS WELL AS I DO THAT DEREK CAN TAKE CARE OF HIMSELF. YOU CAN'T.
WHAT'S THAT SUPPOSED TO MEAN?
HE WILL DO WHAT HE DOES BEST--SURVIVE. I PUT FAR MORE STOCK IN THAT THAN THIS JERK TONTO'S IDLE THREATS. WE NEED YOU TO DO WHAT YOU HAVE TO DO--SUPPORT THIS FAMILY. WHAT'S THE GOOD OF HAVING BOTH OF YOU IN DETENTION OR DEPORTED? WHERE DOES THAT LEAVE US?
HEY.

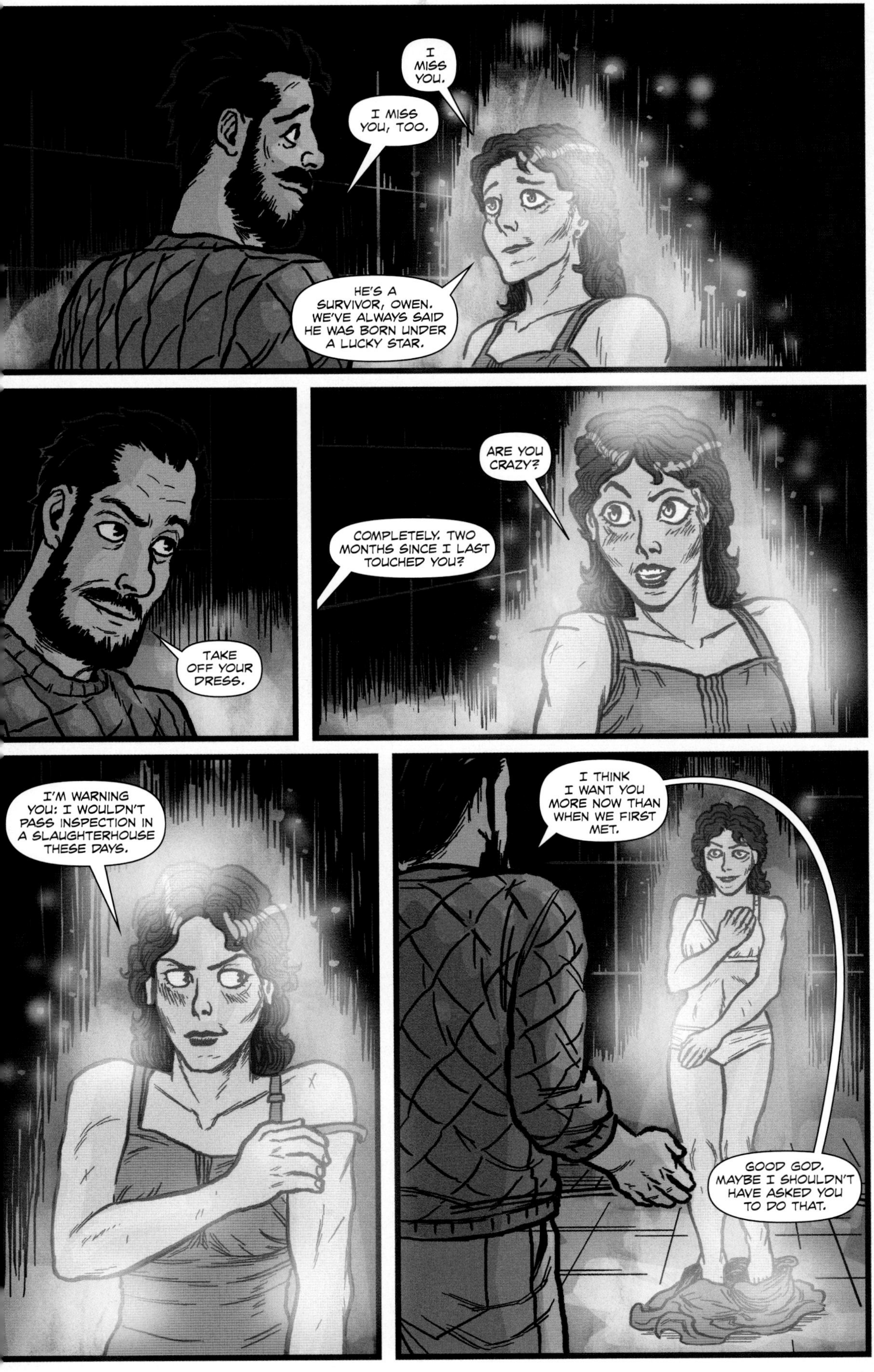
I MISS YOU.
I MISS YOU, TOO.
HE'S A SURVIVOR, OWEN. WE'VE ALWAYS SAID HE WAS BORN UNDER A LUCKY STAR.
TAKE OFF YOUR DRESS.
ARE YOU CRAZY?
COMPLETELY. TWO MONTHS SINCE I LAST TOUCHED YOU?
I'M WARNING YOU: I WOULDN'T PASS INSPECTION IN A SLAUGHTERHOUSE THESE DAYS.
I THINK I WANT YOU MORE NOW THAN WHEN WE FIRST MET.
GOOD GOD. MAYBE I SHOULDN'T HAVE ASKED YOU TO DO THAT.

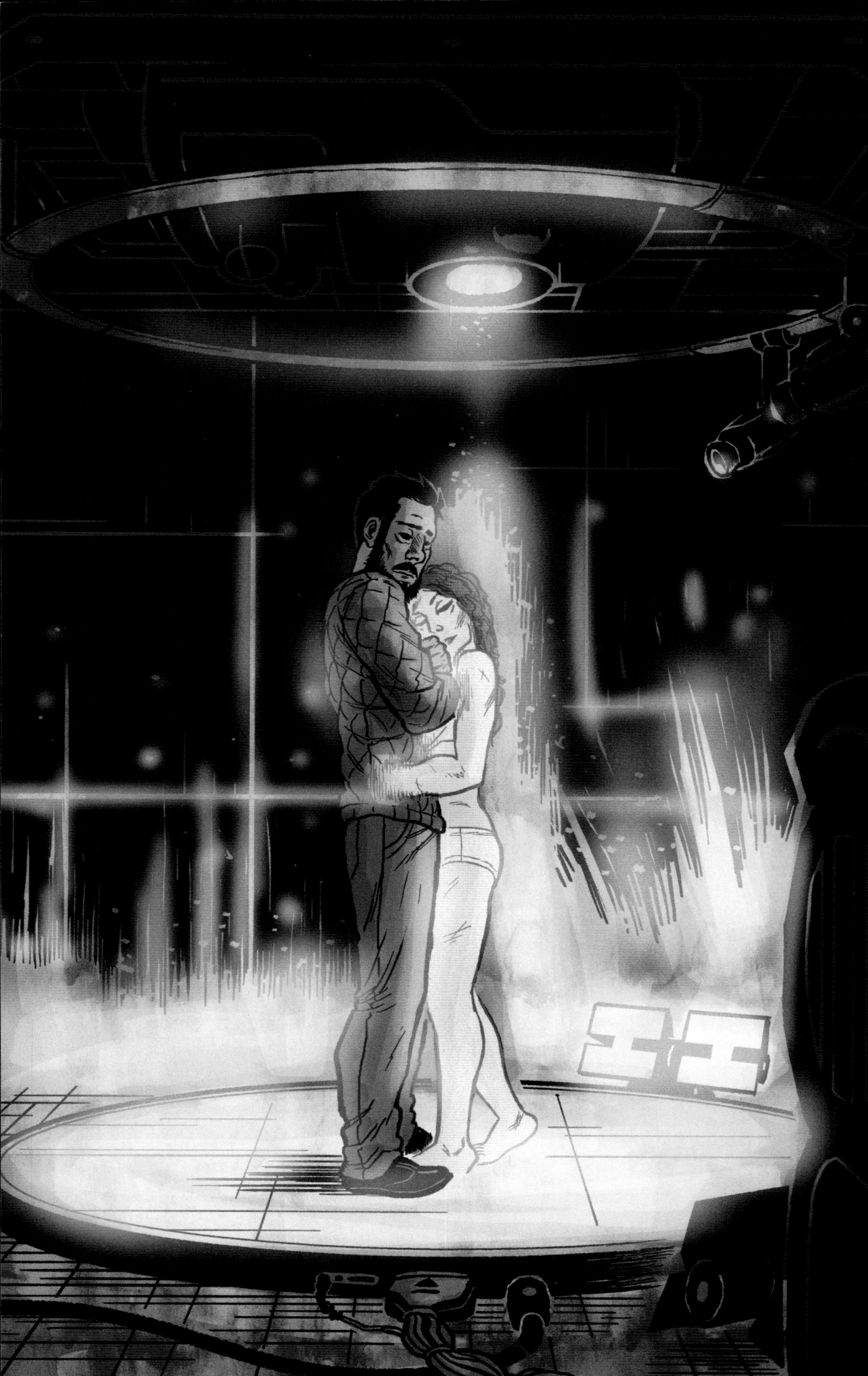

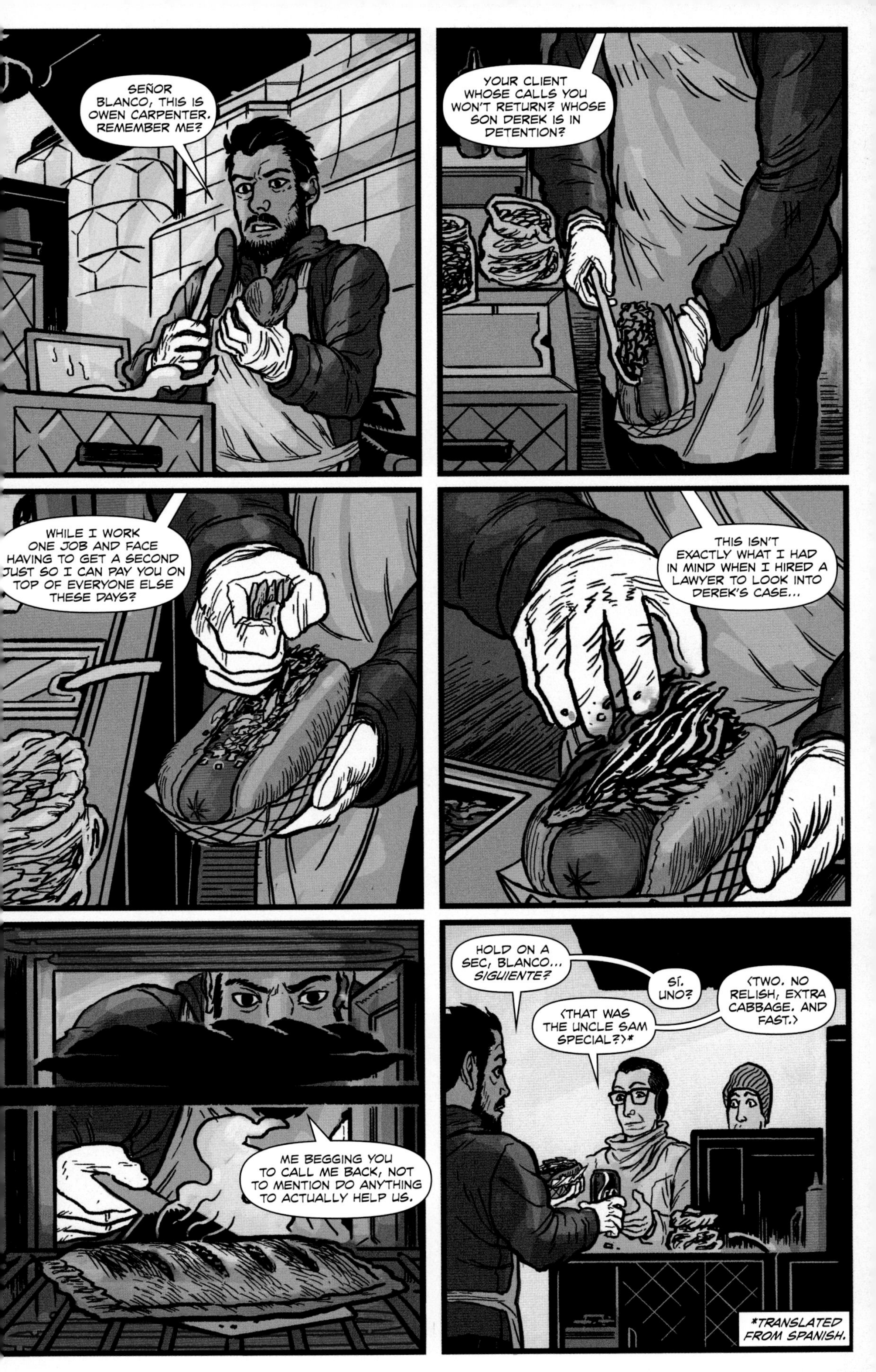
SEÑOR BLANCO, THIS IS OWEN CARPENTER. REMEMBER ME?
YOUR CLIENT WHOSE CALLS YOU WON'T RETURN? WHOSE SON DEREK IS IN DETENTION?
WHILE I WORK ONE JOB AND FACE HAVING TO GET A SECOND JUST SO I CAN PAY YOU ON TOP OF EVERYONE ELSE THESE DAYS?
THIS ISN'T EXACTLY WHAT I HAD IN MIND WHEN I HIRED A LAWYER TO LOOK INTO DEREK'S CASE...
ME BEGGING YOU TO CALL ME BACK, NOT TO MENTION DO ANYTHING TO ACTUALLY HELP US.
HOLD ON A SEC, BLANCO... *SIGUIENTE?*
SÍ. UNO?
<TWO. NO RELISH, EXTRA CABBAGE. AND FAST.>
<THAT WAS THE UNCLE SAM SPECIAL?>*
*TRANSLATED FROM SPANISH.

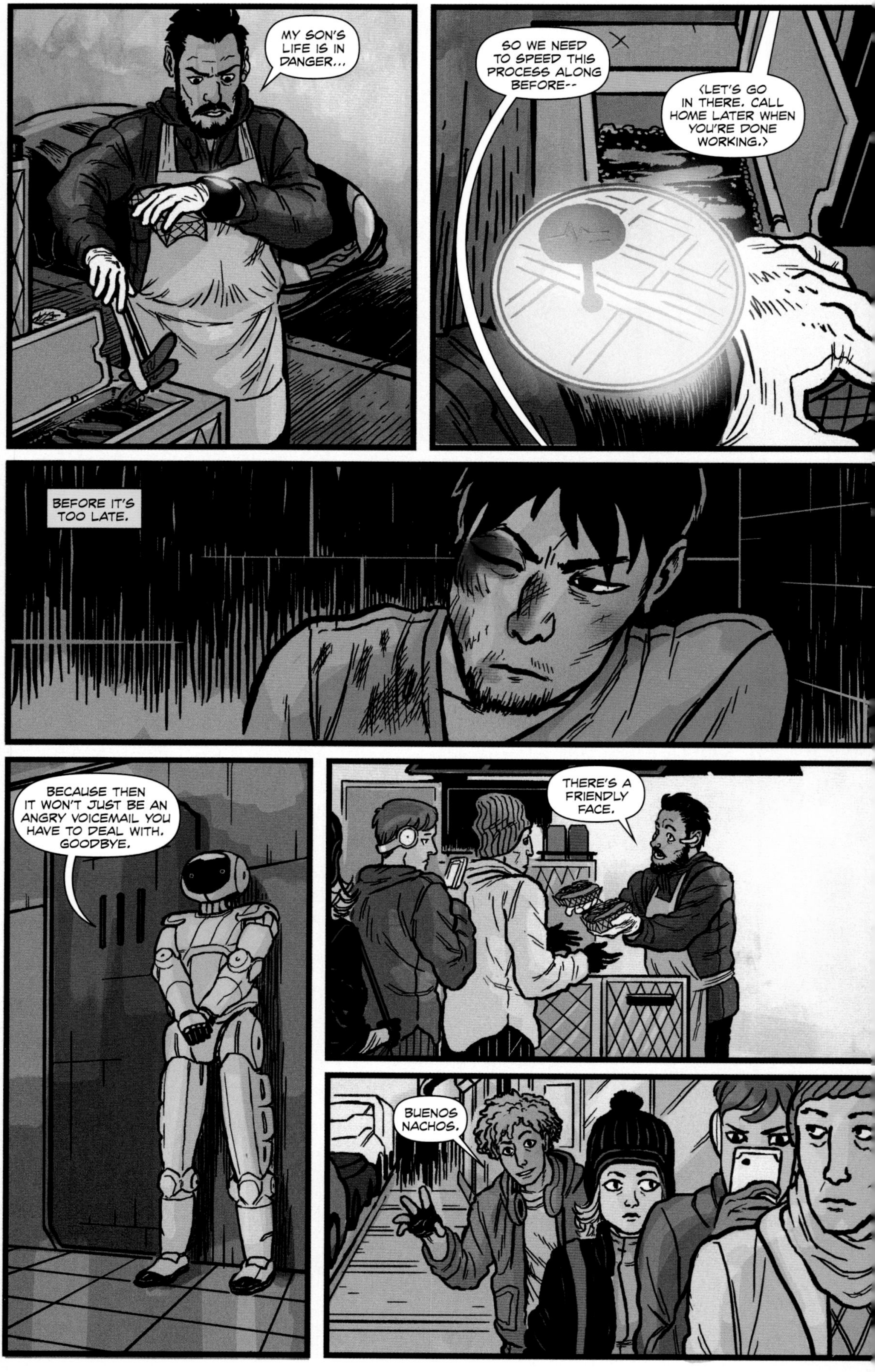
MY SON'S LIFE IS IN DANGER...
SO WE NEED TO SPEED THIS PROCESS ALONG BEFORE--
‹LET'S GO IN THERE. CALL HOME LATER WHEN YOU'RE DONE WORKING.›
BEFORE IT'S TOO LATE.
BECAUSE THEN IT WON'T JUST BE AN ANGRY VOICEMAIL YOU HAVE TO DEAL WITH. GOODBYE.
THERE'S A FRIENDLY FACE.
BUENOS NACHOS.

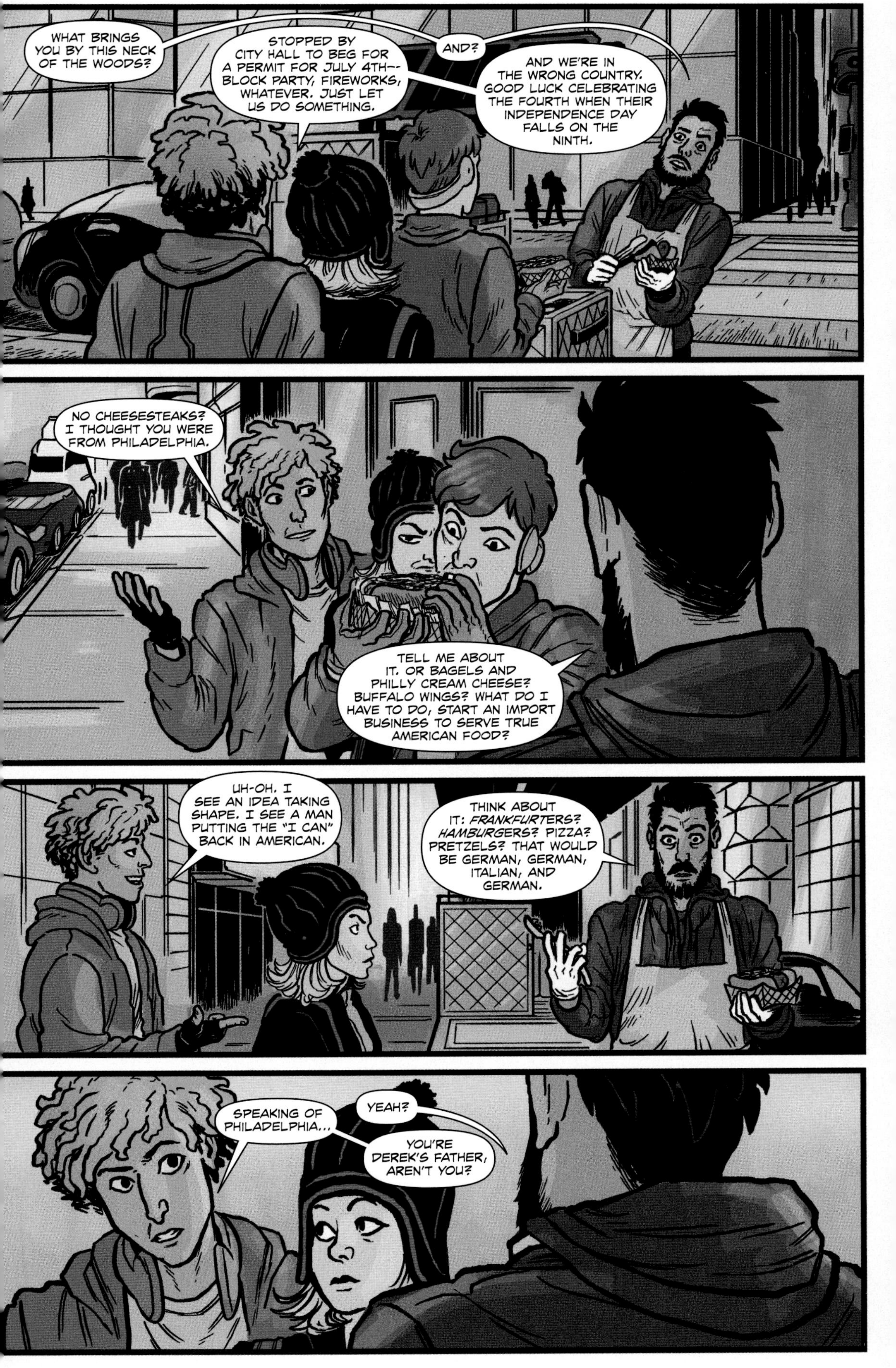
WHAT BRINGS YOU BY THIS NECK OF THE WOODS?
STOPPED BY CITY HALL TO BEG FOR A PERMIT FOR JULY 4TH-- BLOCK PARTY, FIREWORKS, WHATEVER. JUST LET US DO SOMETHING.
AND?
AND WE'RE IN THE WRONG COUNTRY. GOOD LUCK CELEBRATING THE FOURTH WHEN THEIR INDEPENDENCE DAY FALLS ON THE NINTH.
NO CHEESESTEAKS? I THOUGHT YOU WERE FROM PHILADELPHIA.
TELL ME ABOUT IT. OR BAGELS AND PHILLY CREAM CHEESE? BUFFALO WINGS? WHAT DO I HAVE TO DO, START AN IMPORT BUSINESS TO SERVE TRUE AMERICAN FOOD?
UH-OH. I SEE AN IDEA TAKING SHAPE. I SEE A MAN PUTTING THE "I CAN" BACK IN AMERICAN.
THINK ABOUT IT: *FRANKFURTERS*? *HAMBURGERS*? PIZZA? PRETZELS? THAT WOULD BE GERMAN, GERMAN, ITALIAN, AND GERMAN.
SPEAKING OF PHILADELPHIA...
YEAH?
YOU'RE DEREK'S FATHER, AREN'T YOU?

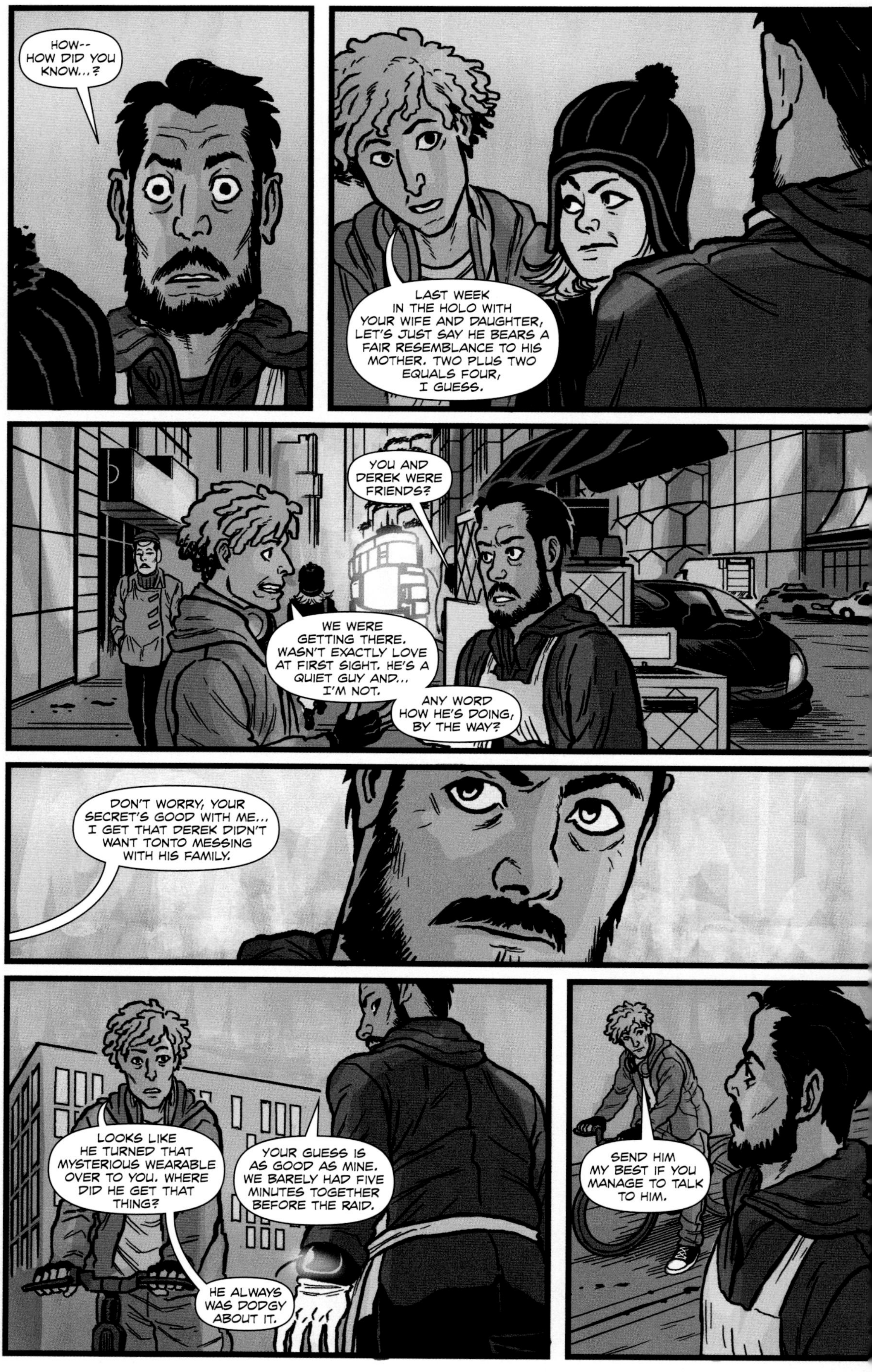
HOW-- HOW DID YOU KNOW...?
LAST WEEK IN THE HOLO WITH YOUR WIFE AND DAUGHTER, LET'S JUST SAY HE BEARS A FAIR RESEMBLANCE TO HIS MOTHER. TWO PLUS TWO EQUALS FOUR, I GUESS.
YOU AND DEREK WERE FRIENDS?
WE WERE GETTING THERE. WASN'T EXACTLY LOVE AT FIRST SIGHT. HE'S A QUIET GUY AND... I'M NOT.
ANY WORD HOW HE'S DOING, BY THE WAY?
DON'T WORRY, YOUR SECRET'S GOOD WITH ME... I GET THAT DEREK DIDN'T WANT TONTO MESSING WITH HIS FAMILY.
LOOKS LIKE HE TURNED THAT MYSTERIOUS WEARABLE OVER TO YOU. WHERE DID HE GET THAT THING?
YOUR GUESS IS AS GOOD AS MINE. WE BARELY HAD FIVE MINUTES TOGETHER BEFORE THE RAID.
HE ALWAYS WAS DODGY ABOUT IT.
SEND HIM MY BEST IF YOU MANAGE TO TALK TO HIM.

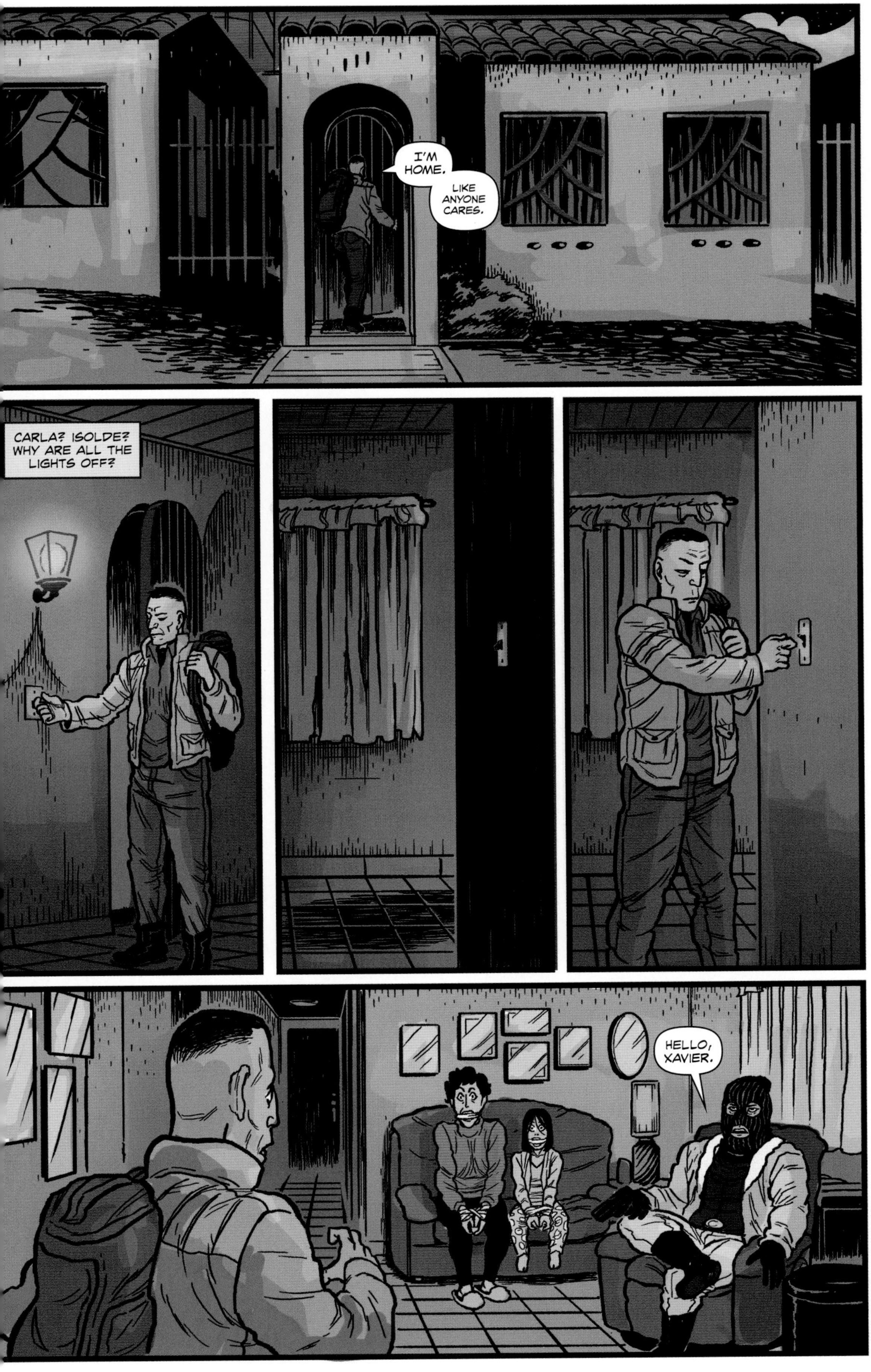
I'M HOME.
LIKE ANYONE CARES.
CARLA? ISOLDE? WHY ARE ALL THE LIGHTS OFF?
HELLO, XAVIER.

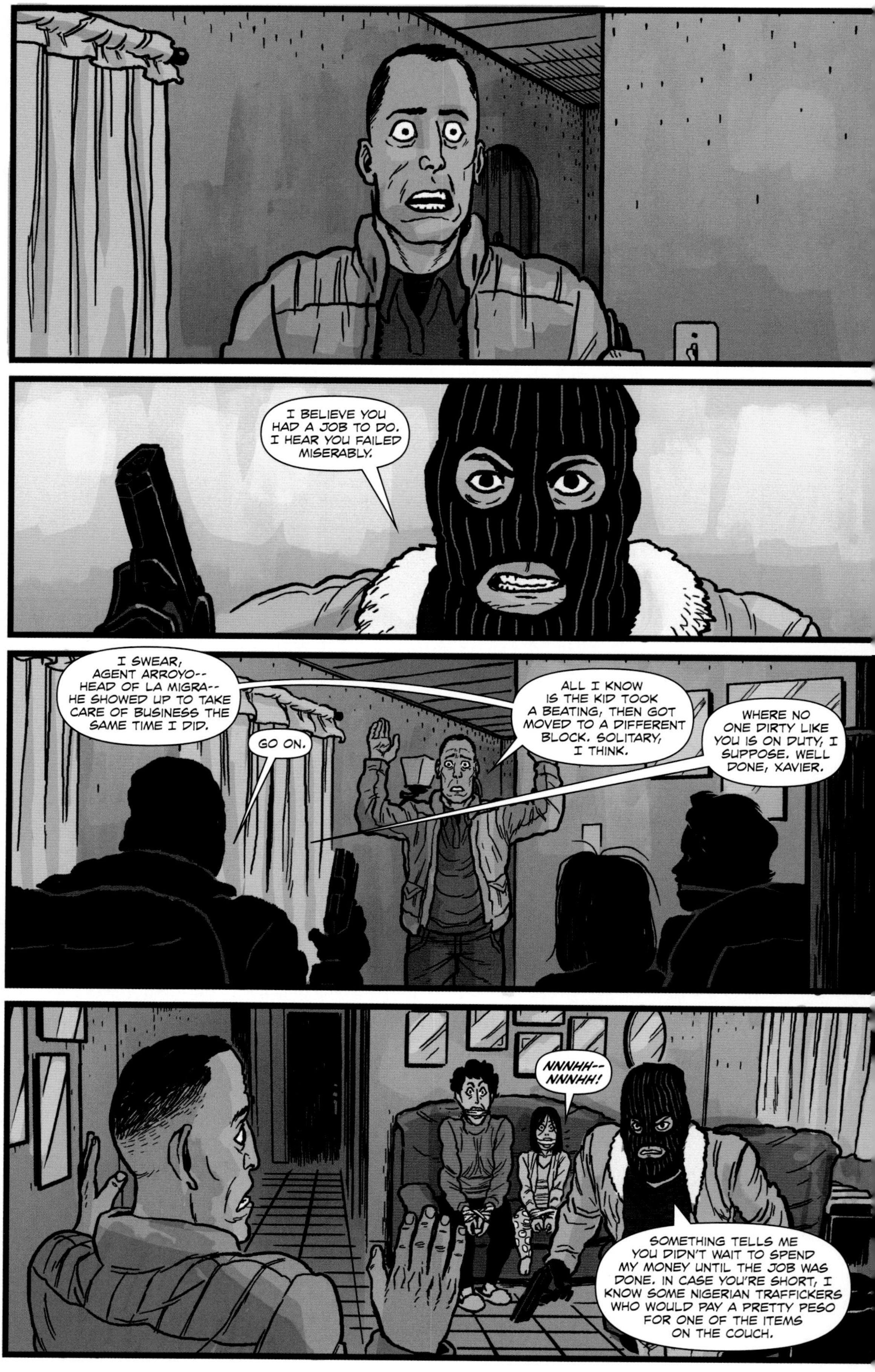
I BELIEVE YOU HAD A JOB TO DO. I HEAR YOU FAILED MISERABLY.
I SWEAR, AGENT ARROYO-- HEAD OF LA MIGRA-- HE SHOWED UP TO TAKE CARE OF BUSINESS THE SAME TIME I DID.
GO ON.
ALL I KNOW IS THE KID TOOK A BEATING, THEN GOT MOVED TO A DIFFERENT BLOCK. SOLITARY, I THINK.
WHERE NO ONE DIRTY LIKE YOU IS ON DUTY, I SUPPOSE. WELL DONE, XAVIER.
NNNHH-- NNNHH!
SOMETHING TELLS ME YOU DIDN'T WAIT TO SPEND MY MONEY UNTIL THE JOB WAS DONE. IN CASE YOU'RE SHORT, I KNOW SOME NIGERIAN TRAFFICKERS WHO WOULD PAY A PRETTY PESO FOR ONE OF THE ITEMS ON THE COUCH.

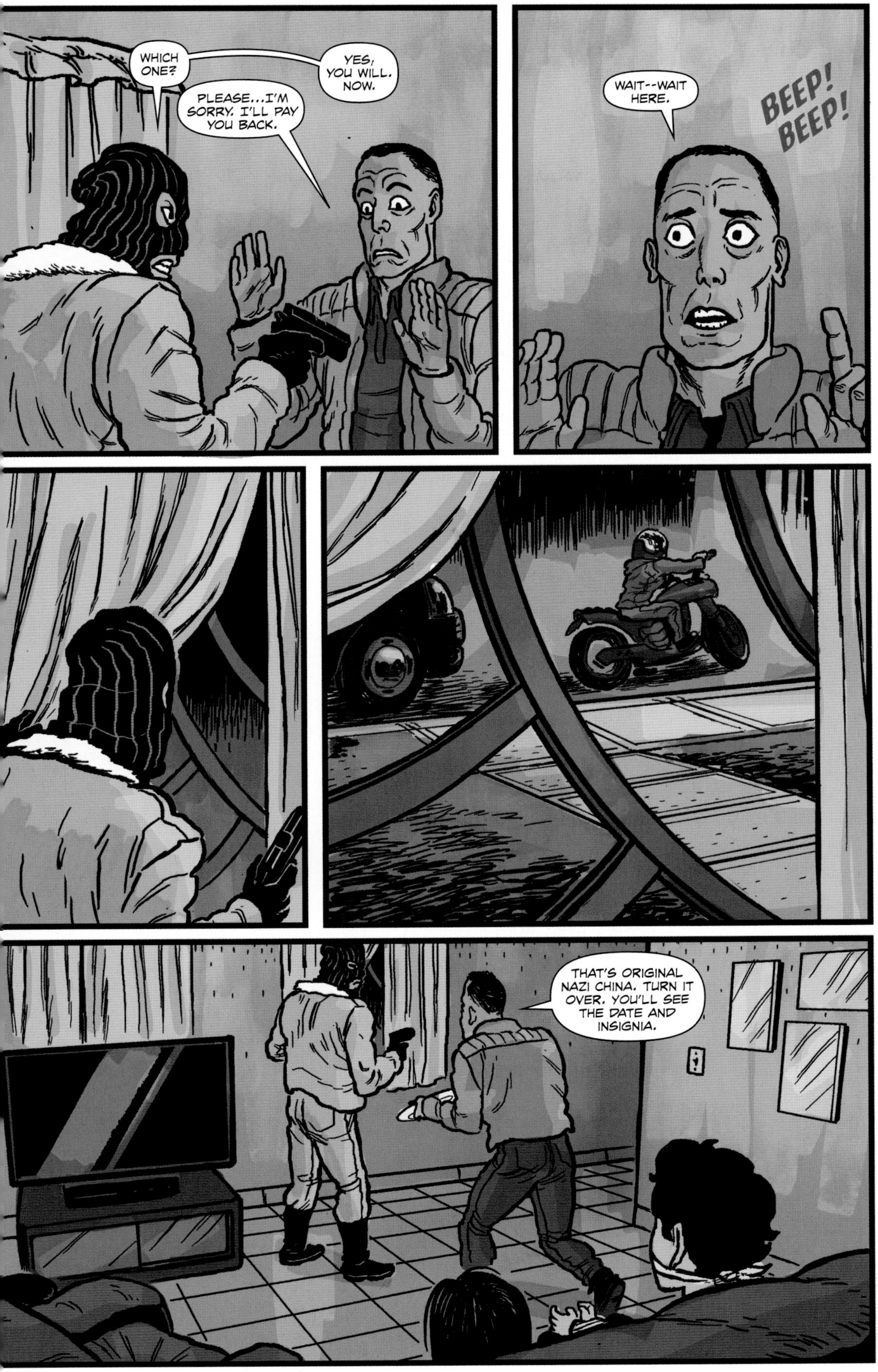
WHICH ONE?
YES, YOU WILL. NOW.
PLEASE...I'M SORRY. I'LL PAY YOU BACK.
WAIT--WAIT HERE.
BEEP! BEEP!
THAT'S ORIGINAL NAZI CHINA. TURN IT OVER. YOU'LL SEE THE DATE AND INSIGNIA.

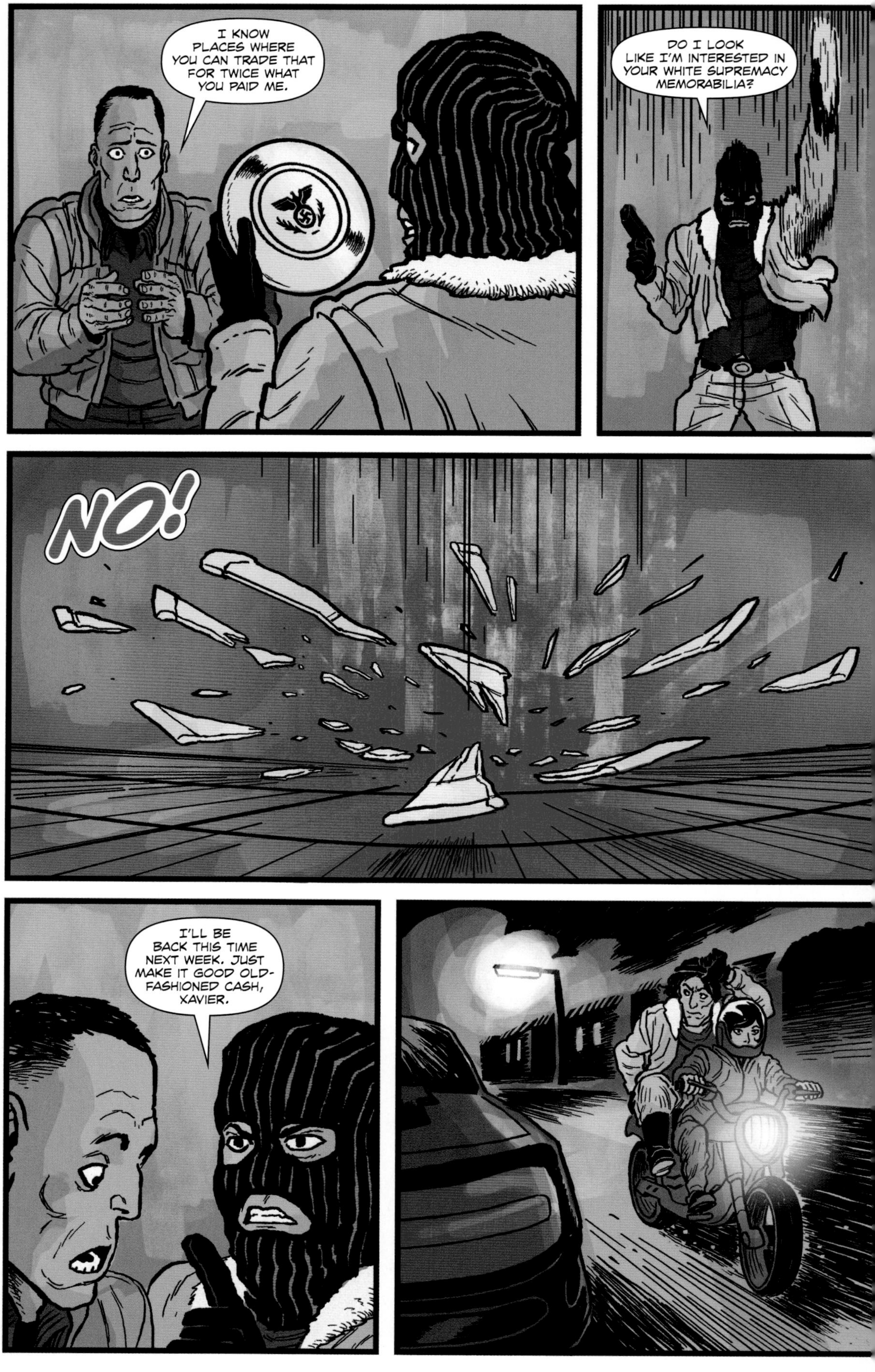
I KNOW PLACES WHERE YOU CAN TRADE THAT FOR TWICE WHAT YOU PAID ME.
DO I LOOK LIKE I'M INTERESTED IN YOUR WHITE SUPREMACY MEMORABILIA?
NO!
I'LL BE BACK THIS TIME NEXT WEEK. JUST MAKE IT GOOD OLD-FASHIONED CASH, XAVIER.

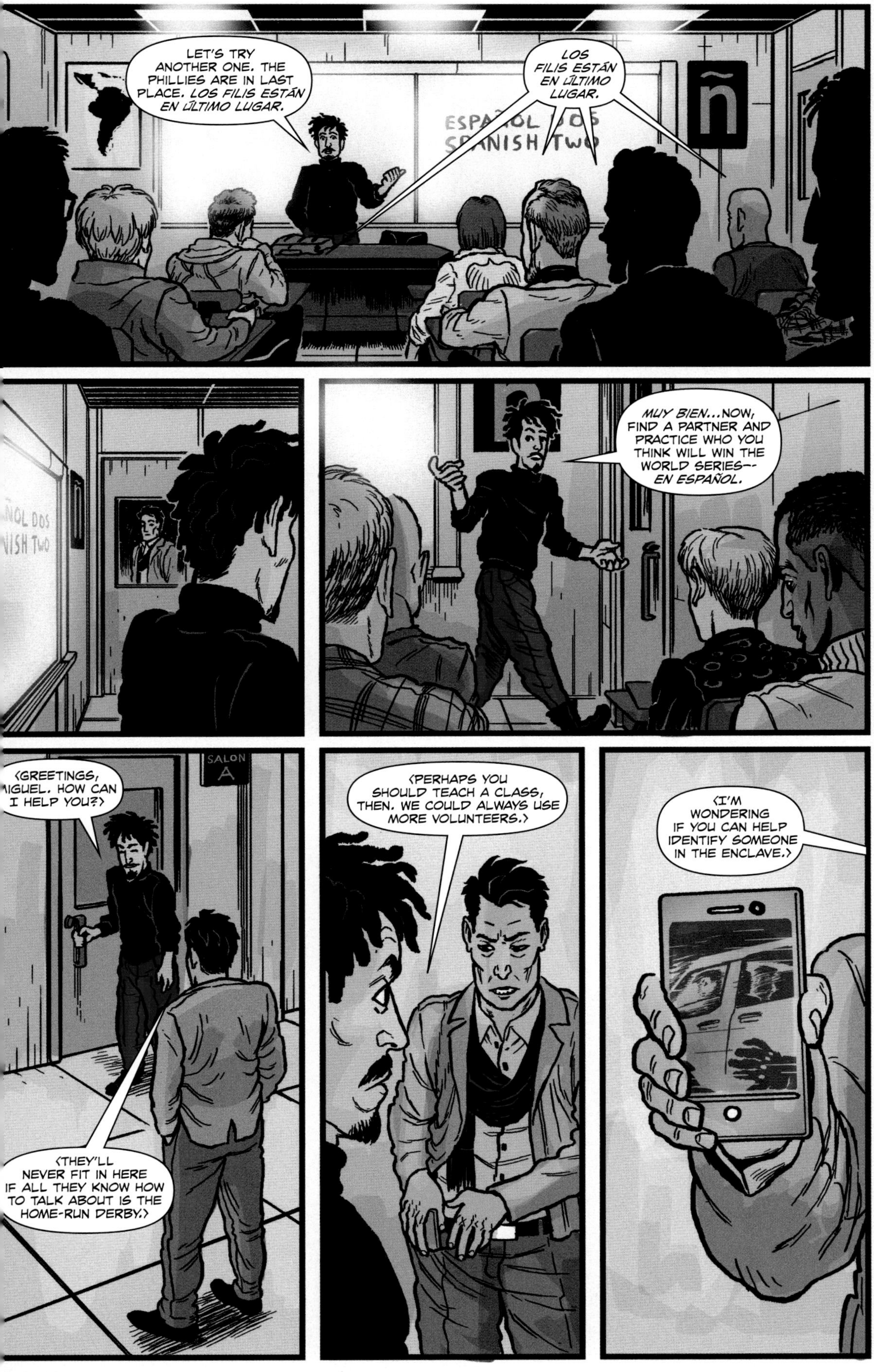
LET'S TRY ANOTHER ONE. THE PHILLIES ARE IN LAST PLACE. *LOS FILIS ESTÁN EN ÚLTIMO LUGAR.*
LOS FILIS ESTÁN EN ÚLTIMO LUGAR.
ESPAÑOL DOS
SPANISH TWO
MUY BIEN...NOW, FIND A PARTNER AND PRACTICE WHO YOU THINK WILL WIN THE WORLD SERIES-- *EN ESPAÑOL.*
SALON A
‹GREETINGS, MIGUEL. HOW CAN I HELP YOU?›
‹THEY'LL NEVER FIT IN HERE IF ALL THEY KNOW HOW TO TALK ABOUT IS THE HOME-RUN DERBY.›
‹PERHAPS YOU SHOULD TEACH A CLASS, THEN. WE COULD ALWAYS USE MORE VOLUNTEERS.›
‹I'M WONDERING IF YOU CAN HELP IDENTIFY SOMEONE IN THE ENCLAVE.›

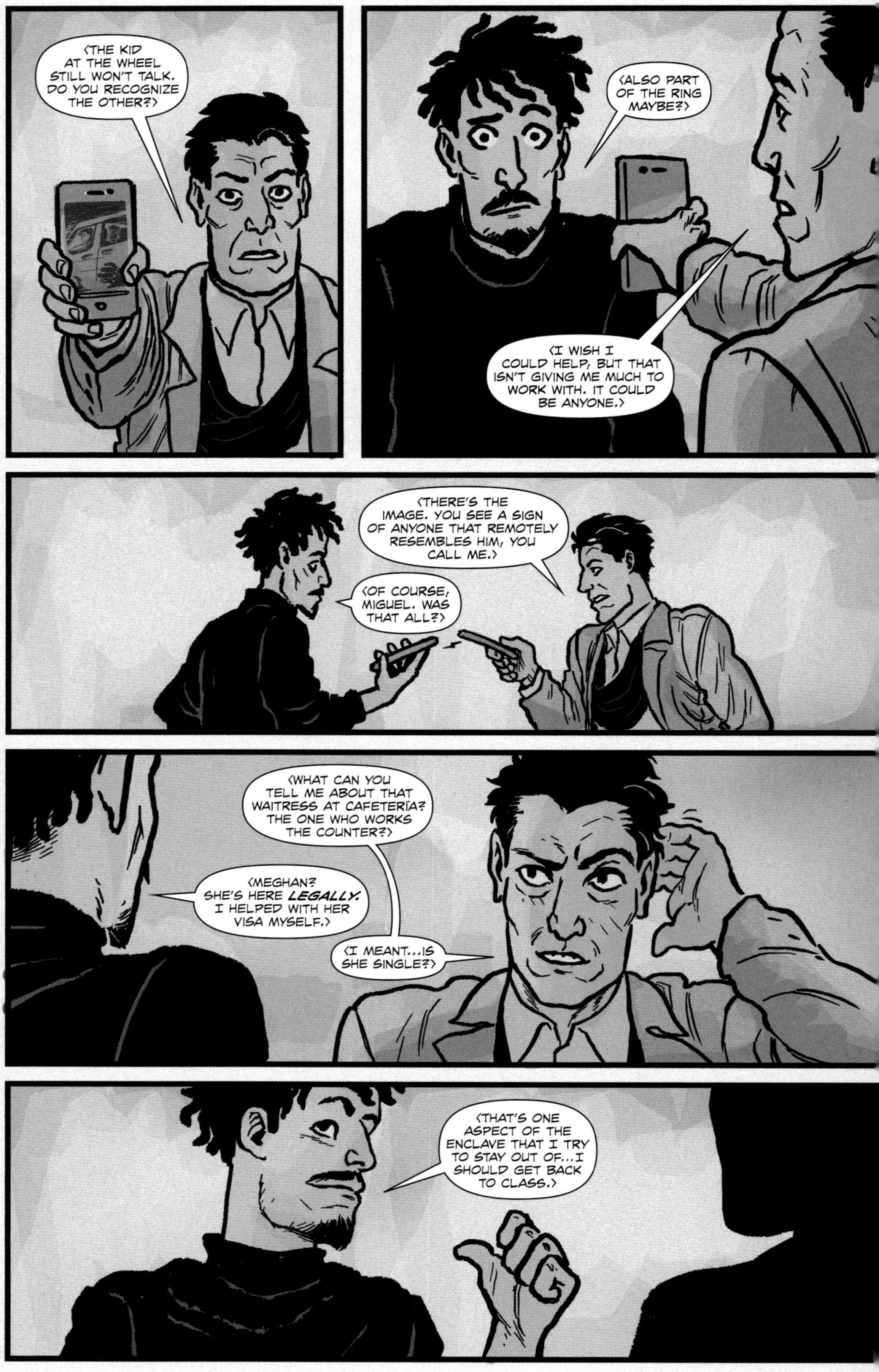
‹THE KID AT THE WHEEL STILL WON'T TALK. DO YOU RECOGNIZE THE OTHER?›
‹ALSO PART OF THE RING MAYBE?›
‹I WISH I COULD HELP, BUT THAT ISN'T GIVING ME MUCH TO WORK WITH. IT COULD BE ANYONE.›
‹THERE'S THE IMAGE. YOU SEE A SIGN OF ANYONE THAT REMOTELY RESEMBLES HIM, YOU CALL ME.›
‹OF COURSE, MIGUEL. WAS THAT ALL?›
‹WHAT CAN YOU TELL ME ABOUT THAT WAITRESS AT CAFETERÍA? THE ONE WHO WORKS THE COUNTER?›
‹MEGHAN? SHE'S HERE *LEGALLY.* I HELPED WITH HER VISA MYSELF.›
‹I MEANT...IS SHE SINGLE?›
‹THAT'S ONE ASPECT OF THE ENCLAVE THAT I TRY TO STAY OUT OF...I SHOULD GET BACK TO CLASS.›

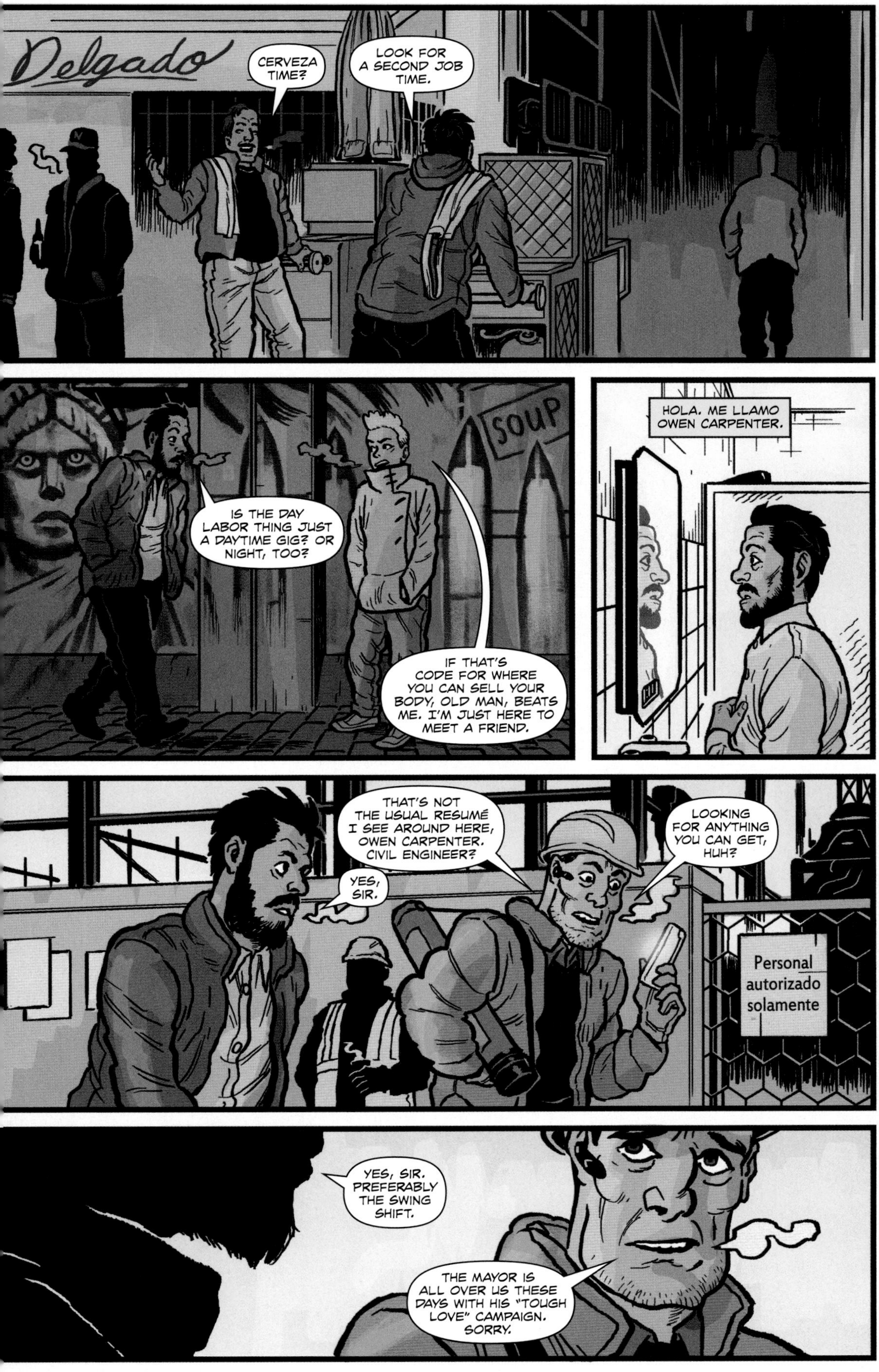
Delgado
CERVEZA TIME?
LOOK FOR A SECOND JOB TIME.
SOUP
IS THE DAY LABOR THING JUST A DAYTIME GIG? OR NIGHT, TOO?
IF THAT'S CODE FOR WHERE YOU CAN SELL YOUR BODY, OLD MAN, BEATS ME. I'M JUST HERE TO MEET A FRIEND.
HOLA. ME LLAMO OWEN CARPENTER.
THAT'S NOT THE USUAL RESUMÉ I SEE AROUND HERE, OWEN CARPENTER. CIVIL ENGINEER?
YES, SIR.
LOOKING FOR ANYTHING YOU CAN GET, HUH?
Personal autorizado solamente
YES, SIR. PREFERABLY THE SWING SHIFT.
THE MAYOR IS ALL OVER US THESE DAYS WITH HIS "TOUGH LOVE" CAMPAIGN. SORRY.

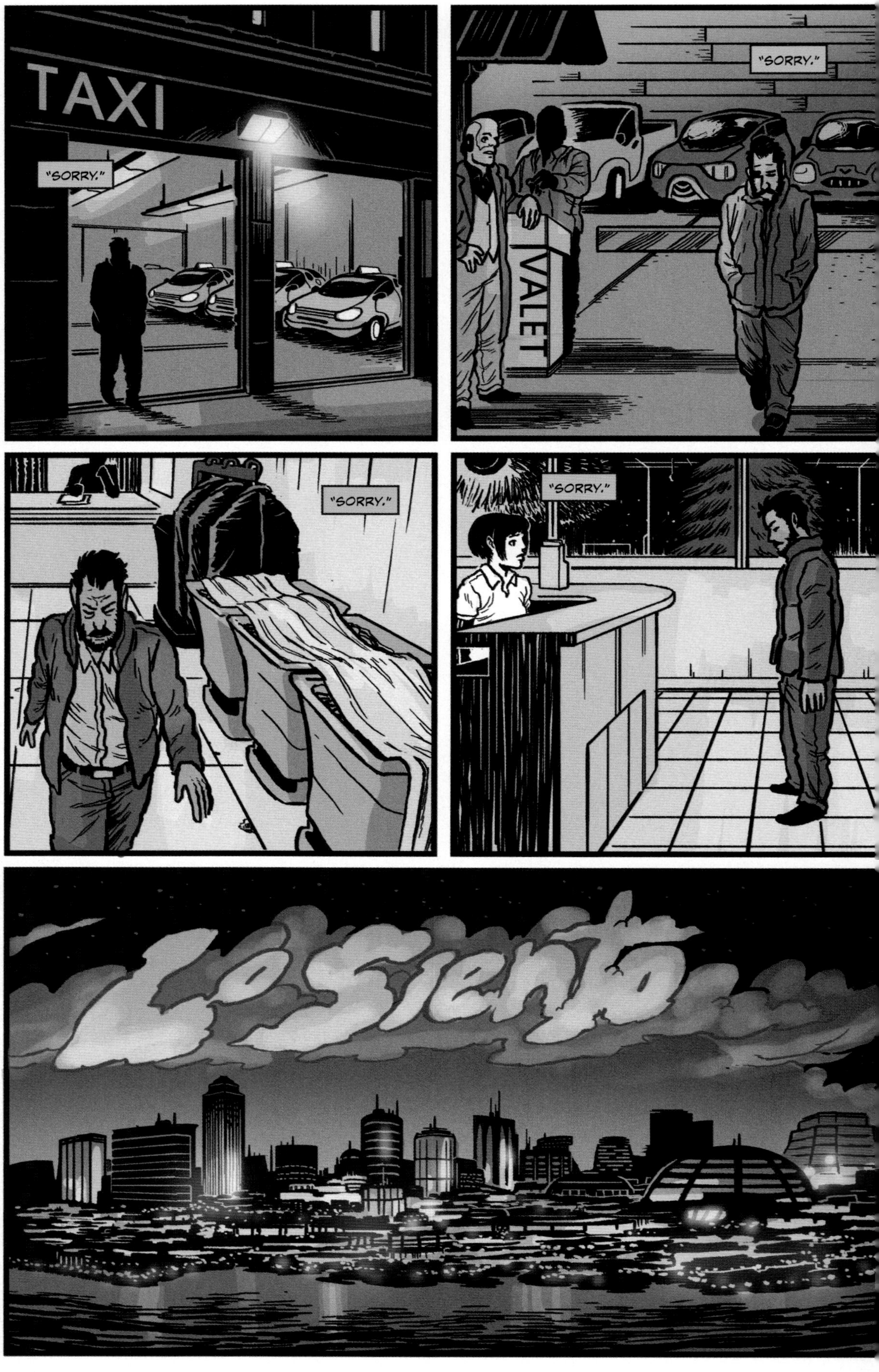
TAXI
"SORRY."
"SORRY."
VALET
"SORRY."
"SORRY."
Lo Siento

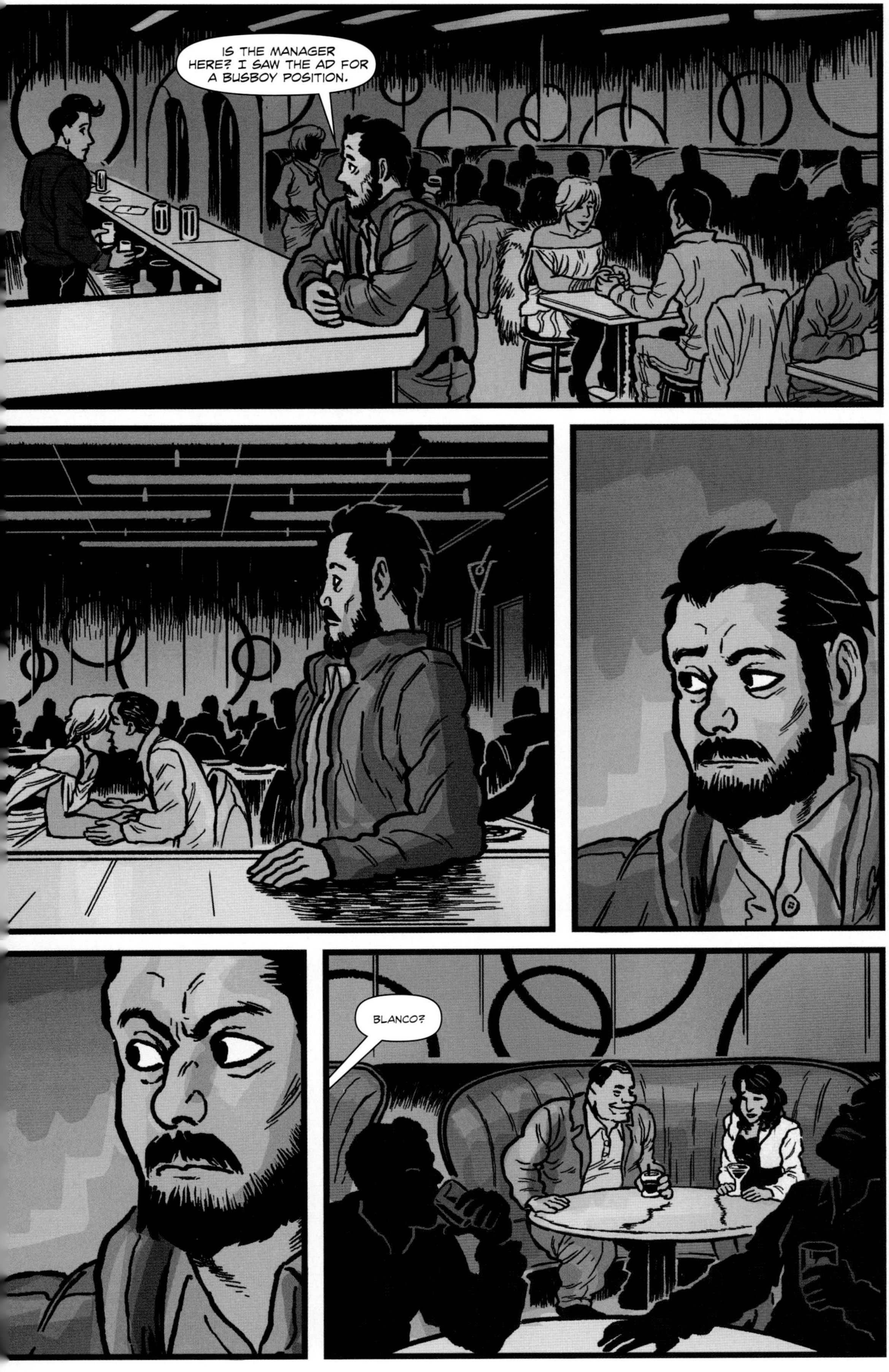
IS THE MANAGER HERE? I SAW THE AD FOR A BUSBOY POSITION.
BLANCO?

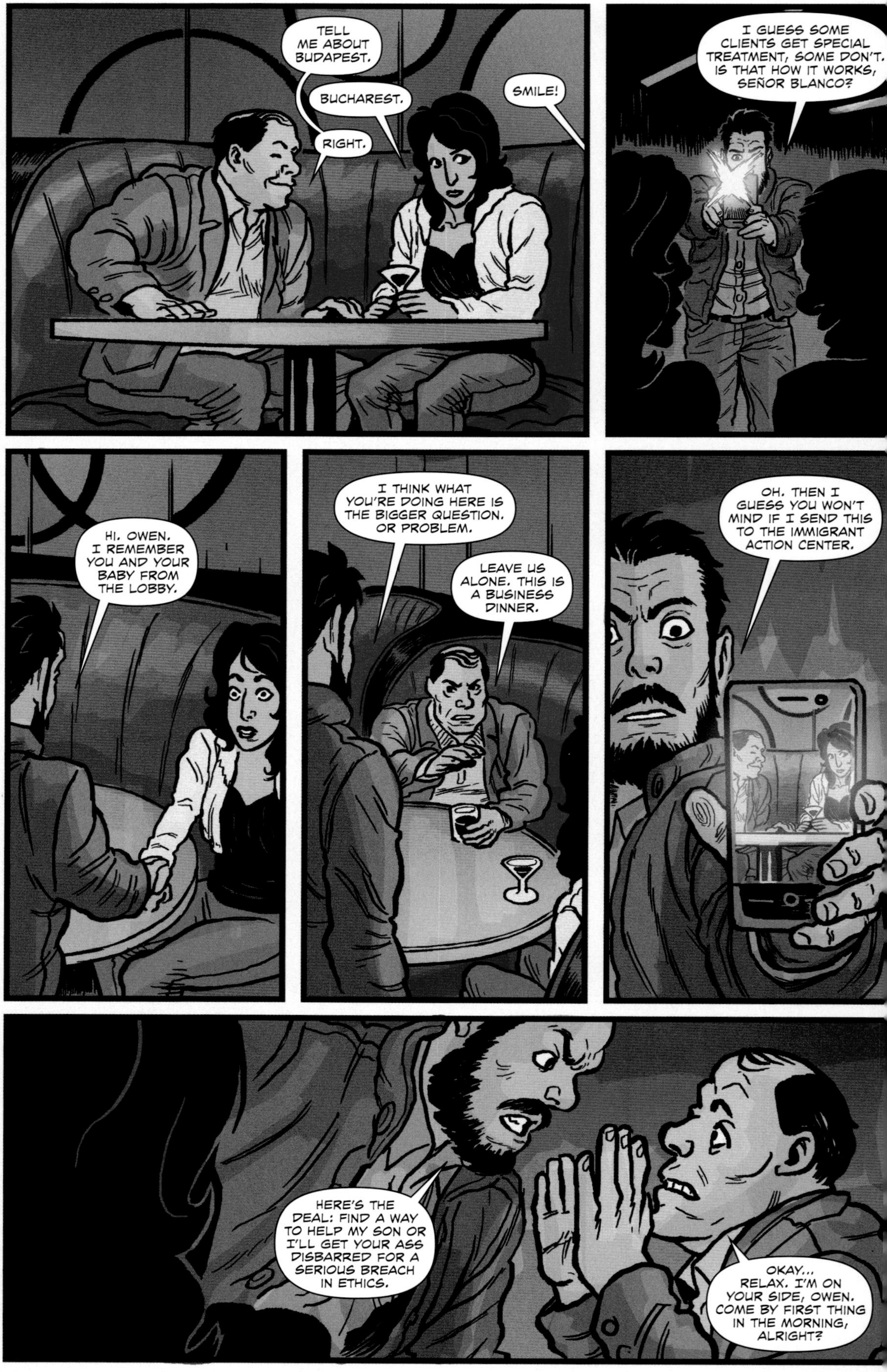
TELL ME ABOUT BUDAPEST.
BUCHAREST.
RIGHT.
SMILE!
I GUESS SOME CLIENTS GET SPECIAL TREATMENT, SOME DON'T. IS THAT HOW IT WORKS, SEÑOR BLANCO?
HI. OWEN. I REMEMBER YOU AND YOUR BABY FROM THE LOBBY.
I THINK WHAT YOU'RE DOING HERE IS THE BIGGER QUESTION. OR PROBLEM.
LEAVE US ALONE. THIS IS A BUSINESS DINNER.
OH. THEN I GUESS YOU WON'T MIND IF I SEND THIS TO THE IMMIGRANT ACTION CENTER.
HERE'S THE DEAL: FIND A WAY TO HELP MY SON OR I'LL GET YOUR ASS DISBARRED FOR A SERIOUS BREACH IN ETHICS.
OKAY... RELAX. I'M ON YOUR SIDE, OWEN. COME BY FIRST THING IN THE MORNING, ALRIGHT?

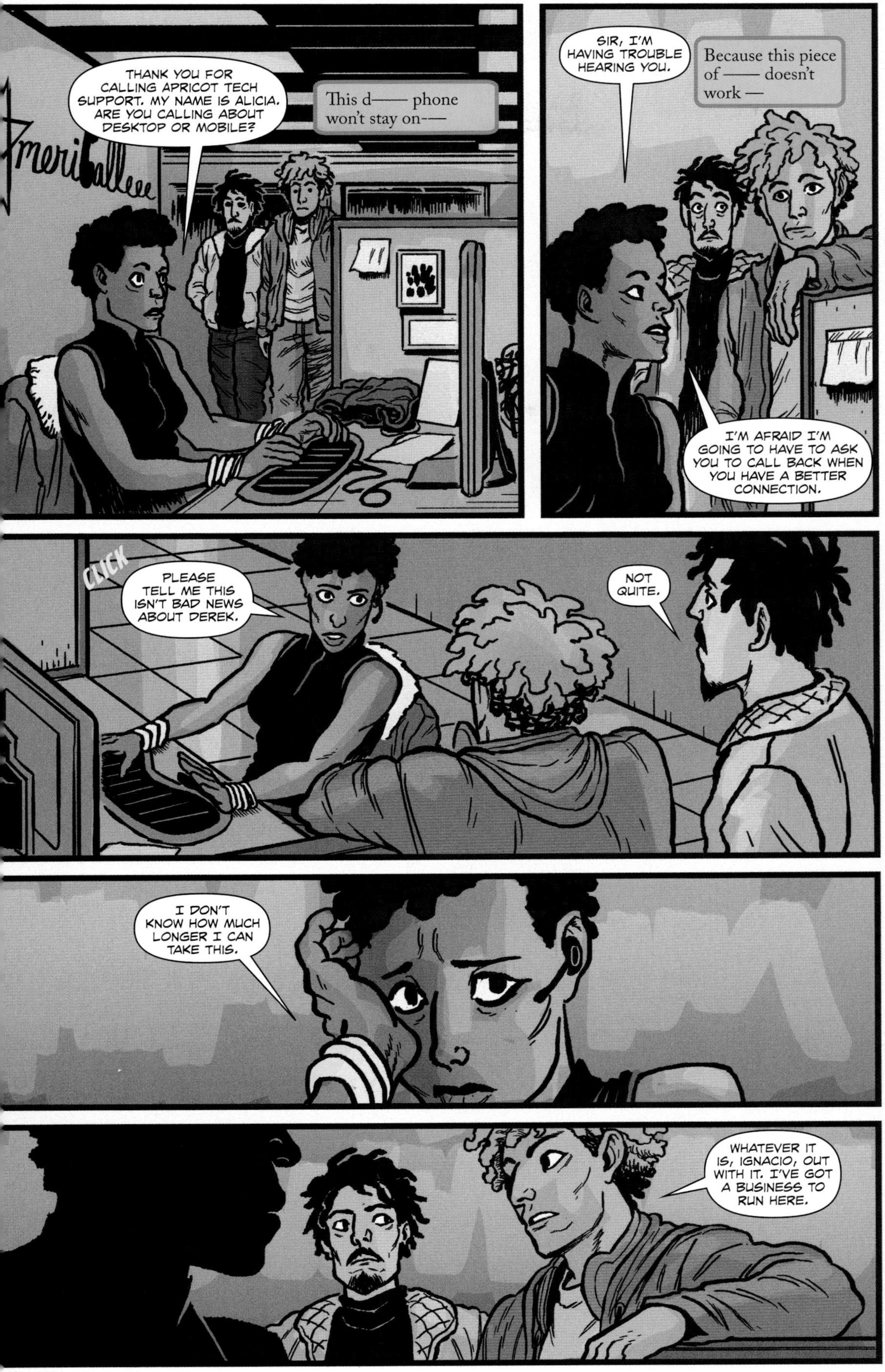
THANK YOU FOR CALLING APRICOT TECH SUPPORT. MY NAME IS ALICIA. ARE YOU CALLING ABOUT DESKTOP OR MOBILE?
This d—— phone won't stay on-—
SIR, I'M HAVING TROUBLE HEARING YOU.
Because this piece of —— doesn't work —
I'M AFRAID I'M GOING TO HAVE TO ASK YOU TO CALL BACK WHEN YOU HAVE A BETTER CONNECTION.
CLICK
PLEASE TELL ME THIS ISN'T BAD NEWS ABOUT DEREK.
NOT QUITE.
I DON'T KNOW HOW MUCH LONGER I CAN TAKE THIS.
WHATEVER IT IS, IGNACIO, OUT WITH IT. I'VE GOT A BUSINESS TO RUN HERE.

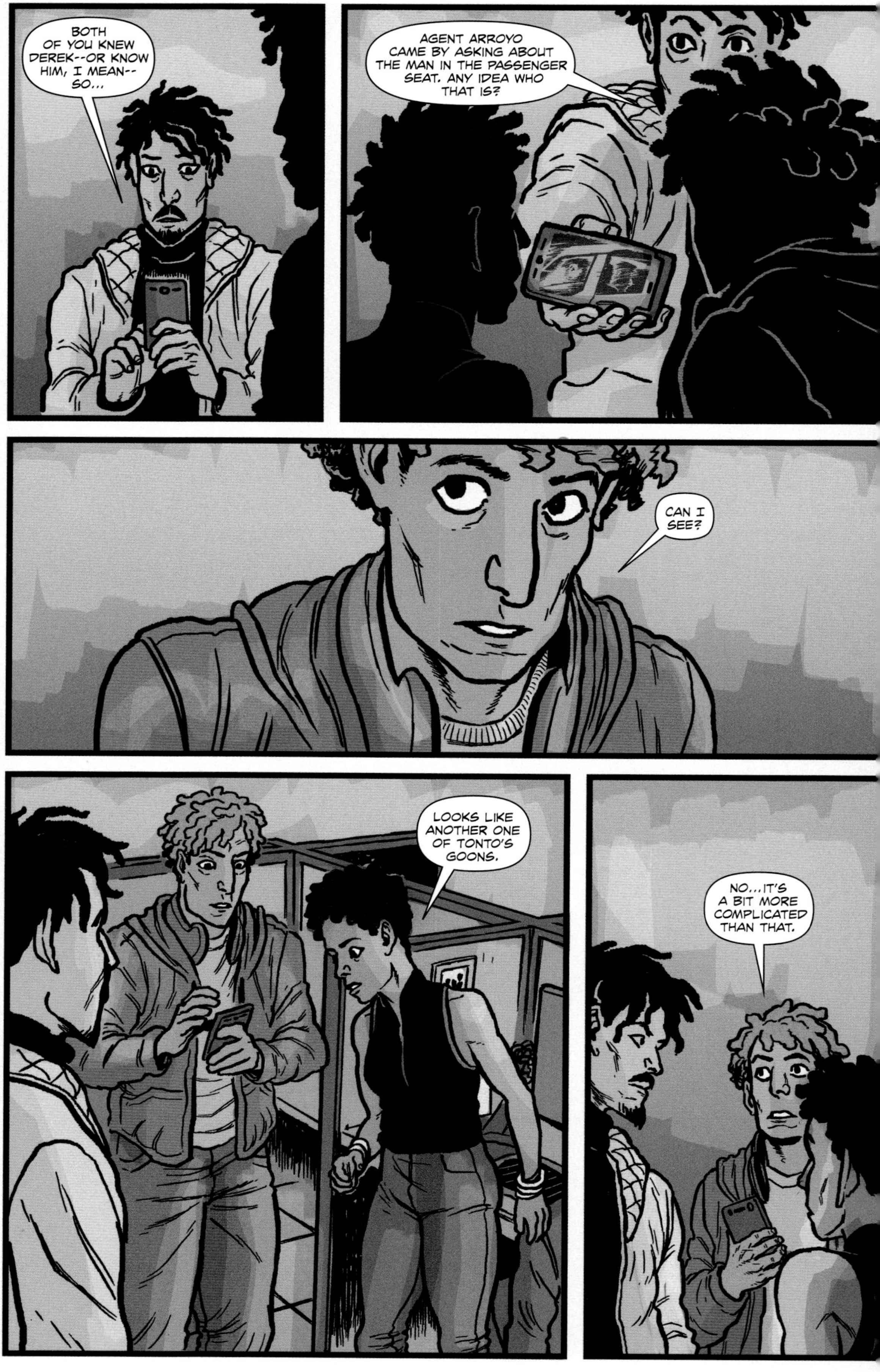
BOTH OF YOU KNEW DEREK--OR KNOW HIM, I MEAN--SO...
AGENT ARROYO CAME BY ASKING ABOUT THE MAN IN THE PASSENGER SEAT. ANY IDEA WHO THAT IS?
CAN I SEE?
LOOKS LIKE ANOTHER ONE OF TONTO'S GOONS.
NO...IT'S A BIT MORE COMPLICATED THAN THAT.

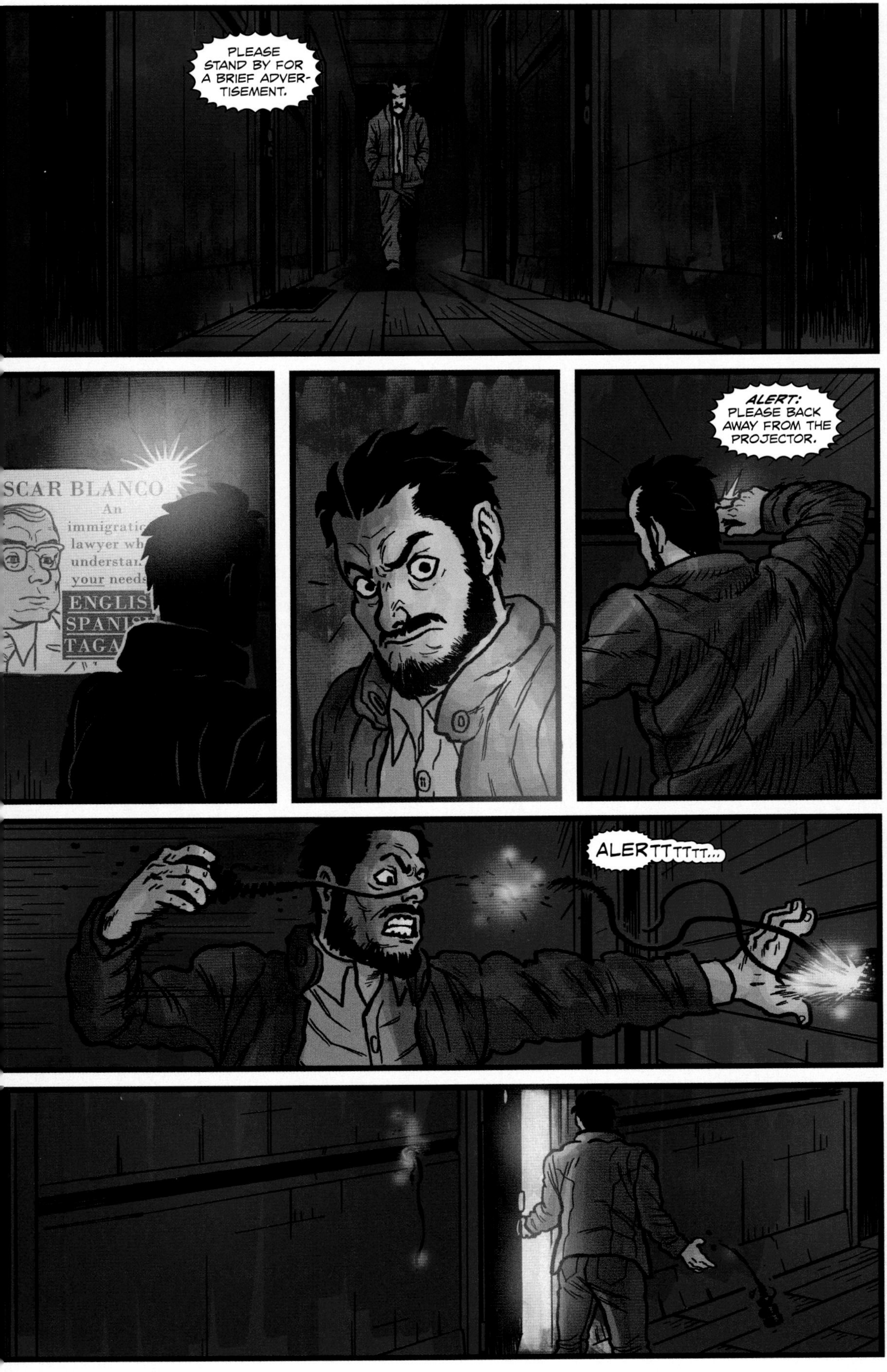
PLEASE STAND BY FOR A BRIEF ADVER-TISEMENT.
SCAR BLANCO
An immigratio lawyer wh understan your needs
ENGLIS
SPANIS
TAGA
ALERT: PLEASE BACK AWAY FROM THE PROJECTOR.
ALERTTTTTT...

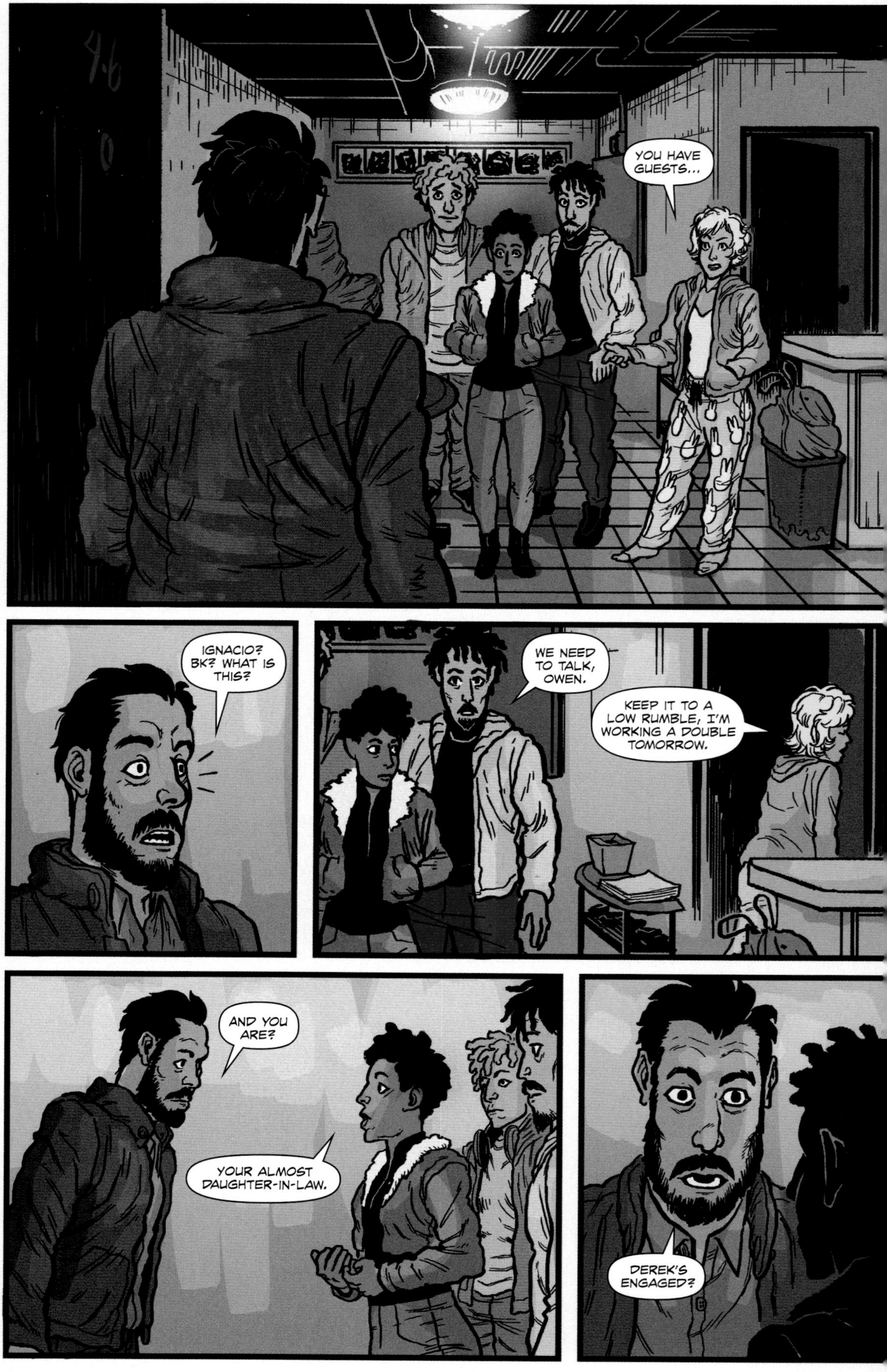
YOU HAVE GUESTS...
IGNACIO? BK? WHAT IS THIS?
WE NEED TO TALK, OWEN.
KEEP IT TO A LOW RUMBLE, I'M WORKING A DOUBLE TOMORROW.
AND YOU ARE?
YOUR ALMOST DAUGHTER-IN-LAW.
DEREK'S ENGAGED?

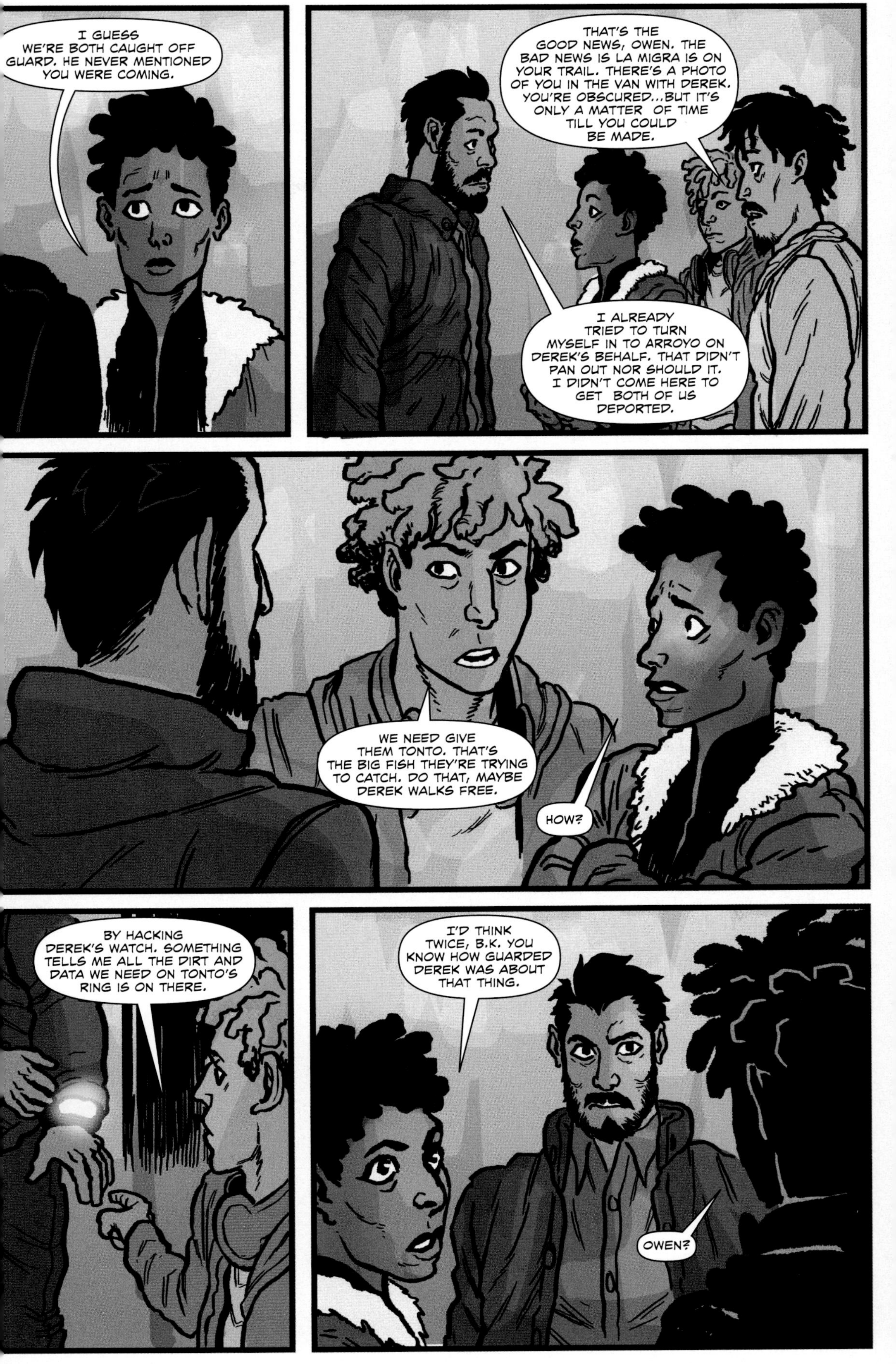
I GUESS WE'RE BOTH CAUGHT OFF GUARD. HE NEVER MENTIONED YOU WERE COMING.
THAT'S THE GOOD NEWS, OWEN. THE BAD NEWS IS LA MIGRA IS ON YOUR TRAIL. THERE'S A PHOTO OF YOU IN THE VAN WITH DEREK. YOU'RE OBSCURED...BUT IT'S ONLY A MATTER OF TIME TILL YOU COULD BE MADE.
I ALREADY TRIED TO TURN MYSELF IN TO ARROYO ON DEREK'S BEHALF. THAT DIDN'T PAN OUT NOR SHOULD IT. I DIDN'T COME HERE TO GET BOTH OF US DEPORTED.
WE NEED GIVE THEM TONTO. THAT'S THE BIG FISH THEY'RE TRYING TO CATCH. DO THAT, MAYBE DEREK WALKS FREE.
HOW?
BY HACKING DEREK'S WATCH. SOMETHING TELLS ME ALL THE DIRT AND DATA WE NEED ON TONTO'S RING IS ON THERE.
I'D THINK TWICE, B.K. YOU KNOW HOW GUARDED DEREK WAS ABOUT THAT THING.
OWEN?

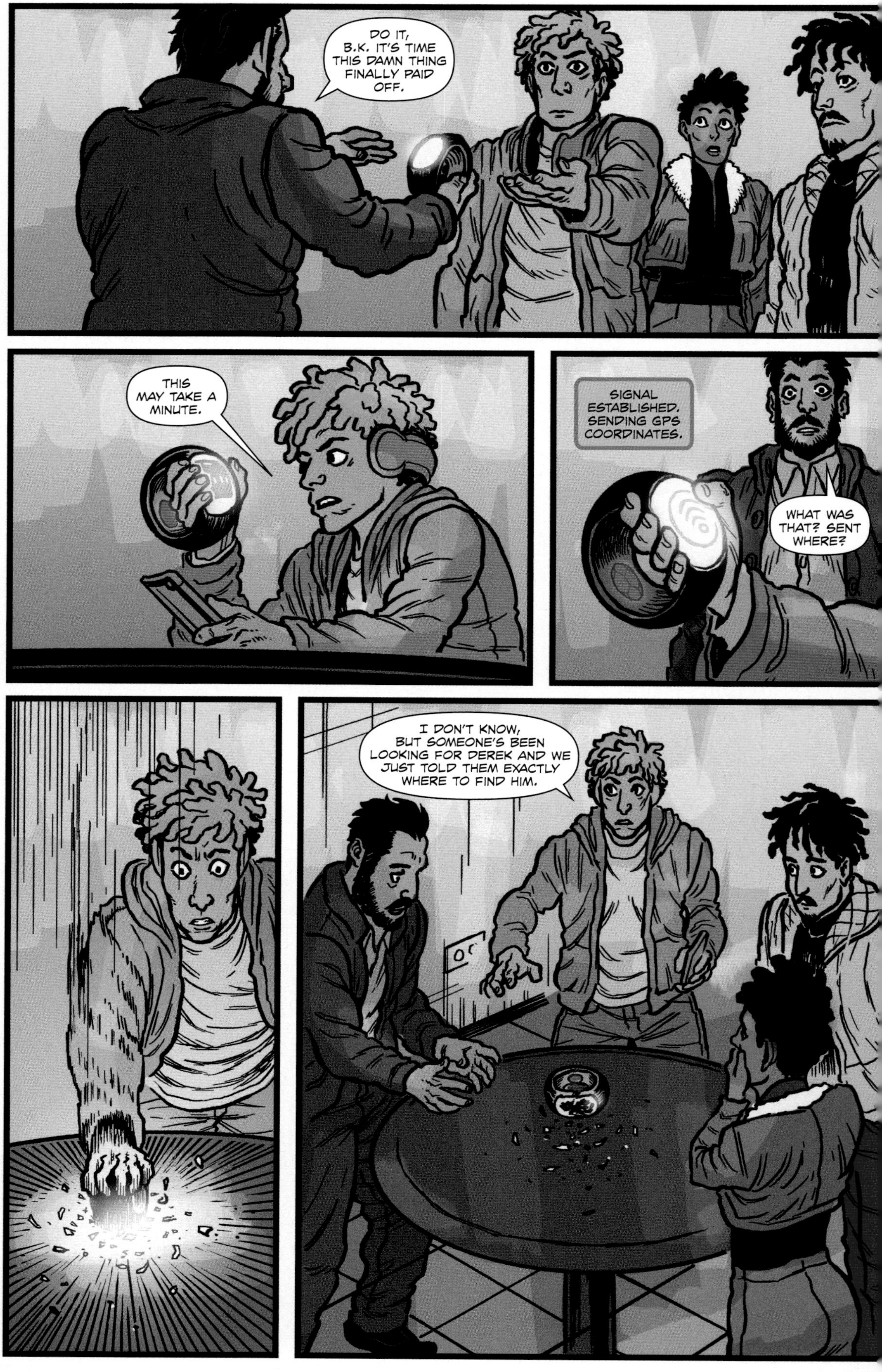
DO IT, B.K. IT'S TIME THIS DAMN THING FINALLY PAID OFF.
THIS MAY TAKE A MINUTE.
SIGNAL ESTABLISHED. SENDING GPS COORDINATES.
WHAT WAS THAT? SENT WHERE?
I DON'T KNOW, BUT SOMEONE'S BEEN LOOKING FOR DEREK AND WE JUST TOLD THEM EXACTLY WHERE TO FIND HIM.

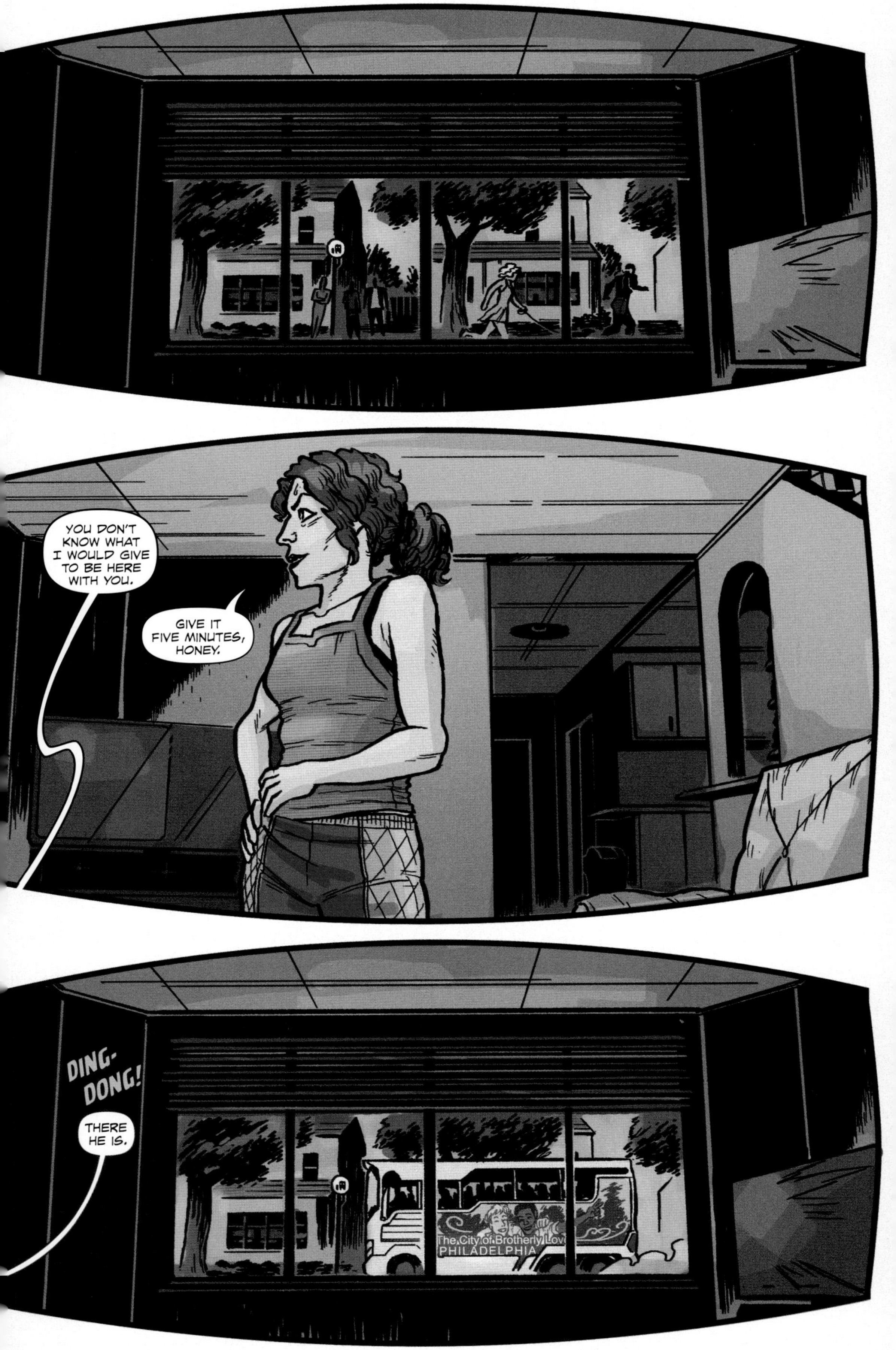
YOU DON'T KNOW WHAT I WOULD GIVE TO BE HERE WITH YOU.
GIVE IT FIVE MINUTES, HONEY.
DING-DONG!
THERE HE IS.
The City of Brotherly Love
PHILADELPHIA

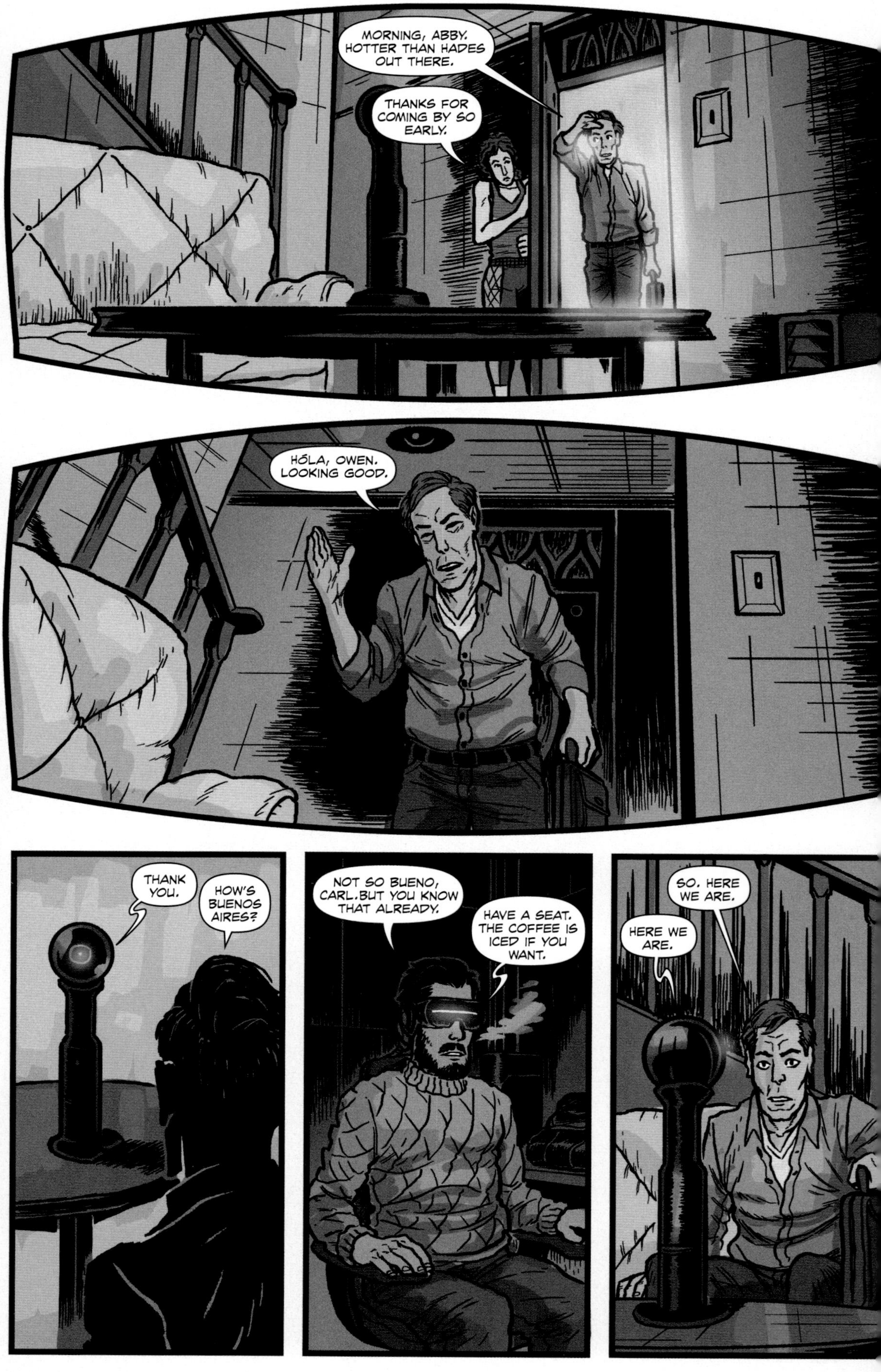
MORNING, ABBY. HOTTER THAN HADES OUT THERE.
THANKS FOR COMING BY SO EARLY.
HÓLA, OWEN. LOOKING GOOD.
THANK YOU.
HOW'S BUENOS AIRES?
NOT SO BUENO, CARL. BUT YOU KNOW THAT ALREADY.
HAVE A SEAT. THE COFFEE IS ICED IF YOU WANT.
SO. HERE WE ARE.
HERE WE ARE.

THEY CAN'T PUT A LIEN ON THE HOUSE, CARL. IT'S PRACTICALLY OUR LAST ASSET.

WISH I COULD AGREE WITH YOU, OWEN. BUT THEY CAN, AND WILL, IF YOU DON'T PAY THE BACK TAXES.

SO WHAT DO YOU SUGGEST? ABBY'S GOT TWO BOARDERS IN THE THIRD BEDROOM JUST TO MAKE THE MORTGAGE, I TOOK ON A SECOND JOB TO SEND HOME WHAT I CAN-- WHICH IS A PITTANCE NOW THAT I'M ON THE HOOK WITH THE SMUGGLERS AND A LAWYER HERE.

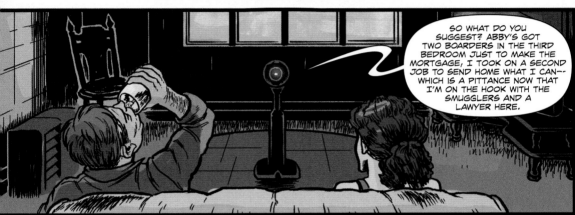

THERE IS CHARLOTTE'S 529 ACCOUNT.

MY DAUGHTER IS NOT NOT GOING TO COLLEGE, CARL, JUST SO THE BANK CAN HAVE ITS POUND OF FLESH.

KEEP IT DOWN, OWEN, UNLESS YOU WANT TO WAKE HER UP SO SHE CAN HEAR YOU.

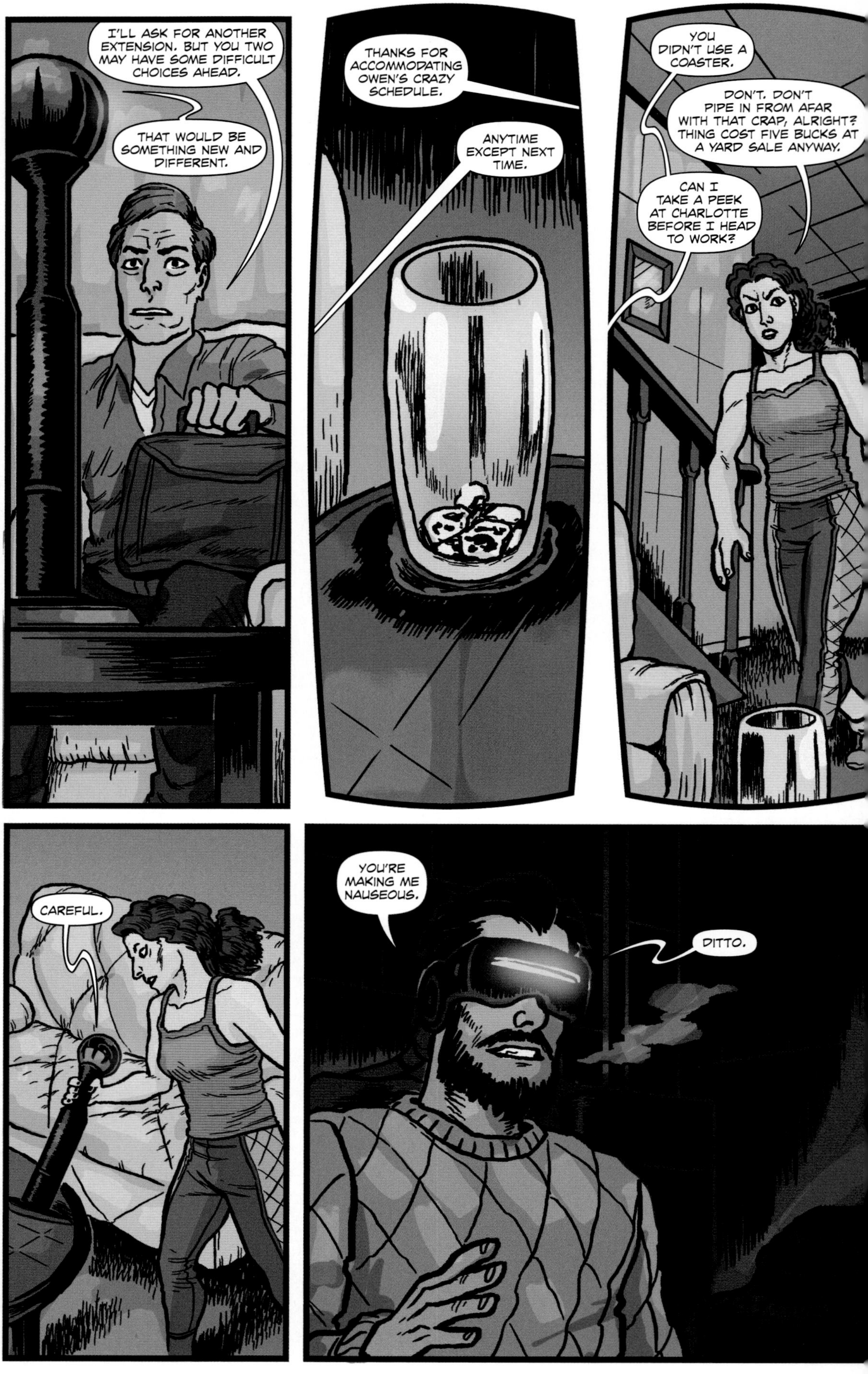
I'LL ASK FOR ANOTHER EXTENSION. BUT YOU TWO MAY HAVE SOME DIFFICULT CHOICES AHEAD.
THAT WOULD BE SOMETHING NEW AND DIFFERENT.
THANKS FOR ACCOMMODATING OWEN'S CRAZY SCHEDULE.
ANYTIME EXCEPT NEXT TIME.
YOU DIDN'T USE A COASTER.
DON'T. DON'T PIPE IN FROM AFAR WITH THAT CRAP, ALRIGHT? THING COST FIVE BUCKS AT A YARD SALE ANYWAY.
CAN I TAKE A PEEK AT CHARLOTTE BEFORE I HEAD TO WORK?
CAREFUL.
YOU'RE MAKING ME NAUSEOUS.
DITTO.

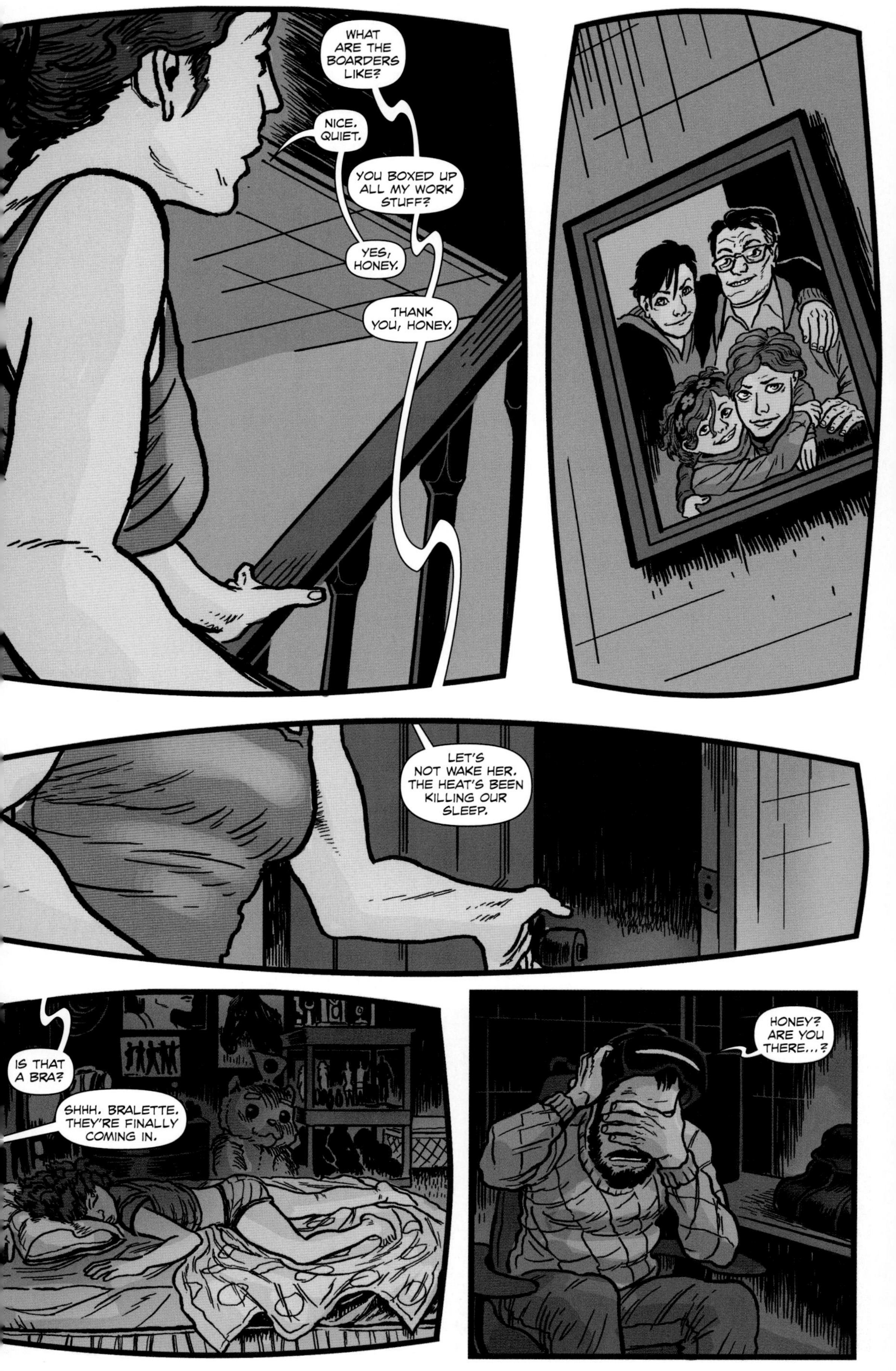
WHAT ARE THE BOARDERS LIKE?
NICE. QUIET.
YOU BOXED UP ALL MY WORK STUFF?
YES, HONEY.
THANK YOU, HONEY.
LET'S NOT WAKE HER. THE HEAT'S BEEN KILLING OUR SLEEP.
IS THAT A BRA?
SHHH. BRALETTE. THEY'RE FINALLY COMING IN.
HONEY? ARE YOU THERE...?

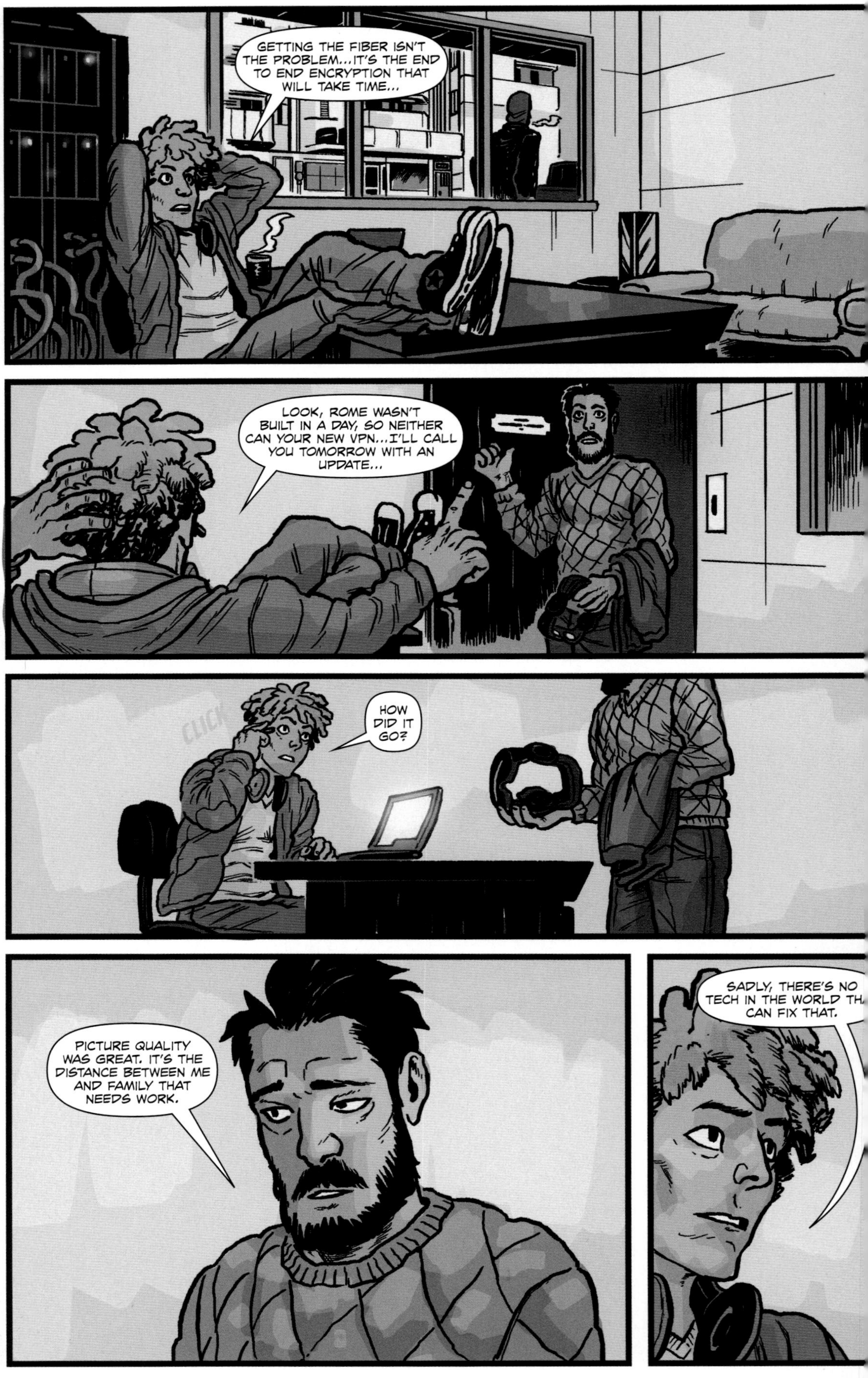
GETTING THE FIBER ISN'T THE PROBLEM...IT'S THE END TO END ENCRYPTION THAT WILL TAKE TIME...
LOOK, ROME WASN'T BUILT IN A DAY, SO NEITHER CAN YOUR NEW VPN...I'LL CALL YOU TOMORROW WITH AN UPDATE...
CLICK
HOW DID IT GO?
PICTURE QUALITY WAS GREAT. IT'S THE DISTANCE BETWEEN ME AND FAMILY THAT NEEDS WORK.
SADLY, THERE'S NO TECH IN THE WORLD THA CAN FIX THAT.

SO, WHERE ARE WE WITH THE FILES YOU PULLED FROM DEREK'S PULSE?

I'LL SHOW YOU...

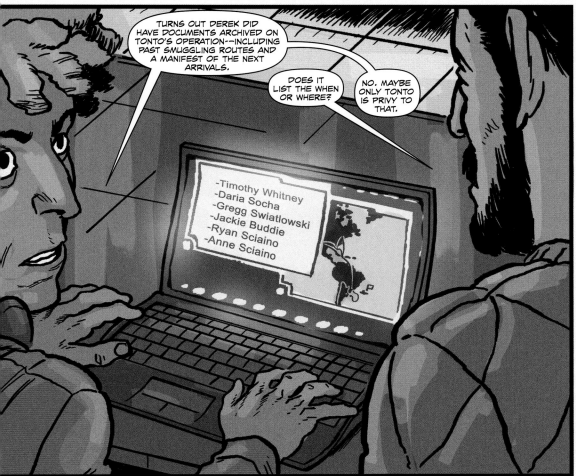

TURNS OUT DEREK DID HAVE DOCUMENTS ARCHIVED ON TONTO'S OPERATION--INCLUDING PAST SMUGGLING ROUTES AND A MANIFEST OF THE NEXT ARRIVALS.

DOES IT LIST THE WHEN OR WHERE?

NO. MAYBE ONLY TONTO IS PRIVY TO THAT.

-Timothy Whitney
-Daria Socha
-Gregg Swiatlowski
-Jackie Buddie
-Ryan Sciaino
-Anne Sciaino

WITHOUT THAT I'VE GOT NOTHING TO OFFER ARROYO.

IT'S A GOOD START. IF DEREK IS WILLING TO TESTIFY AGAINST TONTO, MAYBE--

IT'S NOT ENOUGH TO BUY HIM HIS FREEDOM. NOT YET.

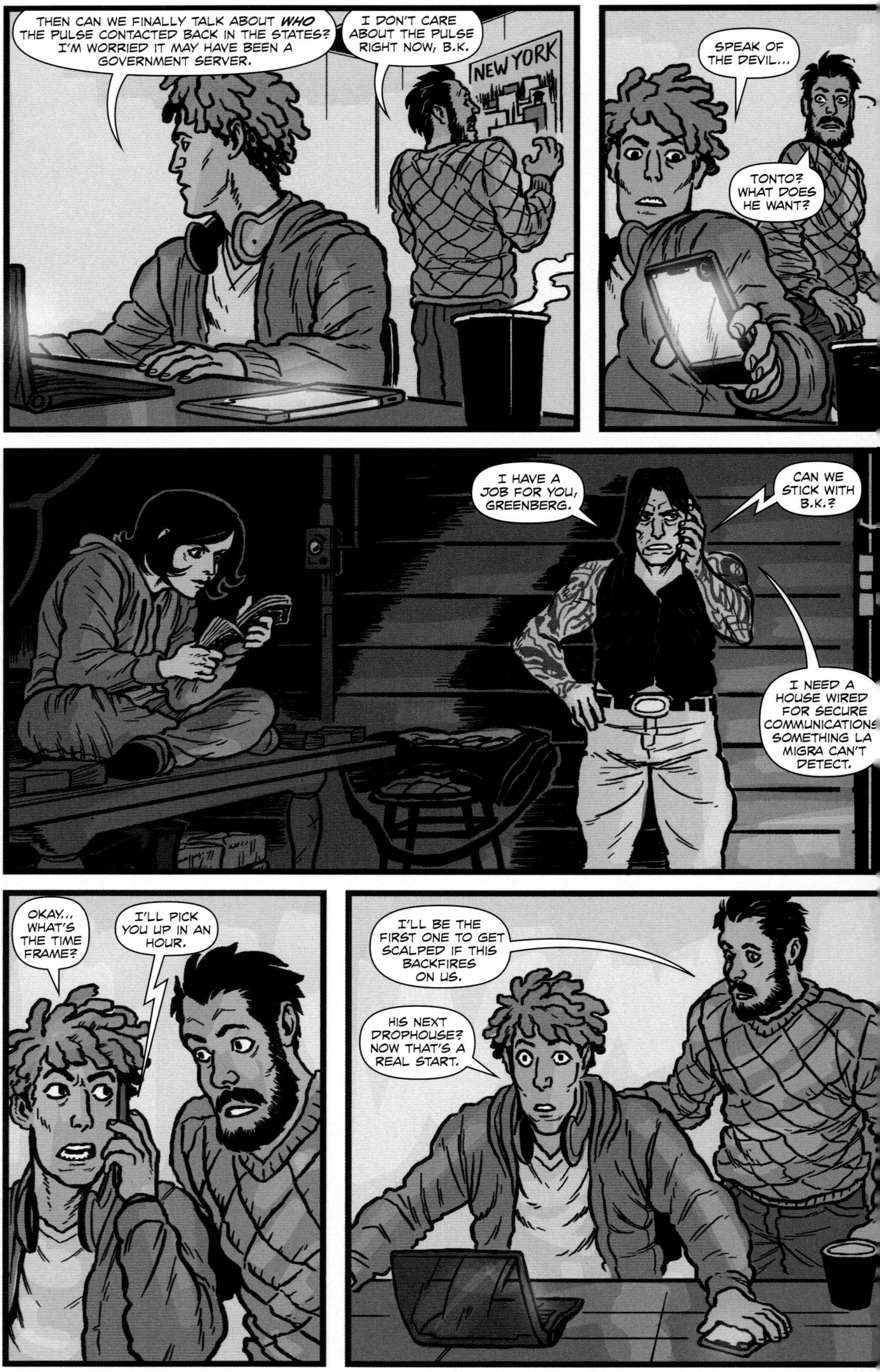
THEN CAN WE FINALLY TALK ABOUT *WHO* THE PULSE CONTACTED BACK IN THE STATES? I'M WORRIED IT MAY HAVE BEEN A GOVERNMENT SERVER.
I DON'T CARE ABOUT THE PULSE RIGHT NOW, B.K.
NEW YORK
SPEAK OF THE DEVIL...
TONTO? WHAT DOES HE WANT?
I HAVE A JOB FOR YOU, GREENBERG.
CAN WE STICK WITH B.K.?
I NEED A HOUSE WIRED FOR SECURE COMMUNICATIONS SOMETHING LA MIGRA CAN'T DETECT.
OKAY... WHAT'S THE TIME FRAME?
I'LL PICK YOU UP IN AN HOUR.
I'LL BE THE FIRST ONE TO GET SCALPED IF THIS BACKFIRES ON US.
HIS NEXT DROPHOUSE? NOW THAT'S A REAL START.

〈HELLO, MIGUEL.〉*

*TRANSLATED FROM SPANISH.

〈EVERYONE IN LA MIGRA SENDS THEIR SYMPATHIES, ELISABETH. HOW IS HE?〉

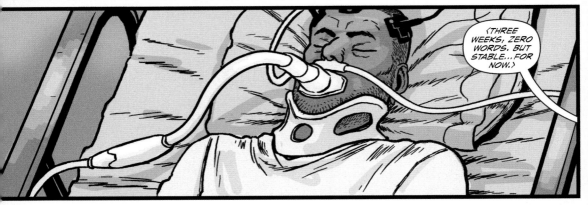

〈THREE WEEKS, ZERO WORDS. BUT STABLE...FOR NOW.〉

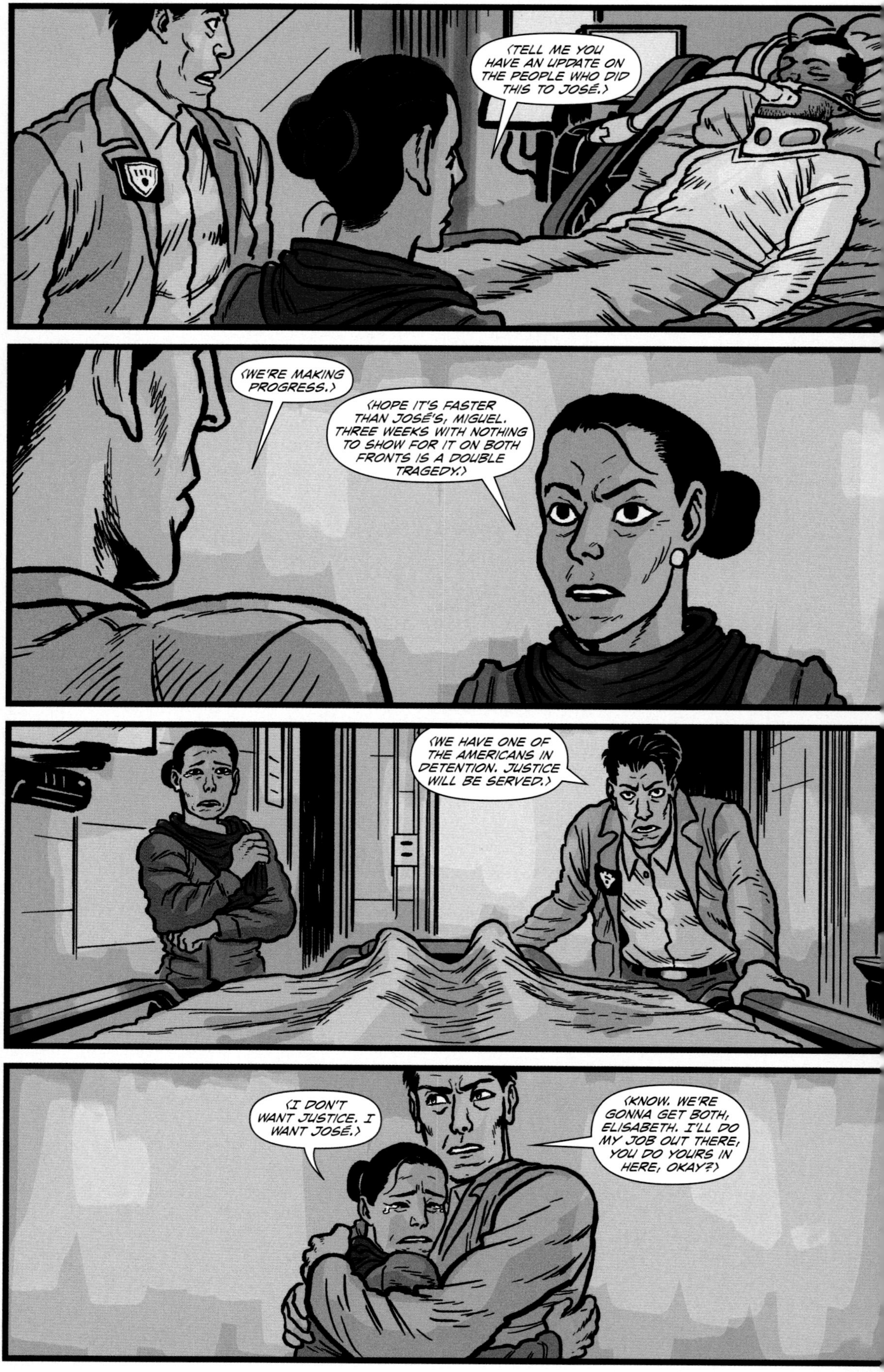
⟨TELL ME YOU HAVE AN UPDATE ON THE PEOPLE WHO DID THIS TO JOSÉ.⟩
⟨WE'RE MAKING PROGRESS.⟩
⟨HOPE IT'S FASTER THAN JOSÉ'S, MIGUEL. THREE WEEKS WITH NOTHING TO SHOW FOR IT ON BOTH FRONTS IS A DOUBLE TRAGEDY.⟩
⟨WE HAVE ONE OF THE AMERICANS IN DETENTION. JUSTICE WILL BE SERVED.⟩
⟨I DON'T WANT JUSTICE. I WANT JOSÉ.⟩
⟨KNOW. WE'RE GONNA GET BOTH, ELISABETH. I'LL DO MY JOB OUT THERE, YOU DO YOURS IN HERE, OKAY?⟩

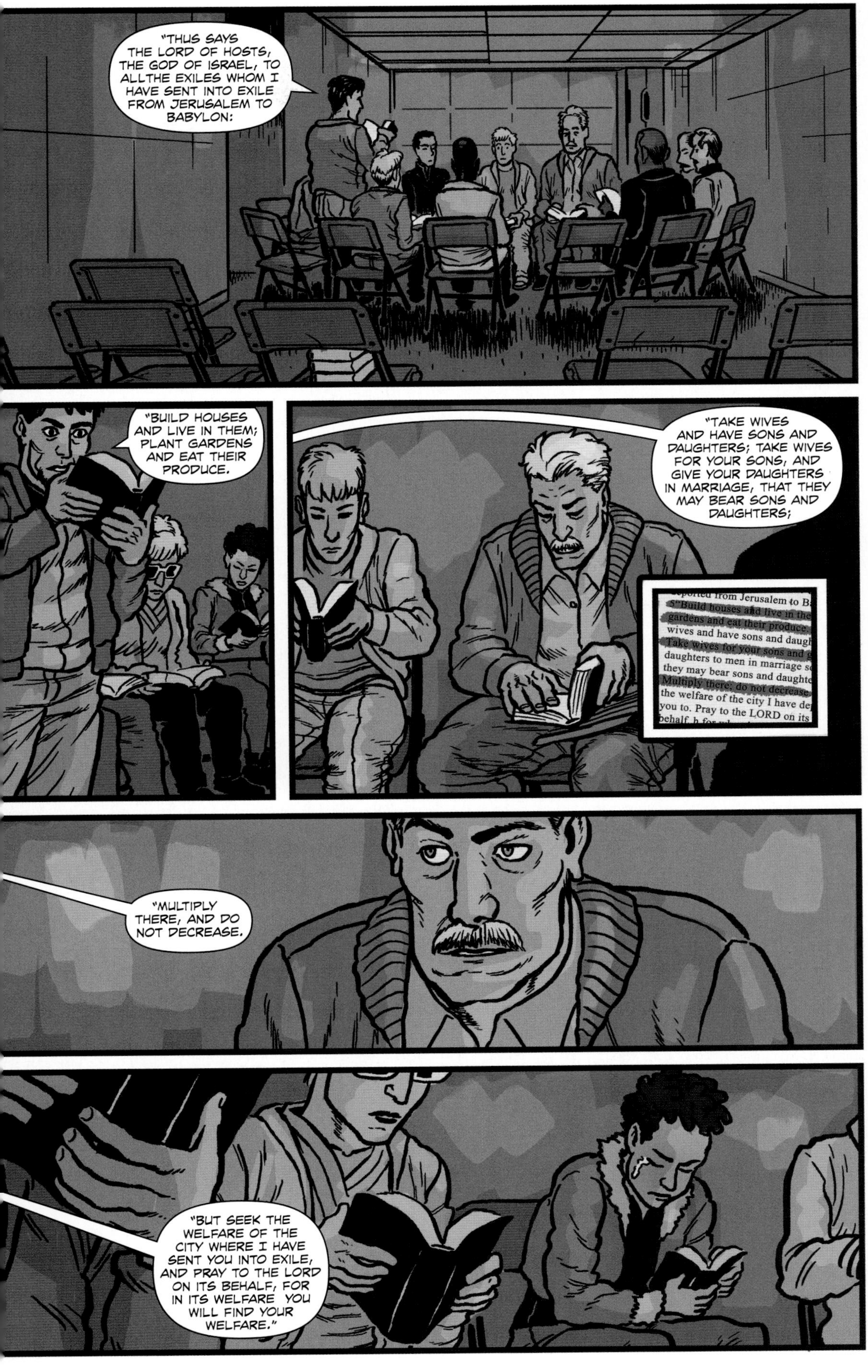
"THUS SAYS THE LORD OF HOSTS, THE GOD OF ISRAEL, TO ALLTHE EXILES WHOM I HAVE SENT INTO EXILE FROM JERUSALEM TO BABYLON:
"BUILD HOUSES AND LIVE IN THEM; PLANT GARDENS AND EAT THEIR PRODUCE.
"TAKE WIVES AND HAVE SONS AND DAUGHTERS; TAKE WIVES FOR YOUR SONS, AND GIVE YOUR DAUGHTERS IN MARRIAGE, THAT THEY MAY BEAR SONS AND DAUGHTERS;
gardens and eat their produce.
wives and have sons and daugh
daughters to men in marriage
they may bear sons and daughte
the welfare of the city I have de
you to. Pray to the LORD on its
"MULTIPLY THERE, AND DO NOT DECREASE.
"BUT SEEK THE WELFARE OF THE CITY WHERE I HAVE SENT YOU INTO EXILE, AND PRAY TO THE LORD ON ITS BEHALF, FOR IN ITS WELFARE YOU WILL FIND YOUR WELFARE."

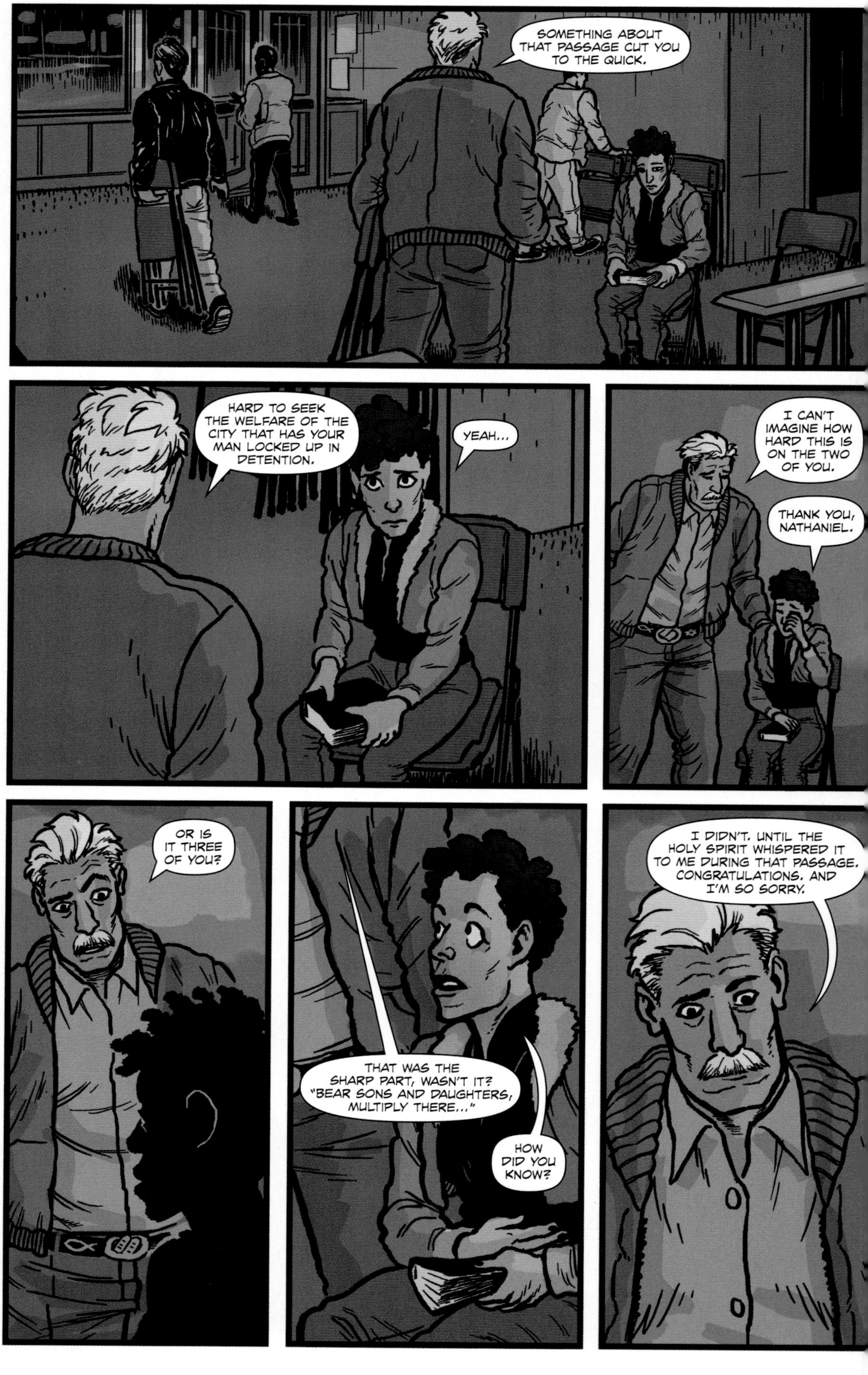
SOMETHING ABOUT THAT PASSAGE CUT YOU TO THE QUICK.
HARD TO SEEK THE WELFARE OF THE CITY THAT HAS YOUR MAN LOCKED UP IN DETENTION.
YEAH...
I CAN'T IMAGINE HOW HARD THIS IS ON THE TWO OF YOU.
THANK YOU, NATHANIEL.
OR IS IT THREE OF YOU?
THAT WAS THE SHARP PART, WASN'T IT? "BEAR SONS AND DAUGHTERS, MULTIPLY THERE..."
HOW DID YOU KNOW?
I DIDN'T. UNTIL THE HOLY SPIRIT WHISPERED IT TO ME DURING THAT PASSAGE. CONGRATULATIONS. AND I'M SO SORRY.

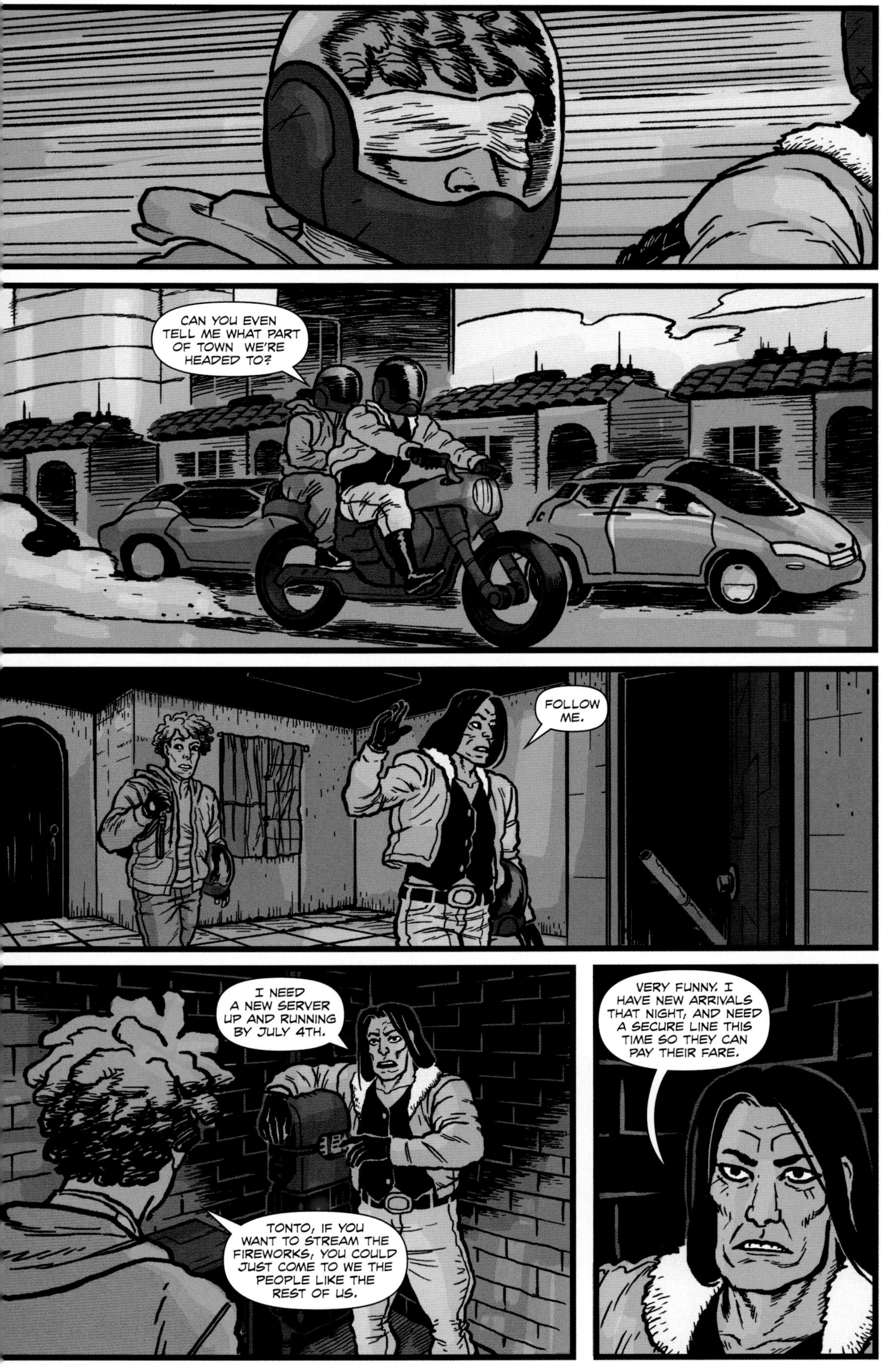
CAN YOU EVEN TELL ME WHAT PART OF TOWN WE'RE HEADED TO?
FOLLOW ME.
I NEED A NEW SERVER UP AND RUNNING BY JULY 4TH.
TONTO, IF YOU WANT TO STREAM THE FIREWORKS, YOU COULD JUST COME TO WE THE PEOPLE LIKE THE REST OF US.
VERY FUNNY. I HAVE NEW ARRIVALS THAT NIGHT, AND NEED A SECURE LINE THIS TIME SO THEY CAN PAY THEIR FARE.

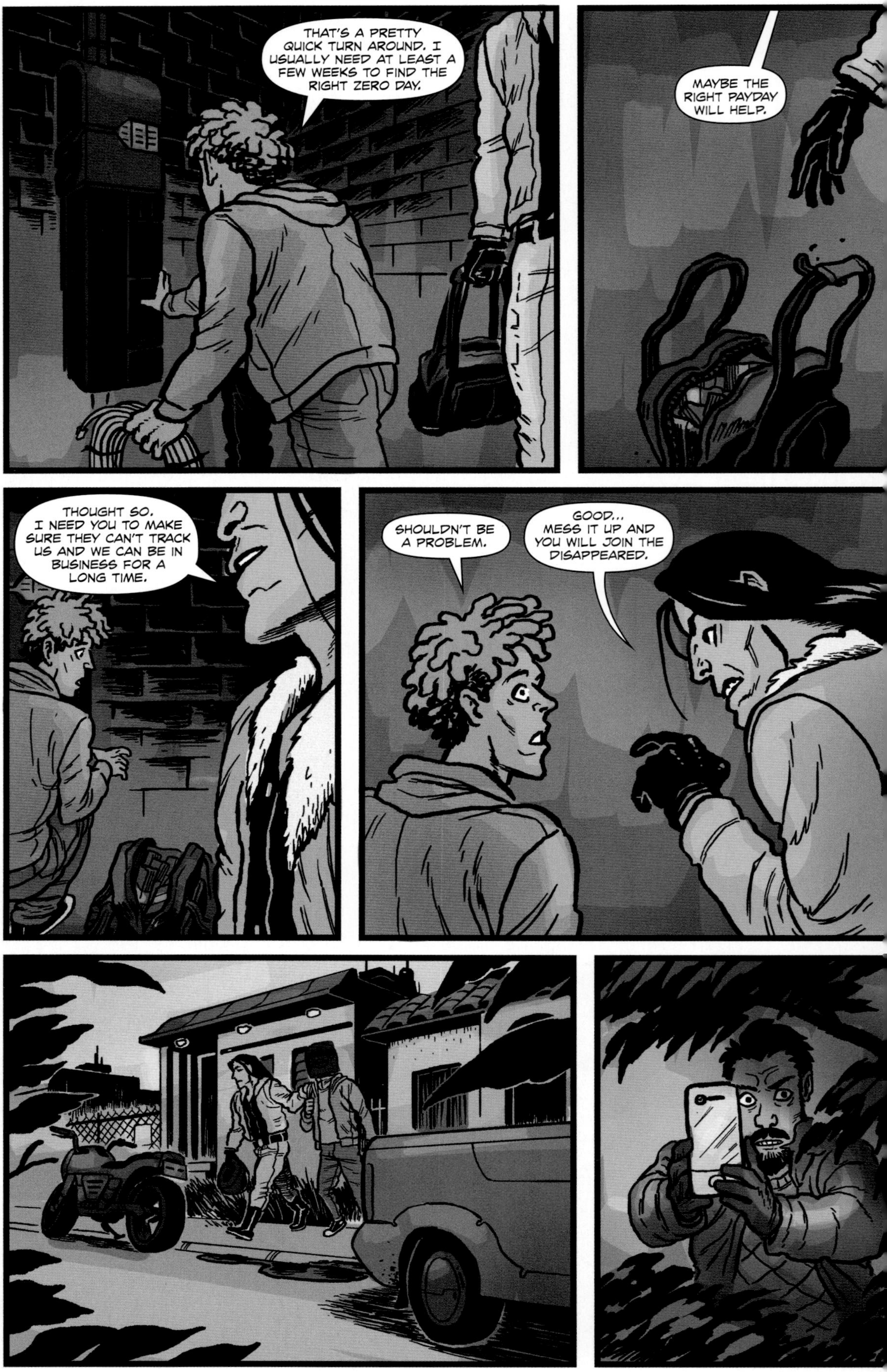
THAT'S A PRETTY QUICK TURN AROUND. I USUALLY NEED AT LEAST A FEW WEEKS TO FIND THE RIGHT ZERO DAY.
MAYBE THE RIGHT PAYDAY WILL HELP.
THOUGHT SO. I NEED YOU TO MAKE SURE THEY CAN'T TRACK US AND WE CAN BE IN BUSINESS FOR A LONG TIME.
SHOULDN'T BE A PROBLEM.
GOOD... MESS IT UP AND YOU WILL JOIN THE DISAPPEARED.

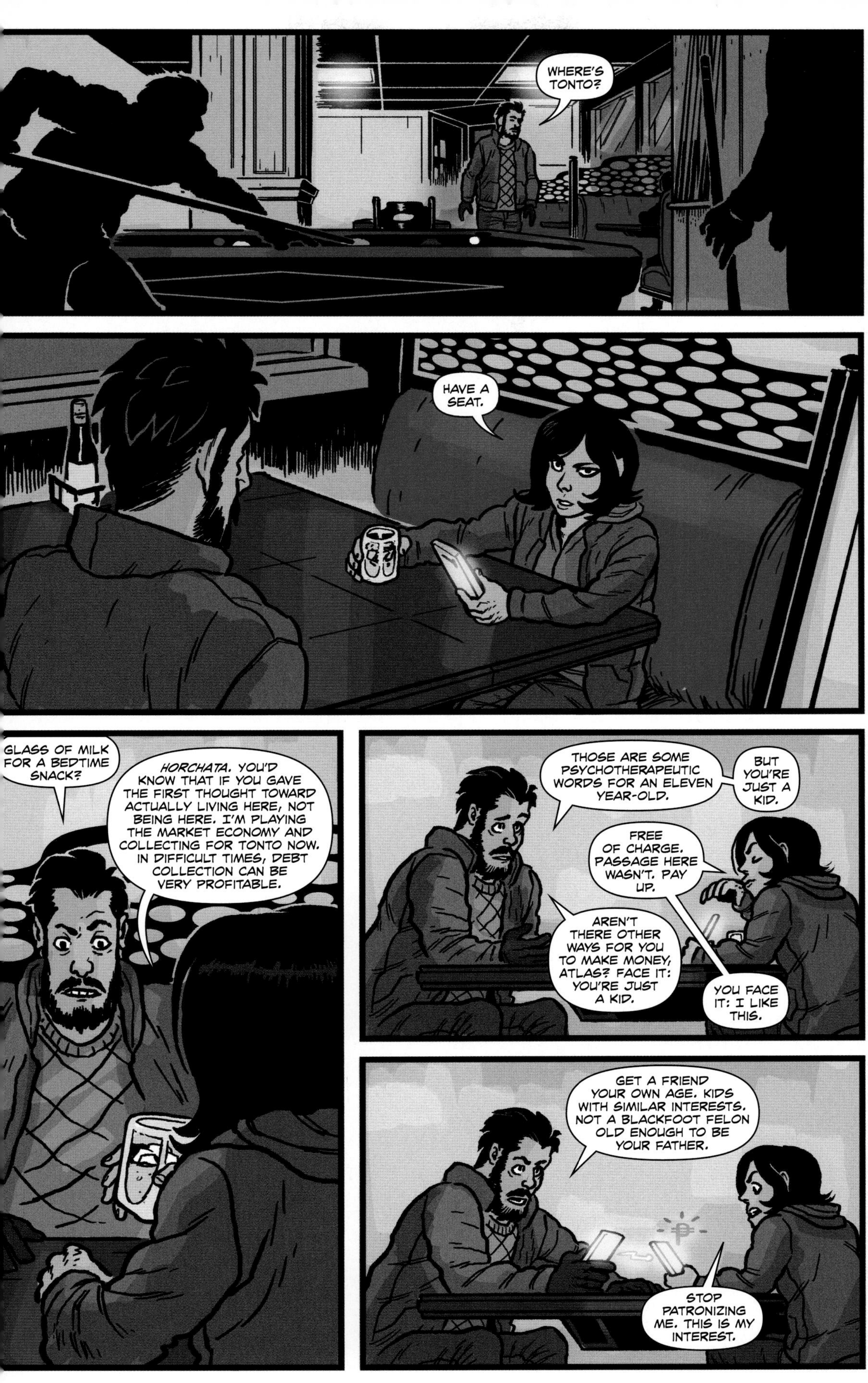
WHERE'S TONTO?
HAVE A SEAT.
GLASS OF MILK FOR A BEDTIME SNACK?
HORCHATA. YOU'D KNOW THAT IF YOU GAVE THE FIRST THOUGHT TOWARD ACTUALLY LIVING HERE, NOT BEING HERE. I'M PLAYING THE MARKET ECONOMY AND COLLECTING FOR TONTO NOW. IN DIFFICULT TIMES, DEBT COLLECTION CAN BE VERY PROFITABLE.
THOSE ARE SOME PSYCHOTHERAPEUTIC WORDS FOR AN ELEVEN YEAR-OLD.
BUT YOU'RE JUST A KID.
FREE OF CHARGE. PASSAGE HERE WASN'T. PAY UP.
AREN'T THERE OTHER WAYS FOR YOU TO MAKE MONEY, ATLAS? FACE IT: YOU'RE JUST A KID.
YOU FACE IT: I LIKE THIS.
GET A FRIEND YOUR OWN AGE. KIDS WITH SIMILAR INTERESTS. NOT A BLACKFOOT FELON OLD ENOUGH TO BE YOUR FATHER.
STOP PATRONIZING ME. THIS IS MY INTEREST.

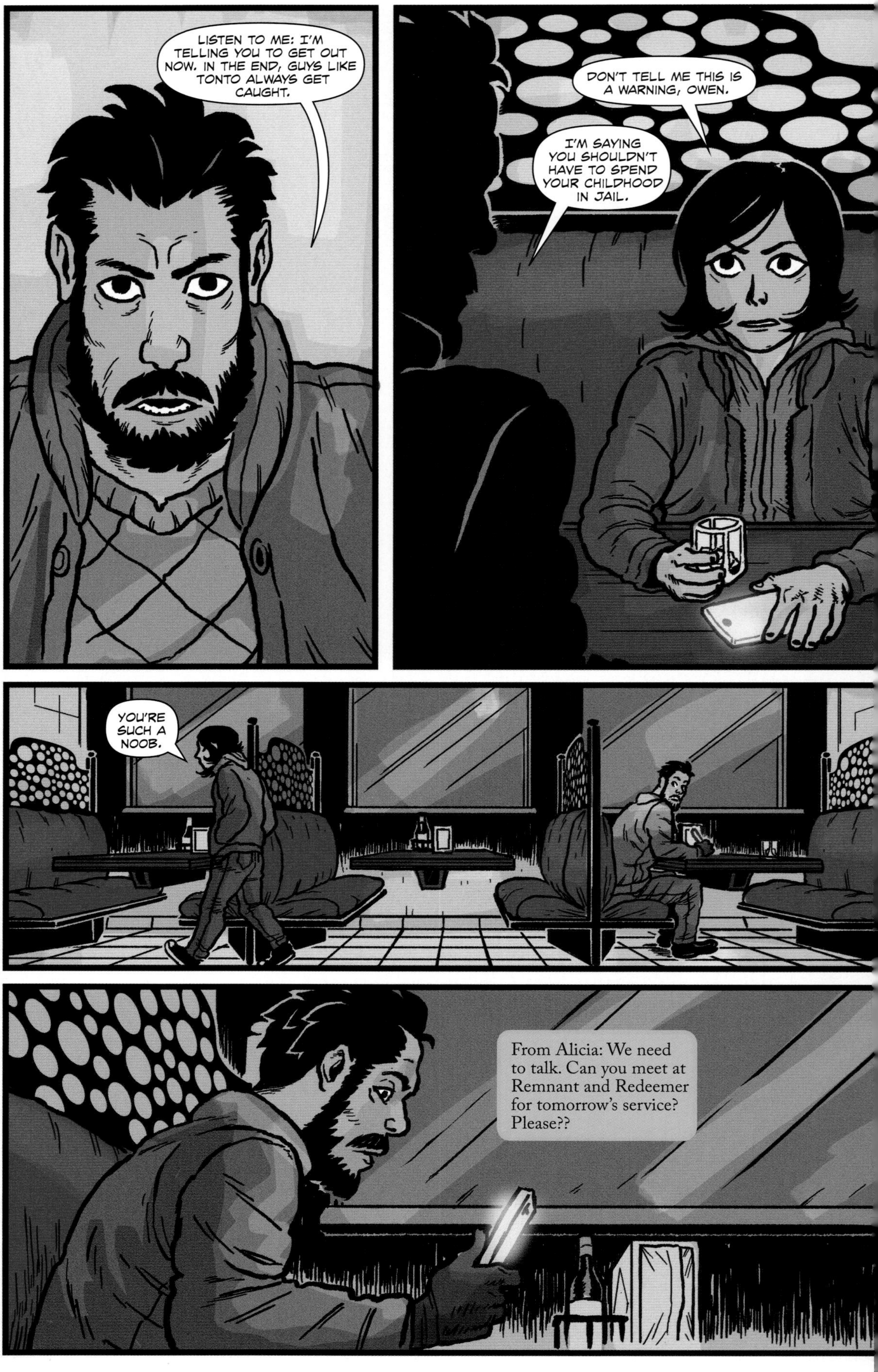
LISTEN TO ME: I'M TELLING YOU TO GET OUT NOW. IN THE END, GUYS LIKE TONTO ALWAYS GET CAUGHT.
DON'T TELL ME THIS IS A WARNING, OWEN.
I'M SAYING YOU SHOULDN'T HAVE TO SPEND YOUR CHILDHOOD IN JAIL.
YOU'RE SUCH A NOOB.
From Alicia: We need to talk. Can you meet at Remnant and Redeemer for tomorrow's service? Please??

SO IF JEREMIAH'S LETTER TO THE EXILES IN BABYLON WAS ALSO WRITTEN TO US, THEN WE'RE TO SEEK THE WELFARE OF WHAT CITY?

his is what the Lord Almighty, the God of Israel, says to all those I carried into exile fro... m to ...b... ...ouses and ...der...

BUENOS AIRES.

AMERICATOWN!

HA-HA! HA-HA! HA-HA! HA-HA! HA-HA!

AMERICATOWN IS BUENOS AIRES, THE WAY JUDEATOWN OR WHATEVER THE JEWS CALLED IT WAS BABYLON.

THE WAY TO SEEK OUR OWN GOOD IS TO SEEK THEIR GOOD. LOVE THY NEIGHBOR? REMEMBER THAT ONE?

"MAYBE RATHER THAN WORRY WHAT THE CITY ISN'T DOING FOR US ON JULY 4TH, WE WOULD DO BETTER TO WORRY WHAT WE'RE DOING FOR THE CITY ON JULY 9TH."

REMANENT &... House of PRAYER

"MAYBE THE BEST WAY TO CELEBRATE AMERICA IS IN THE EXAMPLE IT SET FOR OTHER COUNTRIES LIKE ARGENTINA WHOSE INDEPENDENCE DAY TOOK ITS CUE FROM OURS."

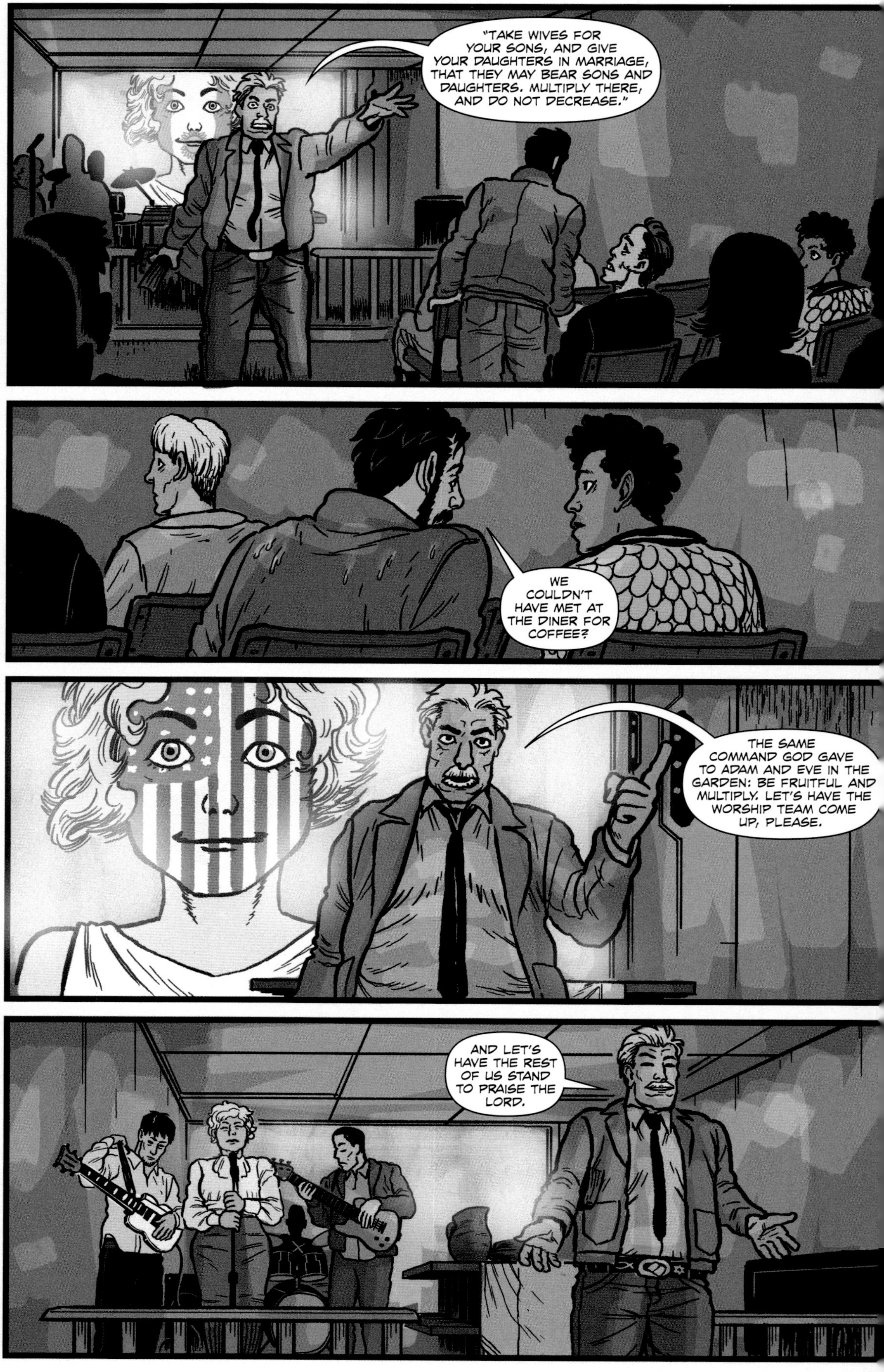
"TAKE WIVES FOR YOUR SONS, AND GIVE YOUR DAUGHTERS IN MARRIAGE, THAT THEY MAY BEAR SONS AND DAUGHTERS. MULTIPLY THERE, AND DO NOT DECREASE."
WE COULDN'T HAVE MET AT THE DINER FOR COFFEE?
THE SAME COMMAND GOD GAVE TO ADAM AND EVE IN THE GARDEN: BE FRUITFUL AND MULTIPLY. LET'S HAVE THE WORSHIP TEAM COME UP, PLEASE.
AND LET'S HAVE THE REST OF US STAND TO PRAISE THE LORD.

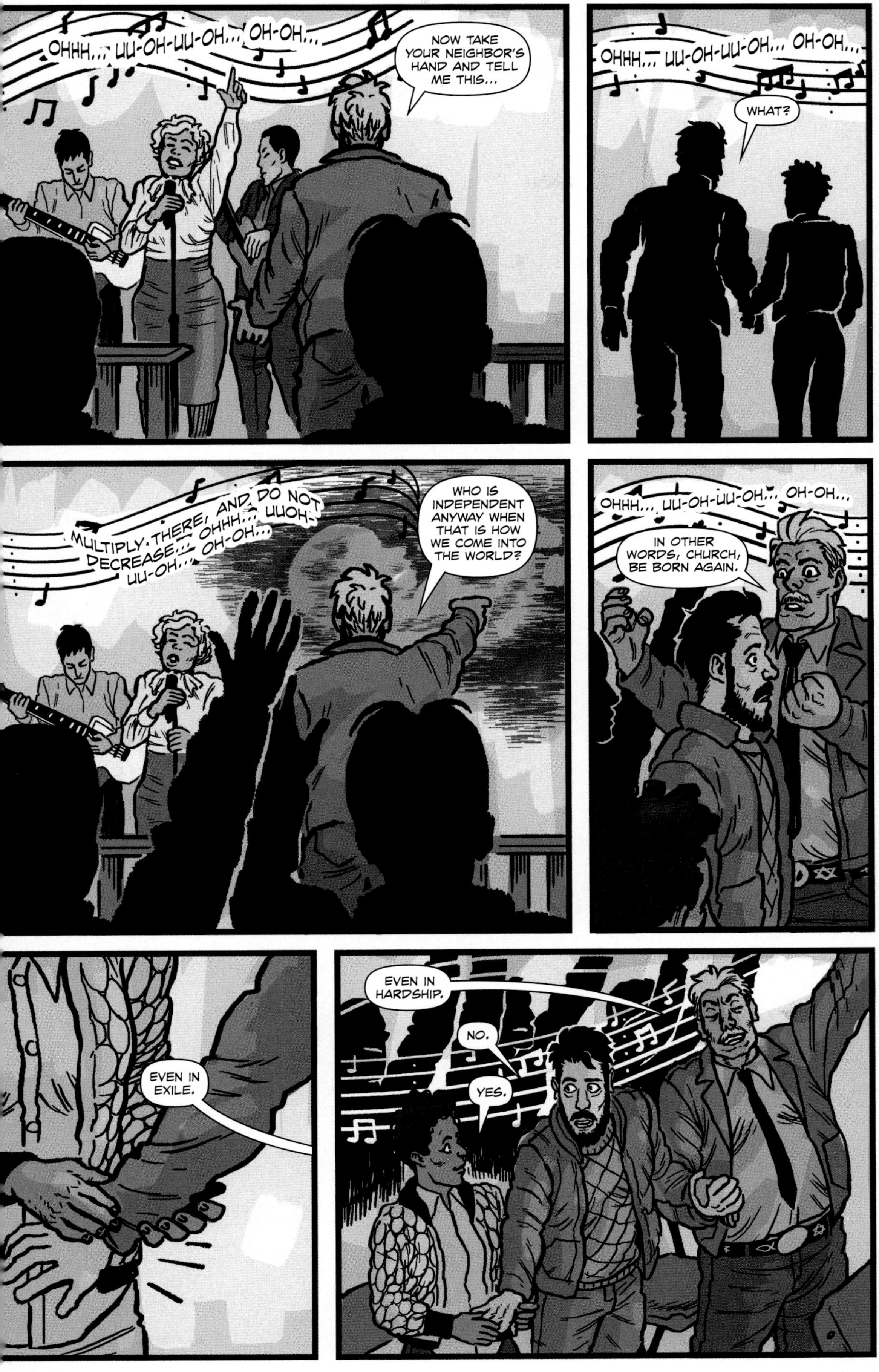
OHHH... UU-OH-UU-OH... OH-OH...
NOW TAKE YOUR NEIGHBOR'S HAND AND TELL ME THIS...
OHHH... UU-OH-UU-OH... OH-OH...
WHAT?
MULTIPLY THERE, AND DO NOT DECREASE... OHHH... UUOH-UU-OH... OH-OH...
WHO IS INDEPENDENT ANYWAY WHEN THAT IS HOW WE COME INTO THE WORLD?
OHHH... UU-OH-UU-OH... OH-OH...
IN OTHER WORDS, CHURCH, BE BORN AGAIN.
EVEN IN EXILE.
EVEN IN HARDSHIP.
NO.
YES.

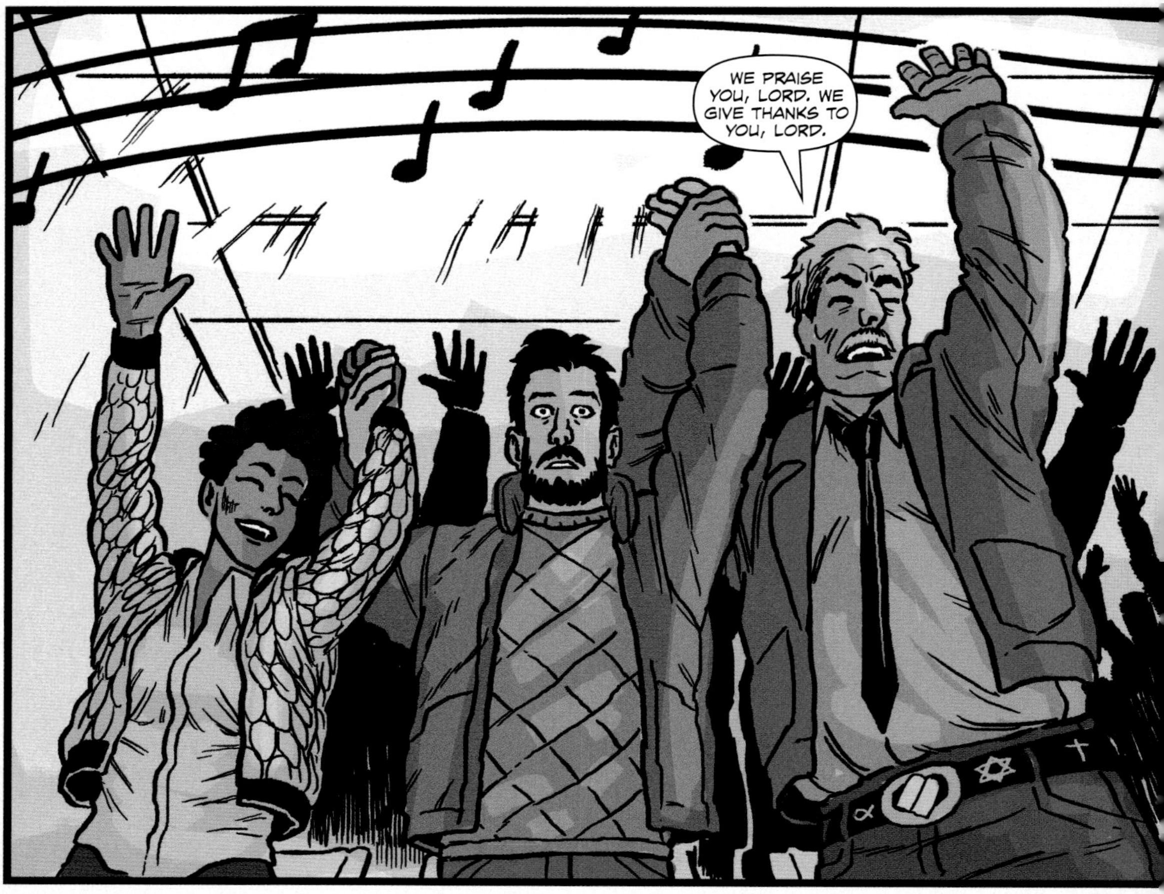
WE PRAISE YOU, LORD. WE GIVE THANKS TO YOU, LORD.

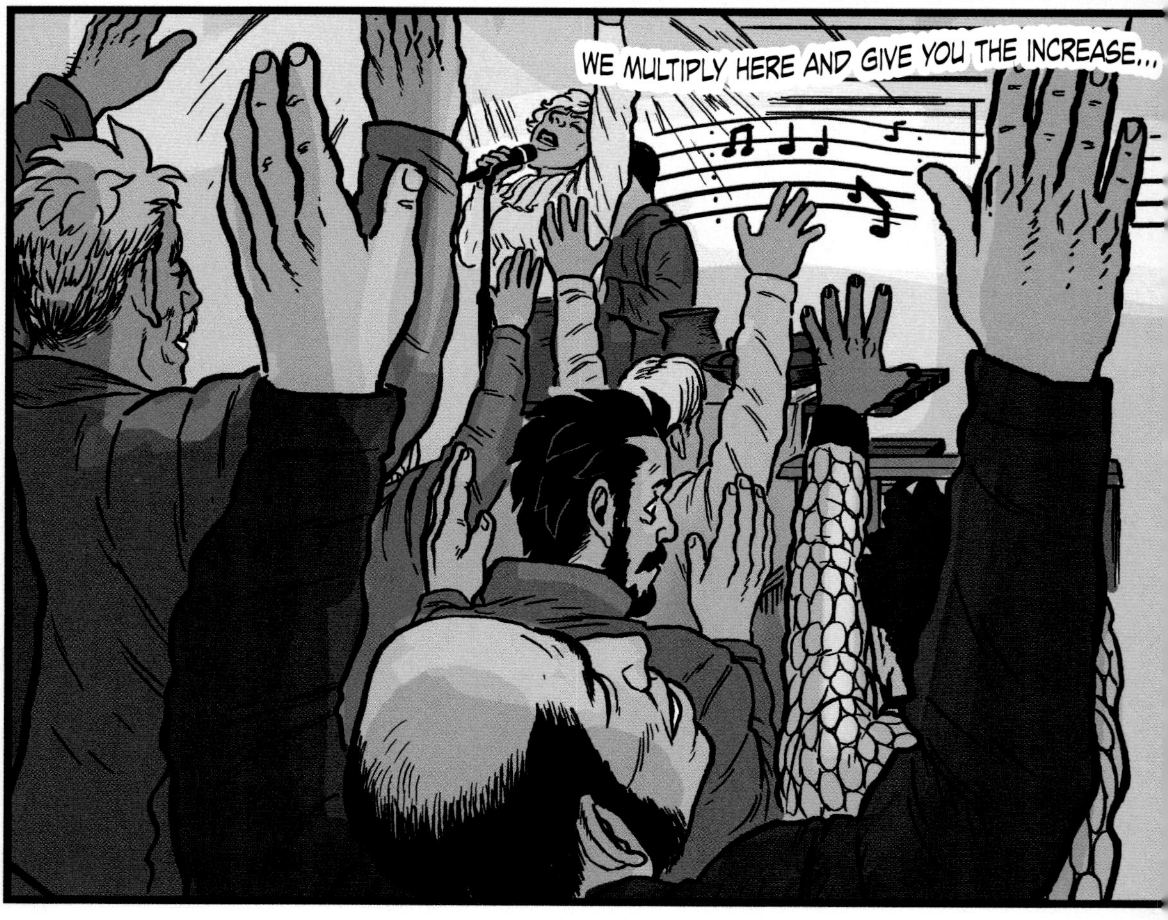
WE MULTIPLY HERE AND GIVE YOU THE INCREASE...

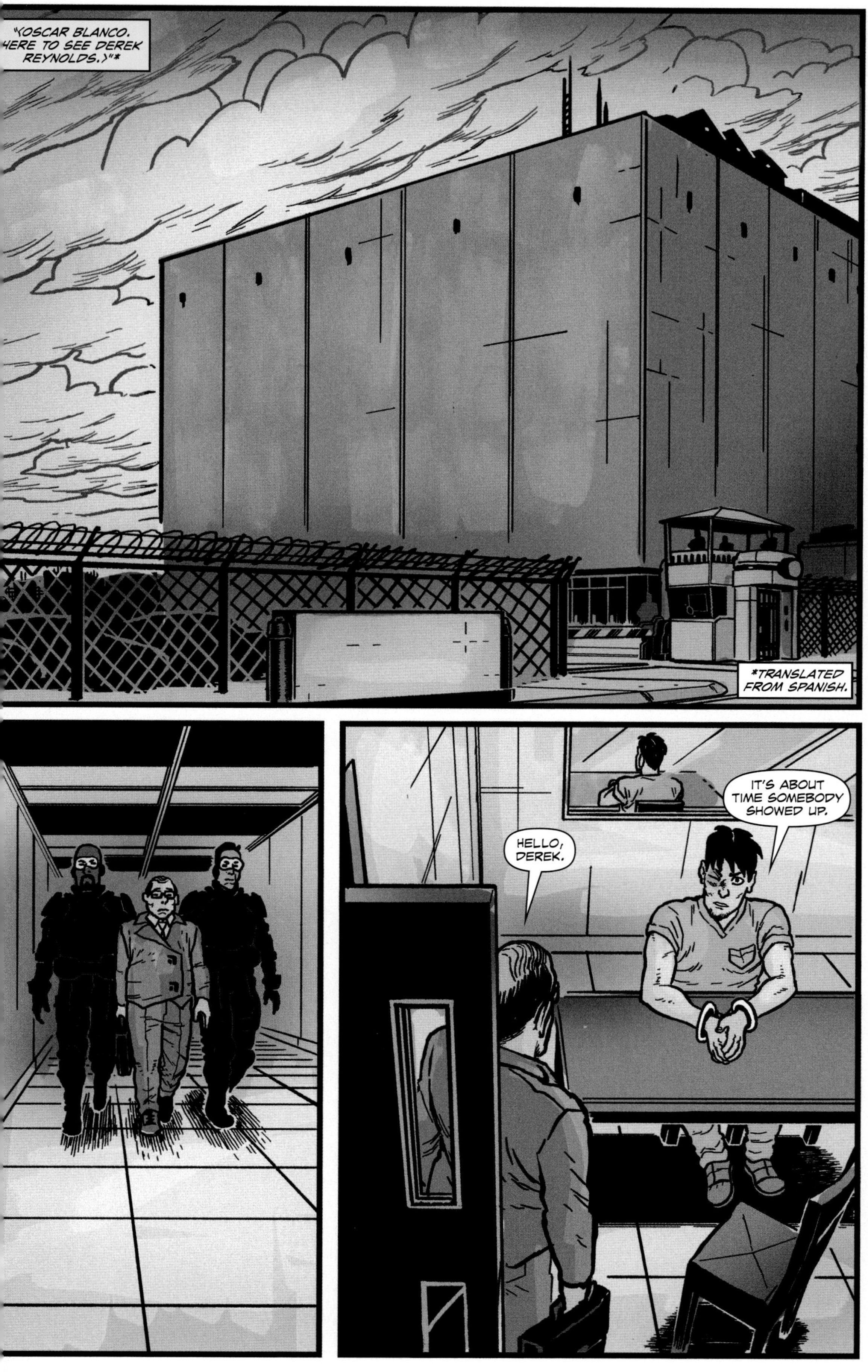
"‹OSCAR BLANCO. HERE TO SEE DEREK REYNOLDS.›"*
*TRANSLATED FROM SPANISH.
IT'S ABOUT TIME SOMEBODY SHOWED UP.
HELLO, DEREK.

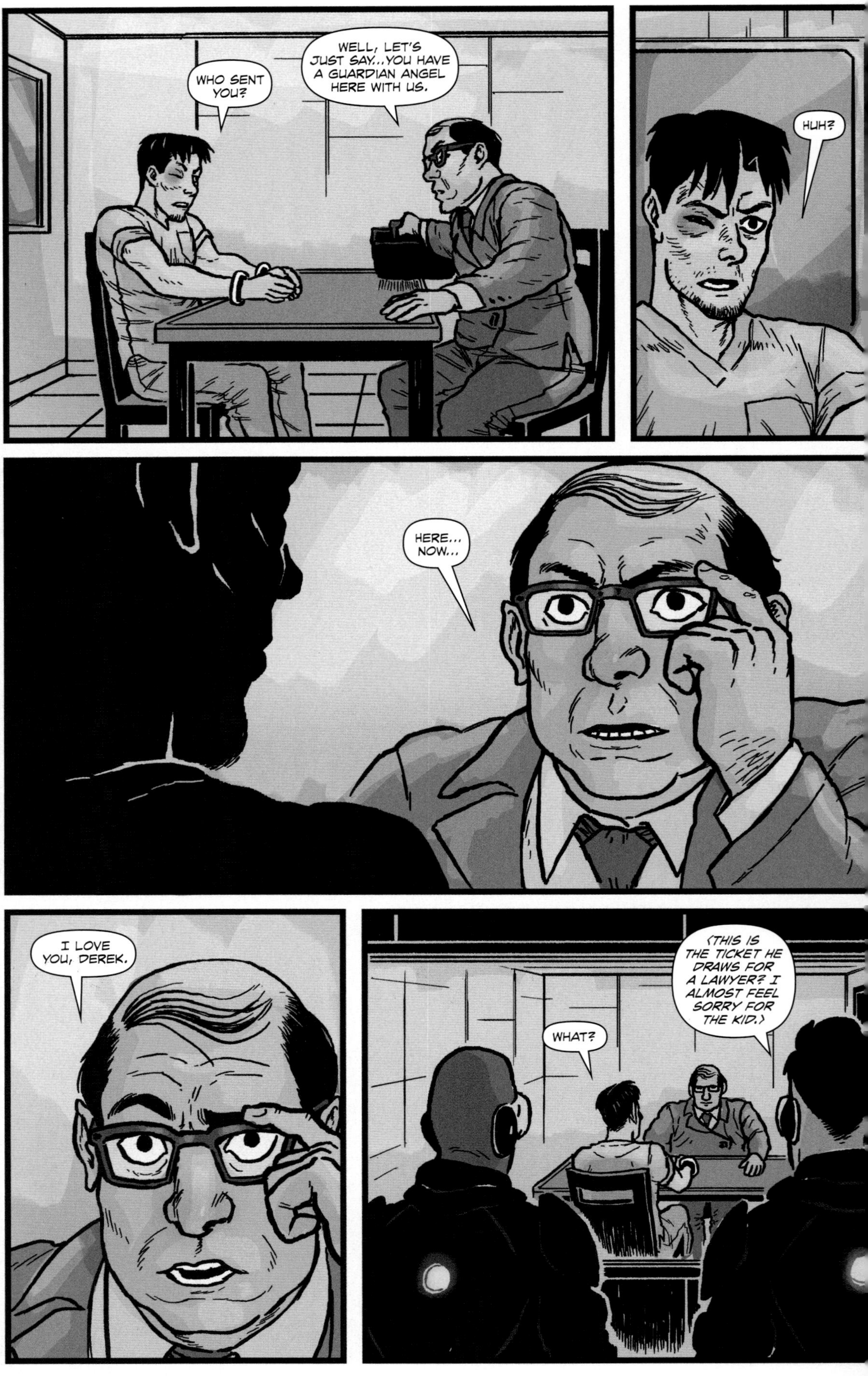
WHO SENT YOU?
WELL, LET'S JUST SAY...YOU HAVE A GUARDIAN ANGEL HERE WITH US.
HUH?
HERE... NOW...
I LOVE YOU, DEREK.
WHAT?
‹THIS IS THE TICKET HE DRAWS FOR A LAWYER? I ALMOST FEEL SORRY FOR THE KID.›

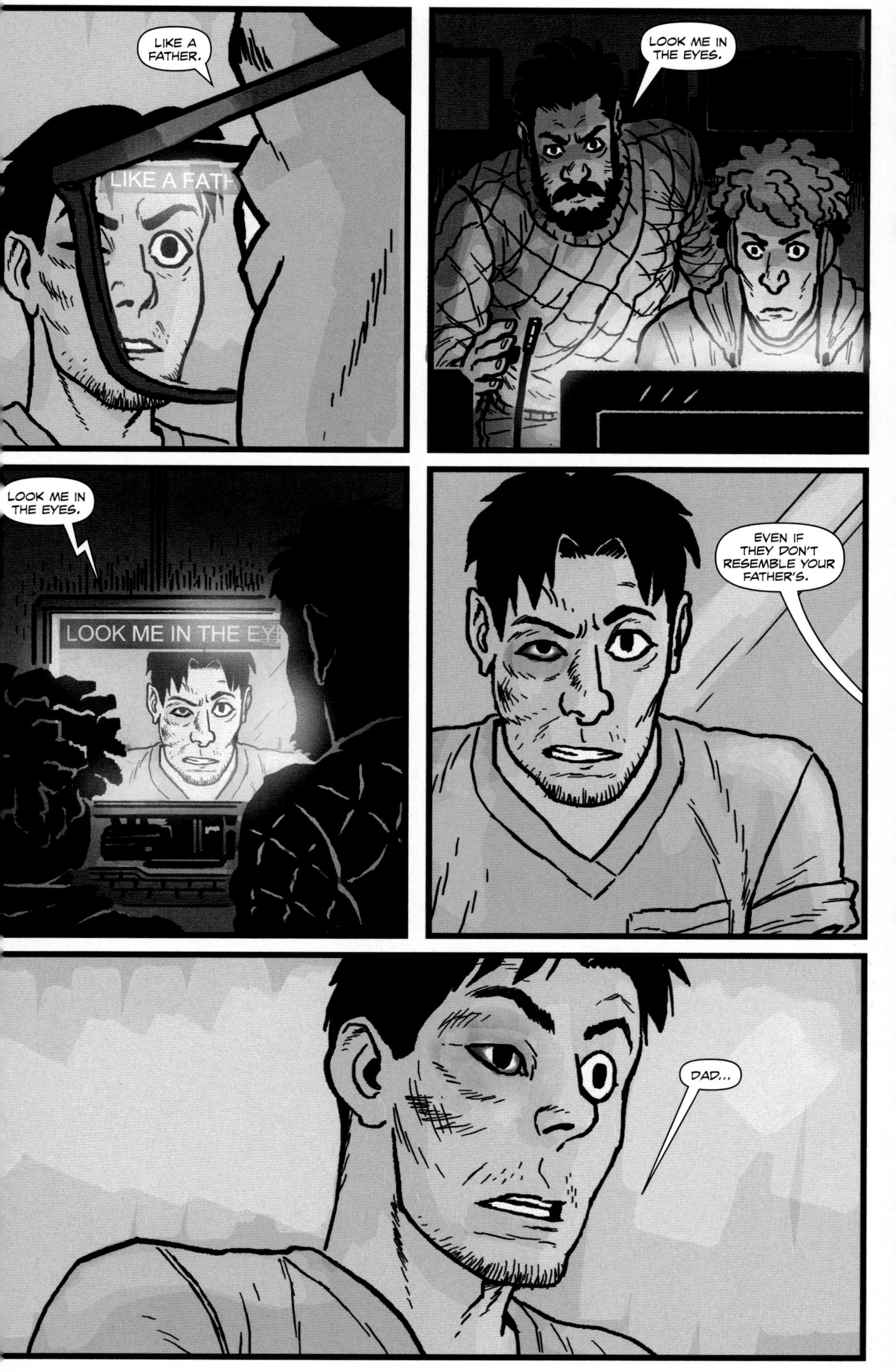
LIKE A FATHER.
LIKE A FATH
LOOK ME IN THE EYES.
LOOK ME IN THE EYES.
LOOK ME IN THE EY
EVEN IF THEY DON'T RESEMBLE YOUR FATHER'S.
DAD...

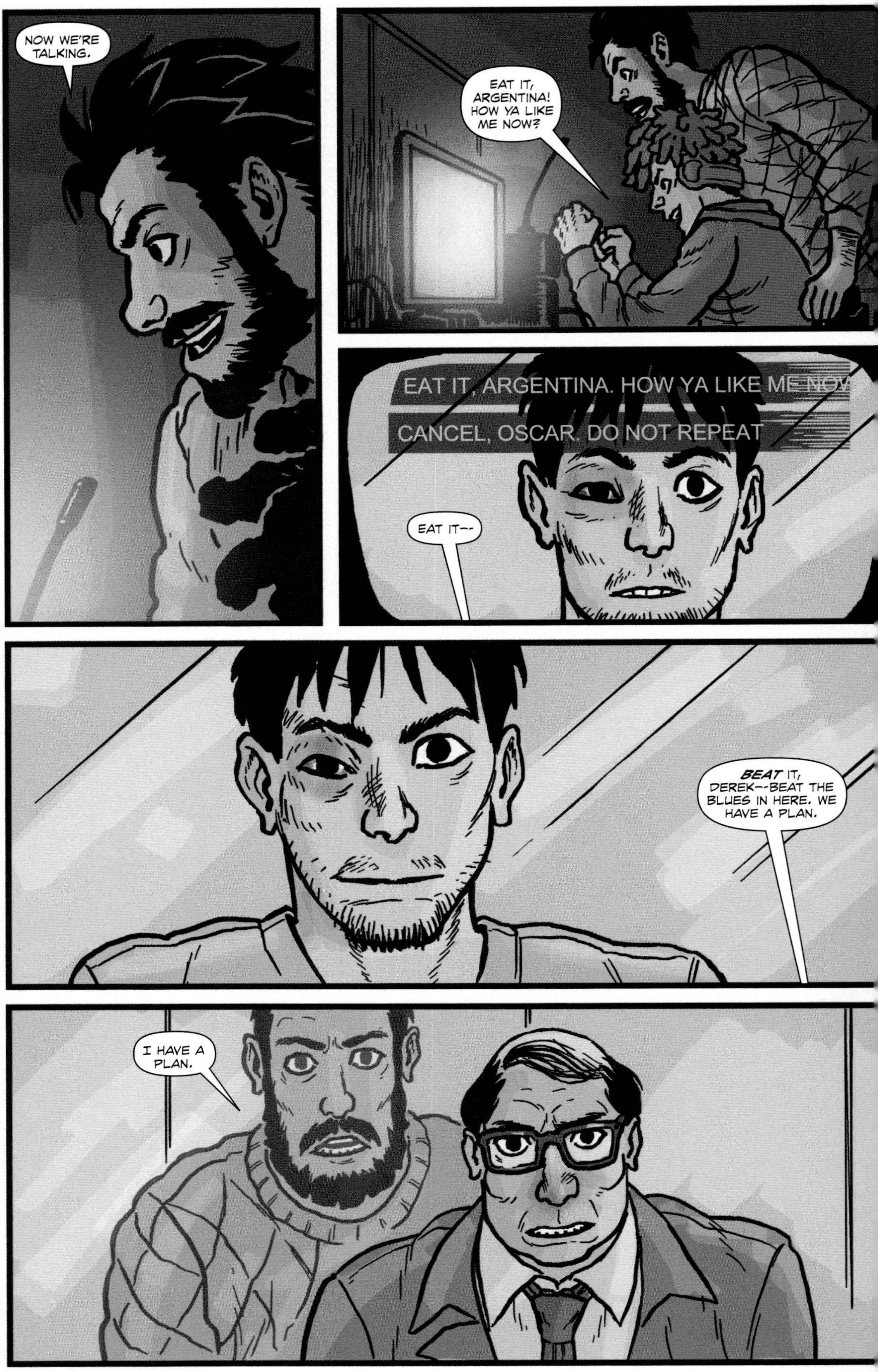
NOW WE'RE TALKING.
EAT IT, ARGENTINA! HOW YA LIKE ME NOW?
EAT IT, ARGENTINA. HOW YA LIKE ME NOW
CANCEL, OSCAR. DO NOT REPEAT
EAT IT--
BEAT IT, DEREK--BEAT THE BLUES IN HERE. WE HAVE A PLAN.
I HAVE A PLAN.

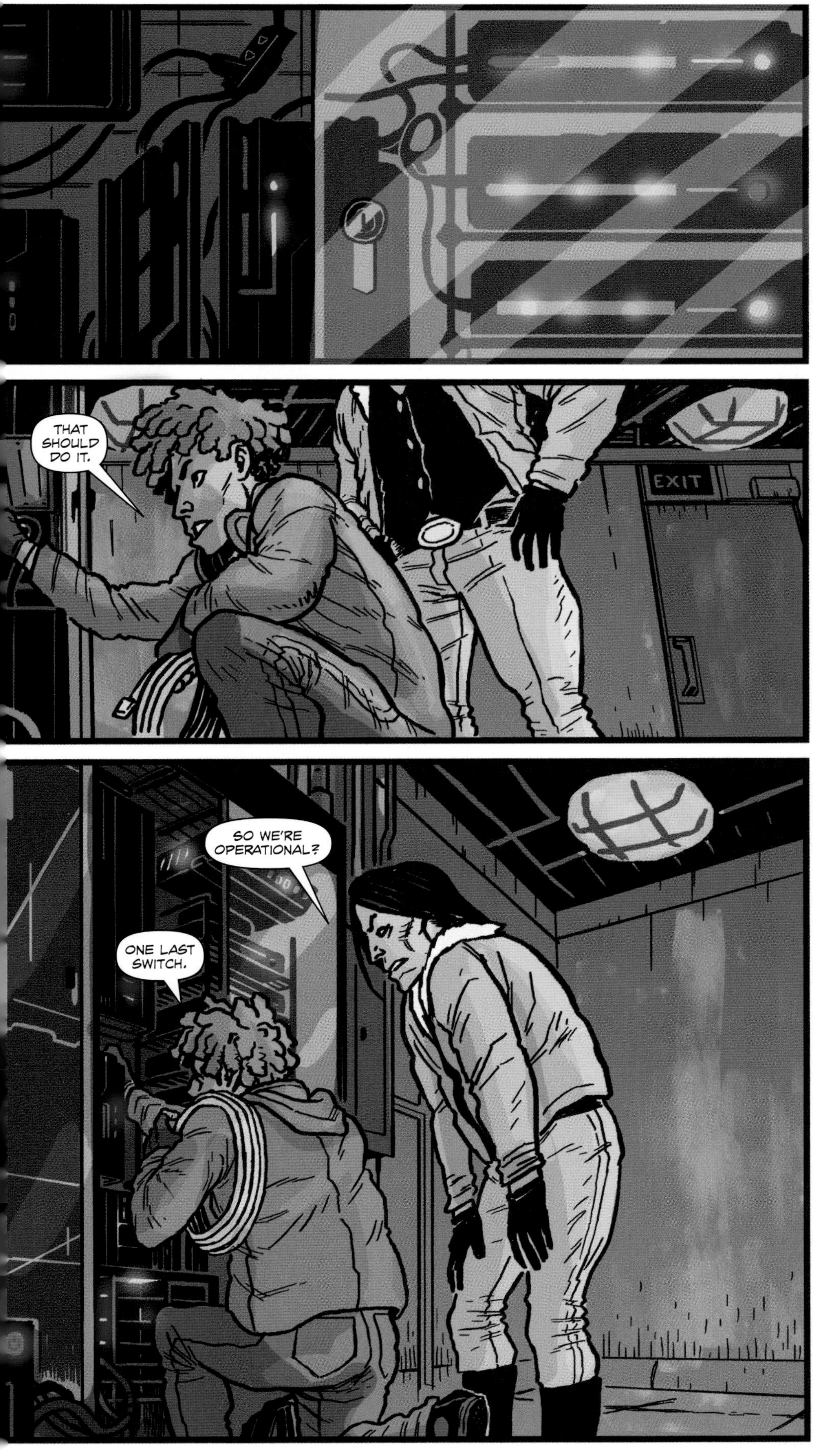
THAT SHOULD DO IT.
EXIT
SO WE'RE OPERATIONAL?
ONE LAST SWITCH.

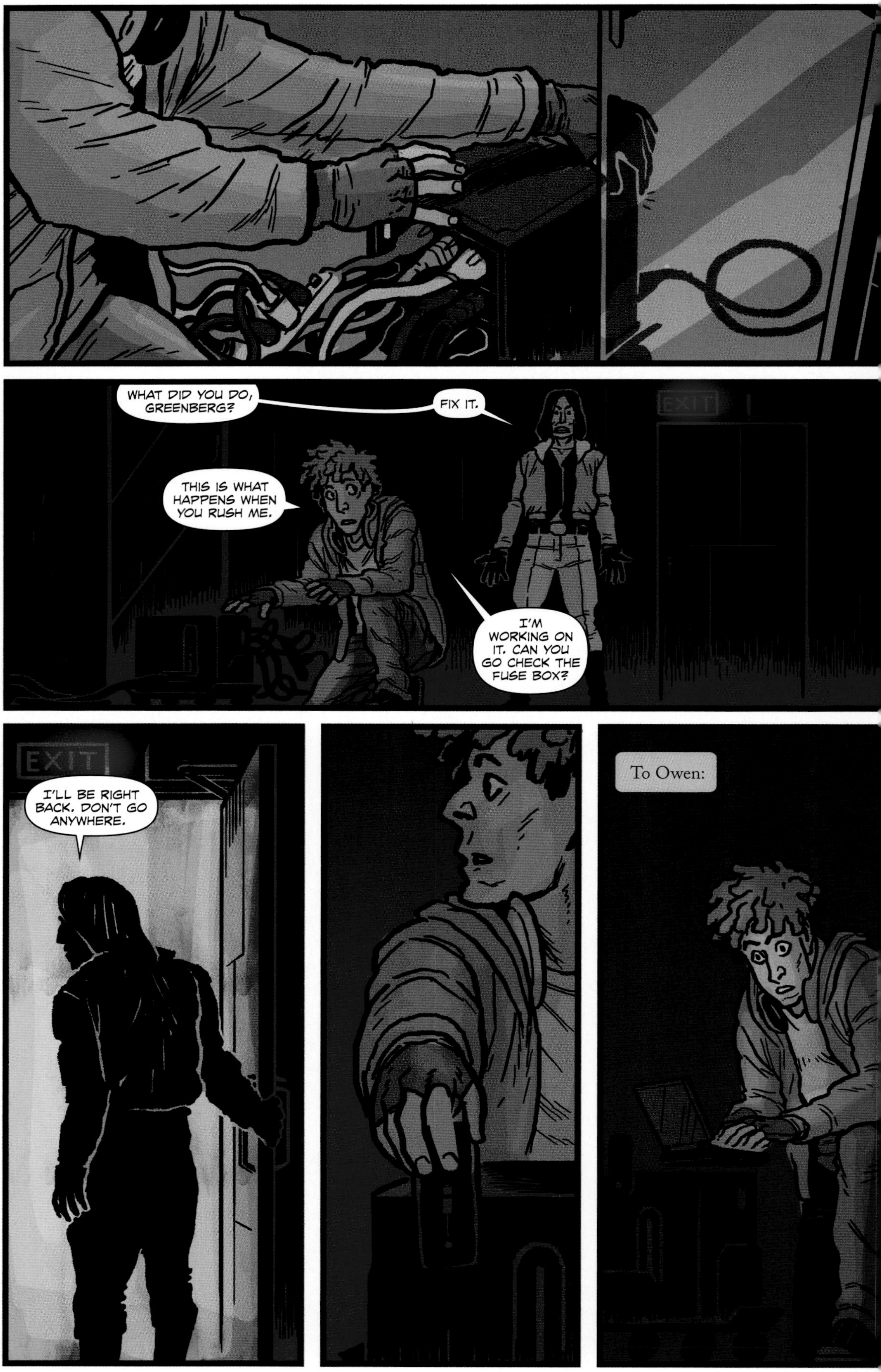
WHAT DID YOU DO, GREENBERG?
FIX IT.
THIS IS WHAT HAPPENS WHEN YOU RUSH ME.
I'M WORKING ON IT. CAN YOU GO CHECK THE FUSE BOX?
EXIT
I'LL BE RIGHT BACK. DON'T GO ANYWHERE.
To Owen:

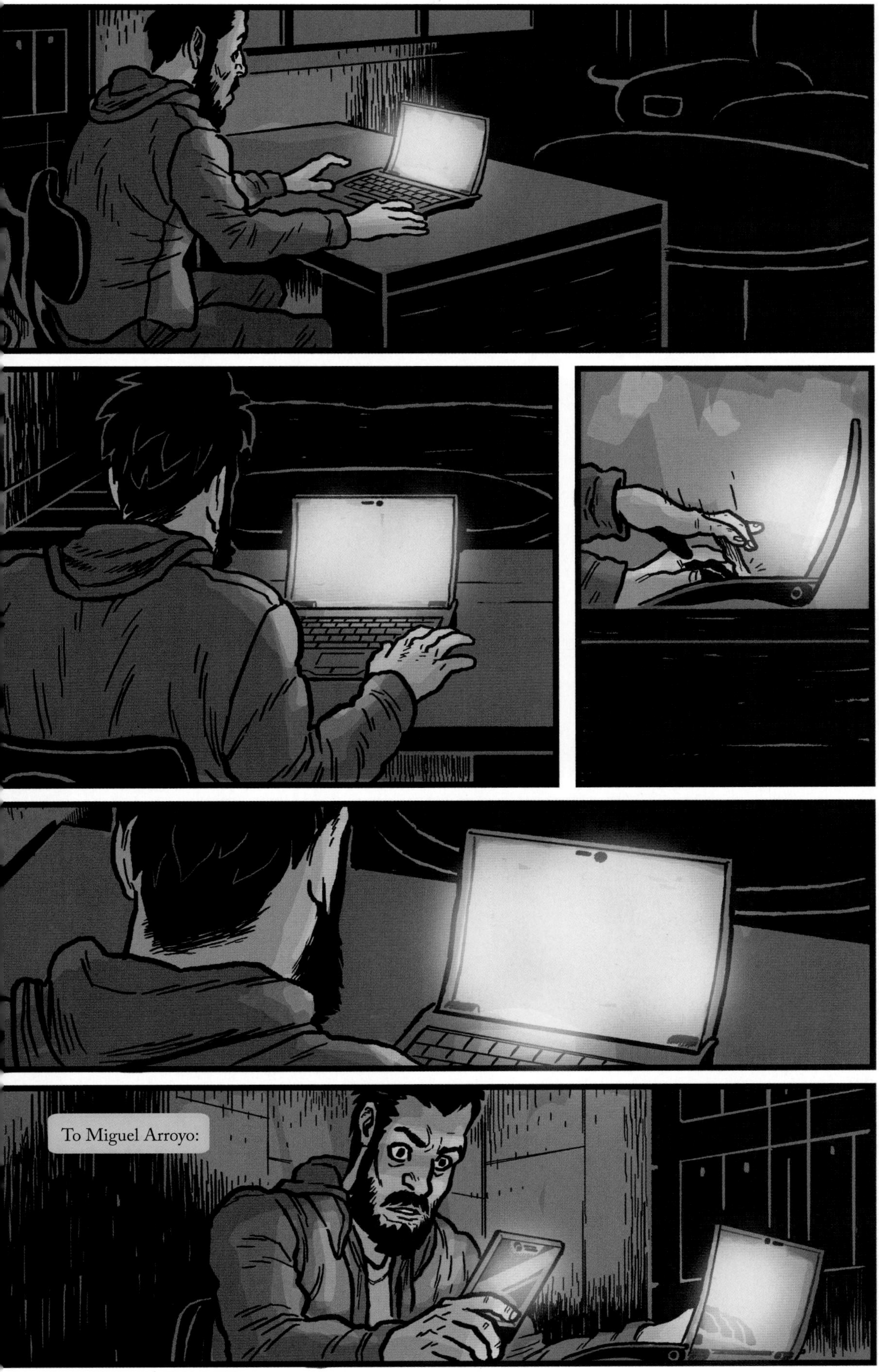
To Miguel Arroyo:

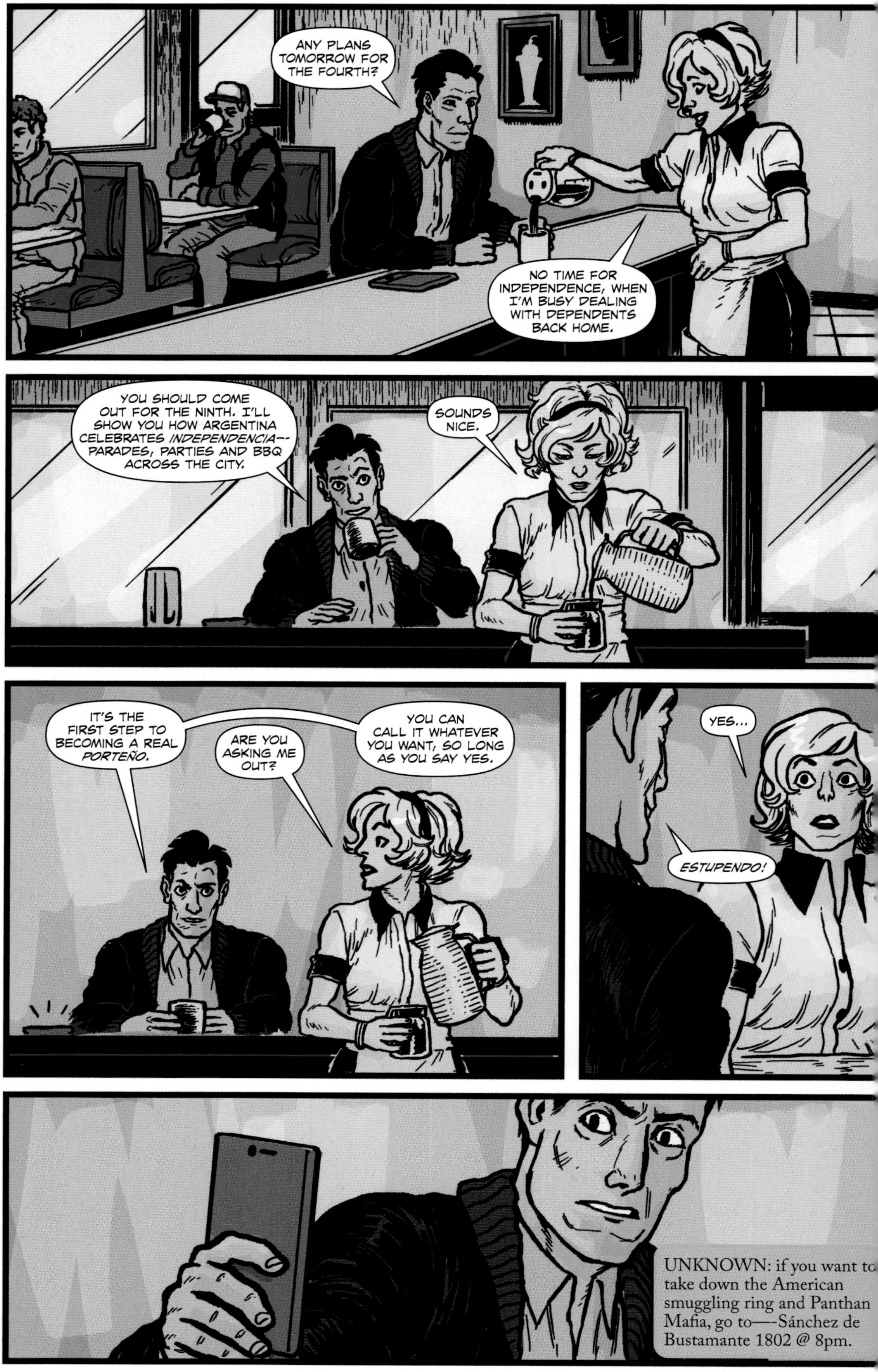

ANY PLANS TOMORROW FOR THE FOURTH?
NO TIME FOR INDEPENDENCE, WHEN I'M BUSY DEALING WITH DEPENDENTS BACK HOME.
YOU SHOULD COME OUT FOR THE NINTH. I'LL SHOW YOU HOW ARGENTINA CELEBRATES *INDEPENDENCIA*-- PARADES, PARTIES AND BBQ ACROSS THE CITY.
SOUNDS NICE.
IT'S THE FIRST STEP TO BECOMING A REAL *PORTEÑO*.
ARE YOU ASKING ME OUT?
YOU CAN CALL IT WHATEVER YOU WANT, SO LONG AS YOU SAY YES.
YES...
ESTUPENDO!
UNKNOWN: if you want to take down the American smuggling ring and Panthan Mafia, go to—-Sánchez de Bustamante 1802 @ 8pm.

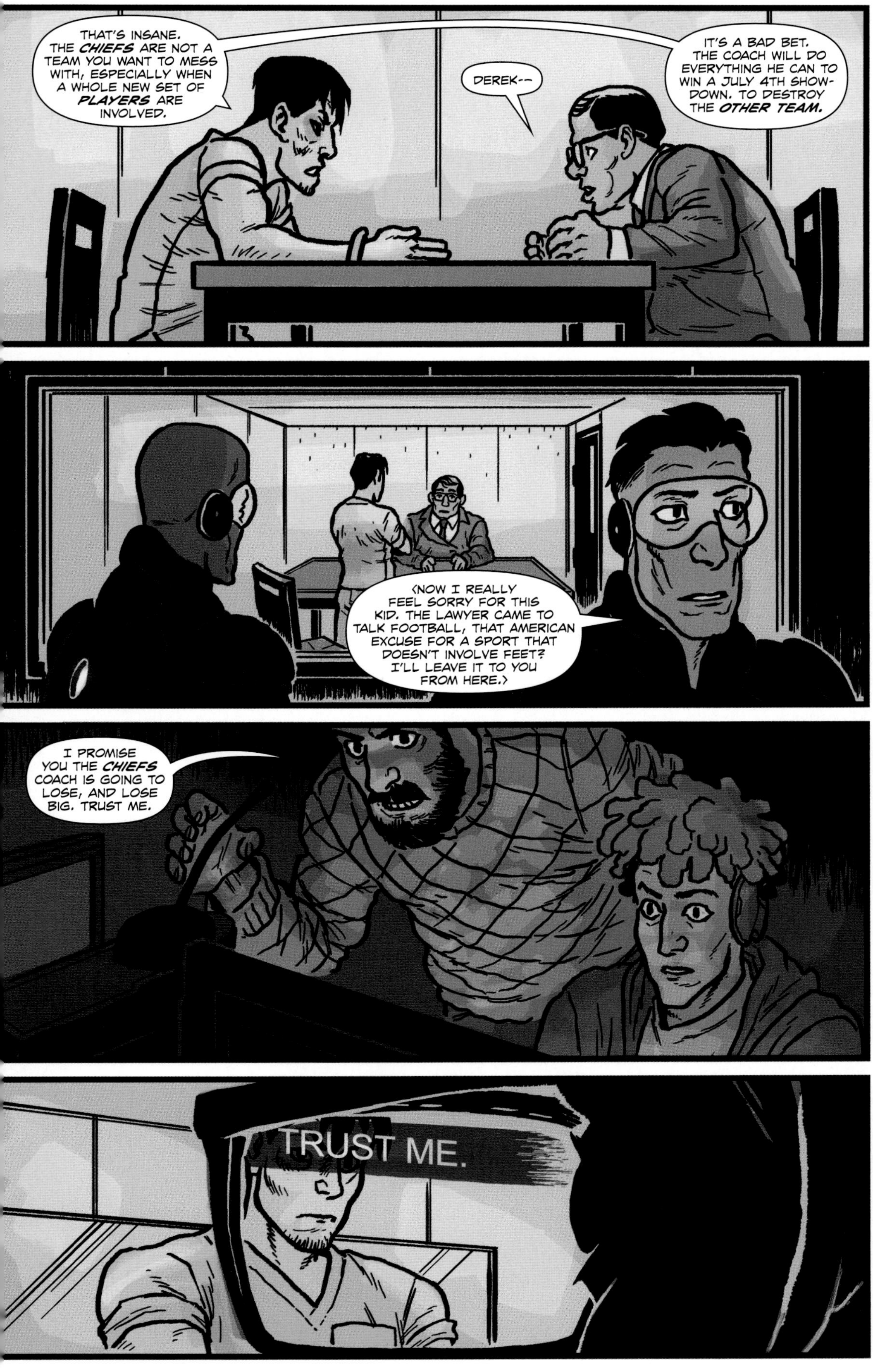
THAT'S INSANE. THE CHIEFS ARE NOT A TEAM YOU WANT TO MESS WITH, ESPECIALLY WHEN A WHOLE NEW SET OF PLAYERS ARE INVOLVED.
DEREK--
IT'S A BAD BET. THE COACH WILL DO EVERYTHING HE CAN TO WIN A JULY 4TH SHOW-DOWN. TO DESTROY THE OTHER TEAM.
<NOW I REALLY FEEL SORRY FOR THIS KID. THE LAWYER CAME TO TALK FOOTBALL, THAT AMERICAN EXCUSE FOR A SPORT THAT DOESN'T INVOLVE FEET? I'LL LEAVE IT TO YOU FROM HERE.>
I PROMISE YOU THE CHIEFS COACH IS GOING TO LOSE, AND LOSE BIG. TRUST ME.
TRUST ME.

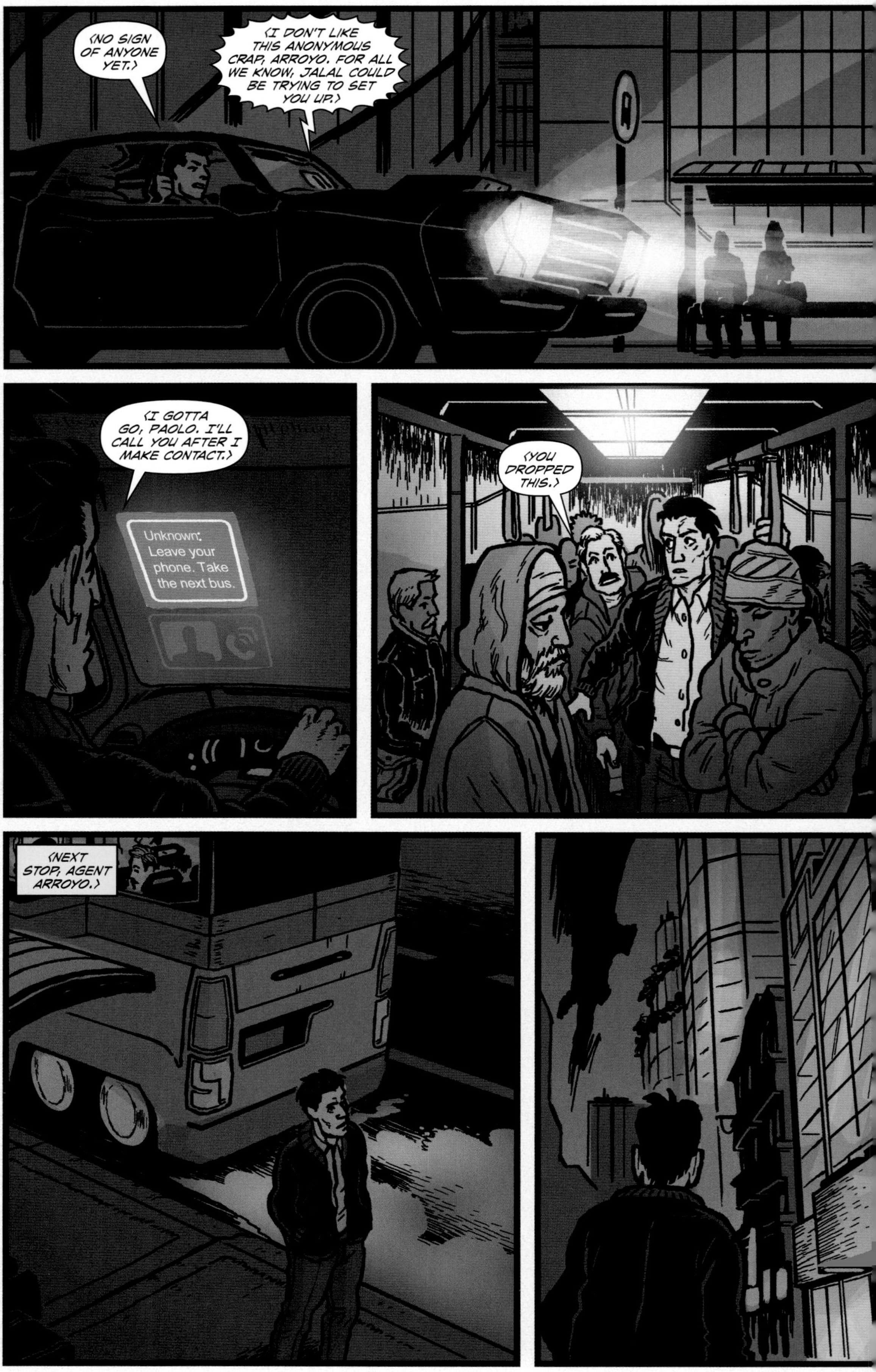

‹NO SIGN OF ANYONE YET.›
‹I DON'T LIKE THIS ANONYMOUS CRAP, ARROYO. FOR ALL WE KNOW, JALAL COULD BE TRYING TO SET YOU UP.›
‹I GOTTA GO, PAOLO. I'LL CALL YOU AFTER I MAKE CONTACT.›
Unknown: Leave your phone. Take the next bus.
‹YOU DROPPED THIS.›
‹NEXT STOP, AGENT ARROYO.›

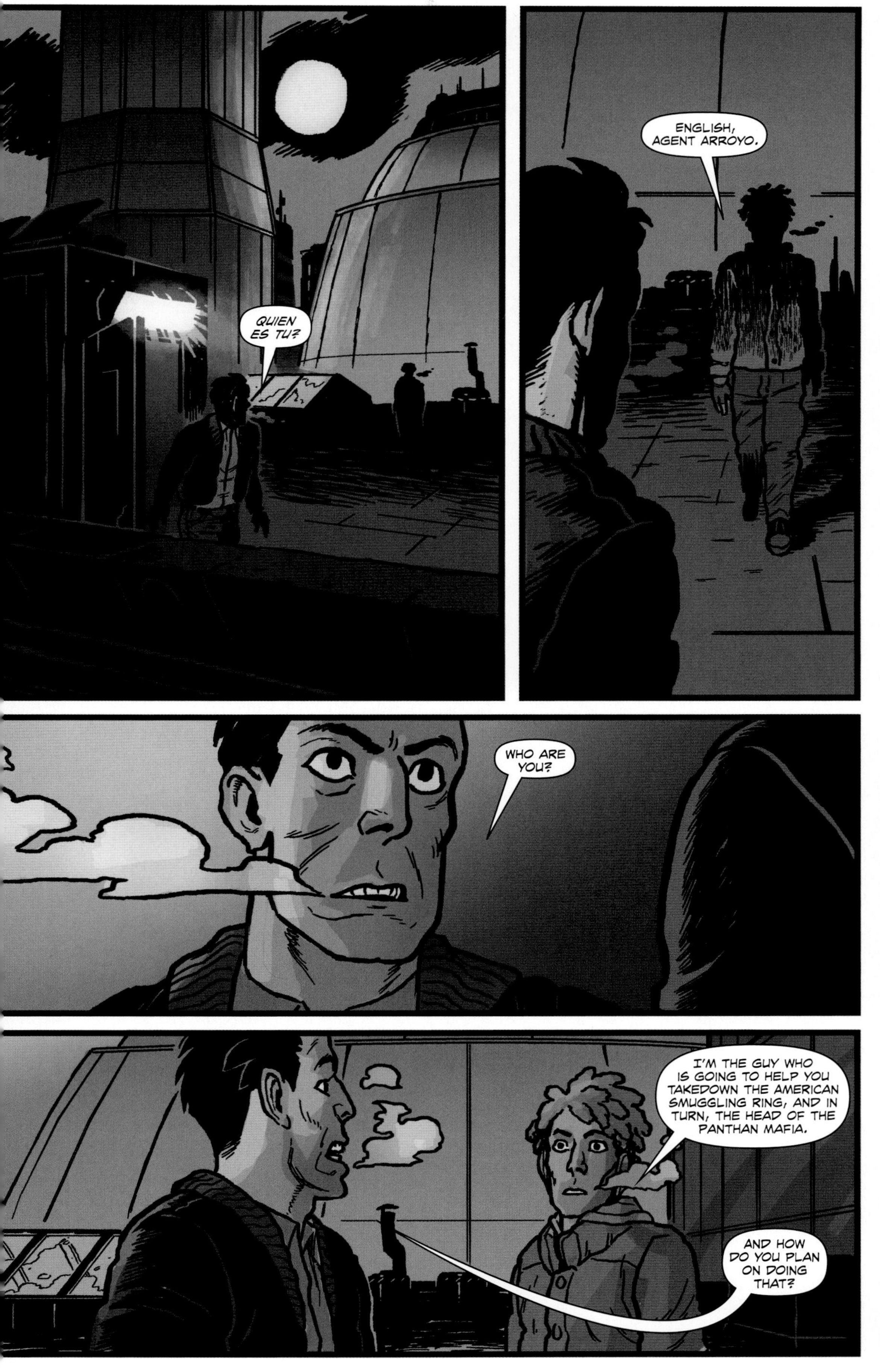
QUIEN ES TU?
ENGLISH, AGENT ARROYO.
WHO ARE YOU?
I'M THE GUY WHO IS GOING TO HELP YOU TAKEDOWN THE AMERICAN SMUGGLING RING, AND IN TURN, THE HEAD OF THE PANTHAN MAFIA.
AND HOW DO YOU PLAN ON DOING THAT?

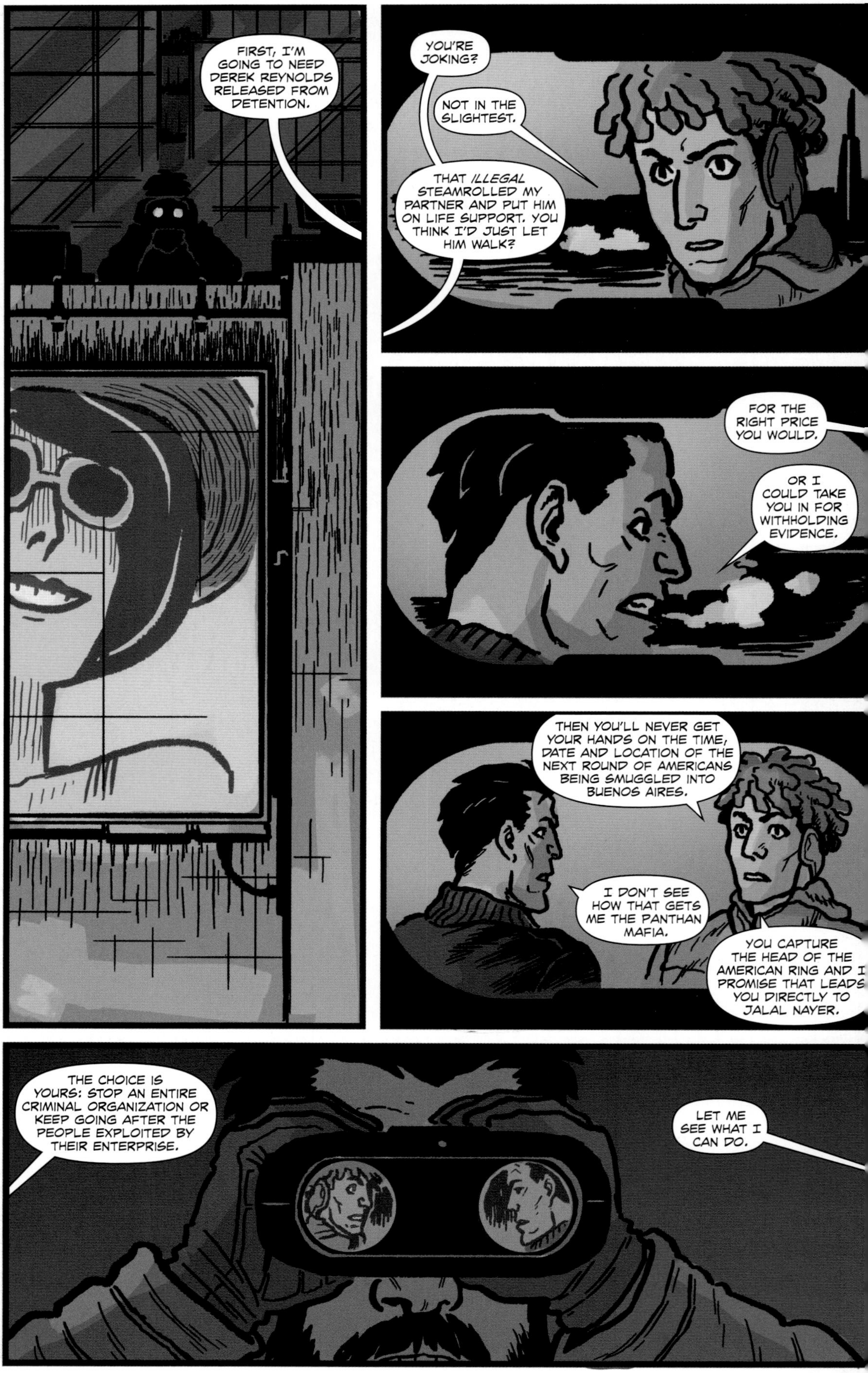
FIRST, I'M GOING TO NEED DEREK REYNOLDS RELEASED FROM DETENTION.
YOU'RE JOKING?
NOT IN THE SLIGHTEST.
THAT ILLEGAL STEAMROLLED MY PARTNER AND PUT HIM ON LIFE SUPPORT. YOU THINK I'D JUST LET HIM WALK?
FOR THE RIGHT PRICE YOU WOULD.
OR I COULD TAKE YOU IN FOR WITHHOLDING EVIDENCE.
THEN YOU'LL NEVER GET YOUR HANDS ON THE TIME, DATE AND LOCATION OF THE NEXT ROUND OF AMERICANS BEING SMUGGLED INTO BUENOS AIRES.
I DON'T SEE HOW THAT GETS ME THE PANTHAN MAFIA.
YOU CAPTURE THE HEAD OF THE AMERICAN RING AND I PROMISE THAT LEADS YOU DIRECTLY TO JALAL NAYER.
THE CHOICE IS YOURS: STOP AN ENTIRE CRIMINAL ORGANIZATION OR KEEP GOING AFTER THE PEOPLE EXPLOITED BY THEIR ENTERPRISE.
LET ME SEE WHAT I CAN DO.

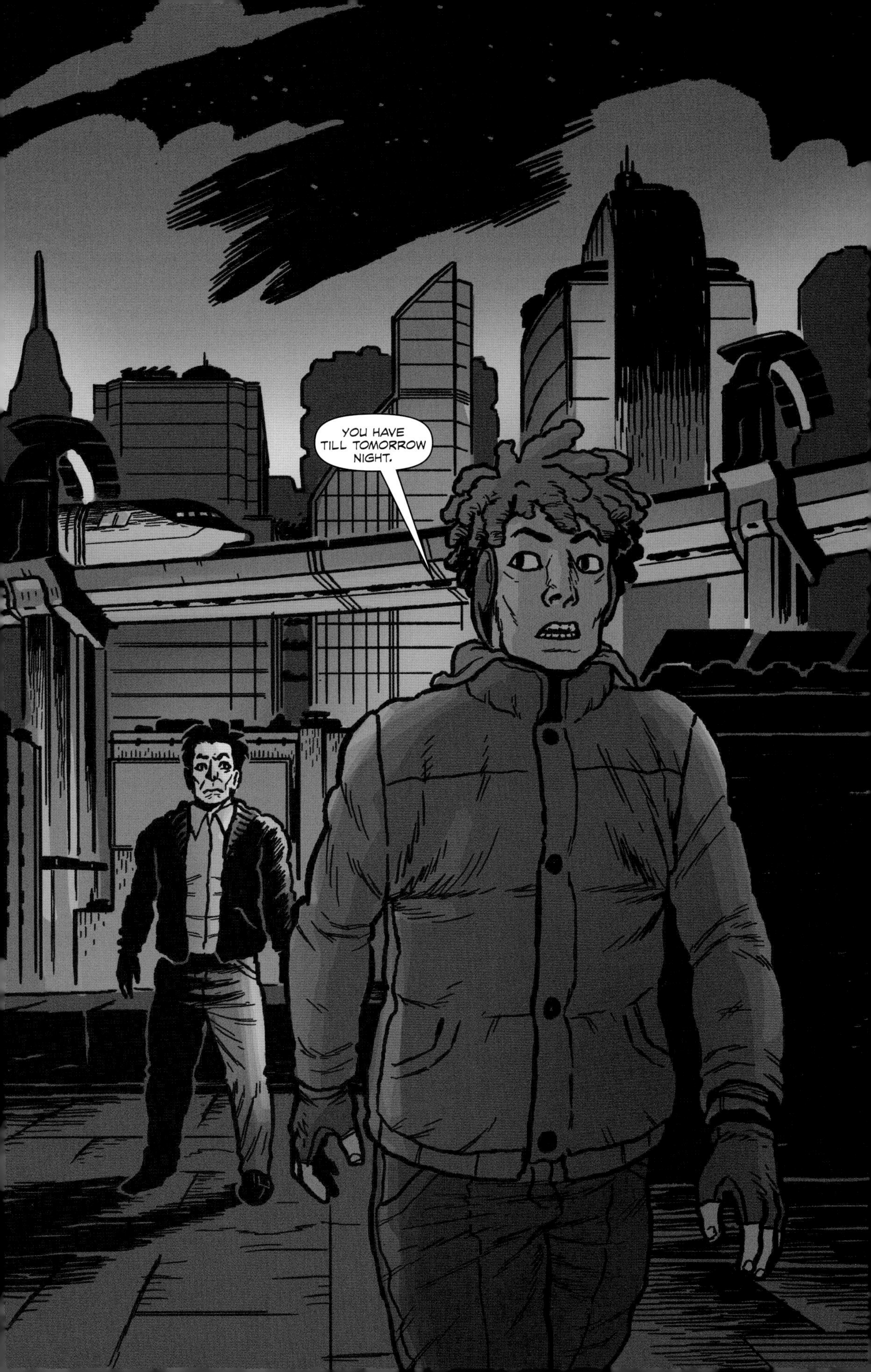
YOU HAVE TILL TOMORROW NIGHT.

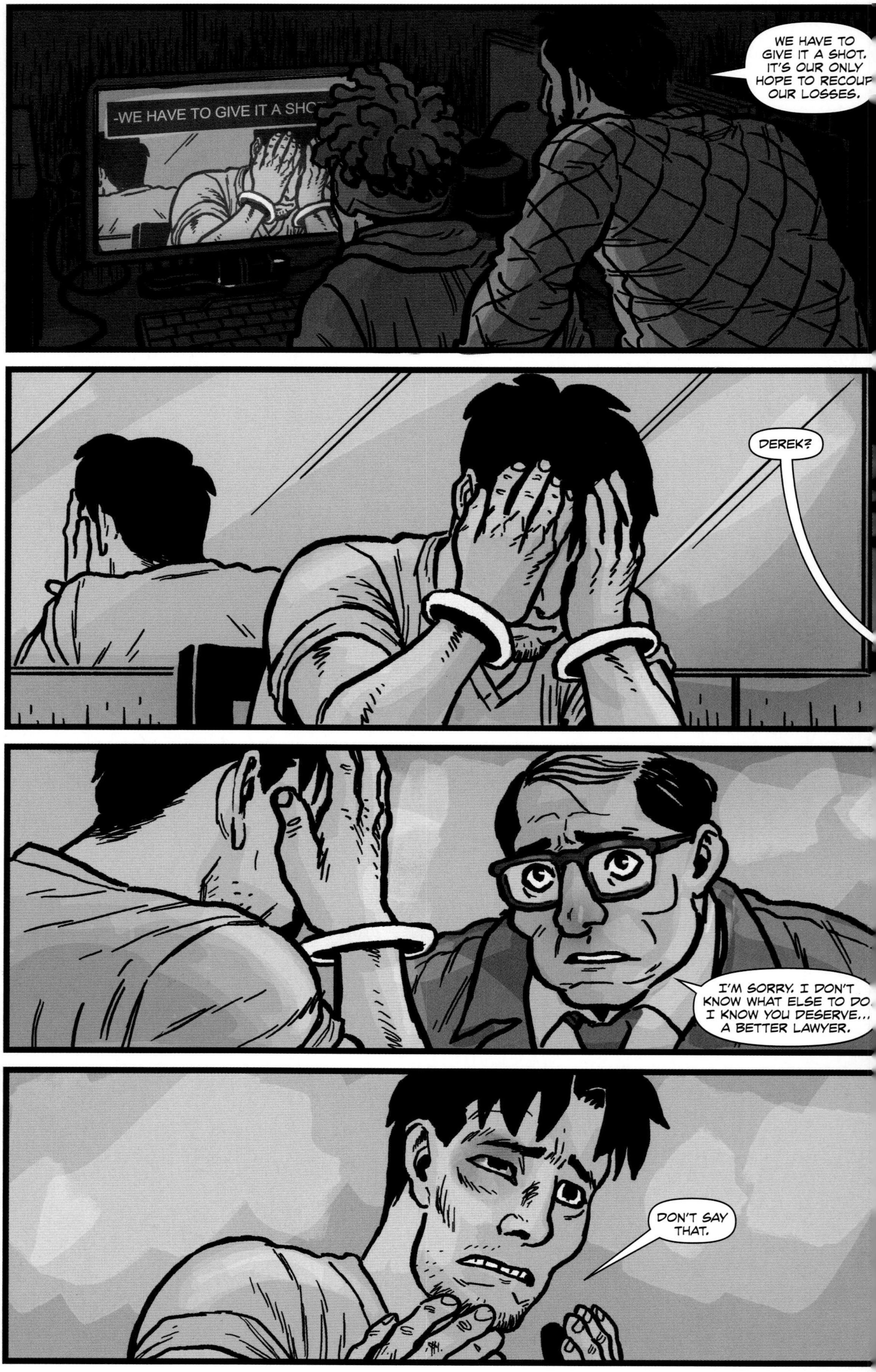
-WE HAVE TO GIVE IT A SHO
WE HAVE TO GIVE IT A SHOT. IT'S OUR ONLY HOPE TO RECOUP OUR LOSSES.
DEREK?
I'M SORRY. I DON'T KNOW WHAT ELSE TO DO. I KNOW YOU DESERVE... A BETTER LAWYER.
DON'T SAY THAT.

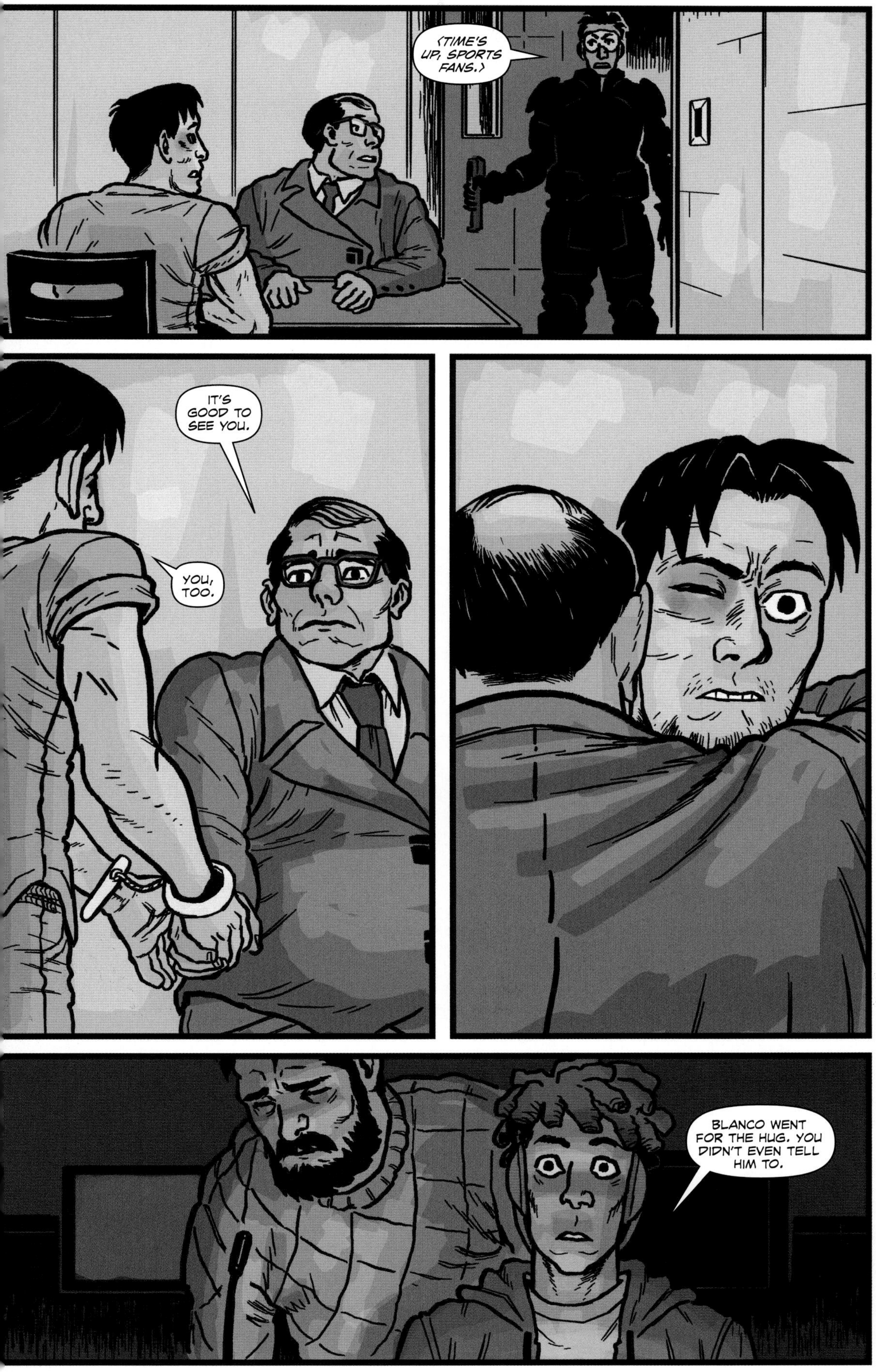
<TIME'S UP, SPORTS FANS.>
IT'S GOOD TO SEE YOU.
YOU, TOO.
BLANCO WENT FOR THE HUG. YOU DIDN'T EVEN TELL HIM TO.

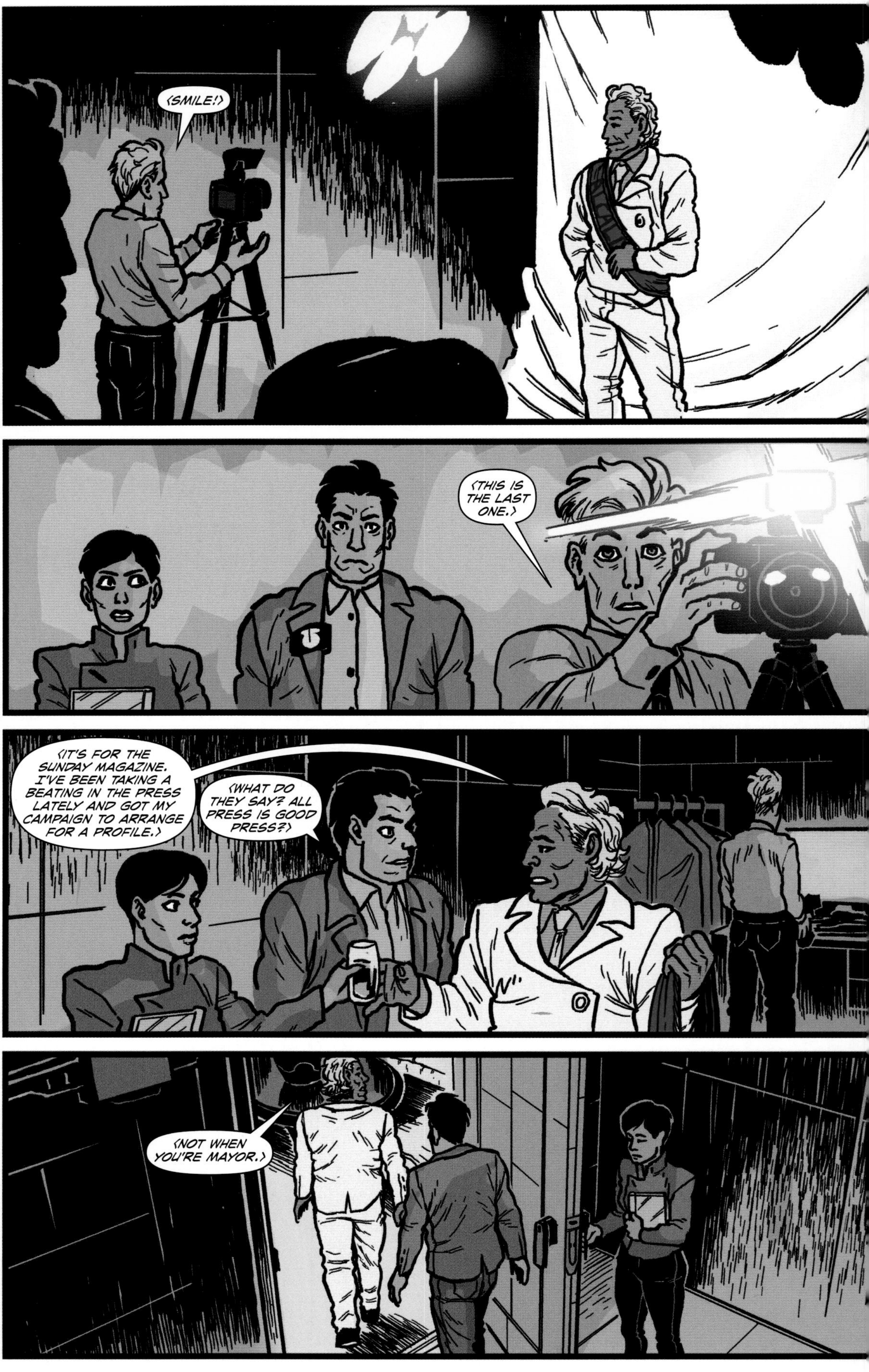
⟨SMILE!⟩
⟨THIS IS THE LAST ONE.⟩
⟨IT'S FOR THE SUNDAY MAGAZINE. I'VE BEEN TAKING A BEATING IN THE PRESS LATELY AND GOT MY CAMPAIGN TO ARRANGE FOR A PROFILE.⟩
⟨WHAT DO THEY SAY? ALL PRESS IS GOOD PRESS?⟩
⟨NOT WHEN YOU'RE MAYOR.⟩

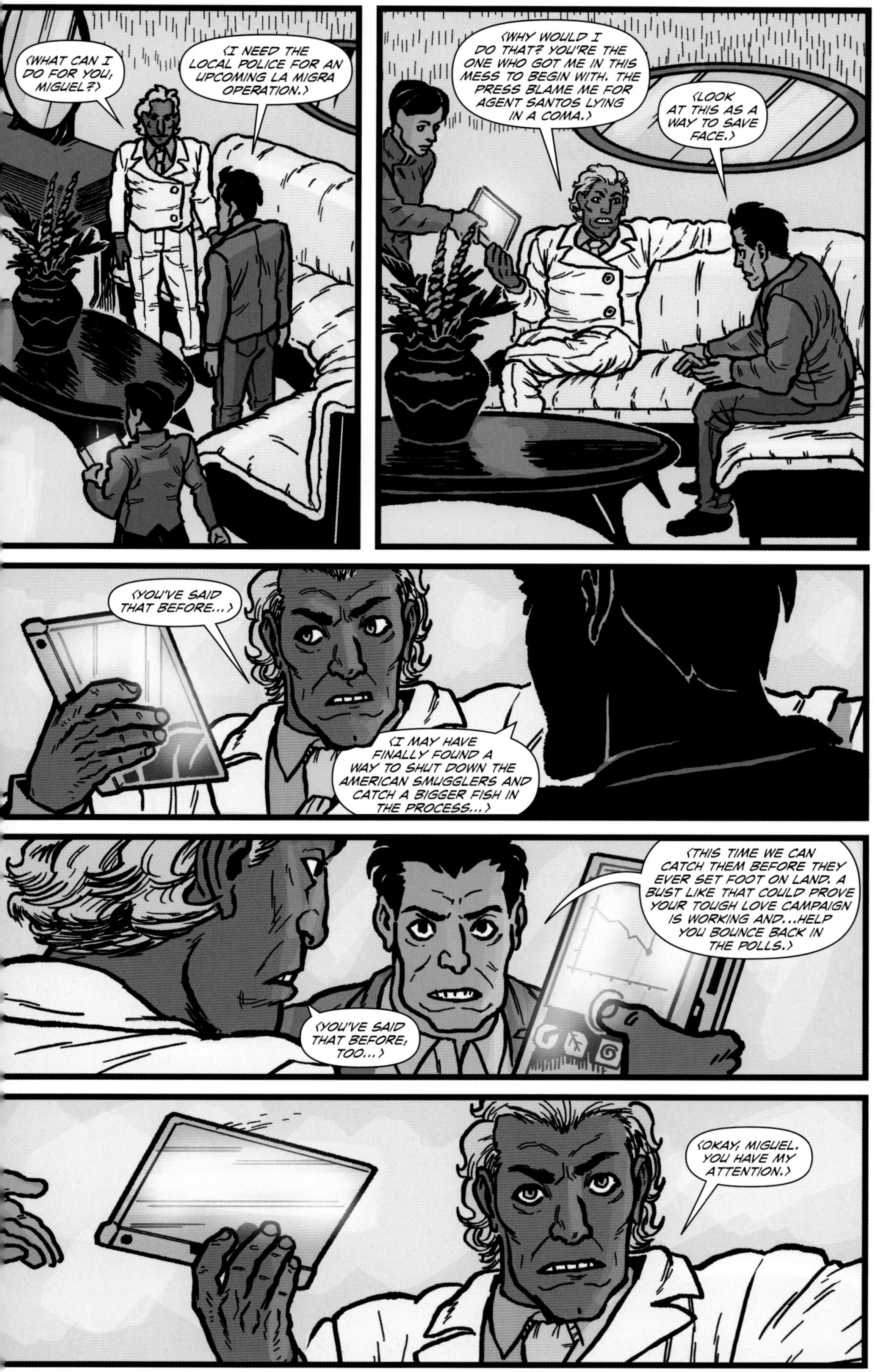
‹WHAT CAN I DO FOR YOU, MIGUEL?›
‹I NEED THE LOCAL POLICE FOR AN UPCOMING LA MIGRA OPERATION.›
‹WHY WOULD I DO THAT? YOU'RE THE ONE WHO GOT ME IN THIS MESS TO BEGIN WITH. THE PRESS BLAME ME FOR AGENT SANTOS LYING IN A COMA.›
‹LOOK AT THIS AS A WAY TO SAVE FACE.›
‹YOU'VE SAID THAT BEFORE...›
‹I MAY HAVE FINALLY FOUND A WAY TO SHUT DOWN THE AMERICAN SMUGGLERS AND CATCH A BIGGER FISH IN THE PROCESS...›
‹THIS TIME WE CAN CATCH THEM BEFORE THEY EVER SET FOOT ON LAND. A BUST LIKE THAT COULD PROVE YOUR TOUGH LOVE CAMPAIGN IS WORKING AND...HELP YOU BOUNCE BACK IN THE POLLS.›
‹YOU'VE SAID THAT BEFORE, TOO...›
‹OKAY, MIGUEL. YOU HAVE MY ATTENTION.›

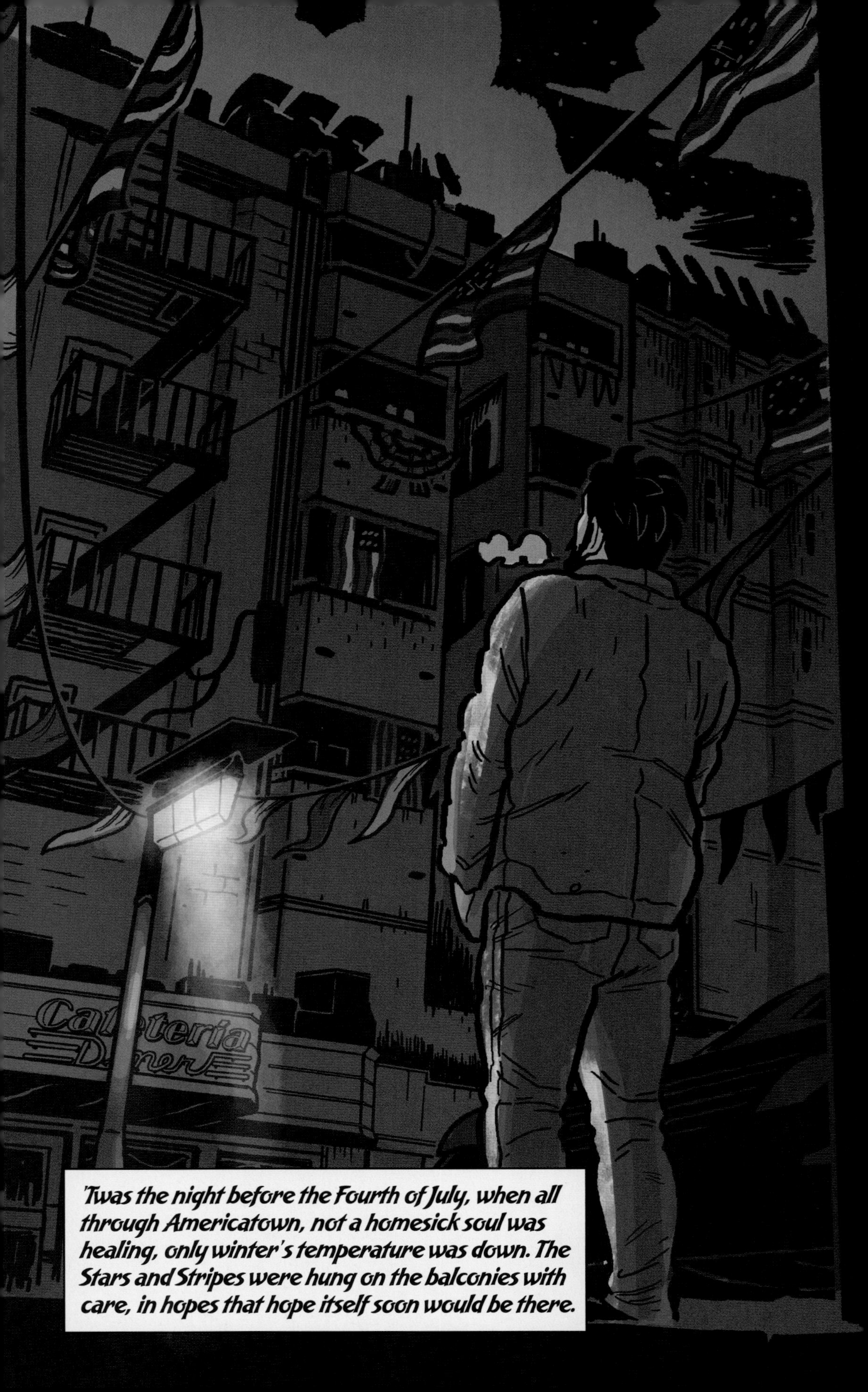
'Twas the night before the Fourth of July, when all through Americatown, not a homesick soul was healing, only winter's temperature was down. The Stars and Stripes were hung on the balconies with care, in hopes that hope itself soon would be there.

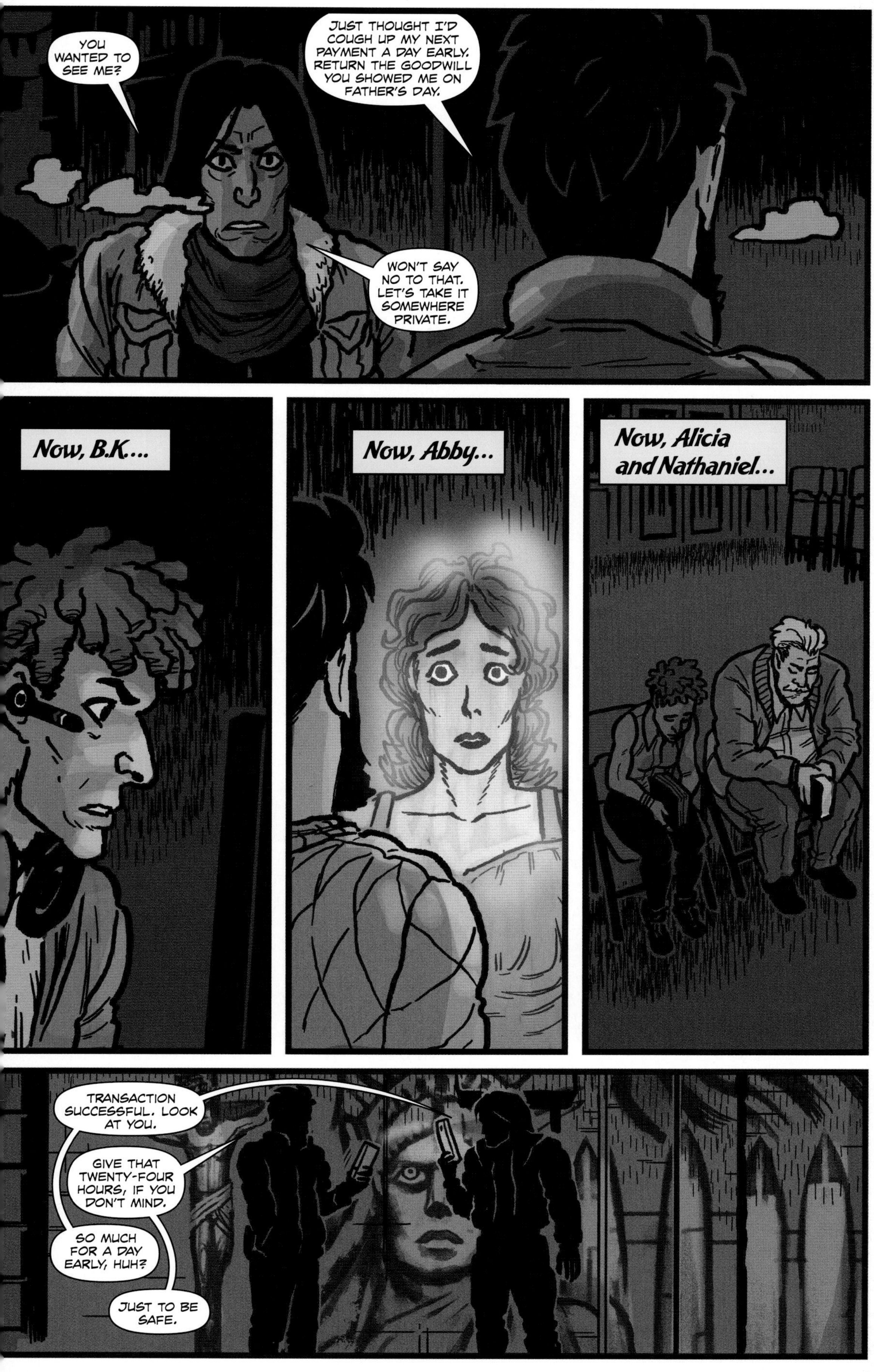
YOU WANTED TO SEE ME?
JUST THOUGHT I'D COUGH UP MY NEXT PAYMENT A DAY EARLY. RETURN THE GOODWILL YOU SHOWED ME ON FATHER'S DAY.
WON'T SAY NO TO THAT. LET'S TAKE IT SOMEWHERE PRIVATE.
Now, B.K....
Now, Abby...
Now, Alicia and Nathaniel...
TRANSACTION SUCCESSFUL. LOOK AT YOU.
GIVE THAT TWENTY-FOUR HOURS, IF YOU DON'T MIND.
SO MUCH FOR A DAY EARLY, HUH?
JUST TO BE SAFE.

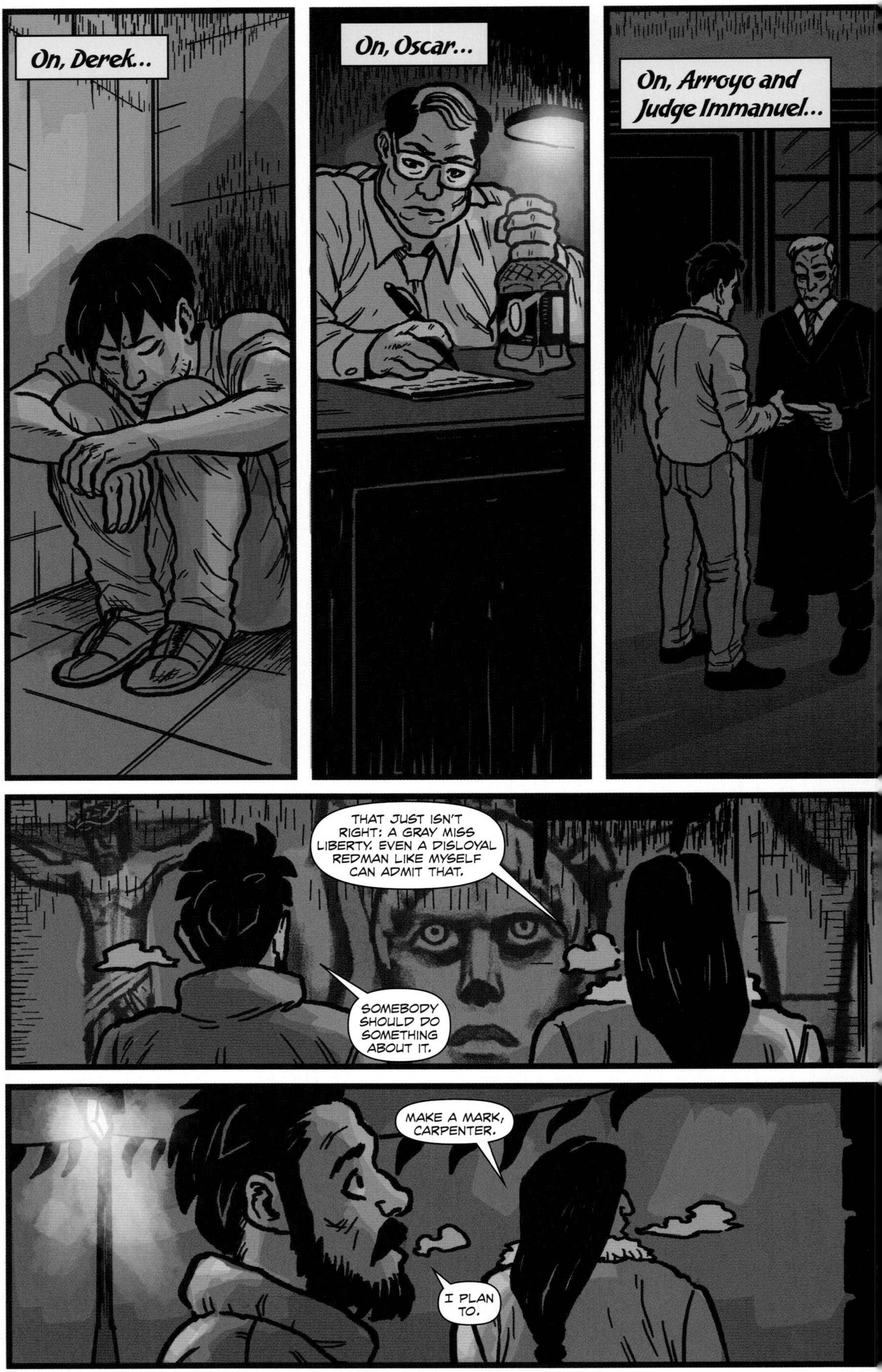
On, Derek...
On, Oscar...
On, Arroyo and Judge Immanuel...
THAT JUST ISN'T RIGHT: A GRAY MISS LIBERTY. EVEN A DISLOYAL REDMAN LIKE MYSELF CAN ADMIT THAT.
SOMEBODY SHOULD DO SOMETHING ABOUT IT.
MAKE A MARK, CARPENTER.
I PLAN TO.

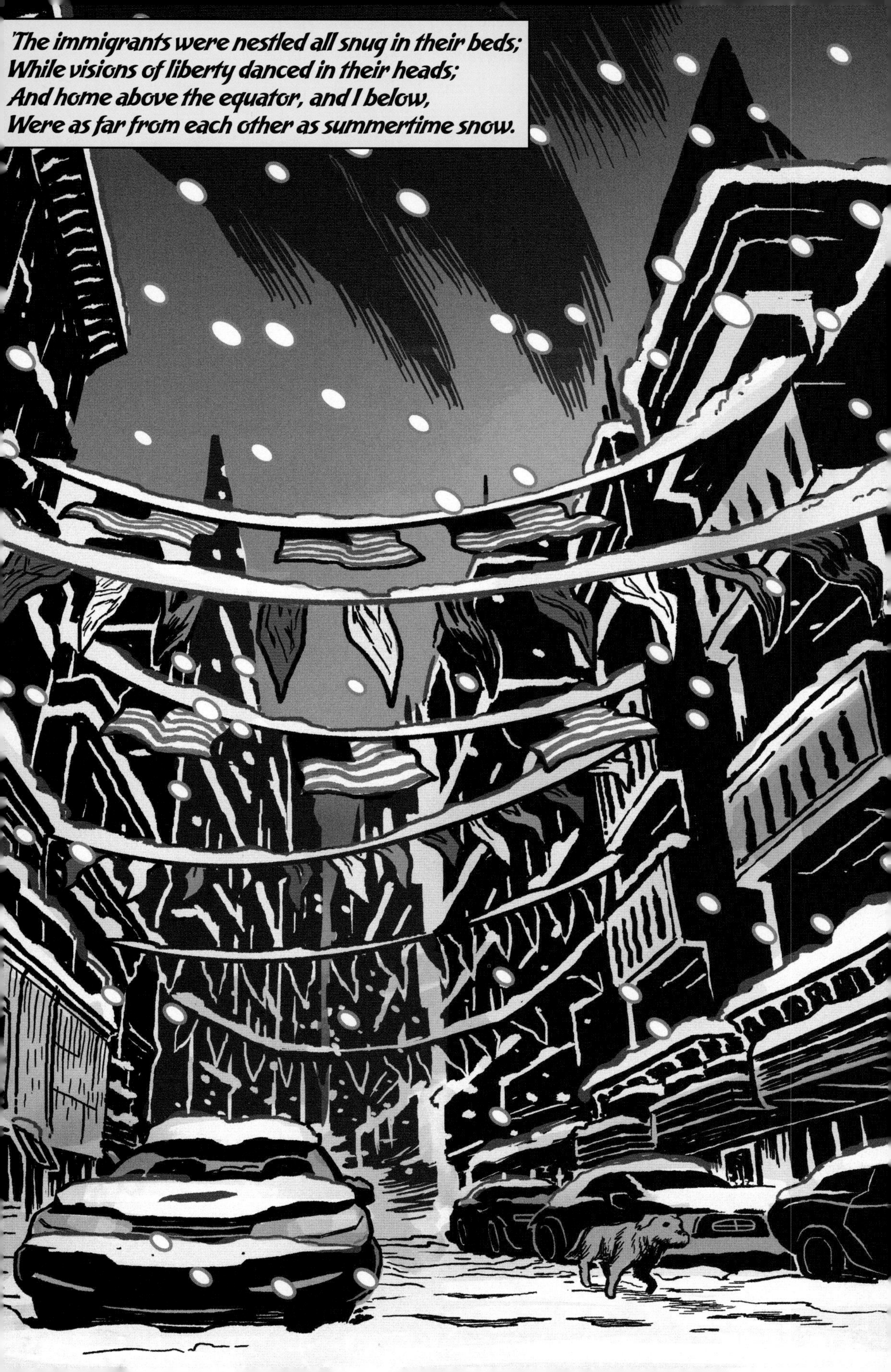
'The immigrants were nestled all snug in their beds;
While visions of liberty danced in their heads;
And home above the equator, and I below,
Were as far from each other as summertime snow.

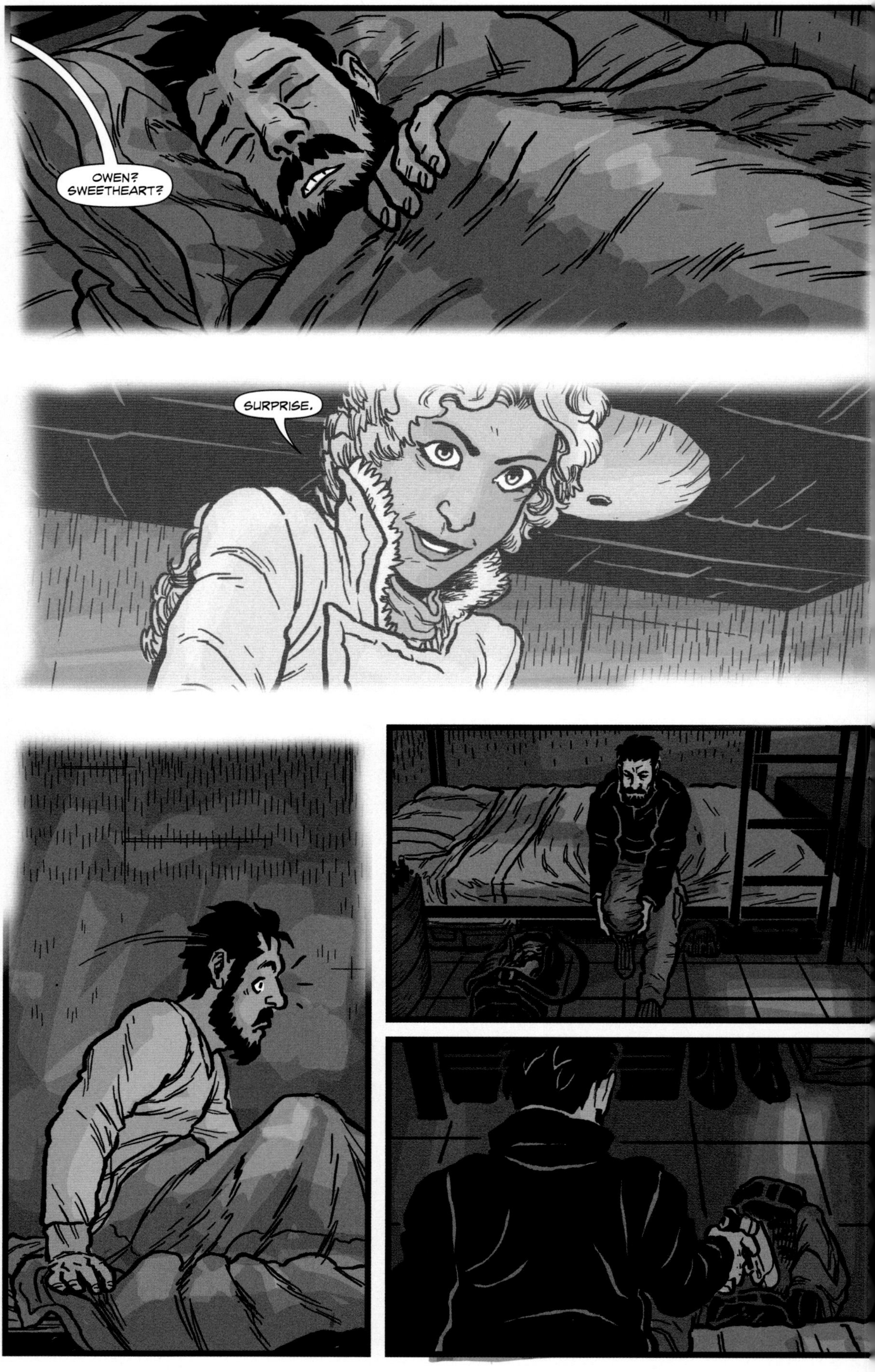
OWEN? SWEETHEART?
SURPRISE.

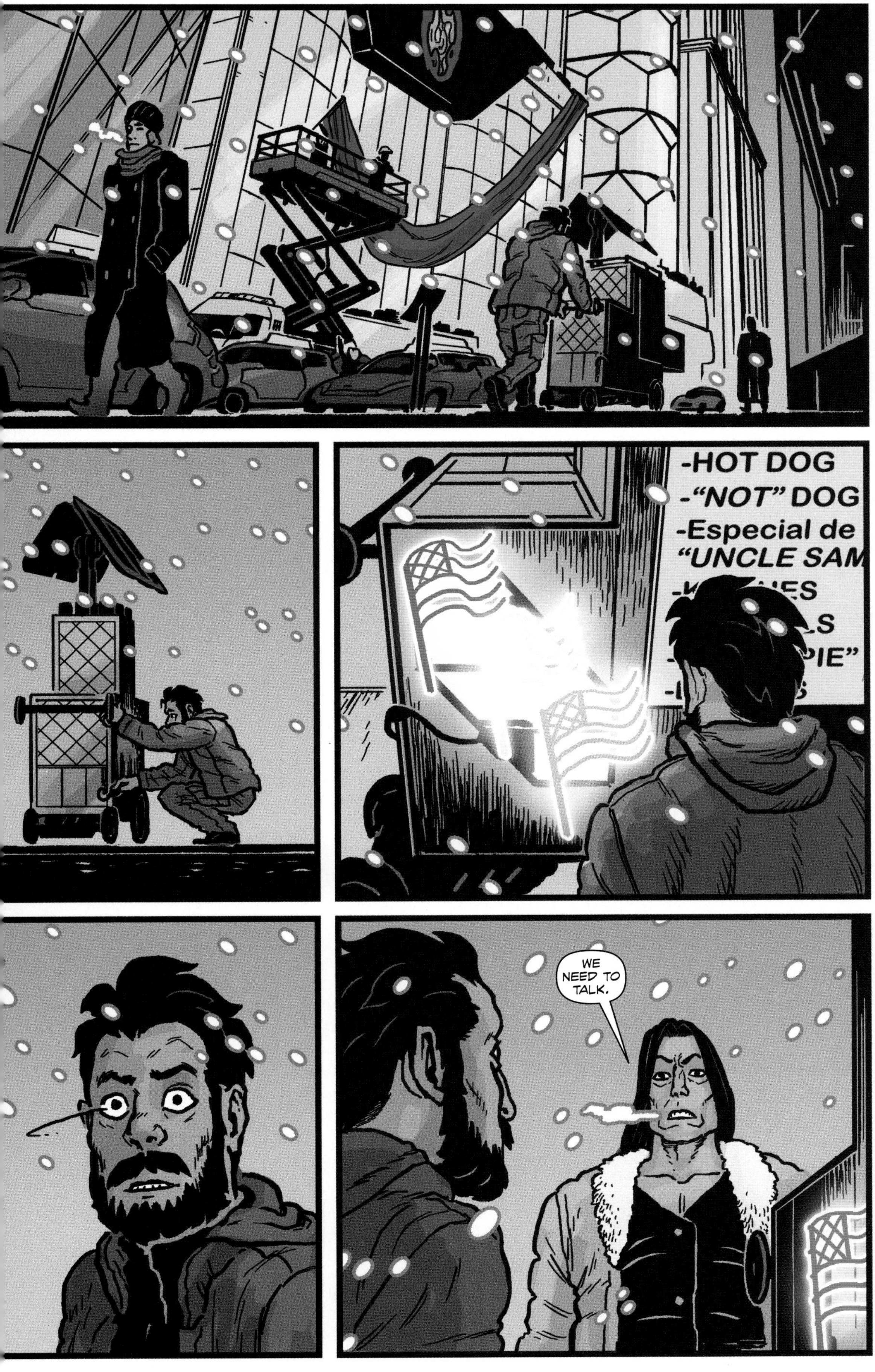
-HOT DOG
-“NOT” DOG
-Especial de
“UNCLE SAM
WE NEED TO TALK.

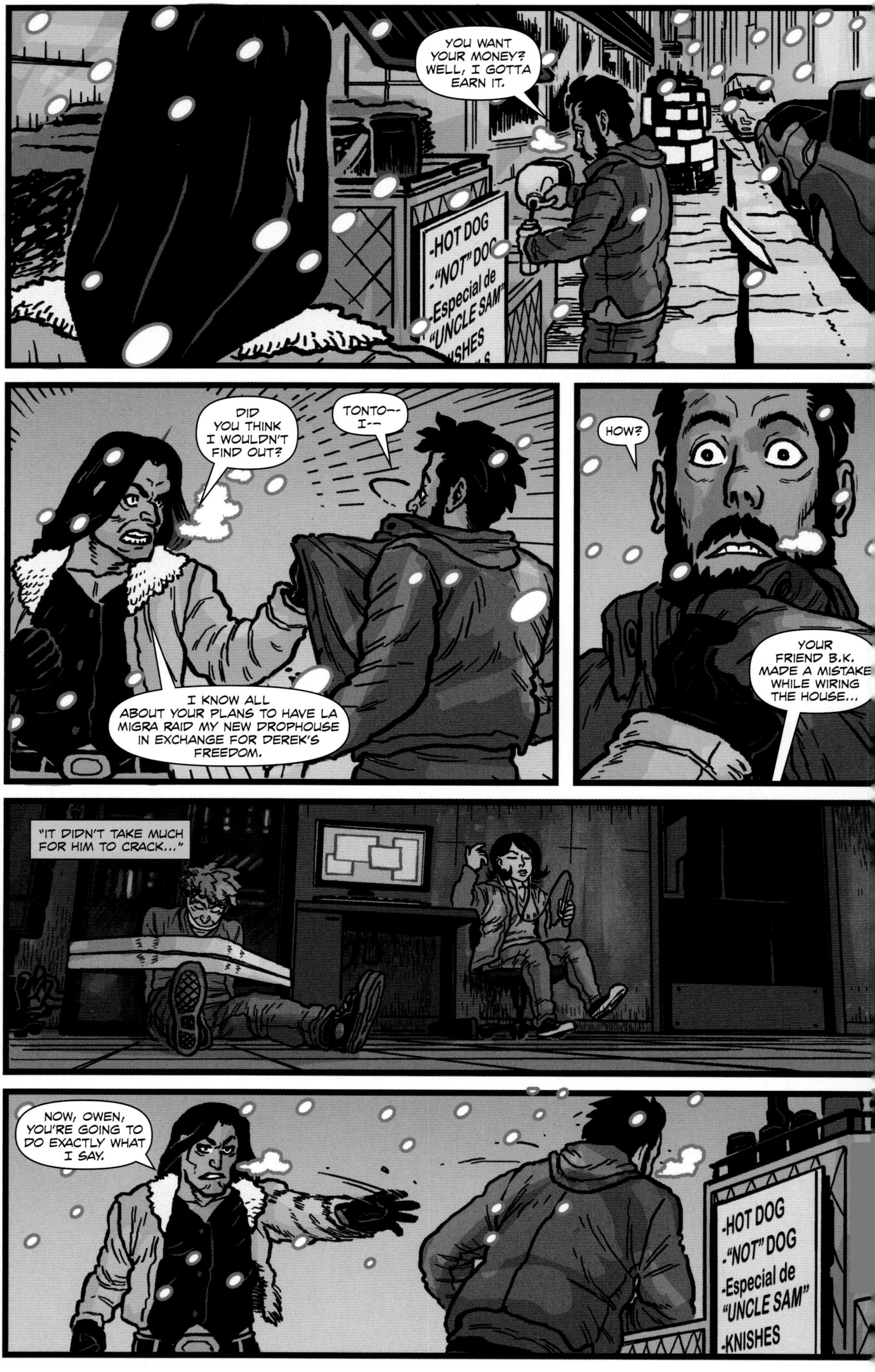
YOU WANT YOUR MONEY? WELL, I GOTTA EARN IT.
-HOT DOG
-"NOT" DOG
-Especial de "UNCLE SAM"
DID YOU THINK I WOULDN'T FIND OUT?
TONTO-- I--
I KNOW ALL ABOUT YOUR PLANS TO HAVE LA MIGRA RAID MY NEW DROPHOUSE IN EXCHANGE FOR DEREK'S FREEDOM.
HOW?
YOUR FRIEND B.K. MADE A MISTAKE WHILE WIRING THE HOUSE...
"IT DIDN'T TAKE MUCH FOR HIM TO CRACK..."
NOW, OWEN, YOU'RE GOING TO DO EXACTLY WHAT I SAY.
-HOT DOG
-"NOT" DOG
-Especial de "UNCLE SAM"
-KNISHES

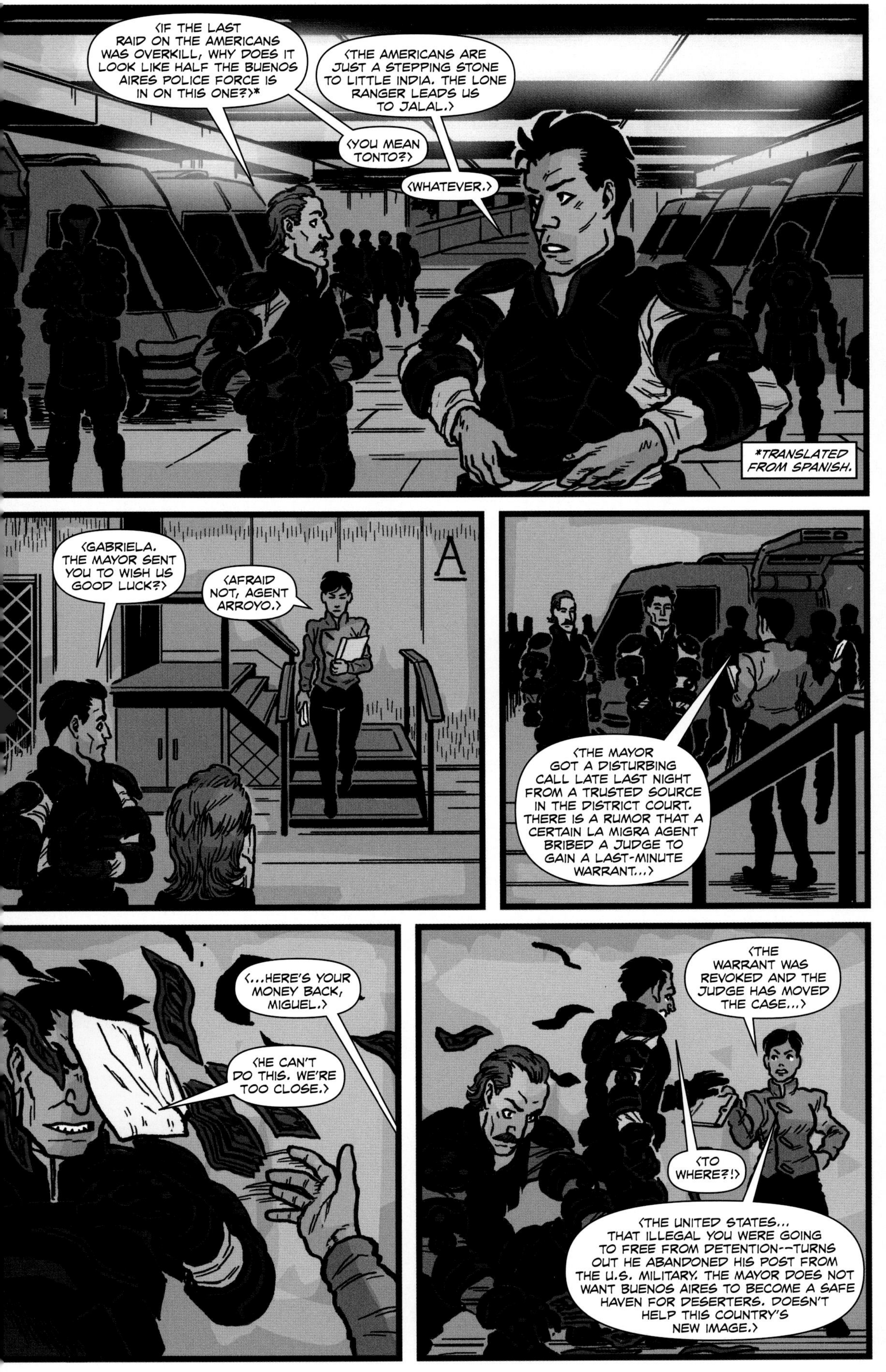
‹IF THE LAST RAID ON THE AMERICANS WAS OVERKILL, WHY DOES IT LOOK LIKE HALF THE BUENOS AIRES POLICE FORCE IS IN ON THIS ONE?›*
‹THE AMERICANS ARE JUST A STEPPING STONE TO LITTLE INDIA. THE LONE RANGER LEADS US TO JALAL.›
‹YOU MEAN TONTO?›
‹WHATEVER.›
*TRANSLATED FROM SPANISH.
‹GABRIELA. THE MAYOR SENT YOU TO WISH US GOOD LUCK?›
‹AFRAID NOT, AGENT ARROYO.›
A
‹THE MAYOR GOT A DISTURBING CALL LATE LAST NIGHT FROM A TRUSTED SOURCE IN THE DISTRICT COURT. THERE IS A RUMOR THAT A CERTAIN LA MIGRA AGENT BRIBED A JUDGE TO GAIN A LAST-MINUTE WARRANT...›
‹...HERE'S YOUR MONEY BACK, MIGUEL.›
‹HE CAN'T DO THIS. WE'RE TOO CLOSE.›
‹THE WARRANT WAS REVOKED AND THE JUDGE HAS MOVED THE CASE...›
‹TO WHERE?!›
‹THE UNITED STATES... THAT ILLEGAL YOU WERE GOING TO FREE FROM DETENTION--TURNS OUT HE ABANDONED HIS POST FROM THE U.S. MILITARY. THE MAYOR DOES NOT WANT BUENOS AIRES TO BECOME A SAFE HAVEN FOR DESERTERS. DOESN'T HELP THIS COUNTRY'S NEW IMAGE.›

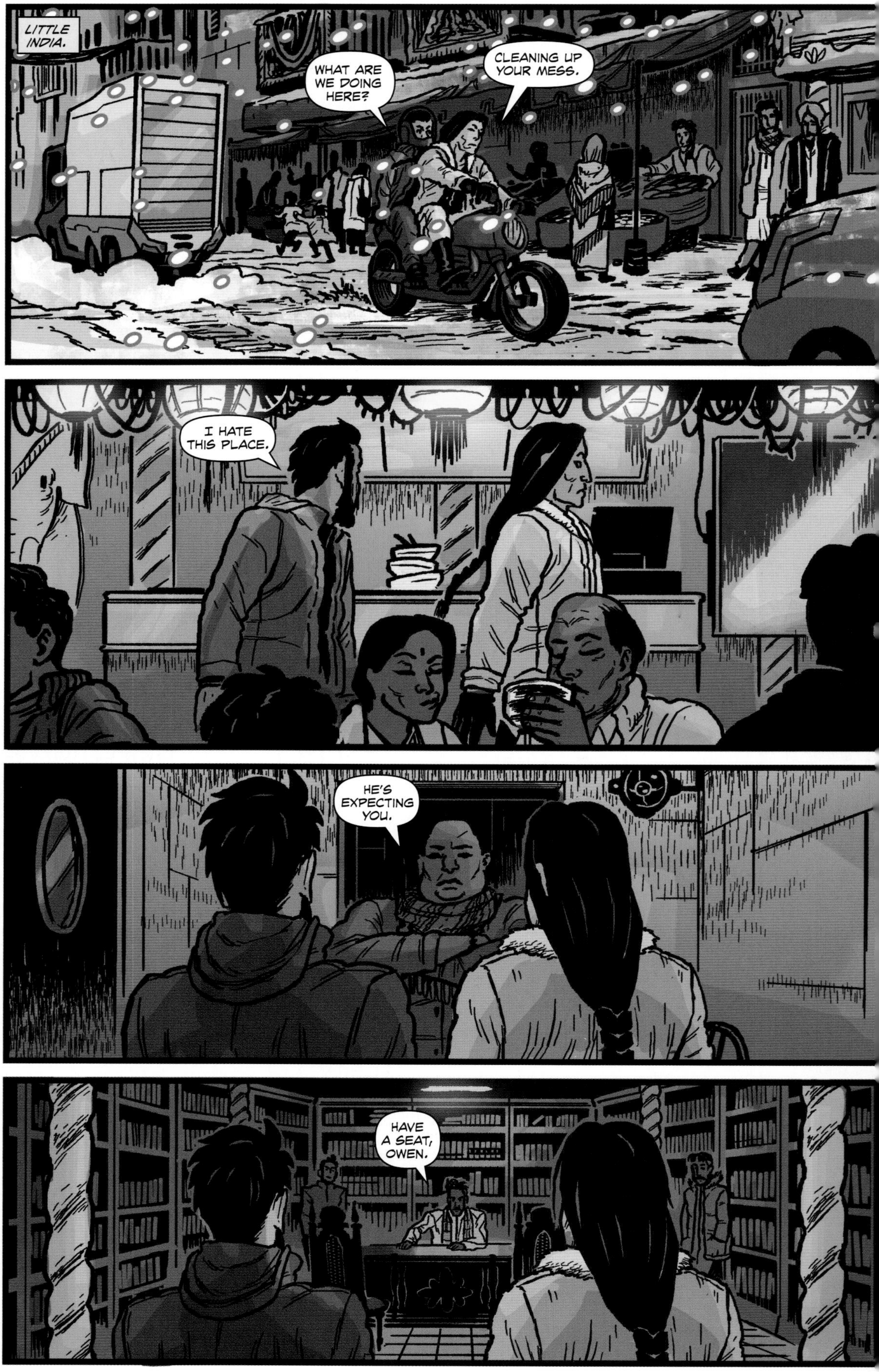
LITTLE INDIA.
WHAT ARE WE DOING HERE?
CLEANING UP YOUR MESS.
I HATE THIS PLACE.
HE'S EXPECTING YOU.
HAVE A SEAT, OWEN.

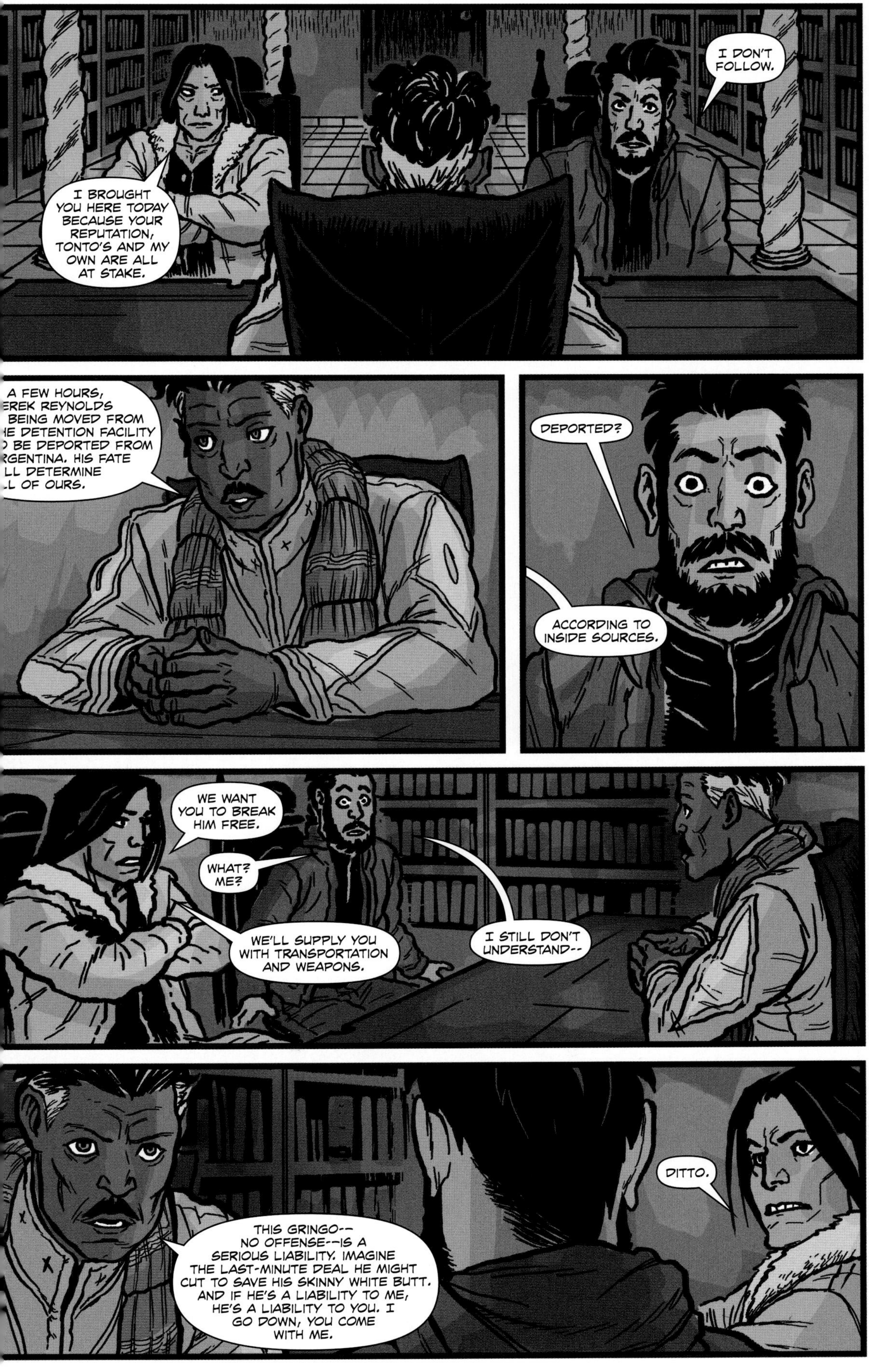
I DON'T FOLLOW.
I BROUGHT YOU HERE TODAY BECAUSE YOUR REPUTATION, TONTO'S AND MY OWN ARE ALL AT STAKE.
A FEW HOURS, EREK REYNOLDS BEING MOVED FROM HE DETENTION FACILITY BE DEPORTED FROM RGENTINA. HIS FATE LL DETERMINE L OF OURS.
DEPORTED?
ACCORDING TO INSIDE SOURCES.
WE WANT YOU TO BREAK HIM FREE.
WHAT? ME?
WE'LL SUPPLY YOU WITH TRANSPORTATION AND WEAPONS.
I STILL DON'T UNDERSTAND--
DITTO.
THIS GRINGO-- NO OFFENSE--IS A SERIOUS LIABILITY. IMAGINE THE LAST-MINUTE DEAL HE MIGHT CUT TO SAVE HIS SKINNY WHITE BUTT. AND IF HE'S A LIABILITY TO ME, HE'S A LIABILITY TO YOU. I GO DOWN, YOU COME WITH ME.

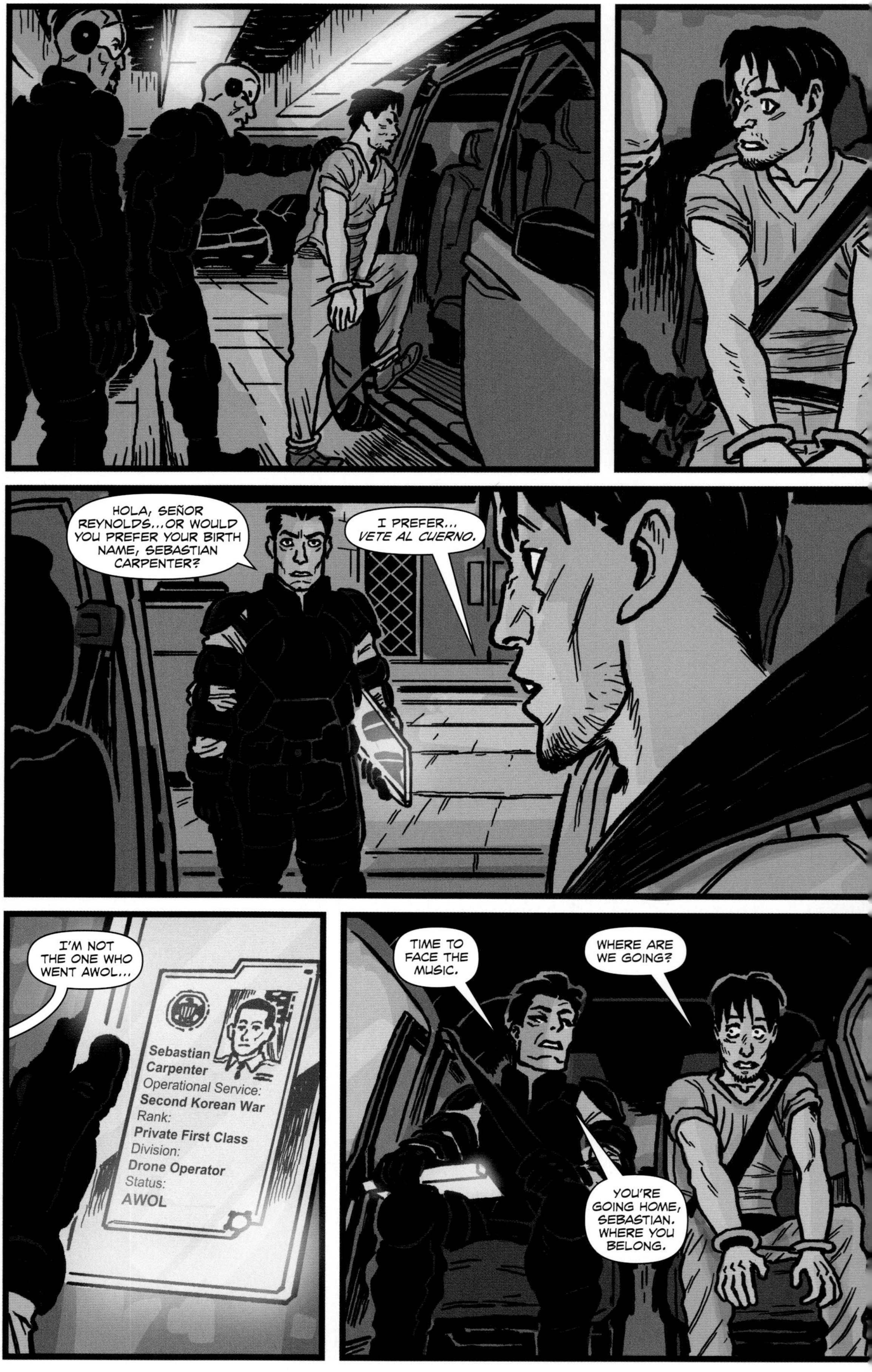
HOLA, SEÑOR REYNOLDS...OR WOULD YOU PREFER YOUR BIRTH NAME, SEBASTIAN CARPENTER?
I PREFER... VETE AL CUERNO.
I'M NOT THE ONE WHO WENT AWOL...
Sebastian Carpenter
Operational Service:
Second Korean War
Rank:
Private First Class
Division:
Drone Operator
Status:
AWOL
TIME TO FACE THE MUSIC.
WHERE ARE WE GOING?
YOU'RE GOING HOME, SEBASTIAN. WHERE YOU BELONG.

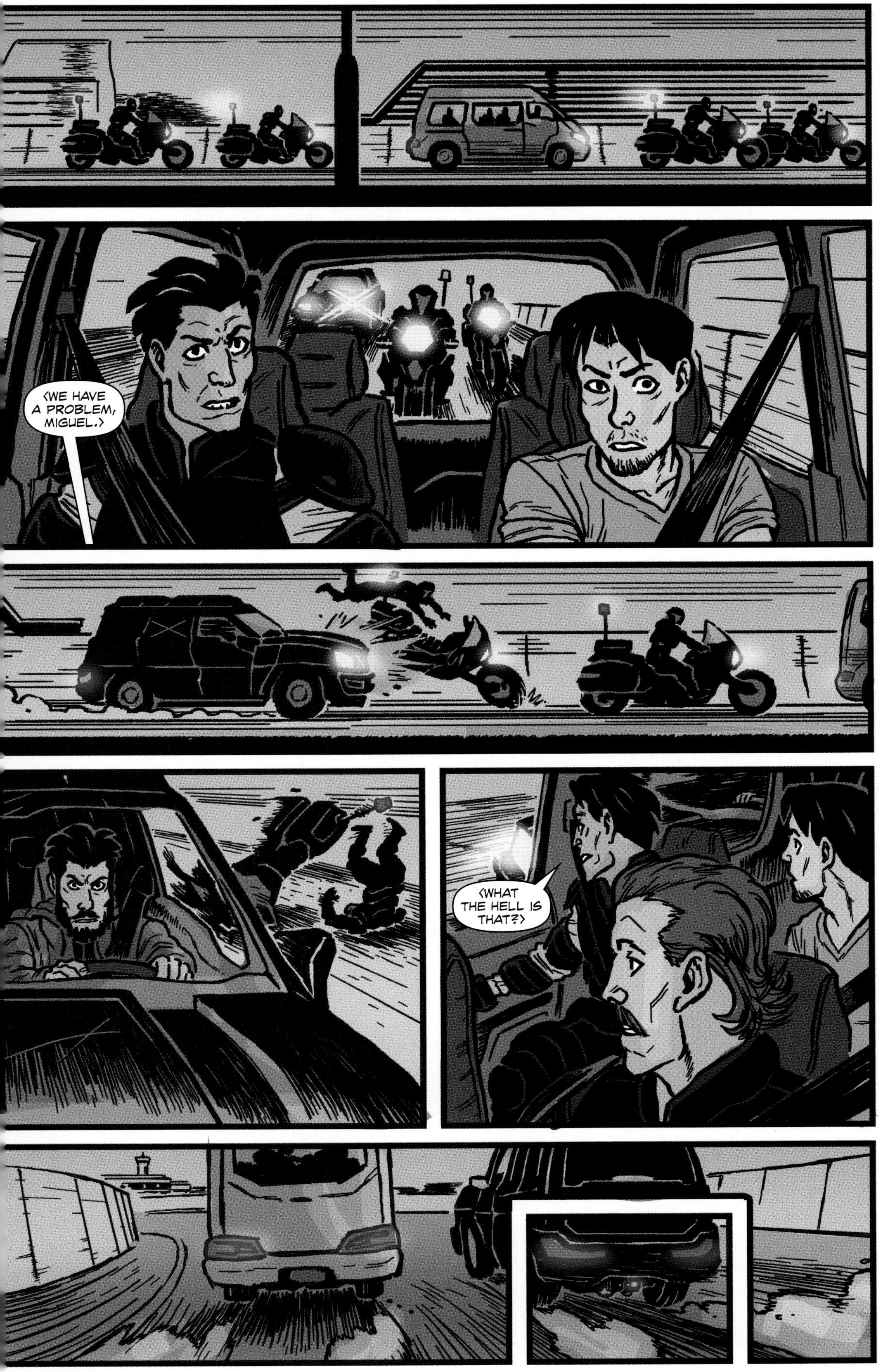

⟨WE HAVE A PROBLEM, MIGUEL.⟩
⟨WHAT THE HELL IS THAT?⟩

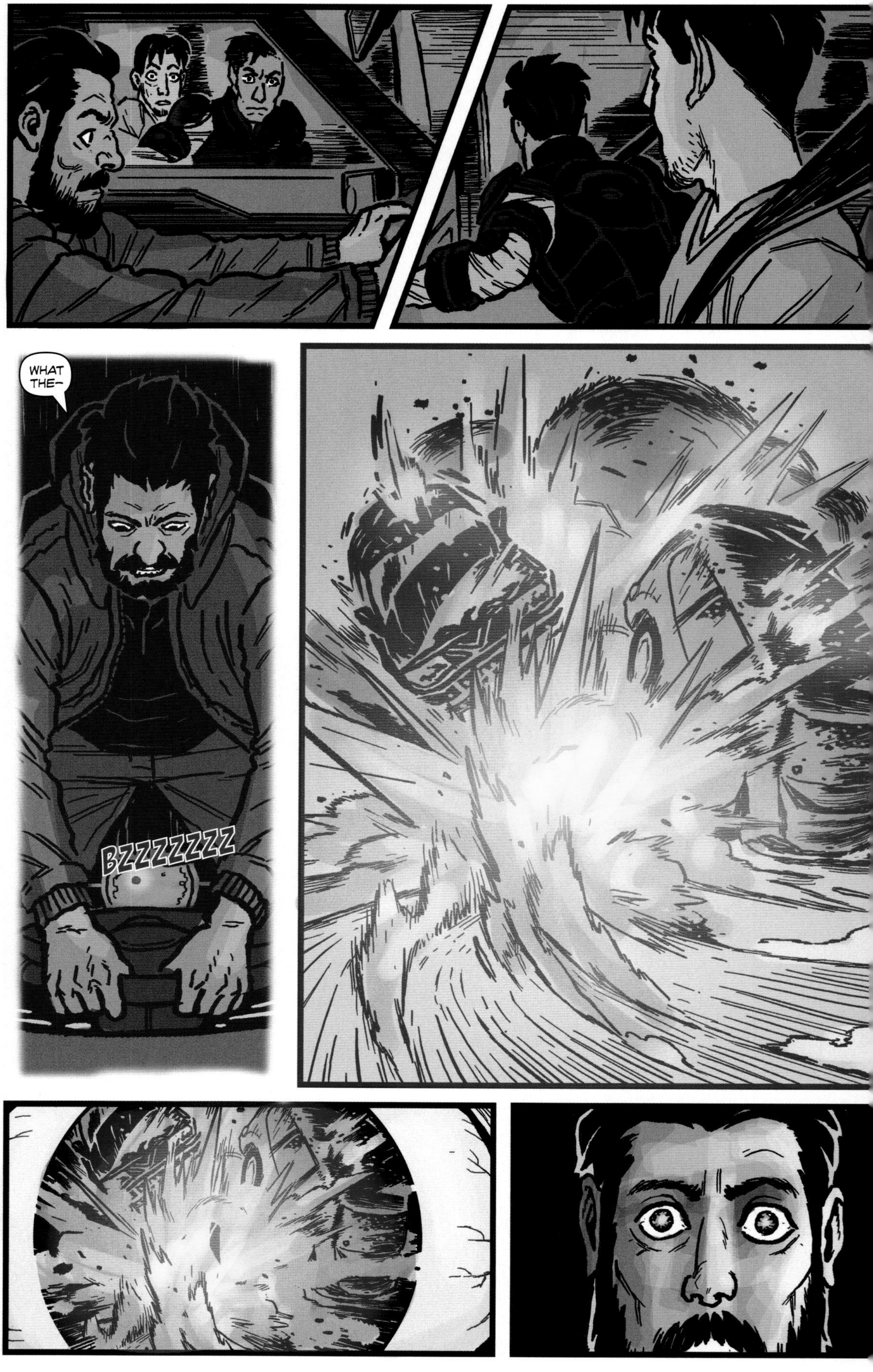
WHAT THE–
BZZZZZZZ

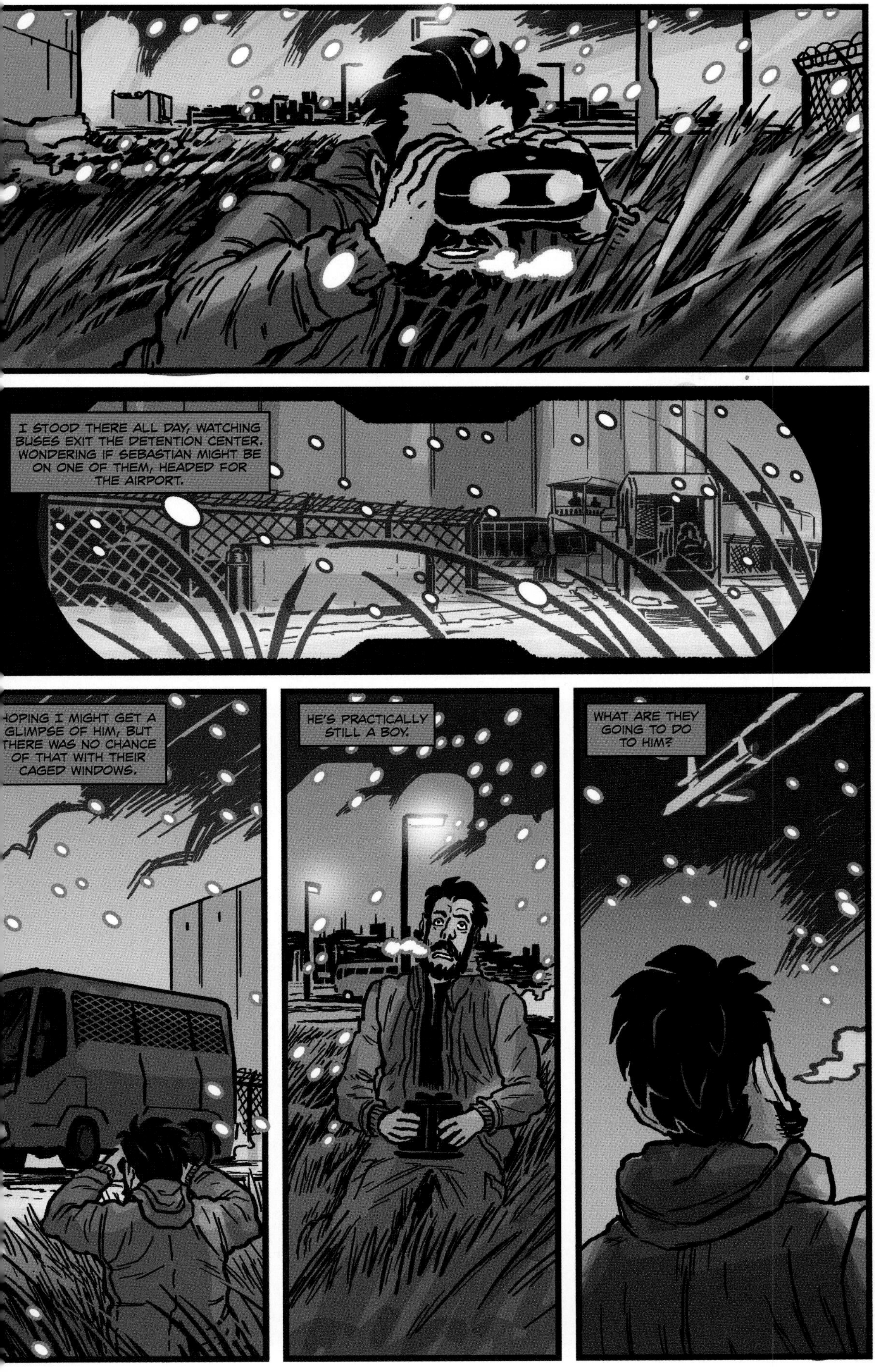
I STOOD THERE ALL DAY, WATCHING BUSES EXIT THE DETENTION CENTER. WONDERING IF SEBASTIAN MIGHT BE ON ONE OF THEM, HEADED FOR THE AIRPORT.
HOPING I MIGHT GET A GLIMPSE OF HIM, BUT THERE WAS NO CHANCE OF THAT WITH THEIR CAGED WINDOWS.
HE'S PRACTICALLY STILL A BOY.
WHAT ARE THEY GOING TO DO TO HIM?

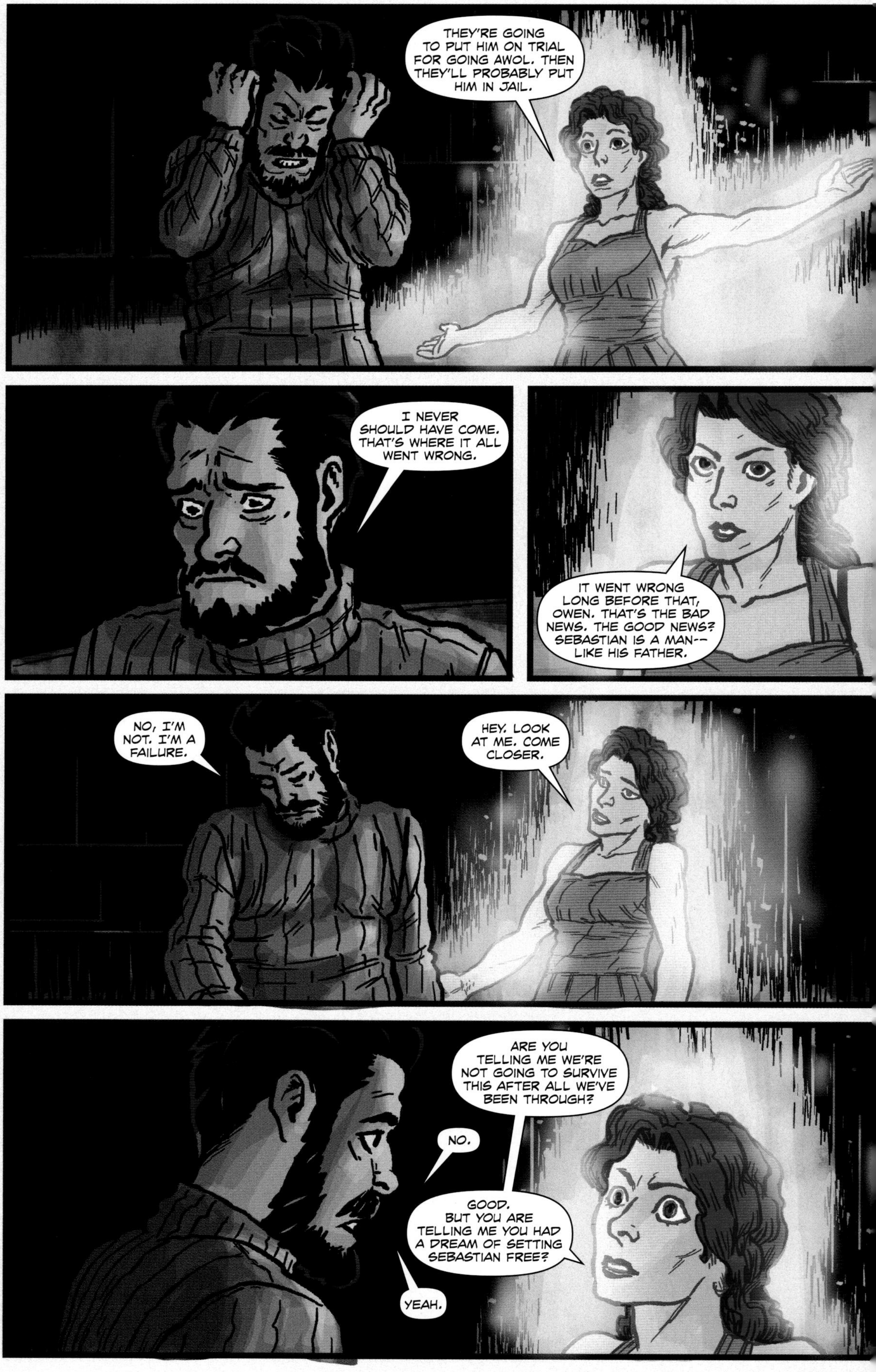
THEY'RE GOING TO PUT HIM ON TRIAL FOR GOING AWOL. THEN THEY'LL PROBABLY PUT HIM IN JAIL.
I NEVER SHOULD HAVE COME. THAT'S WHERE IT ALL WENT WRONG.
IT WENT WRONG LONG BEFORE THAT, OWEN. THAT'S THE BAD NEWS. THE GOOD NEWS? SEBASTIAN IS A MAN-- LIKE HIS FATHER.
NO, I'M NOT. I'M A FAILURE.
HEY. LOOK AT ME. COME CLOSER.
ARE YOU TELLING ME WE'RE NOT GOING TO SURVIVE THIS AFTER ALL WE'VE BEEN THROUGH?
NO.
GOOD. BUT YOU ARE TELLING ME YOU HAD A DREAM OF SETTING SEBASTIAN FREE?
YEAH.

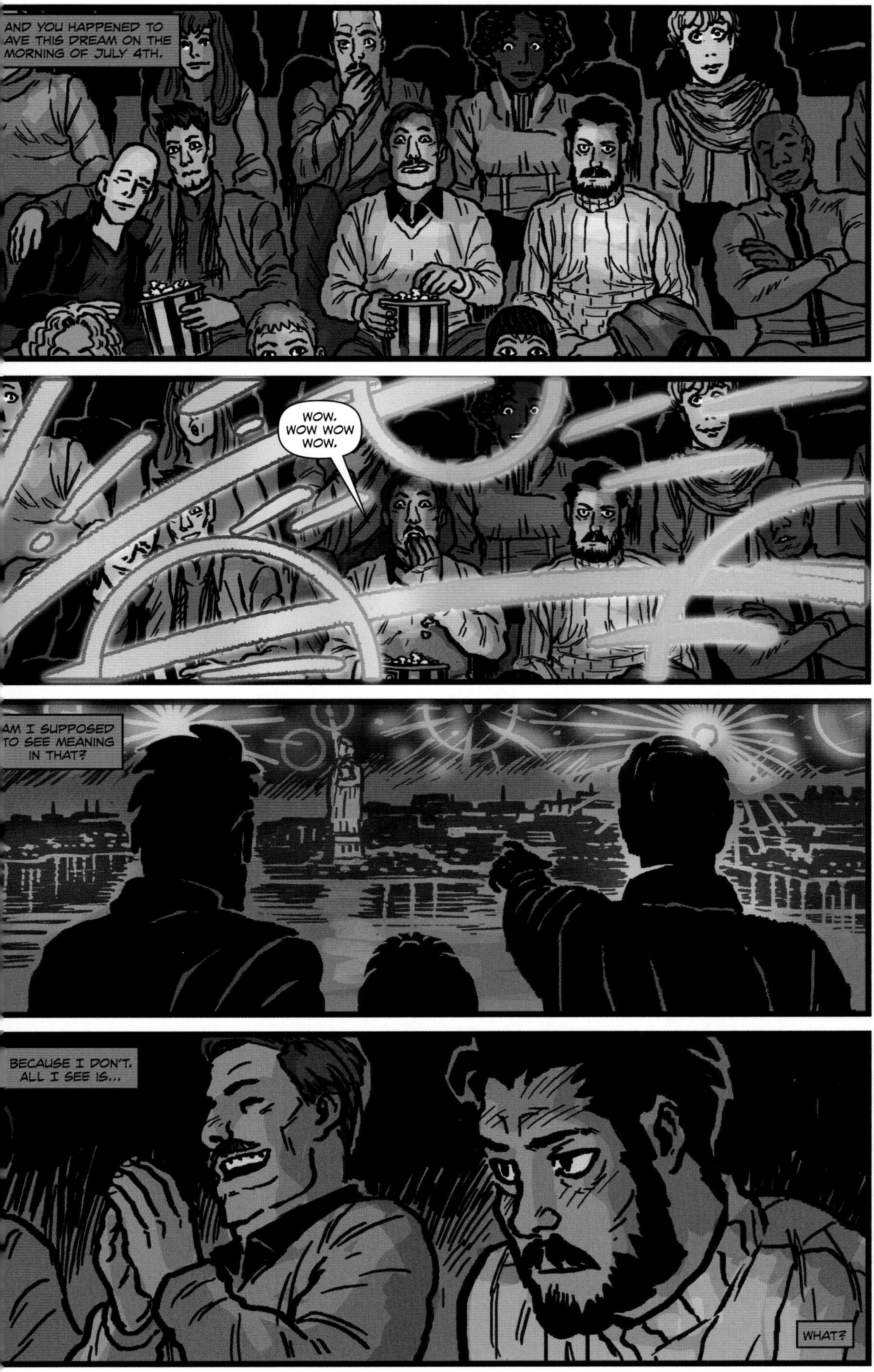
AND YOU HAPPENED TO AVE THIS DREAM ON THE MORNING OF JULY 4TH.
WOW. WOW WOW WOW.
AM I SUPPOSED TO SEE MEANING IN THAT?
BECAUSE I DON'T. ALL I SEE IS...
WHAT?

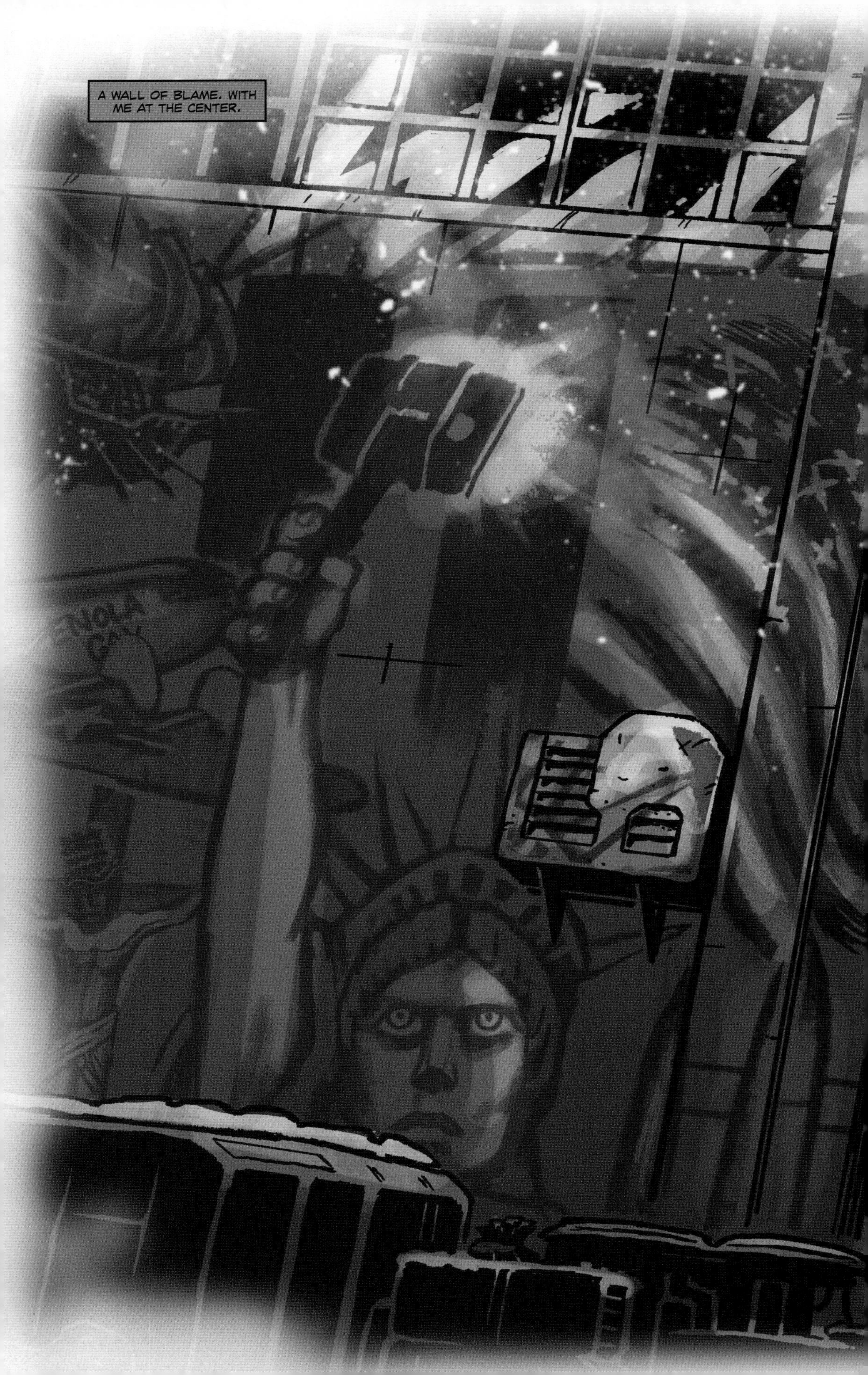
A WALL OF BLAME. WITH ME AT THE CENTER.

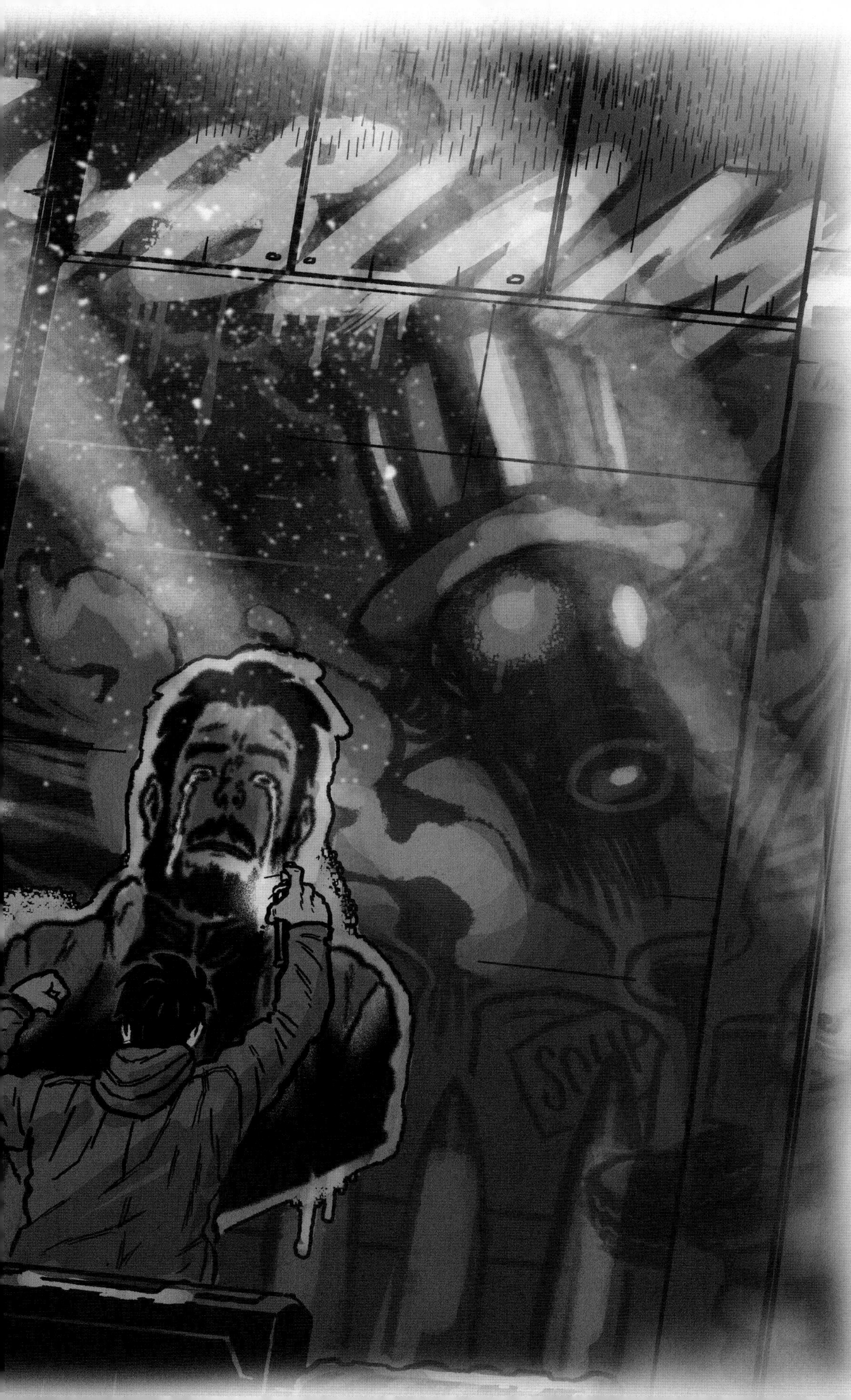
SOUP

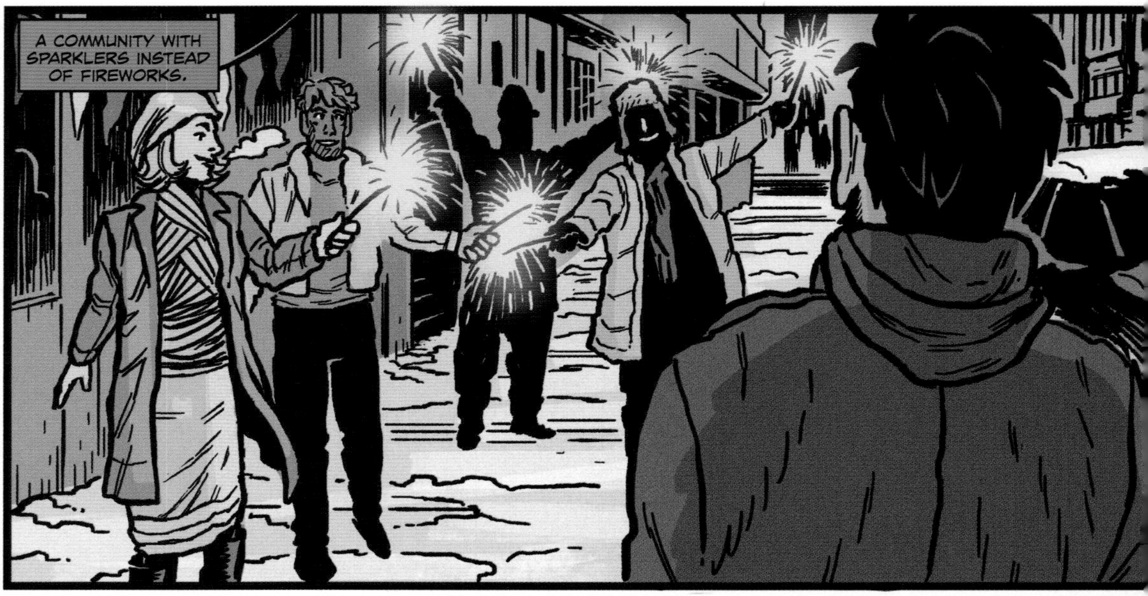
A COMMUNITY WITH SPARKLERS INSTEAD OF FIREWORKS.

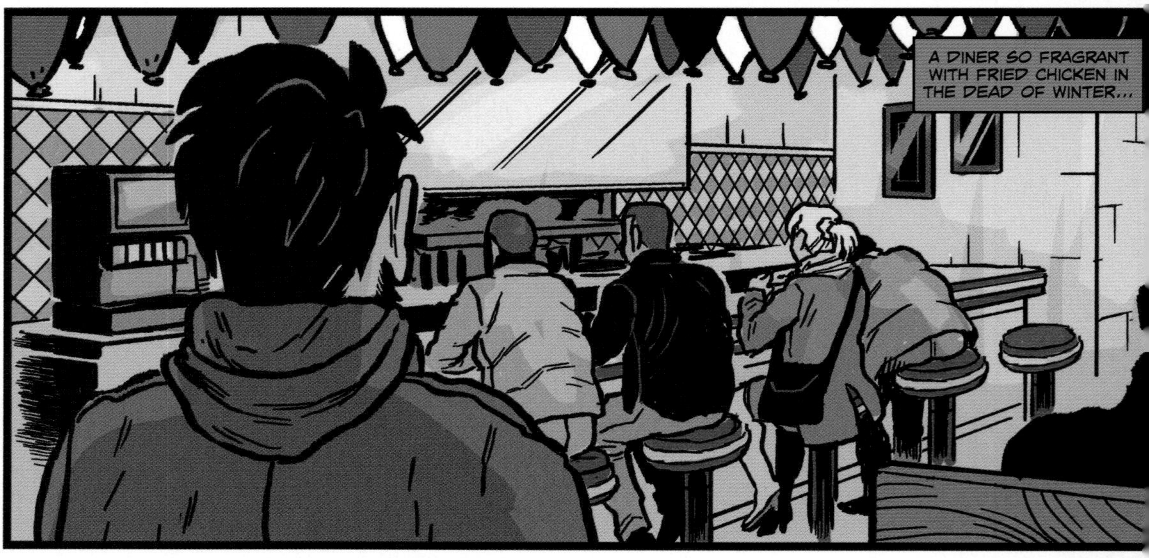
A DINER SO FRAGRANT WITH FRIED CHICKEN IN THE DEAD OF WINTER...

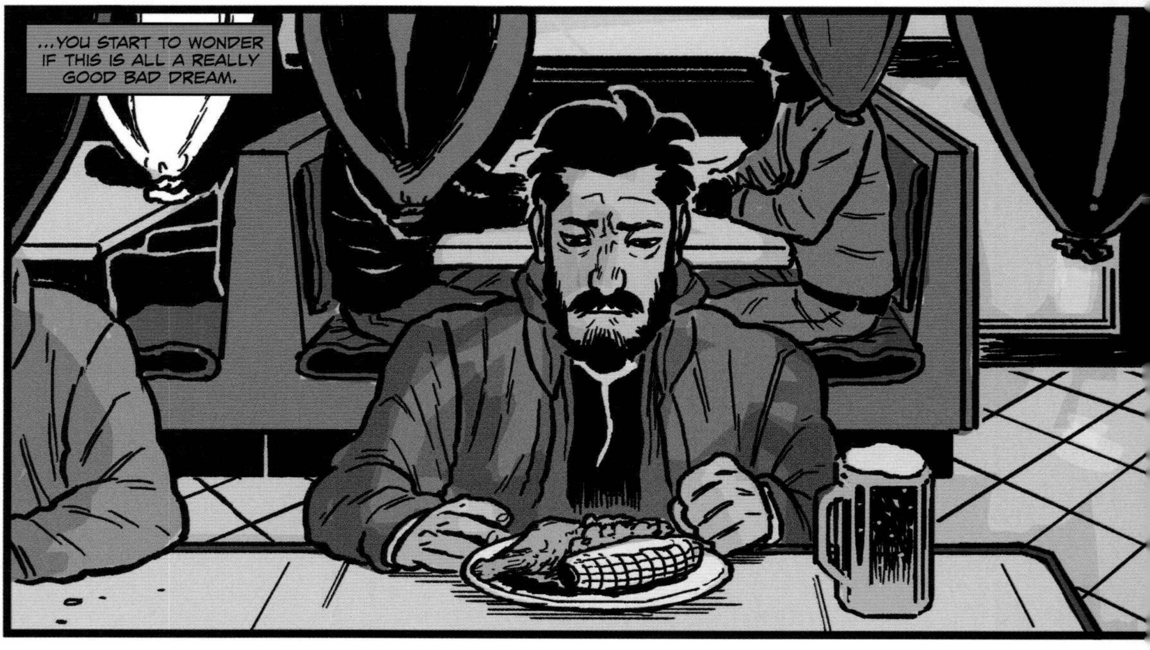
...YOU START TO WONDER IF THIS IS ALL A REALLY GOOD BAD DREAM.

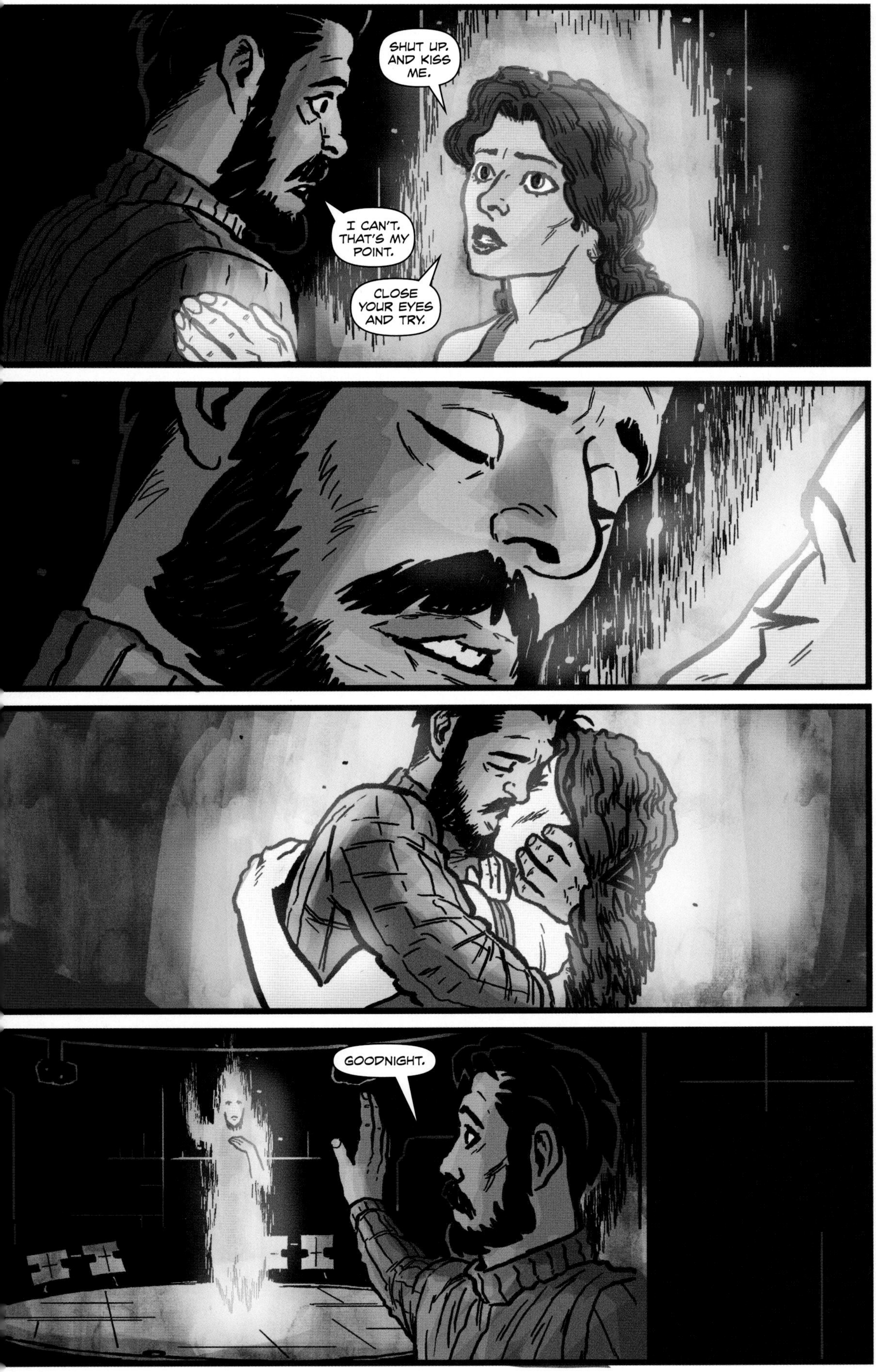
SHUT UP. AND KISS ME.
I CAN'T. THAT'S MY POINT.
CLOSE YOUR EYES AND TRY.
GOODNIGHT.

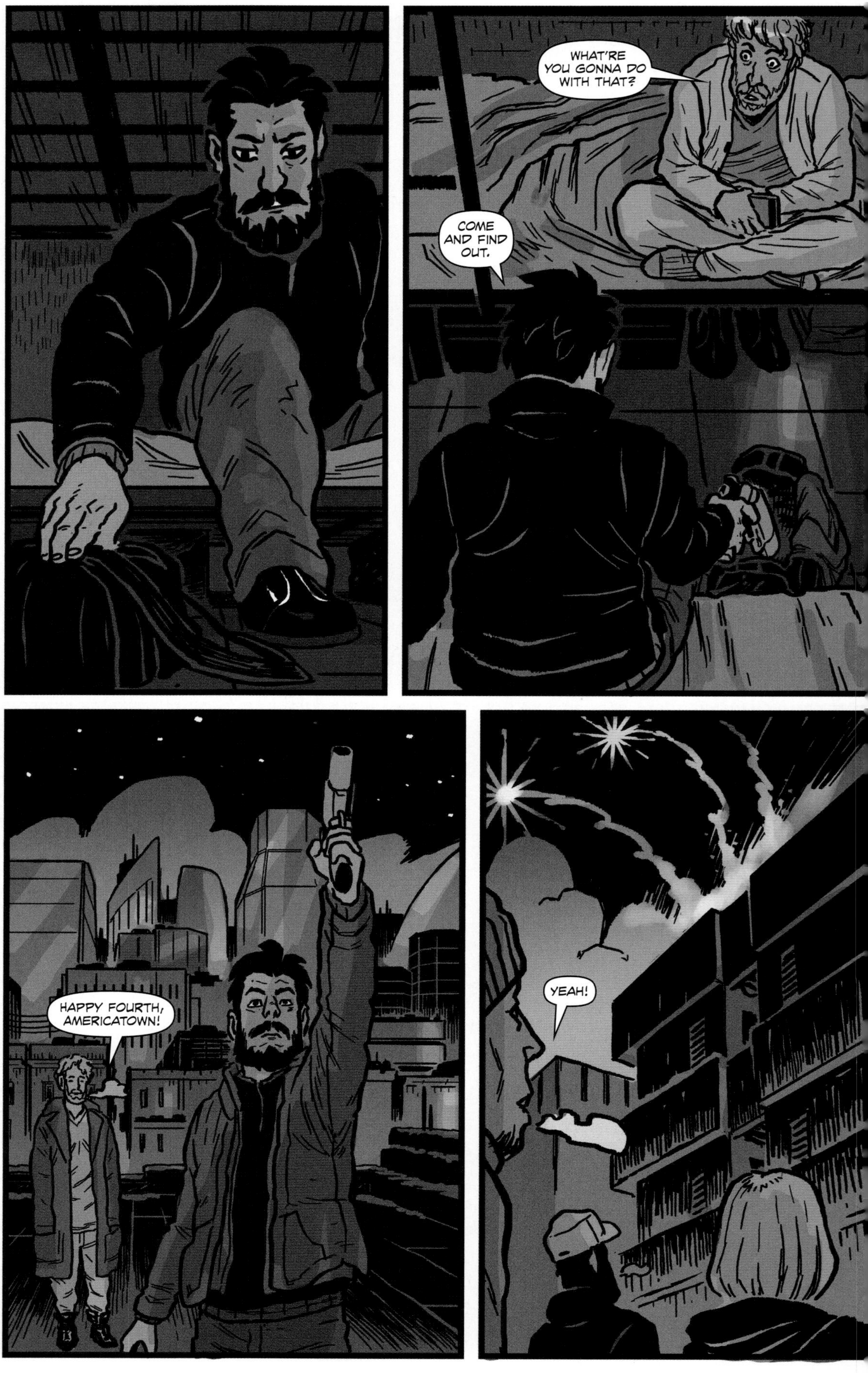
WHAT'RE YOU GONNA DO WITH THAT?
COME AND FIND OUT.
HAPPY FOURTH, AMERICATOWN!
YEAH!

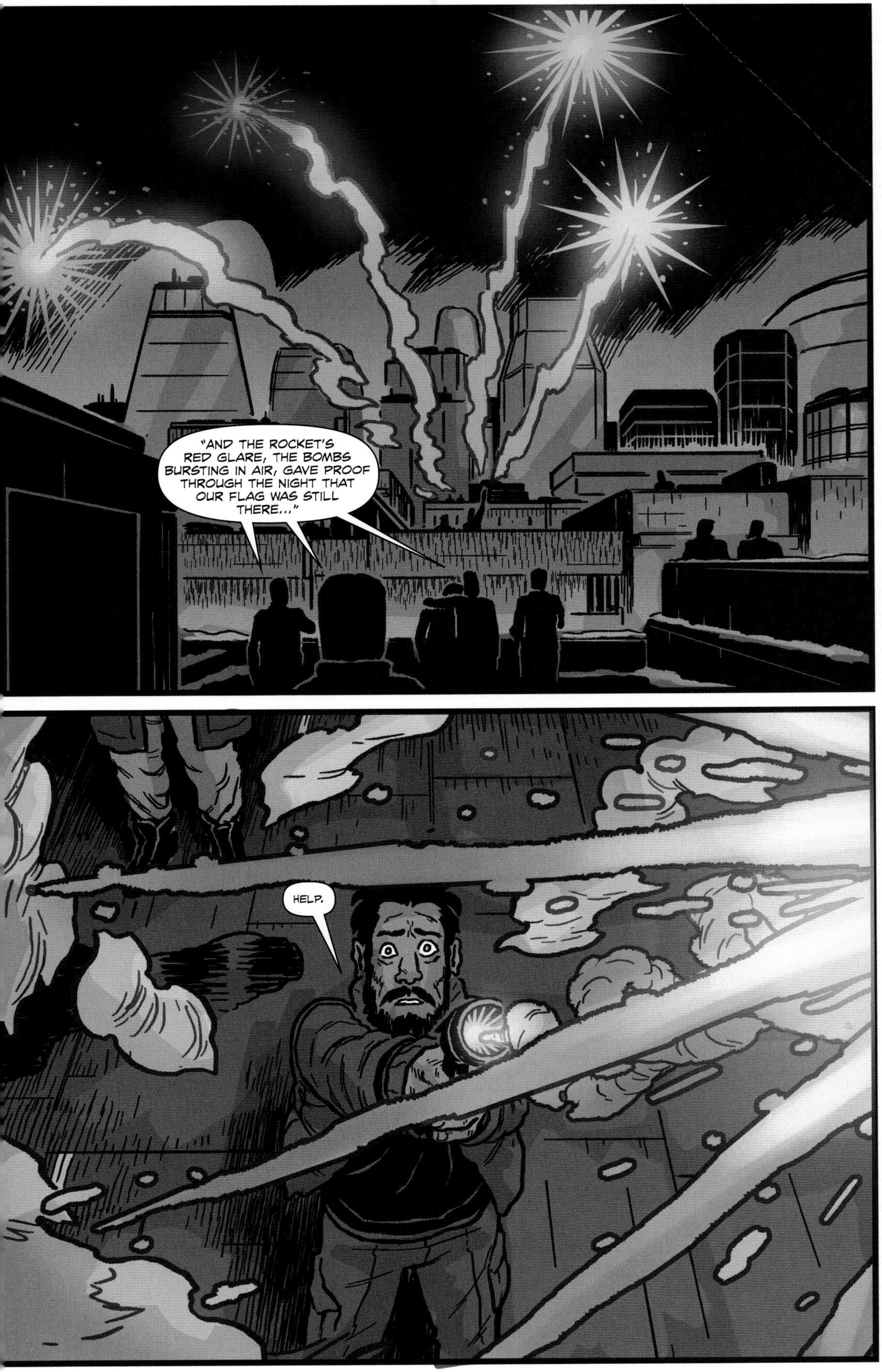
"AND THE ROCKET'S RED GLARE, THE BOMBS BURSTING IN AIR, GAVE PROOF THROUGH THE NIGHT THAT OUR FLAG WAS STILL THERE..."
HELP.

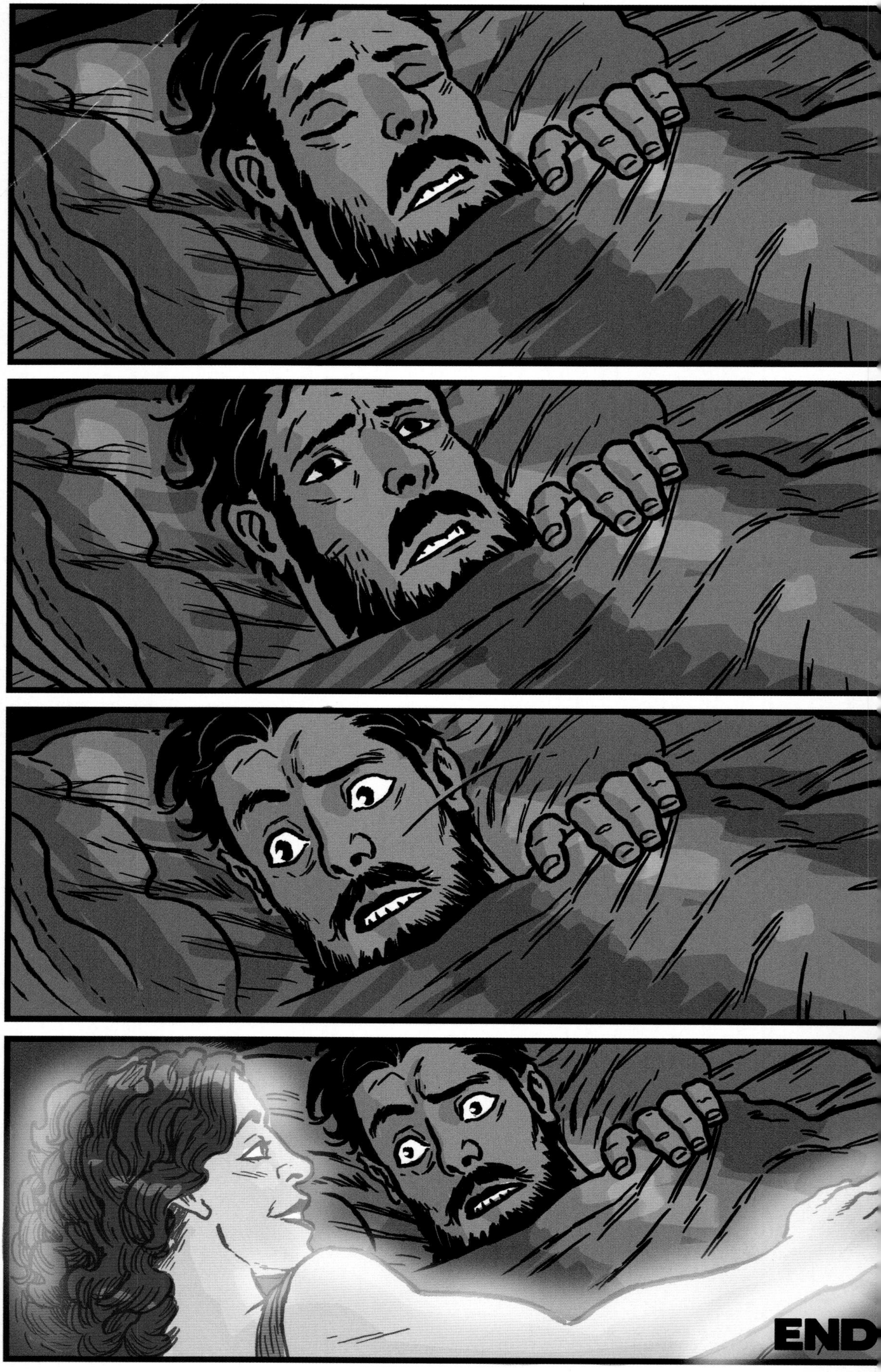
END

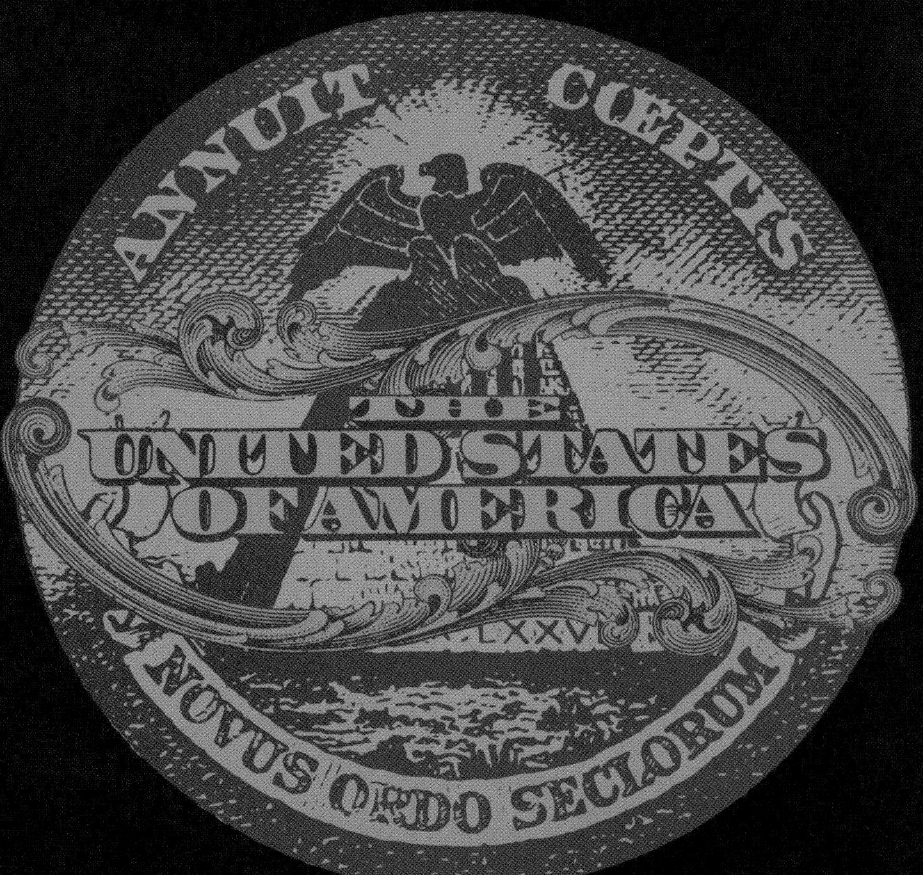
ANNUIT COEPTIS
THE
UNITED STATES
OF AMERICA
NOVUS ORDO SECLORUM

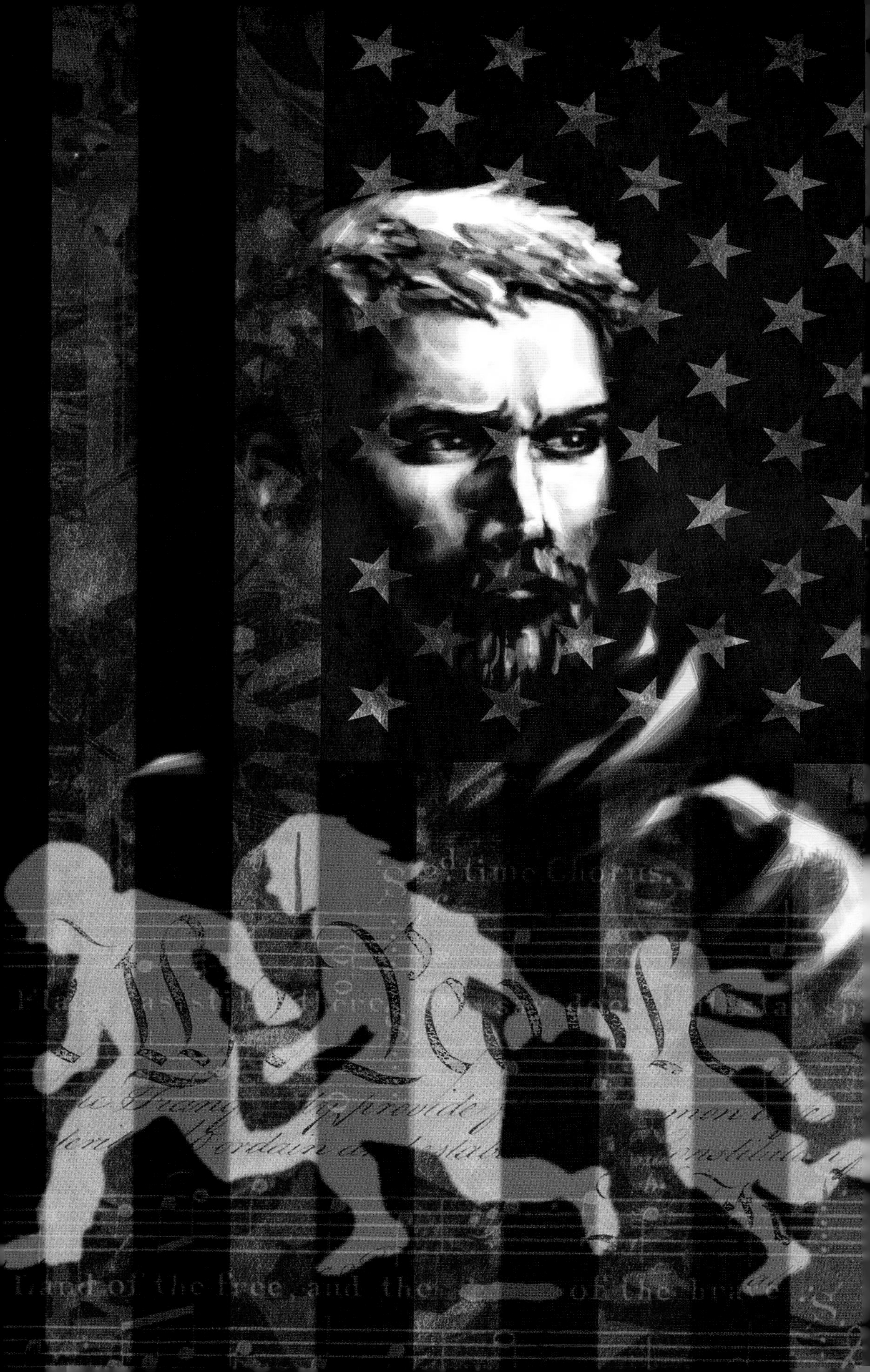
time Chorus.
Land of the free, and the
of the brave

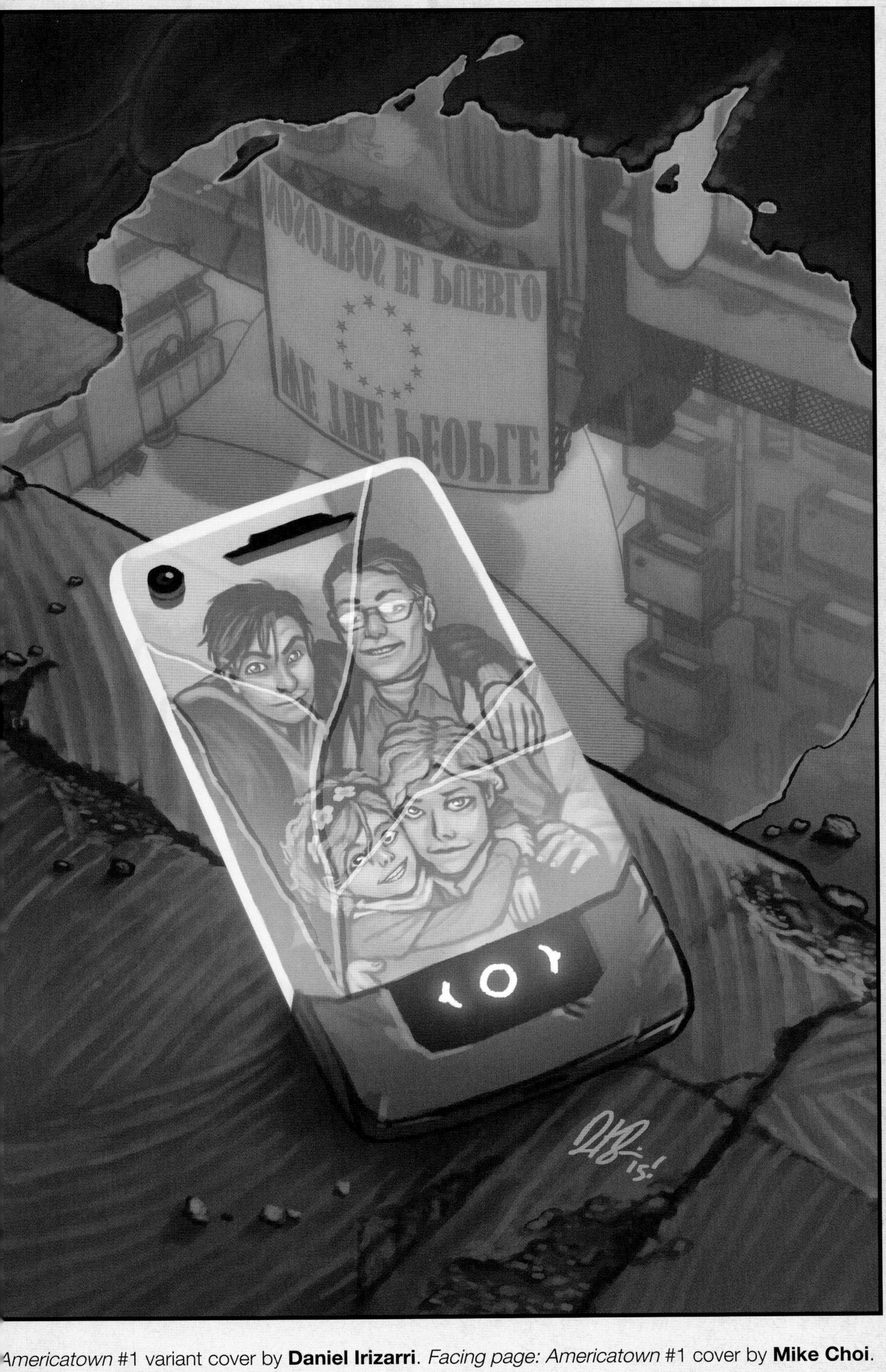

Americatown #1 variant cover by **Daniel Irizarri**. *Facing page: Americatown* #1 cover by **Mike Choi**.

Americatown Boom! Ten Years Anniversary cover by **Sonny Liew**.

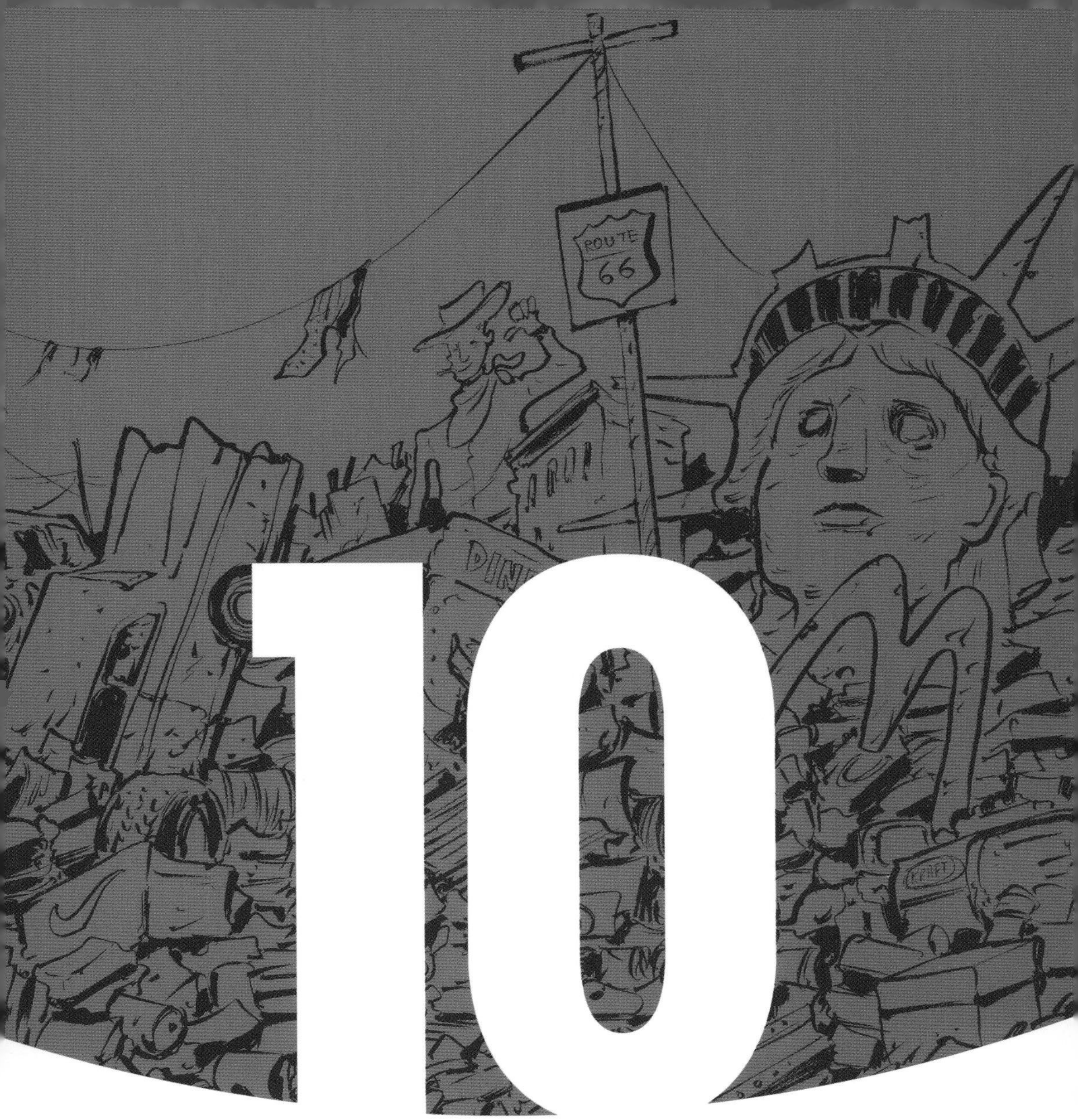
ROUTE
66

10

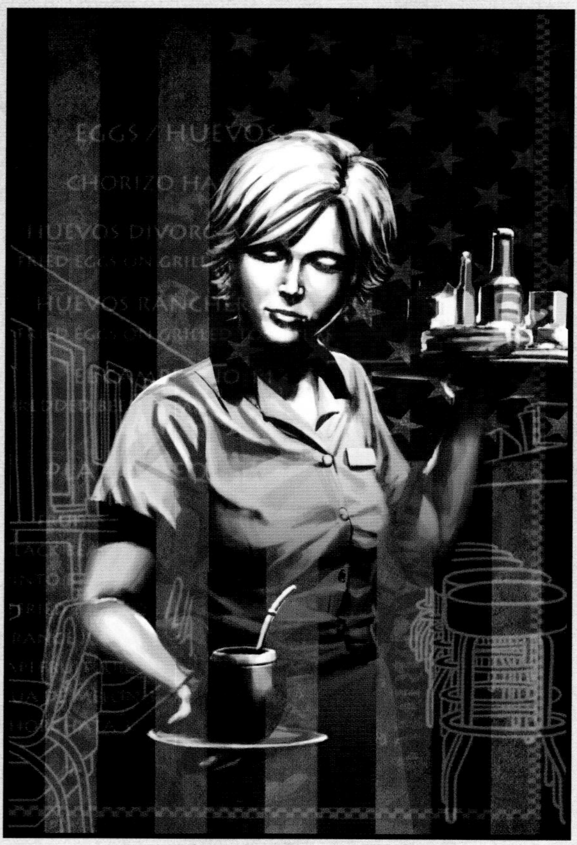
EGGS / HUEVOS

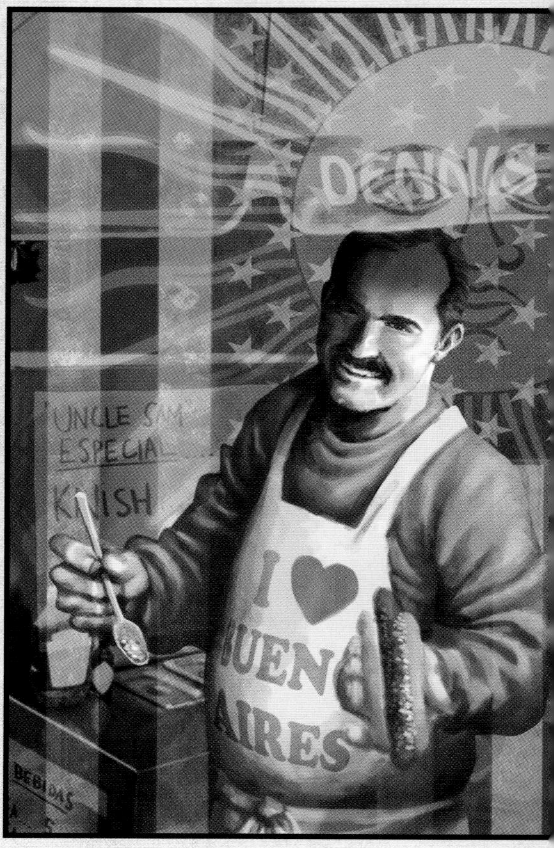
UNCLE SAM
ESPECIAL
KNISH
BEBIDAS

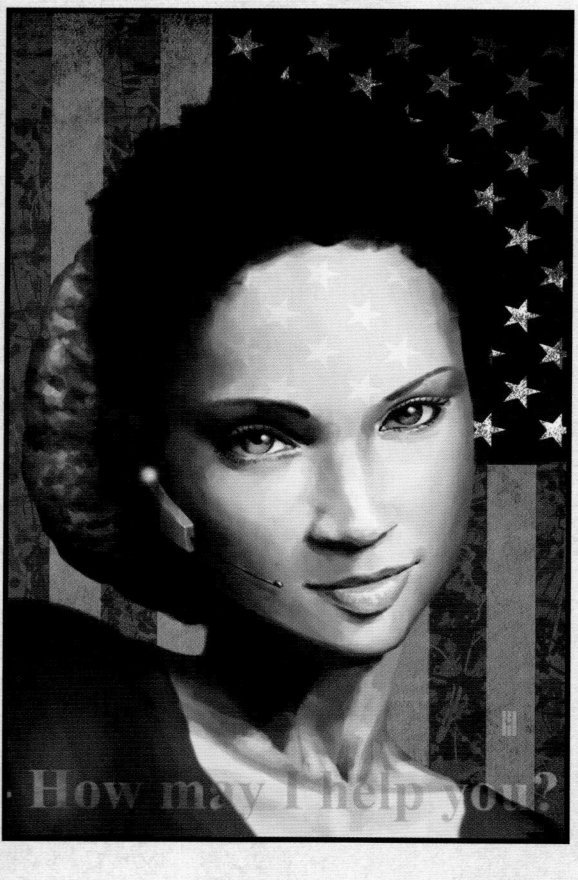
How may I help you?

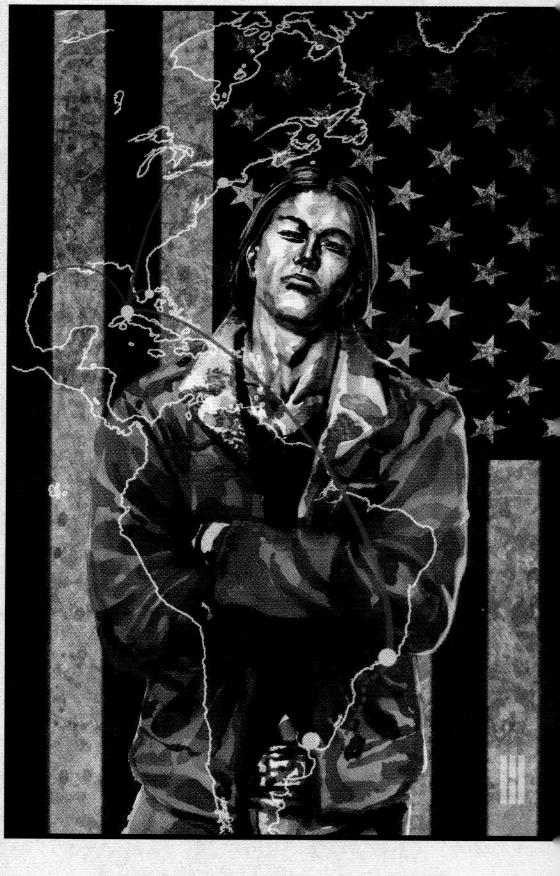

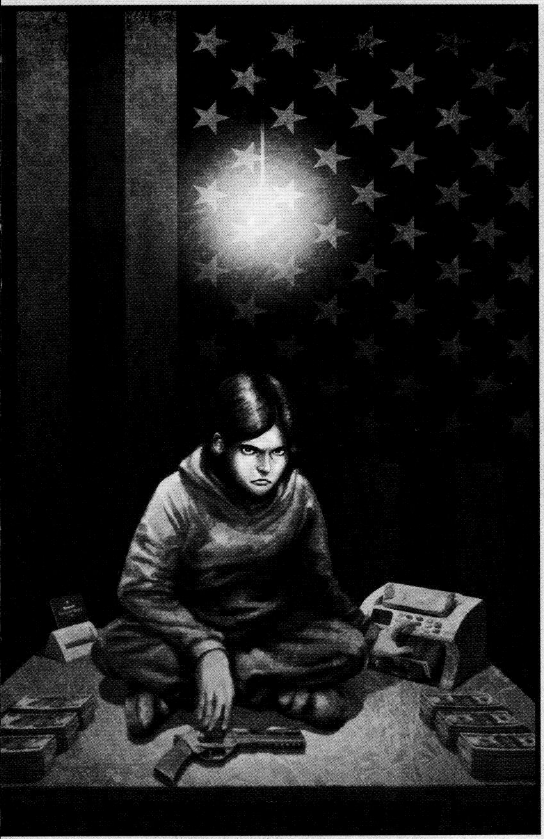

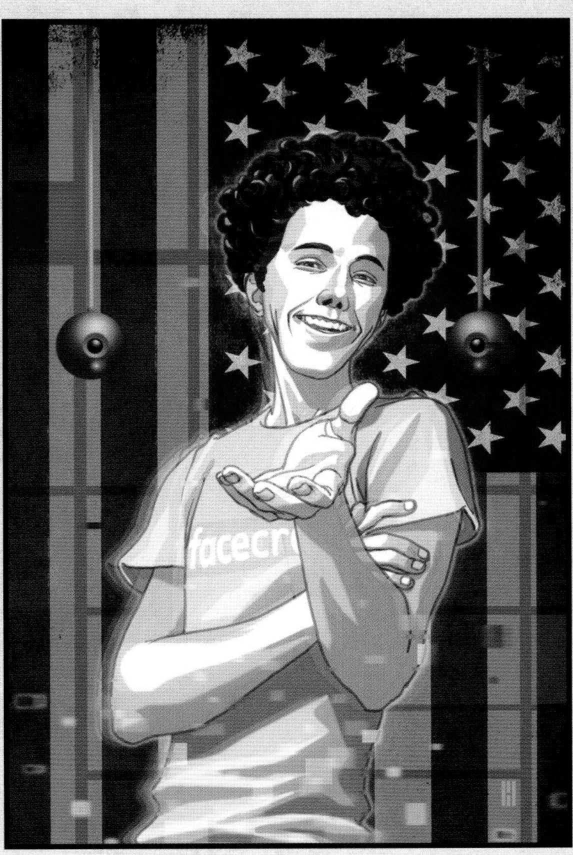
facecr

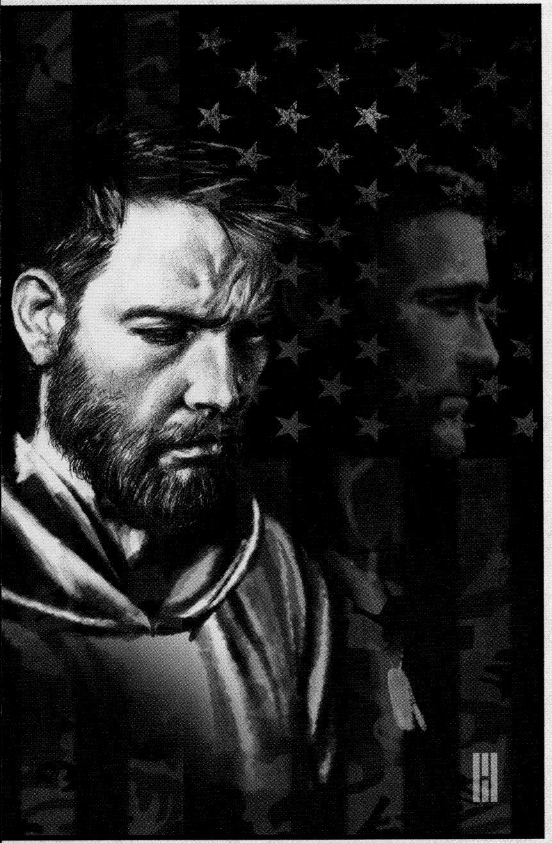

From top left:
Americatown #2-8 covers by
Mike Choi

MORE FROM ARCHAIA

Mouse Guard
David Petersen
Vol. 1, Fall 1152: 978-1-93238-657-8
$24.95 US • $32.99 CA • £18.99 UK

Vol. 2, Winter 1152: 978-1-932386-74-5
$24.95 US • $32.99 CA • £18.99 UK

Vol. 3, The Black Axe: 978-1-936393-06-0
$24.95 US • $32.99 CA • £18.99 UK

Iscariot
S.M. Vidaurri
978-1-60886-761-5
$24.99 US • $32.99 CA • £18.99 UK

Rust: The Boy Soldier
Royden Lepp
978-1-60886-806-3
$10.99 US • $12.99 CA • £8.50 UK

Cursed Pirate Girl
Jeremy A. Bastian
978-1-60886-833-9
$19.99 US • $25.99 CA • £14.99 UK